Weight Loss
for the
Mind

Weight Loss
for the *Mind*

Stuart Wilde

Hay House, Inc.
Carlsbad, California • Sydney, Australia

Copyright © 1994 by Stuart Wilde

Published and distributed in the United States by:

Hay House, Inc., P.O. Box 5100, Carlsbad, CA 92018-5100 • (800) 654-5126
(800) 650-5115 (fax)

Designed by: Wendy Lutge

Library of Congress Cataloging-in-Publication Data

Wilde, Stuart
    Weight loss for the mind / Stuart Wilde.
       p. cm.
    ISBN 1-56170-537-3 (tradepaper)
    1. Conduct of life. I. Title.
BF637.C5W49   1998
131—dc21   97-53043
                            CIP

ISBN 1-56170-537-3

02 01 00 99   8 7 6 5

First Printing, January 1994, by Hay House, Inc.
5th Printing, December 1999

Printed in Canada

Contents

Chapter One

Opinion *and* Feeling

1

*A*s you walk down a city street and look at reality, all the things you see—buildings, houses, cars—are, in fact, an external manifestation of someone's opinion. A building is placed where it is, shaped as it is, because someone had the opinion to construct it that way and to place it on a particular spot.

Internal reality—our perception of life, the psychology and metaphysics of our humanity—is constructed in the same way. It is formed solely by opinion. We perceive what we believe.

We mostly inherit our broad-based opinions and feelings from others, or construct them from common experiences. They make us predictable. They form and define our reality. Those opinions are as real and as solid as the gas station on the corner.

In this booklet, *Weight Loss for the Mind*, we look at the opinions prevalent in our mass psychology and how many of them cause us anguish. With a few simple flips of the mind, and a little psychological and spiritual understanding, you can release 95 percent of all anguish. The other 5 percent you'll probably hang on to for the moment, out of habit.

But you'll gradually dismiss the last 5 percent and free yourself from the opinions you've acquired from others, as well as those you have established yourself. This will liberate you from the collective emotion and the anguish it offers. Serenity flows naturally from a heightened perception. You process and understand things differently.

If you like your spiritual growth, psychological integration, and personal healing on the hurry-up, as I do, then this little book is for you.

Weight is described as the gravity exerted when a particular mass comes into proximity with another. Your physical weight is established by the mass of the earth. If you are overweight, it may not be your fault at all; it could be that the planet is out of balance, and it is exerting a bit too much gravity upon you!

Scientists can't tell us exactly what gravity is. They postulate that it is caused by minute particles called gravitons. As yet, we can't find gravitons so we don't know for certain. But we *can* observe what gravity does.

Gravity is, in fact, the expression of a contradiction. A large mass like our planet contradicts a smaller mass like your body, forcing it to remain within the planet's gravitational influence.

It's interesting that in English we use the same word for the force of gravity and for seriousness. When we say that something is grave, we mean that it impacts our emotions and affects us negatively. We feel the presence of a psychological mass exerting itself upon us. Negative emotion and the force of gravity are really two manifestations of the same force.

The mental and emotional weight you experience as stress, or anguish, is exactly like the force of gravity. It relies on two or more psychological masses in your mind to establish a contradictory relationship with each other. Your reactions to the day-to-day circumstances of life form one mass in your mind, and the ideas that exist around your opinion form the other mass. Across these two masses flows a psychological tension that generates an emotional reaction.

For life's circumstances to generate negative emotion, they have to contradict your opinion. If circumstances don't contradict one of your opinions, your reaction is neutral. When circumstances enhance your opinions, they generate positive emotion for you.

So negative emotion (psychological weight) is only possible when there exists in your mind two opposing mental forces. Imagine them as two large rocks. One is constructed from loosely interconnected ideas, which are grouped initially in your mind by their similarity. They are held together and made solid by personal argument, and form your opinion—your expectations. The other rock is created by your reaction to and perception of life's circumstances. It often stands juxtaposed to the first mass, contradicting it.

Negative emotion, therefore, is nothing more than the experience of being contradicted. You have certain opinions and expectations; and life comes along and contradicts those opinions, thus generating negative emotion.

How do these expectations and opinions arise?

Just as a rock is made up of a series of atoms that give it mass, when your thoughts and ideas are grouped around a personal issue they gradually generate a psychological mass in your mind.

For such a mass to exert power over you, there has to be an underlying opinion to bind the whole thing together. That opinion usually flows from some personal need you think is important.

Opinion is like the nucleus of an atom—it is a *mental* power source. Your ideas hover around it, like the subatomic particles that circle a nucleus. As they orbit your opinion, the personal arguments they give out back it up When enough similar ideas gather to form a solid opinion, they establish a psychological mass in your mind. That mass is extremely solid and difficult to shift.

The human personality relies on these psychological masses to grant it solidity. It's vital for your personality to feel that it is correct and just, and that the ideas it holds are holy and good, and, above all, right. People with crazy and irrational ideas often go to great lengths to justify them.

From the psychological mass created by your opinions flows the view you take on a particular issue. From that impression flow feelings that we call emotion.

The crux of all anguish lies in this issue of opinion and contradiction. Once you get it, and see how it affects your life and your well-being, you can free yourself forever.

If you want a powerful, joyous existence, get a grip on the issue of contradiction—and you are free.

Realization

If your personality were programmed to accept contradictions as natural, and if it did not react, you could not experience negative emotion or anguish.

*** ***

Chapter Two

Contradiction and Expectancy

2

$\mathcal{I}$t's a threefold gain when you understand how these contradictions of life
affect you. First, you can eliminate some of
them immediately. Second, you can design
your life to avoid most of them. Third, you
can develop tools that allow you to accept,
unemotionally, those contradictions you
can't avoid.

Doing these three things, you return to
your natural Godlike state: serene, happy, and
entertained by the wonder and grace of this
strange gift we call life.

How do these contradictions arise?

Most of them are just inherent to our programming. The human personality exists in strange cyberspace, hovering above the ground at five to six feet or slightly more, trapped in nowhere land, someplace in the brain.

Strange, isn't it? We all think we're here. In fact, we are a hovercraft with no landing gear! The human personality never actually lands on earth. Even if you stand on your head, your personality is still somewhere beyond the thickness of your skull above the ground. That sets up an uncomfortable contradiction.

Your personality has to use the body as its link between the infinite cyberspace in which it dwells, and the earthly dimension from which its experiences flow.

The body is finite. Death is the ultimate contradiction. It is natural, therefore, that most people feel a bit insecure.

Life, for many, is a futile attempt to become secure in a dimension that is intrinsically insecure. People constantly fight that, rather than accept the strangeness of the human lesson as a beautiful thing. God must have a marvelous sense of humor—the contradictions of life are awesome and funny and very appealing. I find them heroic.

- *We have to embrace infinity inside a mortal body.*

- *We have to believe in a god we can't see.*

- *We have to learn to love in a dimension where there is so much hatred.*

- *We have to see abundance when people constantly talk of shortages and lack.*

- *We have to discover freedom where control is the state religion.*

- *We have to develop self-worth while people criticize and belittle us.*

- *We have to see beauty where there is ugliness.*

- *We have to embrace kindness and positive attitudes when surrounded by uncertainty.*

- *We have to feel safe in spite of our concerns.*

Yes, the heroism of our condition is most endearing.

Transcendence is nothing more than learning to accept the contradictions of life without resistance.

Embracing these contradictions is not natural to us. In fact, we are taught as children to resist. So, for example, as a small child you were programmed to believe that being wet and cold was a negative experience. If your mother ever left you standing in the rain, you probably reacted emotionally and cried. Now, as an adult, you may have the same programmed negative reaction to getting wet. Around it hover all the variables: Rain ruins your clothes and messes with your hair, rain is uncomfortable as it runs down your neck, rain is cold, cold makes you sick, and so on.

So one mass of energy in your mind says, "We have to be cozy, warm, and comfortable to feel positive, happy, and secure." Then along comes the rain. Now it's belting down, and you're miles from shelter. Suddenly circumstances—the cold, wet conditions—contradict your opinion or desire.

Now, two masses have established a relationship in your mind, each pulling on the other. Negative emotion flows from the contradiction generated by the cold rain. But is it the rain that is negative? Or is it just your reaction to the rain that causes the contradiction? Water falling from above has no intrinsic quality—positive or negative. When you took a shower this morning, you weren't moaning and groaning.

"Ah! But that was hot water."
"So, it's the temperature of the water that's bothering you is it?"
"Precisely."

But what if you just accept cold water as a part of life? Sometimes it rains. You can get angry and resist, or you can relax and just "do" rain. The circumstances haven't changed—your reaction has. As soon as you agree to "do" rain and stop resisting, the rain becomes warmer and gradually more comfortable. Eventually, you can "do" rain indefinitely and even enjoy it.

If you have never "done" rain, try this: Put out your finest clothes, including your most expensive shoes, and wait. When it starts to rain, dress up and step out, walking steadily, head held high. Don't bat an eyelid. Have no opinion, keep walking, love the rain, accept it, make it your friend.

Eventually your resistance falls to zero The rain disappears, in your mind, anyway. While you are "doing" rain, you can amuse yourself by watching others "not doing" rain properly. There's a bit of fun in that.

If you can't bring yourself to "do" rain immediately, at least regularly make the ego do things that contradict it. Start small. Take cold showers. Give away your overcoat; wear fewer clothes.

Stop talking about the weather altogether. Don't comment on conditions, just experience them. After all, when people say it's cold, what do they mean? They mean it is colder than their expectation. In effect, there is no hot and cold, only temperature that rises and falls sometimes.

All of life's circumstances, like the rain, are neutral. Life has no particular quality, positive or negative, other than the labels we give it. Never forget that.

Even death is neutral. We have no way of knowing how we might react to death. Perhaps life is really crummy compared with death. The hand-wringing and anguish we suffer is probably all for nothing. I have a sneaky suspicion that graduating from the earth plane may be one heck of a celebration.

It's the programmed expectancy that stuffs us up and causes us pain. Not the circumstances.

Expectancy sets up the possibility of contradictions.

Yes, we expect the best, but we must learn not to react when we don't get what we want. If you are diligent, and you concentrate and take right action, you'll most likely always get the best result. But you must love life and accept it when it doesn't go your way.

Be heroic, become a warrior. When faced with an adverse situation, don't react, just accept it. Act calmly. Act powerfully. If you don't know what to do immediately, do nothing—wait until the answer comes to you.

Be mature and take the emotion out of situations. Act in the strongest way possible, given the situation. You can easily train your personality to "do" life rather than fight it. Don't be a self-indulgent wimp. Sometimes life isn't cozy, safe, or guaranteed. If you're up to your eyes in muck and bullets, first "do" bullets, then "do" muck.

It's so simple. It's our silly expectancy and the ego's self-importance that demands that things have to be one way or the other. That's what causes us all the pain—not life itself.

Life is mostly guesswork. You will usually guess more or less right, and sometimes you'll guess wrong. When you guess wrong, don't react—love your mistakes, and don't beat yourself up.

Hey! You thought you had enough gas in the car and you didn't, so now you're "doing" walking. So what.

Just walk.

Realization

The circumstances of life have no particular quality, either positive or negative. They are neutral. Don't resist them, even the ones that scare you silly. When faced with adversity, buy the solution—not the emotion.
Teach that to others.

*** ***

Chapter Three

Emotion and Desire

3

When ideas come together in your mind to form an opinion, and when that opinion is seen by you to be pleasing, the personality backs up that opinion by investing it with emotion.

Using emotion, the ego can take an idea (opinion) and make it special, more real, and more important.

Emotion is the tool the personality uses to grant its opinions credibility and value. It's how the personality feels worthwhile. It is also how the personality gets what it wants. It can wield emotion like a baseball bat, manipulating others to react to its needs and desires.

We learn the trick as children. A bit of theatrics, temper tantrums—howling at 120 decibels in the middle of the supermarket—worked marvelously when we wanted an ice cream. Emotion was how we got grownups to take notice.

The more insignificant people feel, the more they will seek to bolster their vulnerability by using emotion. They will bathe in it, constantly talking about their emotions, making them special, and elevating them to a grand scale. They will also be fascinated by the emotions of others, fueling their need, constantly discussing emotional issues, watching emotional TV shows—living in the emotion of local and world events, along with the momentary reactions they have to their own lives. The process makes them feel better temporarily.

However, there are several downsides to the use of emotion in this way. Let's say you watch a news story on TV about a war, and you buy into the emotion of it all. Even though your conscious mind knows you are not involved, a subconscious pollution is taking place that makes you feel less safe and more vulnerable. Watching others reacting to situations that are out of control reminds you of the possibility of your own collapse.

Further, the more you allow yourself to be imbalanced emotionally in your own issues, the greater the ego content. Once the personality has a large part of itself invested emotionally in an issue, any contradiction of its position is seen as a great personal trauma or threat.

Emotion elevates the issues of the ego to a greater importance. It grants the ego power. Other people react to our emotion, especially negative emotion. The ego believes that if it is considered important by others, that will make it more special, less vulnerable, and therefore safer. The more power the ego can garner, the more people will observe it to be different, elevated, above the herd, divine—and beyond the central issue of man, which is death. Sometimes, the use of emotion is nothing more than the personality seeking to avoid what it sees as death by insignificance.

In using emotion initially to help us feel more secure, we actually set ourselves up to experience a greater insecurity and personal affront when things go the wrong way.

Through experiencing life, you gradually form habits and establish preferences from which you develop hopes and expectancy. A hope or expectancy is, in fact, an opinion; when you lace opinion with emotion, you generate desire. When life contradicts your deep-rooted emotional desires, you tend to take it more personally than when a hope is denied.

Here's how the process works in practice. You'll start with a vague hope such as "I'd like a day off work." Around that will float ideas that back up that hope. "I'm entitled to a day off; I've worked hard." Now the personality selects from its memory and reasoning arguments to justify its opinion and make the idea right. However, the hope still has no real weight—it is still in the process of developing mass via personal argument and inner dialogue.

So to give the idea real importance, your personality will begin to invest itself in the idea by lacing it with emotion. The "day off" issue starts to become a vital part of the personality's affirmation of self. "I need a day off. I'm desperate for a day off. Life owes me a day off. Other people have time off. I'm a good person, an important person; my health will suffer if I don't have a day off. Taking the day off is right and proper and just." And so on...

Let's say the reality is that you have loads of obligations, and circumstances won't allow you the luxury of a day off.

At this point, the ego flares up, taking the issue very personally. It will see denial as a personal affront and an assault on its integrity and stability. This will begin to erode the ego's sense of security. The unfulfilled desire becomes an affirmation of the personality's powerlessness. The ultimate powerlessness for the personality is death. So the "day off work" now subconsciously becomes an issue of life and death.

The personality begins to resonate weakness through its insecurity, and its psychological and metaphysical strength breaks down quite quickly. From life's rich tapestry flow circumstances that confirm and sustain that self-perceived weakness.

The physical body reacts to the overall message of weakness, and now you have the makings of a rotten little head cold. The car won't start. Your boss loads you with even more work; a bill you can't pay plops through the mail box. Now you can really feel victimized. A hundred insecurities are triggered in your mind. The natural reaction is to feel threatened. Anger develops. Culprits have to be found. Someone must be doing it to you. Interpersonal wars develop. It's a zoo!

The emotion and weight of it all may lie with you for days or even longer—until the personality experiences a major win or uplift that will allow it to get on top of the situation, and so feel secure and worthwhile and happy. All this performance can be traced back to the thought you had last Thursday, which said, "I'd love a day off work."

It's wonderful how this system works. We start with a vague idea; we back that with reasoning to confirm the idea to ourselves. Then we lace it with emotion, investing ourselves in it. Then we go through a ludicrous emotional power play, laying our life on the line, in an attempt to get what we want. When circumstances call our bluff, we're devastated.

If the emotional content you lace into an idea is sustained over a period of time, and if your desire is continually denied, it can lead to yearning. In metaphysical terms, yearning is the act of leaning toward or leaning over an idea, a hope perhaps.

As I have said in my other books, in leaning emotionally toward your dreams, you actually push them away. The emotion of your desire creates a metaphysical gap between you and the condition or scenario you desire, making it harder for you to pull that desired condition to you. The gap is established because yearning is a powerful affirmation that categorically states, "I do not have the thing I yearn for."

In constantly affirming that you haven't got what you want, you deteriorate and disempower what you do have. More important, you pattern your subtle metaphysical energy with an overlay, like a thumbprint, that is discordant with the very thing you want.

There is one further consideration: The thing you desire—fame, success, money, opportunity, romance, whatever—will usually come to you, in part, through the actions of others. It's your fellow humans who help carry your desires from the nebulous metaphysics of possibility to your immediate reality, where you get to feast upon your dreams.

In yearning, we become self-indulgent. Self-indulgence bothers people. They sense it and feel put upon. They don't like the added burden of your emotional weight impinging upon them. It reminds them of the times they needed things and were denied. They react by feeling themselves the underdog, victimized by your indulgence. They will deny you, hoping to control you or have power over you. In doing so, they hope to drop you from what they see as your unreasonable, superior stance.

Further, pining and yearning can become obsessive. Obsession is a serious disease of the ego—it creates emotional weight, blinding you to opportunities that do exist. It also makes you apathetic. By constantly affirming that you haven't got what you need, the body begins to believe it doesn't have what it needs. That makes it weaker. In the act of perpetually yearning, the ego eventually finds itself in a stagnant void, and the lack of energy gradually eats the body.

If the condition persists, it will eventually kill you.

Don't yearn, act. Take 15 minutes of each day to visualize, as though granted, the condition or circumstance you want. Create a mental setting, see yourself with the object of your desire. Become a part of it, let it become a part of you. Allow it to *be* you. Then rise, head out, and do something that moves you toward your dream—something powerful and positive.

Remember, you have to travel toward your dream. It is very unlikely that, unaided, your dream will find you. It's not impossible, but you might be a long time waiting, maybe forever.

By the way, if you want to increase the intensity of your visualizations and meditations, reach the chapter on "Turbo-Thought" in my book *The Quickening*. In it, I discuss how to use the sexual heat of Kundalini to lace your visions with a metaphysical power that is close to unstoppable.

Please note—if the object of your desire is that another person should act in a certain way, put that out and visualize it—but remember they have their own destiny pattern, and it may not coincide with your desire for them.

If you could hope and dream and want things without wrapping those ideas with emotion, you'd be a very happy person. You wouldn't react if life makes you wait or if life denies you completely. You'd be perfectly at one and balanced all the time. It's the emotion you invest that makes you sad and sets up contradictions. The less you put yourself on the line emotionally, the less pain you suffer.

Realization

Don't use emotion as a self-indulgent tool to attract attention or to make yourself and your ideas important. Instead, act powerfully and concisely. Be active. Create energy, give of yourself. Let others need you, rather than needing them and acting to win their approval.

*** ***

Chapter Four

Eliminating Fear Through Perception

4

$\mathcal{T}$he greatest cause of anguish is fear. Your first step in conquering fear is to learn not to be frightened of fear itself. Start by seeing fear as your friend, not your tormentor. It's okay to be scared at times. In fact, fear keeps you safe. It heightens your perception and allows you to take corrective action when needed. All fear stems initially from the fear of death.

It's the death of *things* that scares us. Not just physical death, but the termination of familiar things—the end of a relationship, a job, a habit. Sometimes it's a rhythm that is about to change, or your location, or a feeling of certainty you've clung to.

It's *change* we resist. Yet change is the spiritual universe's way of keeping you alive and fresh. We live in a rapidly developing world. If you're not changing, life is leaving you behind. Things will get tougher, not easier.

Once you can accept change and endings, and not see them as personal affronts, most of the fear will dissipate. By attempting to hang on to circumstances and conditions whose energy is spent, you strain yourself.

Constantly remind yourself of what you already know. Nothing is guaranteed or certain. It doesn't have to be.

You can be balanced in all circumstances.

Fear of change and fear of the unknown are just malaise of the ego. You don't have to know what will happen in the future in order to feel safe. In fact, the more you evolve and expand your consciousness, the more unpredictable life becomes. The less certain you are, the higher you have climbed.

Cozy, unchanging rhythms are manifestations of the intellect. Often dull and stifling, they are only suited to the lazy or those who lack courage—those who prefer to exist in a confined, defendable area where nothing unexpected can happen. Important fish in little puddles, swimming in their own effluent.

You don't need a puddle, and there's not much oxygen in a pond either. Pick a river.

Flow and go. Be fearless, believe. Let the energy of life carry you spontaneously from stepping stone to stepping stone. Win your freedom. Reach for the open sea. All will be well.

Resistance to change is mostly ego.

If your ego is frightened, ridicule it. Or just chat to it and tell it everything's fine. Then step to your spiritual side. Embrace the spirit, as it has embraced you from the beginning of time, in the warm glow of its celestial light. That's the heroic way.

Realization

All fear is nothing more than the ego's expectancy of an upcoming contradiction. Most of it is not real. Dissipate its power by refusing to buy the emotion. Make fear your friend. Talk to it. Accommodate it as a helper and ally, and most of your fear will change or disappear completely.

*** ***

Chapter Five

Healing Confusion

5

On our vain attempt to achieve security, we do a lot of thinking. We're constantly trying to guess what's going to happen next.

Modern life is full of choices. Given that many things are unpredictable, making the right choice is sometimes a difficult process. Confusion is endemic to the Western tribes. Millions of human hours are given to the process.

Confusion is a mind game that clouds your inner knowing and causes you to vacillate. It makes for indecisive action, poor reasoning, and instability—which manifest as erratic behavior and stress. When you are uncommitted and confused, your results are poor or you fail completely.

Would you like to eliminate confusion from your life forever?

Yes or no?

If your answer is no, please skip this bit. If your answer is yes, please read on.

Confusion comes, first and foremost, from questions. You can't be confused unless you first ask a question. If you are serious about eliminating confusion, begin by reducing the number of questions you ask yourself.

Yes, you can ponder your life. And yes, meditate and feel things through. But it's the diarrhea of questions you ask yourself that drives you nuts.

Do this: Agree from this day forth to eliminate 90 percent of all your questions. Next, agree never to make any decisions solely via logic and intellect. Use your feelings, even though they may seem illogical at times. Given two or three alternatives, you are either going to *know* through your feelings what direction to take, or you'll be unsure.

If you know, go.

If you don't know and you have to mentally grind the options back and forth for days on end, none of the possibilities offered can be right at this time anyway.

They may never be right. Decision should be natural and come from the heart. If it doesn't feel right and you are not sure, do nothing.

Watching and waiting is my way. However, if you have to approach things intellectually because that is your habit, then, rather than pondering and being confused, collect information. Most people who make intellectual and logical decisions suffer hits because of a lack of information. Never advance your troops into a valley without sending a few scouts up to the high ground. You don't want to plow into situations outnumbered, disadvantaged, and unsure.

In passing, here are a few ideas about conflicts—which, after all, are a major source of mental weight. My preferred method is to avoid them, by watching everything, all of the time, and taking early corrective action. Or, by not giving away control in the first place— which is how most of the trouble arises. Almost always, conflicts are various forms of ego-related turf wars.

My next move is always to try to walk away before the conflict gets going, and to agree to release whatever the conflict is about.

My third recommendation deals only with situations where the conflict really is unavoidable. First evaluate your chances of success. Never go into situations where winning is in doubt. If you know you're bound to win, start by pretending to retreat, and get the emotion out of the situation. Your feigned retreat puts others off their guard.

Then, quietly garner all your strength. When you're ready—and not before—come at the conflict with the element of surprise, and with the full force of your power and concentration. All guns blazing. Never use a sledgehammer to crack a nut if you can use a ten-ton pile driver. Victories should be swift, bloodless, and completed in the most efficient manner possible.

Try also to offer the opposition an honorable surrender. That's the kindest way. It's gracious and spiritual to allow their ego an intellectual escape route even if it is mostly hooey. You don't want to destroy people. The object of this journey is to expand goodness. You are not here to judge and punish others.

In relation to confusion, remember this: Everything gives off energy. When your feelings can't read a situation properly, that tells you the circumstances you're considering lack energy. Either the situation is wrong for you, or you are not ready, or this is not the proper time.

What you choose to do in life is not usually as important as the level of power and concentration you bring to your action, and the timing you choose when exerting that power. Timing and concerted action are the keys to success. Selecting direction is tertiary to timing and power.

In helping others resolve their confusion, never ask the individual what they think, always ask how they *feel* about an issue. Then ask them what they want. Help them discover whether they really want what it is they think they want. As I said, most wanting is ego.

Then get them to look at whether their want is reasonable, given their energy and circumstances. And, finally, is it likely? Most individuals are professional dreamers who, in fact, only need the dreaming—they don't need the responsibility or the action required to materialize their dreams.

When a dream becomes a reality, the experience of it naturally changes. Usually, reality is a letdown compared with the vision. The idea of their dream actually becoming a part of their lives is often too daunting. So, many ensure they are never disappointed by underperforming or selecting actions that ensure their dream remains just that—only a dream.

Realization

Confusion is a manifestation of an unsettled intellect. The intellect is dominated by the ego. So confusion is mostly the ego's chatter harassing your life. Train the ego to ask fewer questions and answer most of the others with, "I don't know, and I don't care."

*** ***

Chapter Six

Healing Frustration

6

*F*rustration comes from expectancy, the emotional outcropping of which is desire. We use past rhythms and experiences, hoping to extrapolate from that the timing of some future event. Sometimes that works and often it doesn't. Most frustration stems from slotting hopes and plans into preselected time frames that you consider necessary to your happiness and well-being. That's not a mature way to conduct your life.

You know things usually take longer than you think they will, because it's easier to think something through than it is to carry it out in practice. Important things always take longer than you expect. That's because they are usually more complex, and because often the circumstance or condition you desire eludes you until you have matured and grown to where you can not only handle it, but claim it.

The other main cause of frustration is people. We usually try to slot people into patterns that suit us. That is a futile exercise in self-destruction. You can certainly encourage people and hope they might change, but in the end you either love them unconditionally for what they are or you have to agree to walk.

In my early 20s, I owned a clothing company. We hired a great designer who was the mainstay of the corporation. She was indispensable. Exercising power over us, she totally controlled the fate of the company—and she knew it. After a while, her ego kicked in with a vengeance, and she became temperamental, capricious, and unreliable. As she wobbled, the whole company wobbled with her. She caused endless trouble because we had no real control.

From that day forth, I decided I would never suffer the same situation again. Now, everyone in my life is dispensable. I hold no permanent emotion to any situation or person—including family and friends. Everything can be released. Nothing is obligatory. When people know that is your attitude, they tend to be more equitable and realistic. They certainly are more caring, more diligent.

WEIGHT LOSS FOR THE MIND

You can work with people, and you can be loving and patient while they grow and respond to positive input. But in the end, if they won't change or—in the case of an employee—toe the line and support the cause, then you have to let them go. Never get into a situation where someone is so indispensable you can't get rid of them.

This is especially true of romance, where one tends to give away control more easily. Nobody should ever be essential to you. Falling in love is fun, but don't let it blind you to the fact that there are five billion characters out there to bat at. Make sure the focus of your affection is constantly reminded that he or she isn't too vital and that, though you may love them and you may have chosen them, you are also aware of the vast field of opportunity lying just beyond the front door.

It's fine to rely on people if you are really sure of the person you are relying on. But most individuals aren't too solid, especially under pressure. If you have to rely on people, be sure you spread the risk. No one person should hold the key to your life. It always amazes me how people will entrust their entire life's savings to some character or organization they hardly know. Take many small, calculated risks rather than plunge all of yourself on the one bet.

A mistake we frequently make when dealing with people is to expect them to remain the same. We remember them as they used to be. In fact, people change, minute by minute, second by second. They suffer mood swings, energy shifts, emotional waves, and psycho logical changes. That often makes them unpredictable, erratic, and irresponsible. In many cases, relying on others means giving away your power. Sometimes you have little or no choice. However, you should design your life to avoid it as much as possible.

The other source of frustration for many is the experience of not getting what they want. The solution to that is to not want whatever it is you think you want. If you can't manage that, at least want fewer things. The more things you have to have, the more vulnerable you become. If you are mature and evolved, you'll need nothing from anyone—and what little you do need you can provide for yourself.

Remember, most of the things you think you need are ego trips designed to bolster your image and your perception of security. Many of them are not particularly vital. You'll waste a lot of energy satisfying your ego only to find that, as soon as it's got what it wants, it ignores all your efforts and promptly nails another list of demands to your forehead.

The ego will always try to force you to slave for its vision. I wouldn't stand for that BS if I were you.

Realization

Frustration stems from the nasty habit of allowing the ego to decide the timing and delivery of its desires. If you blindfold the ego with discipline and never show it the menu of life, it doesn't bitch about the food—it's thrilled that you are eating to keep alive.

*** ***

Chapter Seven

Healing Guilt

7

*G*uilt is silly, self-indulgent, and weak. It's often an emotional outcropping of a poor self-image.

You didn't come to earth because you are perfect—quite the reverse. You came because you needed to learn lessons that are available here. If you've stuffed up some aspect of your life, all it means is that you attended the seminar of life and got the message.

There is no real sin—only high energy and low energy. If your actions were less than best, you can forgive yourself and resolve to do better next time. Probably there won't be a next time. You usually only have to stuff up once to get the point. Certainly you might have acted better, but you didn't. Forgive yourself. You're not a bloody angel. If you were, you wouldn't be here.

The past is past and can't be fixed. The only tragedy is when you carry a negative memory of it into the future. Absolve yourself. If needs be, create a solemn ceremony, light a candle, say a prayer or meditate, and release yourself from previous stuff-ups. If you've hurt people in some way, write them a mental letter and mail it to their heart—tell them you're sorry. Or, better still, pop 'round and apologize to them personally. That's very cathartic for them and for you.

Don't forget, the way people perceive you is clouded by their own program and by what is often an extreme lack of perception. They see you in whatever terms benefit and confirm their opinion. How you *actually* are is mostly a secret. It lies deep within your spiritual self and often is not seen by others. Cling to that reality, and never mind what people think. Trying to win the approval of others by doing a goody-goody routine is often just a carry-over from the child within who seeks parental acceptance. It's not necessary for a mature adult.

Worrying about what people think disempowers your values. It places control in *their* opinions and *their* reactions.

Let people think what they like. They will anyway. You don't have to be a politician and act just to win favor. Instead, act as honorably and correctly as possible. Either people will approve or they won't. Leave it up to them, and remember not to ask them. That way you won't have to stuff around finding out what they think of you, processing their reactions, and explaining yourself to them. That's energy down the drain. Don't mess with it.

Finally, guilt is one of the emotional cudgels people use to establish control, especially in family situations. Don't use guilt to control others and never succumb to the ploy yourself. Call it as you see it. When others see that you won't play ball, they'll back off. Once they hook you emotionally via guilt, it's hard to break free. Any escape you do engineer will usually involve a big fight. The trick is to politely and lovingly sidestep their emotional net before it ensnares you.

Realization

To pine for an alternative past is a waste of energy. In the pristine world of your infinite spiritual self, there is no sin or negative energy. There is only compassion, learning, and unconditional love and forgiveness. Remind yourself and those around you of this fact. In the light of God, everything is healed and seen to be perfect.

*** ***

Chapter Eight

Healing Anger

8

*Y*ou can't develop a lightness of being without sooner or later healing your anger. So let's get rid of that pronto!

As I said in my book *Whispering Winds of Change*, all anger comes initially from an impending sense of loss or an actual loss.

When the ego has a part of its importance invested in material things, it will take the disappearance of those items as an affront. So, when the stereo goes missing, the ego will feel that a part of itself has been taken away. It will rant and rave while it stares longingly at the gap on the carpet where the stereo once stood.

Alternatively, you could understand and accept that the stereo is not really part of you. You can whistle your favorite tune and say to yourself, "Ah! I see they have come for the stereo!"

Often anger arises from losses that are not tangible—for example, the loss of importance or status, the loss of certainty, the loss of a familiar rhythm, the loss of opportunity, and a host of other possible or actual losses. As often as not, the anger generated is over the *possibility* of a loss rather than one that is actually suffered. Often the loss never materializes. It's the very thought of its possibility that drives you bonkers.

The answer is, don't attach too strongly to your possessions and the familiar circumstances of your life. If you do suffer a loss, just agree to suffer the loss. Usually when things retreat from your life, it seems traumatic initially, but in the long term, it is often very helpful. There is a deep spiritual process that keeps you cleansed and light and unencumbered. It is the very process that carries stuff away. Allow it. Thank it for granting you freedom—now you don't have to worry about someone pinching the stereo as you don't have one to worry about.

Once you have accepted the loss of whatever it is you've lost, you can, if you wish, set upon a course of action to retrieve the item or condition. But, before setting off, be sure the item is worth the effort of its retrieval. People become obsessed with their ego's view of justice. It creates prisons for them.

I chuckle over those stories of people who spend five years and half-a-million dollars going to court over some trivial issue; and finally the judge pronounces them right and awards them one dollar in damages. And the plaintiff struts to the front steps of the courthouse, all puffed up, silly as a mad goat, half-a-million poorer, pontificating about how they've been vindicated. Those twits get what they deserve—nothing. There is no percentage in being right; that's ego. The only percentage is in being free.

Don't allow anger to stay with you for long. It's very destructive. In a metaphysical sense, it's nuclear war. It is better to express your anger verbally than to internalize it silently. Long-term, that can make you very sick. Better still, process your anger by scrutinizing the emotional flare you are experiencing. Get to the depth and meaning of it by searching for the loss.

In addition to the silent anger we sometimes feel, there is the theatrical anger people use to terrify and manipulate others into a prescribed course of action. The anger is not real. It is pretense, designed to cause the appropriate effect. You should not adopt the technique, because it shows you up as manipulative and phony. When others use it against you, often it's hard to call their bluff—they will swear black and blue that their feigned reaction is real. They can't admit that some, or all, of their reaction is staged for the politics of the moment and for the benefit of their audience.

The human personality is often covert and dishonest. It's adept at maneuvering situations and people to its advantage.

It's a rare character who doesn't have any issues to defend, or hidden agenda they are trying to satisfy. It's even more rare to find someone who tells you openly what they feel or want. To cover their real intention, which may shift moment to moment, people lie or use half-truths. They try to obscure the real issue with red herrings; or use emotion to validate a dishonest or dubious position.

So someone might say, "I am very angry. You have really hurt my feelings." Usually what they mean is, "I perceive you might or you have actually caused me some kind of loss. I can't allow you to set a precedent. Contradictions are an affront to my ego's sense of self. By blaming you for hurting my feelings, I am hoping to manipulate you into either backing off in the current situation or at least promising to toe the line in the future.

By using theatrical anger and referring to my feelings, I can elevate my position in this issue to a greater importance than your side of the issue."

The correct response is to tell the person that you've understood what they are saying—and then walk away, saying nothing more. If you feel it best to discuss the issue with them, take a line similar to this: "I understand you when you say you feel hurt and angry, but I don't understand why you think I should be responsible for your reactions. In order for me to better understand your position, why don't you explain to me what it is you feel you've lost."

Realization

Once you see that most anger is just a theatrical routine, you can diminish it to the irrelevance it deserves. All anger comes from loss. All loss is a security issue. All security issues are various manifestations of ego. Understand that and most anger becomes unnecessary.

*** ***

Chapter Nine

Elevating Your Spirit

9

The way to eliminate the weight or anguish of your life quickly is to begin to discipline and control the ego. There is no emotional pain that is not ego-driven. We don't want to eliminate the ego completely. Otherwise we'd be wandering around the house each morning, drinking coffee for hours, saying, "Who the hell am I?" We need the ego to sustain a sense of identity.

However, if you'll start by calling ego's bluff, and understanding the games it gets you into, you can develop strategies for managing

things better. You really don't need any quali-
fication or high-powered university degree to
understand the psychology of the ego's
machinations. Its ways are predictable and
easy to understand.

Watch when it suckers you into importance. Stifle it when it seeks more and more
gratification. Ignore it when it offers a hundred questions. Answer most of its questions—let it know that you're not interested
and that you just don't care.

When you experience frustration, look for
the vision that's denied. Look at the time
frames you've invested that vision with.
Develop patience. If you see yourself as an infinite being, you have all eternity. You can wait
forever if need be.

When angry, look for the loss. When you're sad, also look for the loss—sadness is just another manifestation of the same reaction. It's okay to be sad sometimes. Just agree to whatever loss is making you sad, then look for freshness and beauty and the life force. Happiness returns in a moment.

Remember, all mental weight comes from the interaction of two or more opposing forces in your mind—your reaction to circumstance and your opinion or desire. You can fix most of the contradictions by controlling circumstances better and learning not to react when they don't suit. If you have less resistance, your opinions and desires will be less rigid. You'll learn to flow through life rather than fight your way along.

Learning to accept the contradictions of life is just a flip of the mind. Train your mind to be less dogmatic by offering it lots of self-imposed contradictions. Throw yourself into the icy lake of realism; don't let the ego play that cozy, safe, guaranteed game with you. You should never forget that your guarantee in life lies in the fact that you have none. That should spur you to action. Ignore the guarantee, and get on with the journey. In the end, your energy—your perception and your ability—is all you have. Raise your energy and there's your guarantee. Discipline yourself and don't let little emotional upsets become large theatrical self-indulgences that destroy your stability. Change all the things you can easily change, accept most of the ones you can't change, and walk away from the rest.

Change your opinions, control the ego, and the light of spirit flows naturally from within your serenity. The more level and equitable your life becomes, the more the inner light of God shines through your mind— bypassing the ego and showing you a beauty and perception of life that most never even seek, let alone attain.

The light is always there, just beyond the veil of the brain's oscillations and the world of opinion, intellect, and rigidity. One glimpse is enough. No words can properly describe the magnificence of the incandescent light of God. For within it is the very breath of life itself, and from it flows not just an overwhelming sense of love and security, but a sacred knowledge that beckons to us to reach beyond all earthly terms. Laced within that heavenly light is a glow, tempered in a diaphanous hue, the softness of which flows upon you more tenderly than the softest touch possible. It is through this softness that the human heart is settled. All anguish and fear is gently dispersed in the rapture of such a goodness, the likes of which can only overwhelm the human mind in awe.

Dominate the ego, call the spirit forward in as much humility and poise as you can muster, and let that be your guide and your healer. Let the grace of it sweep through your life.

Yes. And imagine this often weary and frightened heart—all fear melted away, all anguish receding in the ghost of time. Yes, and see that same heart—fragile in its beauty, diligent in its task, beating quietly in the human breast, destined to eventual failure yet soldiering on in all circumstances—lovingly providing sustenance to the organism in silence.

Yes, and in that same heart, obligated and labored as it is by its chore, there is space for even more expansion and further obligation. It yearns and seeks and begs to be given it.

What obligation, we ask?

The obligation to carry a spark of the God-force within itself. Not just for the benefit of the organism to which it is indentured, but to shine—ever so faintly perhaps, but shine all the while—for the benefit of others. So all shall see and remember, lest the reason for everything be forgotten in the turmoil of ego and spite, importance and power.

Yes, and if we listen quietly, we will hear the heart as it calls from its hidden place saying, "Give me the light to carry, honor me with the obligation. Let me be the beast of burden and offer the enormity of that incandescence to my brothers and sisters. Let me shine to quiet the fears of our people, elevating and inspiring them, invigorating them in momentary glimpses of the heavenly light and a better world."

Yes. And that heavenly light beckons all the while, yet never insisting. Silently reminding each to glimpse beyond sorrow and pain, beyond the illusion of our insecurity, to glimpse no less into the very depth of God's embrace.

Such is the wonder of it, not mortal can be but engulfed by its majesty. The nobility of which, flowing as a stream of light—sometimes gold, sometimes violet—passes through the human heart, silencing the mind, engulfing the emotions in a profound sensation. Pure love. Eternal love.

The quiet heart—so sweet and kind and full of compassion—reaches back within, seeking to find for itself a place to rest within that violet light of eternity. That humble wish, its grace, its simplicity, when granted, is like a gentle kiss—the goodness of which tumbles upon you with the softness of a snowflake you imagine has fallen from the very hand of God.

Yes, and think again, what is life if not just a collection of experiences? And what are you if not just a memory of your reaction to those experiences? Better, therefore, to remember it well, proud, and heroic. Put aside the silly foibles of the ego that tarnish the memory of you.

Accept and rejoice that such a great gift as this was bestowed by God, personally, upon you. The gift of Life.

Accept the spirit within and let it heal you. Then walk through the lives of your people, teaching them the same process. And one day, some day, you may look back at your planet from a great place, and you may smile. For you'll see the goodness of it all, gently spreading eon by eon to cover all of our people. And you'll remember that you were there in the early days, when the renaissance of that goodness was first launched.

"Yes" you'll say, "I remember my life. I remember it well."

"It was most fine."

*** ***

About the Author

Author and lecturer **Stuart Wilde** is one of the real characters of the self-help, human potential movement. His style is humorous, controversial, poignant, and transformational. He has written 13 books, including those that make up the very successful Taos Quintet, which are considered classics in their genre. They are: *Affirmations*, *The Force*, *Miracles*, *The Quickening*, and *The Trick to Money Is Having Some*. Stuart's books have been translated into 12 languages.

International Tour and Seminar Information

For information on Stuart Wilde's latest tour
and seminar dates in the USA and Canada,
contact:

White Dove International
P.O. Box 1000
Taos, NM 87571
(505) 758-0500
(505) 758-2265 (fax)

Stuart's Website: **www.powersource.com/wilde**

*** ***

We hope you enjoyed this Hay House book. If you would like to receive a free catalog featuring additional Hay House books and products, or if you would like information about the Hay Foundation, please contact:

Hay House, Inc.
P.O. Box 5100
Carlsbad, CA 92018-5100
(760) 431-7695 or **(800) 654-5126**
(760) 431-6948 (fax) or **(800) 650-5115 (fax)**

Please visit the Hay House Website at:
www.hayhouse.com

*** ***

Could any gentleman's
attentions be more welcome
than those of a daring hero
who is honor-bound
to protect her?

But could any
love be more
perilous?

"*R*uskin's friends are no friends of mine. I understand he'd been bothering you—in what way?"

"He was . . . attracted.".

Tony kept his eyes on Alicia's. "And you?"

Irritation flashed in her eyes. "I was not."

He felt his lips ease. "I see."

They remained, gazes locked, for two heartbeats, then he reached out and took her hand, raised her fingers to his lips. Kissed, and felt the tremor that raced through her.

She drew in a quick breath, tensed to step back.

He reacted. Tightening his grip on her fingers, he drew her nearer. Bent his head and touched his lips to hers in the lightest, most fleeting kiss.

Just a brushing of lips, more promise than caress.

He intended it to be that, not a real kiss but a tantalizing temptation.

Raising his head, he watched her lids rise, saw surprise, shock, and curiosity fill her eyes. Then she realized, stiffened, drew back.

Releasing her, he said, "I meant it. I truly enjoyed the afternoon."

He wondered if she understood what he was saying.

Before she could question him—before he could be tempted to say or do anything more—he bowed and turned to the door.

A Gentleman's Honor

STEPHANIE LAURENS

AVON BOOKS

An Imprint of HarperCollins*Publishers*

This is a work of fiction. Names, characters, places, and incidents are products of the author's imagination or are used fictitiously and are not to be construed as real. Any resemblance to actual events, locales, organizations, or persons, living or dead, is entirely coincidental.

AVON BOOKS
An Imprint of HarperCollins*Publishers*
10 East 53rd Street
New York, New York 10022-5299

First Avon Books paperback printing: October 2003

Avon Trademark Reg. U.S. Pat. Off. and in Other Countries, Marca Registrada, Hecho en U.S.A.
HarperCollins® is a registered trademark of HarperCollins Publishers Inc.

Printed in the U.S.A.

10 9 8 7 6 5 4 3 2 1

A Gentleman's Honor

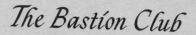

The Bastion Club

"a last bastion against the matchmakers of the ton"

MEMBERS

Christian Allardyce,
Marquess of Dearne

Anthony Blake,
Viscount Torrington

Jocelyn Deverell,
Viscount Paignton

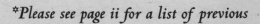

*Please see page ii for a list of previous

Charles St. Austell,
Earl of Lostwithiel

Gervase Tregarth,
Earl of Crowhurst

Jack Warnefleet,
Baron Warnefleet of Minchinbury

#1 ~~Tristan Wemyss,~~ Leonora
~~Earl of Trentham~~ Carling

titles in the Bastion Club series.

ONE

The Bastion Club
Montrose Place, London
March 15, 1816

"WE'VE A MONTH BEFORE THE SEASON BEGINS, AND AL-ready the harpies are hunting in packs." Charles St. Austell sank into one of the eight straight-backed chairs around the mahogany table in the Bastion Club's meeting room.

"As we predicted." Anthony Blake, sixth Viscount Tor-rington, took the chair opposite. "The action in the marriage mart seems close to frenetic."

"Have you seen much of it, then?" Deverell sat beside Charles. "I have to admit I'm biding my time, lying low until the Season begins."

Tony grimaced. "My mother might be resident in Devon, but she has a worthy lieutenant in my godmother, Lady Amery. If I don't appear at her entertainments at least, I can be assured of receiving a sharp note the next morning, inquiring why."

There were laughs—resigned, cynical, and commiserating—from the others as they took their seats. Christian Allardyce, Gervase Tregarth, and Jack Warnefleet all sat, then, in concert, all eyes went to the empty chair beside Charles.

"Trentham sends his regrets." At the head of the table,

Christian didn't bother keeping a straight face. "He didn't sound all that sincere. He wrote that he had more pressing engagements, but wished us joy in our endeavors. He expects to be back in town in a week, however, and looks forward to supporting the six of us through our upcoming travails."

"Kind of him," Gervase quipped, but they were all grinning.

Trentham—Tristan Wemyss—had been the first of their number to successfully achieve his goal, the same goal they all were intent on attaining. They all needed to marry; that common aim had spawned this, their club, their last bastion against the matchmakers of the ton.

Of the six of them as yet unwed, gathered this evening to share the latest news, Tony felt sure he was the most desperate, although why he felt so restless, so frustrated, as if poised for action yet with no enemy in sight, he couldn't fathom. He hadn't felt so moody in years. Then again, he hadn't been a civilian, an ordinary gentleman, for years, either.

"I vote we meet every fortnight," Jack Warnefleet said. "We need to keep abreast of events, so to speak."

"I agree." Gervase nodded across the table. "And if any of us has anything urgent to report, we call a meeting as needed. Given the pace at which matters move in the ton, two weeks is the limit—by then, the ground has shifted."

"I've heard the patronesses of Almack's are thinking of opening their season early, such is the interest."

"Is it true one still has to wear knee breeches?"

"On pain of being turned away." Christian raised his brows. "Although I've yet to ascertain just why that would be painful."

The others laughed. They continued trading information—on events, the latest fashions and tonnish distractions—eventually moving on to comment and caution on individual matrons, matchmaking mamas, dragons, gorgons, and the like—all those who lay in wait for unsuspecting eligible gentlemen with a view to matrimonially ensnaring them.

"Lady Entwhistle's one to avoid—once she sinks her talons into you, it's the devil of a job to break free."

It was their way of coping with the challenge before them.

They'd all spent the last decade or more in the service of His Majesty's government as agents acting in an unofficial capacity scattered throughout France and neighboring states, collecting information on enemy troops, ships, provisions, and strategies. They'd all reported to Dalziel, a spymaster who lurked, a spider in the center of his web, buried in the depths of Whitehall; he oversaw all English military agents on foreign soil.

They'd been exceedingly good at their jobs, witness the fact they were all still alive. But now the war was over, and civilian life had caught up with them. Each had inherited wealth, title, and properties; all were wellborn, yet their natural social circle, the haut ton—the gilded circle to which their births gave entrée and in which their titles, properties, and the attendant responsibilities made participation obligatory—was an arena of operations largely unknown to them.

Yet in gathering information, evaluating it, exploiting it—in that they were experts, so they'd established the Bastion Club to facilitate mutual support for their individual campaigns. As Charles had described it with typical dramatic flair, the club was their secured base from which each would infiltrate the ton, identify the lady he wanted as his wife, and then storm the enemy's position and capture her.

Sipping his brandy, Tony recalled that he'd been first to point out the need for a safe refuge. With a French mother and French godmother intent on encouraging any and all comers to bat their lashes at him—both ladies were aware such a tactic was guaranteed to make him take the matter of finding a wife into his own hands without delay—it had been he who had sounded the warning. The ton was not safe for such as they.

Set on in the gentlemen's clubs, hounded by fond papas as well as gimlet-eyed matrons, all but buried beneath the avalanche of invitations that daily arrived at their doors, life in the ton as an unmarried, wealthy, titled, *eminently* eligible gentleman was these days fraught with danger.

Too many had fallen on the battlefields of the Peninsula, and more recently at Waterloo.

They, the survivors, were marked men.

They were outnumbered, but they'd be damned if they'd be outgunned.

They were experts in battle, in tactics, and strategy; they weren't about to be taken. If they had any say in it, *they* would do the taking.

That was, at the heart of it, the *raison d'être* of the Bastion Club.

"Anything more?" Christian glanced around the table. All shook their heads; they drained their glasses.

"I have to make an appearance at Lady Holland's soirée." Charles pulled a face. "I gather she feels she lent Trentham a helping hand, and now wants to try her luck with me."

Gervase raised his brows. "And you're giving her the chance?"

On his feet, Charles met his gaze. "My mother, sisters, and sisters-in-law are in town."

"Oh, ho! I see. Thinking of taking up residence here for the nonce?"

"Not at present, but I won't deny the thought has crossed my mind."

"I'll come with you." Christian strolled around the table. "I want to have a word with Leigh Hunt about that book he's writing. He's sure to be at Holland House."

Tony stood.

Christian glanced his way. "Are you still glorying in solitary state?"

"Yes, thank heaven—the mater's fixed in Devon." Tony resettled his coat with a graceful shrug. "I have, however, been summoned by my godmother to a soirée at Amery House. I'll have to put in an appearance." He looked around the table. "Anyone going that way?"

Gervase, Jack, and Deverell shook their heads; they'd decided to retire to the club's library and spend the rest of the evening in companionable silence.

Tony bade them farewell; grinning, they wished him luck. Together with Christian and Charles, he went downstairs and into the street. They parted on the pavement; Christian and Charles made for Kensington and Holland House, while Tony headed for Mayfair

Reluctance dragged at him; he ignored it. Any experienced commander knew there were some forces it was wise never to waste energy opposing. Such as godmothers. French godmothers especially.

"Good evening, Mrs. Carrington. A pleasure to meet you again."

Alicia Carrington smiled easily and gave Lord Marshalsea her hand. "My lord. I daresay you recall my sister, Miss Pevensey?"

As his lordship's gaze was riveted on Adriana, standing a few steps away, Alicia's question was largely rhetorical. His lordship, however, had clearly decided that gaining Alicia's support was crucial to securing Adriana's hand; while acknowledging Adriana, he remained by Alicia's side and made conversation in a distant, distracted fashion.

That last, something Alicia viewed with amusement, was due to his lordship's absorption with Adriana, talking animatedly with a coterie of admirers all vying for her favor. Adriana was an English rose gowned in pink silk a shade darker than that generally worn by young ladies, the better to exploit her luxuriant dark curls. Those sheened in the chandeliers' glow, creating the perfect frame for her bewitching features, her large brown eyes set under finely arched black brows, her peaches-and-cream complexion and lush, rosebud lips.

As for Adriana's figure, deliberately understated in the demure gown that hinted at rather than defined, it enticed. Even gowned in sackcloth, Alicia's sister was a package guaranteed to capture gentlemen's eyes, which was the reason they were here in London, in the very heart of the ton.

Masquerading.

At least, Alicia was; Adriana was who she purported to be.

While making the appropriate responses to Lord Marshalsea, Alicia monitored all those who paid court to her younger sister. Everything to date had gone exactly as they, sitting in the tiny parlor of their small house in Little Compton, in rural Warwickshire, which along with the surrounding few acres were all they—she, Adriana, and their three brothers—jointly owned, had planned, yet not even in their admittedly unfettered imaginations had they envisioned that events, people, and opportunities would fall out so well.

Their plan, desperate and reckless though it was, might just succeed. Succeed in securing a future for their three brothers—David, Harry, and Matthew—and for Adriana. For herself, Alicia hadn't thought that far; time enough to turn her mind to her own life once she'd seen her siblings safe.

Lord Marshalsea grew increasingly restless; taking pity on him, Alicia eased him into Adriana's circle, then stepped back, effacing herself as a good chaperone should. She eavesdropped, listening as Adriana handled the gentlemen surrounding her with her customary confidence. Although neither she nor Adriana had had any previous experience of the ton, of the ways of society's elite, since their appearance in town and their introduction to those exalted circles some weeks ago, they'd managed without the slightest hiccup.

Eighteen months of intensive research and their own sound common sense had stood them in good stead. Having three much younger brothers whom they'd largely reared had eradicated any tendency to panic; both jointly and individually, they'd risen to every challenge and triumphed.

Alicia was proud of them both, and increasingly hopeful of an excellent outcome to their scheme.

"Mrs. Carrington—your servant, ma'am."

The drawled words jolted her from the rosy future. Concealing her dismay, calmly turning, lips curving, she gave her hand to the gentleman bowing before her. "Mr. Ruskin. How pleasant to meet you here."

"The pleasure, I assure you, dear lady, is all mine."

Straightening, Ruskin delivered the comment with an intent look and a smile that sent a warning slithering down her spine. He was a largish man, half a head taller than she and heavily built; he dressed well and had the manners of a gentleman, yet there was something about him that, even hampered by inexperience, she recognized as less than savory.

For some ungodly reason, Ruskin had from their first meeting fixed his eye on her. If she could understand why, she'd do something to deflect it; her ever-fertile imagination painted him a snake, with her as his mesmerized prey. She'd pretended ignorance of the tenor of his attentions, had tried to be discouraging. When he'd shocked her by obliquely suggesting a *carte blanche*, she'd pretended not to understand; when he'd later alluded to marriage, she'd feigned deafness and spoken of something else. To no avail; he still sought her out, increasingly pointedly.

Thus far she'd avoided any declaration, thereby avoiding having outright to refuse it. Given her masquerade, she didn't want to risk an overt dismissal, didn't want to draw any attention her way; the most she dared do was behave coolly.

Ruskin's pale gaze had been traveling her face; it rose to trap hers. "If you would grant me the favor of a few minutes in private, my dear, I would be grateful."

He still held her fingers; keeping her expression non-committal, she eased her hand free and used it to gesture to Adriana. "I'm afraid, sir, that with my sister in my care, I really cannot—"

"Ah." Ruskin sent a glance Adriana's way, a comprehensive survey taking in the besotted lordlings and gentlemen gathered around her, and Miss Tiverton, whom Adriana had taken under her wing, thereby earning Lady Hertford's undying gratitude. "What I have to say will, I daresay, have some impact on your sister."

Looking back at Alicia, Ruskin met her eyes; his smile remained easy, a gentleman confident of his ground. "However, your concern is . . . understandable."

His gaze lifted; he scanned the room, filled with the fashionable. Lady Amery's soirée had attracted the cream of the ton; they were present in force, talking, exchanging the latest *on-dits*, exclaiming over the latest juicy scandal.

"Perhaps we could repair to the side of the room?" Ruskin brought his gaze back to her face. "With this noise, no one will hear us; we'll be able to talk, and you'll be able to keep your ravishingly lovely young sister safe . . . and in view."

Steel rang beneath his words; Alicia dismissed any thought of refusing him. Inclining her head, feigning serene indifference, she laid her fingers on his sleeve and allowed him to steer her through the crowd.

What unwelcome challenge was she about to face?

Behind her calm facade, her heart beat faster; her lungs felt tight. Had she imagined the threat in his tone?

An alcove behind a chaise filled with dowagers provided a small oasis of relative privacy. As Ruskin had said, she could still see Adriana and her court clearly. If they kept their voices low, not even the dowagers, heads close swapping scandal, would overhear.

Ruskin stood beside her, calmly looking out over the crowd. "I would suggest, my dear, that you hear me out— hear *all* I have to say—before making any reply."

She glanced briefly at him, then stiffly inclined her head. Lifting her fingers from his sleeve, she gripped her fan.

"I think . . ." Ruskin paused, then continued, "I should mention that my home lies not far from Bledington—ah, yes! I see you understand."

Alicia struggled to mask her shock. Bledington lay southwest of the market town of Chipping Norton; Little Compton, their village, lay to the northwest—as the crow flew there could be no more than eight miles between Little Compton and Bledington.

But Ruskin and she had never met in the country. Her family had lived a circumscribed existence, until recently never venturing beyond Chipping Norton. In embarking on her masquerade, she'd been certain no one in London would know her.

Ruskin guessed her thoughts. "We never met in the country, but I saw you and your sister when I was home last Christmas. The pair of you were crossing the market square."

She glanced up.

He caught her eye, and smiled wolfishly. "I determined, then, to have you."

Involuntarily, her eyes widened.

His smile turned self-deprecatory. "Indeed—quite romantic." He looked back at the crowd. "I asked and was told your name—Miss Alicia Pevensey."

He paused, then shrugged. "If you hadn't appeared in London, no doubt nothing would have come of it. But you did appear, a few months later—as a widow of more than a year's standing. I wasn't fooled for a moment, but

I comprehended your need of the ruse, and appreciated your courage in implementing it. It was a bold move, but one with every chance of success. I saw no reason to do other than wish you well. As my admiration for your astuteness grew, my interest in you on a personal level firmed.

"However"—his voice hardened—"when I offered you my protection, you refused. On reflection, I decided to do the honorable thing and offer for your hand. Again, however, you turned up your nose—quite why I have no notion. You seem uninterested in attaching a husband, solely concerned with watching over your sister as she makes her choice. Presumably, given you transparently have no need of funds, you've determined to make your own decision in your own time."

His gaze returned to her face. "I would suggest, my dear *Mrs. Carrington*, that your time has run out."

Alicia fought down the faintness, the giddiness that threatened; the room seemed to be whirling. She drew a slow breath, then asked, her tone commendably even, "What, precisely, do you mean?"

His expression remained intent. "I mean that your performance as a hoity widow in dismissing my suit was so convincing I checked my information. Today, I received a letter from old Dr. Lange. He assures me that the Pevensey sisters—*both* Pevensey sisters—remain unwed."

The room gyrated, heaved, then abruptly stopped.

Disaster stared her in the face.

"Indeed." Ruskin's predatory smile dawned, yet his self-deprecation remained. "But fear not—having concluded that marrying you would be an excellent notion, nothing I've learned has changed my mind."

His gaze hardened. "So let us be clear, my dear. *Mrs. Carrington* cannot continue in the ton, but if you consent to become Mrs. William Ruskin, I see no reason the ton should ever learn that Mrs. Carrington did not exist. I'm renewing my offer for your hand. Should you accept, there's no reason your plan to establish the lovely Adriana will suffer so much as a hiccup." His smile faded; he held her gaze. "I trust I make myself plain?"

Triumph had turned to ashes; her mouth was dry. Moistening her lips, she fought to keep her tone even. "I believe I understand you perfectly, sir. However . . . I would ask for a little time to consider my reply."

His brows rose; his untrustworthy smile returned. "Of course. You may have twenty-four hours—there isn't much to consider, after all."

She sucked in a breath, frantically gathered her wits to protest.

His gaze, hard, trapped hers. "Tomorrow evening you can formally accept me—tomorrow night, I'll expect to share your bed."

Shock held her immobile, staring at his face; she searched his eyes but found no hint of any emotion worth appealing to.

When she made no reply, he bowed punctiliously. "I'll call on you tomorrow evening at nine."

Turning, he left her, strolling into the crowd.

Alicia stood frozen, her wits careening, her skin icy, her stomach hollow.

A burst of raucous laughter from the dowagers, ineffectually smothered, jerked her back to earth. She glanced across the room at Adriana. Her sister was holding her own, but had noticed her distraction; their gazes met, but when Adriana arched a brow, Alicia shook her head.

She had to regain control—of their plan, of her life. Marry Ruskin, or . . . she could barely take it in.

Faintness still gripped her; she felt hot one minute, cold the next. Seeing a footman passing, she requested a glass of water. He brought it promptly, eyeing her warily as if she might swoon; she forced a weak smile and thanked him.

A chair stood against the wall two yards away. She

walked to it and sat, sipping her water. After a few minutes, she flicked open her fan and waved it before her face.

She had to think. Adriana was safe for the moment . . .

Blocking out all thought of the threat Ruskin had made, she focused on him, on what he'd said—on what he knew and what he didn't. Why he was acting as he was, what insights that gave her, how she might press him to change his mind.

They—she, Adriana and the three boys—desperately needed Adriana to make a good match. Not with just any gentleman, but one with reasonable wealth and a sufficiently good heart not only to forgive them the deception they were practicing but to provide for the boys' schooling.

They were as near to penniless as made no difference. They were wellborn, but had no close connections; there were just the five of them—or more correctly Alicia and Adriana to look after them all. David was only twelve years old, Harry ten, and Matthew eight. Without an education, there would be no future for them.

Adriana had to be given the chance to make the match they felt certain she could. She was stunningly beautiful; the ton had already labeled her a "diamond of the first water" among other admiring epithets. She would be a hit, a wild success; once the Season proper commenced, she could take her pick from the wealthy eligibles, and she was wise enough, despite her years, to make the right choice, with Alicia's help.

One gentleman would be the right one for her, for them all, and then the family—Adriana and the three boys—would be safe.

Alicia had no other goal before her; she hadn't had for the past eighteen months, since their mother died. Their father had died years before, leaving the family with little money and few possessions.

They'd scrimped, saved, and survived. And now they'd

risked all on this one throw that fate, in creating Adriana's undoubted beauty, had given them. In order to do so, Alicia had behaved in ways she wouldn't otherwise countenance; she'd taken risks she otherwise never would have—and thus far won.

She'd become Mrs. Carrington, a wealthy and fashionable widow, the perfect chaperone to introduce Adriana to the ton. Hiring a professional chaperone had been out of the question—not only did they not have the funds, but to the ton, especially the upper echelons, a wealthy widow presenting her ravishing younger sister was a significantly different prospect to two provincial spinsters with a hired chaperone, one whose relative standing would have illuminated theirs.

With her masquerade in place, they'd cleared every hurdle and succeeded in insinuating themselves into the ton. The ultimate success beckoned; all was going so well . . .

There *had* to be a way around Ruskin and his threat.

She could marry him, but the recoil the thought evoked made her cast that as a last resort; she'd return to it if and only if there was no other way.

One thing Ruskin had said clanged in her mind. He thought they had money. He'd discovered she'd never married, but he hadn't learned she was first cousin to a pauper.

What if she told him?

Would that make him turn aside from his plan, or simply place another weapon in his hands? If he learned she came with no money but only costs and responsibilities, would she decide not to marry her after all, but instead force her to become his mistress?

The thought made her nauseous. She gulped the last of her water, then rose to set the glass down on a nearby sideboard. The movement had her facing down the side of the room just as Ruskin stepped out through a pair of glass doors.

Moving into the crowd, she looked more closely. The doors, left ajar, led outside, presumably to a terrace.

The very fact she'd seen him go out into a place that would afford greater privacy hardened her resolve; she would go and speak with him. Despite what seemed an unhealthy wish to "have her," there might be some other reward he would accept in return for his silence.

It was worth a try. She did have acquaintances with money she could—or at least thought she might be able to—call on. At the very least, she might be able to talk him into giving her more time.

Tacking through the crowd, she came up beside Adriana.

With a smile at her cavaliers, her sister turned to her. "What's wrong?"

Alicia wondered again at her sister's facility for seeing straight through her. "Nothing I can't manage—I'll tell you about it later. I'm just going out onto the terrace to talk to Mr. Ruskin. I'll be back shortly.

The look in Adriana's eyes said she had many more questions but accepted she couldn't ask them now. "All right, but be careful. He's a toad, if not worse."

"I say, Mrs. Carrington, will you and Miss Pevensey be attending the opening night at the Theatre Royal?"

Young Lord Middleton was as eager as a spaniel; Alicia returned a vague answer, exchanged a few more comments, then slid out of the group and headed for the glass doors.

As she'd surmised, they gave onto a terrace overlooking the gardens. The doors had been left ajar to let air into the crowded and overheated drawing room; slipping through, she drew them almost closed behind her, then, shrugging her shawl over her shoulders, looked about.

It was mid-March and chilly; she was glad of the shawl. Not surprisingly, there were no others strolling in the still and frosty night. She glanced around, expecting to see Ruskin, perhaps indulging in a cigarillo, but the terrace, overhung with shadows, was empty. Walking to the balustrade, she surveyed the gardens. No Ruskin. Had he chosen to leave the soirée by this route?

She glanced down along the path that, from its direction, she assumed led to a gate giving onto the street.

A flash of movement caught her eye.

She peered, and glimpsed a man-sized shadow in the gloom beneath a huge tree beside the path. The tree was massive, the shadows beneath it dense, but she thought the man had just sat down. Perhaps there was a seat there, and Ruskin had gone to sit and smoke, or to think.

Of tomorrow night.

The idea had her stiffening her spine. Pulling her shawl tight, she descended the steps and set off along the path.

With every step Tony took along Park Street, his resistance to attending his godmother's soirée and smiling and chatting and doing the pretty with a gaggle of young ladies with whom he had nothing in common—and who, if they knew the man he truly was, would probably faint—waxed stronger. Indeed, his reluctance over the whole damn business was veering toward the despondent.

Not by the wildest, most exaggerated flight of fancy could he imagine being married to any of the young beauties thus far paraded before him. They were . . . too young. Too innocent, too untouched by life. He felt no connection with them whatsoever.

The fact that they—each and every one—would happily accept his suit if he chose to favor them, and think themselves blessed, raised definite questions as to their intelligence. He was not, had never been, an easy man; one look should tell any sane woman that. He would not be an easy husband. The position of his wife was one that would demand a great deal of its holder, an aspect of which the sweet young things seemed to have no inkling.

His wife . . .

Not so many years ago, the thought of searching for

her would have had him laughing. He hadn't imagined finding a wife was something that would unduly exercise him—when he needed to marry, the right lady would be there, miraculously waiting.

He hadn't, then, appreciated just how important, how vital her role *vis à vis* himself would be.

Now he was faced with that anticipated need to marry—and an even greater need to find the right wife— but the right lady had thus far shown no inclination even to make an appearance. He had no idea what she might look like, or be like, what aspects of her character or personality would be the vital clue—the crucial elements in her that he needed.

He wanted a wife. The restlessness that seemed to enmesh his very soul left him in no doubt of that, but exactly *what* he wanted, let alone why . . . that was the point on which he'd run aground.

Identify the target. The first rule in planning any successful sortie.

Until he succeeded in satisfying that requirement, he couldn't even start his campaign; the frustration irked, fueling his habitual impatience. Hunting a wife was ten times worse than hunting spies had ever been.

His footsteps echoed. Another, distant footfall sounded; his agent's senses, still very much a part of him, flaring to full attention, he looked up.

Through the mist wreathing the street, he saw a man, well muffled in coat and hat and carrying a cane, step away from the garden gate of . . . Amery House. The man was too far away to recognize and walked quickly away in the opposite direction.

Tony's godmother's house stood at the corner of Park and Green Streets, facing Green Street. The garden gate opened to a path leading up to the drawing-room terrace.

By now the soirée would be in full swing. The thought of the feminine chatter, the high-pitched laughter, the giggles, the measuring glances of the matrons, the calculation in so many eyes, welled and pressed down on him.

On his left, the garden gate drew nearer. The temptation to take that route, to slip inside without any announcement, to mingle and quickly look over the field, then perhaps to retreat before even his godmother knew he was there, surfaced . . . and grew.

Closing his hand on the wrought-iron latch, he lifted it. The gate swung soundlessly open; passing through, he closed it quietly behind him. Through the silent garden, heavily shadowed by large and ancient trees, the sound of conversation and laughter drifted down to him.

Mentally girding his loins, he drew in a deep breath, then quickly climbed the steep flight of steps that led up to the level of the garden.

Through ingrained habit, he moved silently.

The woman crouching by the side of the man lying sprawled on his back, shoulders propped against the trunk of the largest tree in the garden, didn't hear him.

The tableau exploded into Tony's vision as he gained the top of the steps. Senses instantly alert, fully deployed, he paused.

Slim, svelte, gowned for the evening in silk, her dark hair piled high, with a silvery shawl wrapped about her shoulders and clutched tight with one hand, the lady slowly, very slowly, rose. In her other hand, she held a long, scalloped stilletto; streaks of blood beaded on the wicked blade.

She held the dagger by the hilt, loosely grasped between her fingers, pointing downward. She stared at the blade as if it were a snake.

A drop of dark liquid fell from the dagger's point.

The lady shuddered.

Tony stepped forward, driven by an urge to take her in his arms; catching himself, he halted. Sensing his presence, she looked up.

A delicate, heart-shaped face, complexion as pale as snow, dark eyes wide with shock, looked blankly at him.

Then, with a visible effort, she gathered herself. "I think he's dead."

Her tone was flat; her voice shook. She was battling hysterics; he was thankful she was winning.

Tamping down that impulsive urge to soothe her, shield her, a ridiculously primitive feeling but unexpectedly powerful, he walked closer. Forcing his gaze from her, he scanned the body, then reached for the dagger. She surrendered it with a shudder, not just of shock but of revulsion.

"Where was it?" He kept his tone impersonal, businesslike. He crouched down, waited.

After an instant, she responded, "In his left side. It had fallen almost out . . . I didn't realize . . ." Her voice started to rise, became thready, and died.

Stay calm. He willed the order at her; a cursory examination confirmed she was right on both counts. The man was dead; he'd been knifed very neatly, a single deadly thrust between the ribs from the back. "Who is he—do you know?"

"A Mr. Ruskin—William Ruskin."

He glanced at her sharply. "You knew him."

He hadn't thought it possible, but her eyes widened even more. "No!"

Alicia caught her breath, closed her eyes, fought to summon her wits. "That is"—she opened her eyes again—"only to speak to. Socially. At the soirée . . ."

Waving back at the house, she dragged in a breath and rushed on, "I came out for some air. A headache . . . there was no one out here. I thought to wander . . ." Her gaze slid to Ruskin's body. She gulped. "Then I found him."

Ruskin had threatened her, her plan, her family's future. He'd been blackmailing her—and now he was dead. His blood oozed in a black pool by his side, stained the dagger now in the stranger's hand. It was a struggle to take everything in, to know even what she felt, let alone how best to react.

The unknown gentleman rose. "Did you see anyone leaving?"

She stared at him. "No." She glanced around, suddenly aware of the deep silence of the gardens. Abruptly, she swung her gaze back to him.

Tony sensed her sudden thought, her rising panic. Was irritated by it. "No—*I* didn't kill him."

His tone reassured her; her sudden tenseness faded.

He glanced again at the corpse, then at her; he waved back up the path. "Come. We must go in and tell them."

She blinked, but didn't move.

He reached for her elbow. She permitted him to take it, let him turn her unresisting, and steer her back toward the terrace. She moved slowly, clearly still in shock. He glanced at her pale face, but the shadows revealed little. "Did Ruskin have a wife, do you know?"

She started; he felt the jerk through his hold on her arm. From beneath her lashes, she cast him a shocked glance. "No." Her voice was tight, strained; she looked ahead. "No wife."

If anything, she'd paled even more. He prayed she wouldn't swoon, at least not before he got her inside. Appearing at his godmother's soirée via the terrace doors with a lady senseless in his arms would create a stir even more intense than murder.

She started shaking as they went up the steps, but she clung to her composure with a grim determination he was experienced enough to admire.

The terrace doors were ajar; they walked into the drawing room without attracting any particular attention. Finally in good light, he looked down at her, studied her features, the straight, finely chiseled nose, lips a trifle too wide, yet full, lush and tempting. She was above average in height, her dark hair piled high in gleaming coils exposing the delicate curve of her nape and the fine bones of her shoulders.

Instinct quivered; deep within him, primitive emotion stirred. Sexual attraction was only part of it; again, the urge to draw her close, to keep her close, welled.

She looked up, met his gaze. Her eyes were more green than hazel, large and well set under arched brows; they were presently wide, their expression dazed, almost haunted.

Fortunately, she seemed in no danger of succumbing to the vapors. Spying a chair along the wall, he guided her to it; she sank down with relief. "I must speak with Lady Amery's butler. If you'll remain here, I'll send a footman with a glass of water."

Alicia lifted her eyes to his face. To his velvet black eyes, to the concern and the focus she sensed behind his expression, behind the masklike, chiseled, haughtily angular planes. His was the most strikingly attractive masculine face she'd ever seen; he was the most startlingly attractive man she'd ever met, elegant, graceful, and strong. It was his strength she was most aware of; when he'd taken her arm and walked beside her, her senses had drunk it in.

Looking up at him, into his eyes, she drew on that strength again, and felt the horror they'd left outside recede even further. The reality around them came into sharper focus; a glass of water, a moment to compose herself, and she'd manage. "If you would . . . thank you."

That "thank-you" was for far more than the glass of water.

He bowed, then turned and headed across the room.

Suppressing an inner wrench, not just reluctance but real resistance to leaving her, Tony found a footman and dispatched him to revive her, then, ignoring the many who tried to catch his eye, he found Clusters, the

Amerys' butler, and pulled him into the library to explain the situation and give the necessary orders.

He'd been visiting Amery House since he'd been six months old; the staff knew him well. They acted on his orders, summoning his lordship from the cardroom and her ladyship from the drawing room, and sending a footman running for the Watch.

He wasn't entirely surprised by the ensuing circus; his godmother was French, after all, and in this instance she was ably supported by the Watch captain, a supercilious sort who saw difficulties where none existed. Having taken the man's measure with one glance, Tony omitted mentioning the lady's presence. There was, in his view, no reason to expose her to further and unnecessary trauma; given the dead man's size and the way she'd held the dagger, it was difficult if not impossible to convincingly cast her as the killer.

The man he'd seen leaving the grounds via the garden gate was much more likely to have done the deed.

Besides, he didn't know the lady's name.

That thought was uppermost in his mind when, finally free of the responsibility of finding a murdered man, he returned to the drawing room and discovered her gone. She wasn't where he'd left her; he scouted the rooms, but she was no longer among the guests.

The crowd had thinned appreciably. No doubt she'd been with others, perhaps a husband, and they'd had to leave. . . .

The possibility put a rein on his thoughts, dampened his enthusiasm. Extricating himself from the coils of a particularly tenacious matron with two daughters to marry off, he stepped into the hall and headed for the front door.

On the front steps, he paused and drew in a deep breath. The night was crisp; a sharp frost hung in the air.

His mind remained full of the lady.

He was conscious of a certain disappointment. He hadn't expected her gratitude, yet he wouldn't have minded a chance to look into those wide green eyes again, to have them focus on him when they weren't glazed with shock.

To look deep and see if she, too, had felt that stirring, that quickening in the blood, the first flicker of heat.

In the distance a bell tolled the hour. Drawing in another breath, he went down the steps and headed home.

Home was a quiet, silent place, a huge old house with only him in it. Along with his staff, who were usually zealous in preserving him from all undue aggravation.

It was therefore a rude shock to be shaken awake by his father's valet, whom he'd inherited along with the title, and informed that there was a gentleman downstairs wishful of speaking with him even though it was only nine o'clock.

When asked to state his business, the gentleman had replied that his name was Dalziel, and their master would assuredly see him.

Accepting that no one in his right mind would claim to be Dalziel if they weren't, Tony grumbled mightily but consented to rise and get dressed.

Curiosity propelled him downstairs; in the past, he and his peers had always been summoned to wait on Dalziel in his office in Whitehall. Of course, he was no longer one of Dalziel's minions, yet he couldn't help feeling that alone would not account for Dalziel's courtesy in calling on him.

Even if it was just past nine o'clock.

Entering the library where Hungerford, his butler, had left Dalziel to kick his heels, the first thing he became aware of was the aroma of fresh coffee; Hungerford had served Dalziel a cup.

Nodding to Dalziel, elegantly disposed in an armchair, he went straight to the bellpull and tugged. Then he turned and, propping an arm along the mantelpiece, faced Dalziel, who had set down his cup and was waiting.

"I apologize for the early hour, but I understand from Whitley that you discovered a dead body last night."

Tony looked into Dalziel's dark brown eyes, half-hidden by heavy lids, and wondered if such occurrences ever slipped past his attention. "I did. Pure chance. What's your—or Whitley's—interest?"

Lord Whitley was Dalziel's opposite number in the Home Office; Tony had been one, possibly the only, member of Dalziel's group ever to have liaised with agents run by Whitley. Their mutual targets had been the spy networks operating out of London, attempting to undermine Wellington's campaigns.

"The victim, William Ruskin, was a senior administrative clerk in the Customs and Revenue Office." Dalziel's expression remained uninformative; his dark gaze never wavered. "I came to inquire whether there was any story I should know?"

A senior administrative clerk in the Customs and Revenue Office; recalling the stiletto, an assassin's blade, Tony was no longer truly sure. He refocused on Dalziel's face. "I don't believe so."

He knew that Dalziel would have noted his hesitation; equally, he knew that his erstwhile commander would accept his assessment.

Dalziel did, with an inclination of his head. He rose. Met Tony's eyes. "If there's any change in the situation, do let me know."

With a polite nod, he headed for the door.

Tony saw him into the hall and handed him into the care of a footman; retreating to the library, he wondered, as he often had, just who Dalziel really was. Like recognized like; he was certainly of the aristocracy, with his finely hewn Norman features, pale skin and sable hair, yet Tony had checked enough to know Dalziel wasn't his last name. Dalziel was slightly shorter and leaner than the men he had commanded, all ex-Guardsmen, yet he projected an aura of lethal purpose that, in a roomful of larger men, would instantly mark him as the most dangerous.

The one man a wise man would never take his eye from.

The door to the street shut; a second later, Hungerford appeared with a tray bearing a steaming cup of coffee. Tony took it with a grateful murmur; like all excellent butlers, Hungerford always seemed to know what he required without having to be told.

"Shall I ask Cook to send up your breakfast, my lord?"

He nodded. "Yes—I'll be going out shortly."

Hungerford asked no more, but silently left him.

Tony savored the coffee, along with the premonition Dalziel's appearance and his few words had sent tingling along his nerves.

He was too wise to ignore or dismiss the warning, yet, in this case, he wasn't personally involved.

But she might be.

Dalziel's query gave him the perfect excuse to learn more of her. Indeed, given Whitehall's interest, it seemed incumbent upon him to do so. To assure himself that there wasn't anything more nefarious than murder behind Ruskin's death.

He needed to find the lady. *Cherchez la femme.*

TWO

❦

HE REGRETTED NOT ASKING HER NAME, BUT INTRODUC-
tions over a dead body simply hadn't occurred to him, so
all he had was her physical description. The notion of
asking his godmother occurred, only to be dismissed; alerting *Tante* Felicité to any interest on his part—especially
when he wasn't sure of his ground—didn't appeal, and
the lady might have arrived with others. Felicité might
not know her personally.

Over breakfast, he applied his mind to the question of
how to track the lady down. The idea that occurred
seemed a stroke of genius. Ham and sausages disposed
of, he strode into his hall, shrugged on the coat Hungerford held, and headed for Bruton Street.

The lady's gown had been a creation of considerable
elegance; although he hadn't consciously noted it at the
time, it had registered in his mind. The vision leapt
clearly to his inner eye. Pale green silk superbly cut to
compliment a lithe rather than buxom figure; the fall of
the silk, the drape of the neckline, all screamed of an expert modiste's touch.

According to Hungerford, Bruton Street was still home
to the ton's most fashionable modistes. Tony started at
the nearer end, calmly walking into Madame Francesca's
salon and demanding to see Madame.

Madame was delighted to receive him, but regretfully—and it truly was regretfully—could not help him.

That refrain was repeated all the way down the street. By the time he reached Madame Franchot's establishment at the other end, Tony had run out of patience. After enduring fifteen minutes of Madame's earnest inquiries regarding his mother's health, he escaped, no wiser.

Going slowly down the stairs, he wondered where the devil else one of his lady's ilk might obtain her gowns. Reaching the street door, he opened it.

And saw, large as life, walking along the opposite side of the street, the lady herself. So she did come to Bruton Street.

She was walking briskly, absorbed in conversation with a veritable stunner—a younger lady of what even to Tony's jaded eye registered as quite fabulous charms.

He waited inside the doorway until they walked farther on, then went out, closed the door, crossed the street, and fell in in their wake, some twenty yards behind. Not so close that the lady might sense his presence, or see him immediately behind her should she glance around, yet not so far that he risked losing them should they enter any of the shops lining the street.

Somewhat to his surprise, they didn't. They walked on, engrossed in their discussion; reaching Berkeley Square, they continued around it.

He followed.

"There was nothing you could have done—he was already dead and you saw nothing to the point." Adriana stated the facts decisively. "Nothing would have been gained and no point served by you becoming further involved."

"Indeed," Alicia agreed. She just wished she could rid herself of the niggling concern that she *should* have waited in Lady Amery's drawing room, at least for the gentleman to return. He'd been uncommonly sensible and supportive; she should have thanked him properly. There was also the worry that he might have become embroiled in difficulties over finding a dead body—she had no idea of the correct procedures, or even if there *were* correct procedures—yet he'd seemed so competent, doubtless she was worrying over nothing.

She was still jumpy, nervy, hardly surprising but she couldn't allow even a murder to distract her from their plan. Too much depended on it.

"I do hope Pennecuik can get that lilac silk for us—it's a perfect shade to stand out among the other pastels." Adriana glanced at her. "I rather think that design with the frogged jacket would suit—do you remember it?"

Alicia admitted she did. Adriana was trying to distract her, to deflect her thoughts into more practical and productive avenues. They'd just come from visiting Mr. Pennecuik's warehouse, located behind the modistes' salons at the far end of Bruton Street. Mr. Pennecuik supplied the trade with the very best materials; he now also supplied Mrs. Carrington of Waverton Street with the stuffs for the elegant gowns in which she and her beautiful sister, Miss Pevensey, graced the ton's entertainments.

A most amicable arrangement had been reached. Mr. Pennecuik supplied her with the most exclusive fabrics at a considerable discount in return for her telling all those who asked—as hordes of matrons did and would when they clapped eyes on Adriana—that insisting on the best fabric was the key to gaining the most from one's modiste, and the fabrics from Mr. Pennecuik's were unquestionably the best.

As she patronized no modiste, the presumption was that she employed a private seamstress. The truth was she and Adriana, aided by their old nurse, Fitchett, sewed all their gowns. No one, however, needed to know that, and so everyone was pleased with the arrangement.

"Dark purple frogging." Alicia narrowed her eyes, creating the gown in her mind. "With ribbons of an in-between shade to edge the hems."

"Oh, yes! I saw that on a gown last night—it looked quite stunning."

Adriana prattled on. Alicia nodded and hmmed at the right points; inwardly, she returned to the nagging possibility that continued to disturb her.

The gentleman had stated he wasn't the murderer. She'd believed him—still did—but didn't know why. It would have been so easy . . . he might have heard her on the path, propped Ruskin against the tree, hid in the shadows and waited for her to "discover" Ruskin, then walked up and "discovered" her. If anyone asked, she would be honor-bound to state he'd come up after she'd found Ruskin already dead.

Already stabbed.

The memory of the dagger sliding out . . . she shivered.

Adriana glanced at her, then tightened their linked arms, pressing closer. "Stop thinking about it!"

"I can't." It wasn't Ruskin she was thinking most about, but the man who had emerged from the shadows; despite all, it was he who lingered most strongly in her mind.

Determinedly she redirected her thoughts to the crux of her worries. "After all our luck to date, I can't help but worry that some whisper of my involvement with so scandalous a thing as murder will out, and will affect your chances." She met Adriana's gaze. "We all have so much riding on this."

Adriana's smile was truly charming; she was no giddy miss, but a sensible female not easily influenced by man or fate. "Just show me the field and leave the rest to me. I assure you I'm up to it, and while I'm swishing my skirts, you can retreat into the shadows if you wish. But truly, I think it unlikely any news of this murder, much less your part in it, will surface, beyond, of course, the customary 'How unfortunate.' "

Alicia grimaced.

"Now," Adriana continued, "I gather from Miss Tiverton that there'll be quite a different crowd at Lady Mott's tonight. Apparently, her ladyship has a wide acquaintance in the counties, and what with everyone coming up to town early, there's sure to be many at her ball tonight. I think the cerise-and-white stripes will be best for me tonight, and perhaps the dark plum for you."

Alicia let Adriana fill her ears with sartorial plans. Turning into Waverton Street, they headed for their door.

From the corner of the street, Tony watched them climb the steps and enter, waited until the door shut, then ambled past. No one watching him would have noticed his interest.

At the end of Waverton Street he paused, smiled to himself, then headed home.

Lady Mott's ball had been talked of as a small affair.

The ballroom was certainly small. The ball, however, was such a crush Alicia was grateful that the size of Adriana's court gave them some protection.

As was her habit, after delivering Adriana to her admirers, she stepped back to the wall. There were chairs for chaperones a little way along, but she'd quickly realized that, not truly being chaperone material, it behooved her to avoid those who were; they were too inquisitive.

Besides, standing just feet away, she was near if Adriana needed help in dealing with any difficult suitor or avoiding the more wolfish elements who had started to appear at the periphery of her court.

Such gentlemen Alicia showed no hesitation in putting to rout.

The strains of the violins heralded a waltz, one Adriana had granted to Lord Heathcote. Alicia was watching, relaxed yet eagle-eyed as her sister prettily took his lordship's arm, when hard fingers closed about her hand.

She jumped, swallowed a gasp. The fingers felt like iron.

Outraged, she swung around, and looked up—into the dark, hard-featured face of the gentleman from the shadows.

Her lips parted in shock.

One black brow arched. "That's a waltz starting— come and dance."

Her wits scattered. By the time she'd regathered them, she was whirling down the room, and it was suddenly seriously difficult to breathe.

His arms felt like steel, his hand hard and sure on her back. He moved gracefully, effortlessly, all harnessed power, hard muscle and bone. He was tall, lean, yet broad-shouldered; the notion that he'd captured her, seized her and swept her away, and now had her in his keeping, flooded her mind.

She shook it aside, yet the sensation of being swept up by a force beyond her control, engulfed by a strength entirely beyond her power to counter, shocked her, momentarily dazed her.

Tangled her tongue.

Left her mentally scrambling to catch up—and filch the reins of her will back from his grasp.

The look on his face—one of all-seeing, patronizing, not superiority but control—helped enormously.

She dragged in a breath, conscious of her bodice tightening alarmingly. "We haven't been introduced!" The first point that needed to be made.

"Anthony Blake, Viscount Torrington. And you are?"

Flabbergasted. Breathless again. The timbre of his voice, deep, low, vibrated through her. His eyes, deepest black under heavy lids, held hers. She had to moisten her lips. "Alicia . . . Carrington."

Where *were* her wits?

"*Mrs*. Carrington." She dragged in another breath, and felt the reel her wits had been whizzing through start to slow.

His eyes hadn't left hers. Then he slipped his shoulder from under her hand, and that hand, her left, was trapped in his. His fingers shifted, finding the gold band on her ring finger.

His lips twisted fleetingly; he replaced her hand on his shoulder and continued to whirl her smoothly down the room.

She stared at him, beyond astonished. Inwardly thanking the saints for Aunt Maude's ring.

Then she blinked, cleared her throat, and looked over his shoulder into safe oblivion. "I must thank you for your help last evening—I hope the matter was concluded without any undue difficulties. I do ask you to excuse my early retreat." She risked a glance at his face. "I fear I was quite overcome."

In her experience most men accepted that excuse without question.

He looked as if he didn't believe it for a moment.

"*Quite* overcome," she reiterated.

The cynical scepticism—she was sure it was that—in his narrowing eyes only deepened.

Theatrically, she sighed. "I was attending with my *un-married* younger sister. She's in my care. I had to take her home—my responsibility to her came first, above all else, as I'm sure you'll understand."

For a full minute, not a muscle moved in his classically sculpted face, then his brows rose. "I take it Mr. Carrington was not present?"

A whisper of caution tickled her spine; she kept her eyes on his. "I'm a widow."

"Ah."

There seemed a wealth of meanings in the single syllable; she wasn't sure she approved of any of them. Her tone sharp, she inquired, "And what do you mean by that?"

He opened his eyes wider, the heavy lids lifting; his lips, thin, mobile, the lower somewhat fuller, seemed to ease. His black gaze held hers trapped; he made no move to answer her question.

Not with words.

She suddenly felt quite warm.

Flustered—she was actually flustered.

The music reached its conclusion; the dance ended. She'd never been so thankful of any event in her life. She stepped out of his arms, only to feel his hand close once more about hers.

His gaze on her face, he set her hand on his sleeve. "Allow me to escort you back to your sister."

She had little choice but to accept; she did so with a haughty inclination of her head, and permitted him to steer her up the room, tacking through the crowd to where Adriana had returned to the safety of her court.

Taking up her position a few steps away, close by the wall, she lifted her hand from Torrington's sleeve and turned to dismiss him.

His gaze had gone to Adriana; he glanced back at her. "Your sister is very lovely. I take it you're hoping to establish her creditably?"

She hesitated, then nodded. "There seems no reason she shouldn't make an excellent match." Especially now Ruskin was gone. The recollection had her meeting Torrington's black gaze; it seemed fathomless, but far from cold.

Oddly intriguing. His gaze seemed to hold her, yet she didn't, in fact, feel trapped. Just held. . . .

"Tell me." His expression eased a fraction more. "Have you seen the latest offering at the Opera House? Have you been in town long enough to do so?"

He glanced away; she blinked. "No. The opera is one experience we've yet to enjoy." Studying him, she couldn't see him enthralled by opera or a play. Couldn't resist asking, "Have you succumbed to its lure recently?"

His lips twitched. "Opera isn't my weakness."

Weakness—did he have one? Given all she could sense, it seemed unlikely. She realized she was gazing at him, trying hard not to stare, not to show any consciousness of him, of the potent masculine aura of which, as the confines of the crowded ballroom necessitated them standing mere inches apart, she was very much aware.

She'd been going to dismiss him. She drew in a breath.

"I thought you'd want to know that the proper authorities were informed of Mr. Ruskin's sad end." Those fascinating black eyes returned to hers; he'd lowered his voice so only she could hear. "In the circumstances, I saw no need to implicate you. You knew nothing of the situation leading to Ruskin's death—or so I understood."

She nodded. "That's correct." As if in support of his judgment, she added, "I have no idea why he was stabbed, or by whom. I had no connection with him beyond a few social exchanges."

Torrington's black gaze remained steady on her face, then he inclined his head and looked away. "So from which part of the country do you and your sister hail?"

Given he'd just informed her he'd been instrumental in protecting her from precisely the sort of imbroglio she'd been frantic to avoid, she felt compelled to answer. "Warwickshire. Not far from Banbury." She and Adriana had decided it would be wise henceforth to avoid all mention of Chipping Norton.

"Your and Miss Pevensey's parents?"

"Are no longer alive."

That earned her a glance, black and sharp. "She has no guardian other than yourself?"

"No." She lifted her chin. "Be that as it may, I believe we'll muddle through."

He registered her acerbic tone; he glanced again at Adriana. "So you're solely responsible for . . ." He looked back at her. "Do you have any idea what you've taken on?"

She raised her brows, no longer amused. "As I said, I believe we'll manage nicely. We have until now, and quite well, I would say."

His black gaze held hers with a disturbing intensity. "I

would have thought your husband would have had some hand in that."

She blushed. "Yes, of course, but he's been dead for some years."

"Indeed?" Torrington's black eyes gleamed. "Might one inquire from what he died?"

"An inflamation of the lung," she snapped, not at all sure to what in his question she was reacting. She looked away at the surrounding crowd, tried to realign her thoughts with the requirements of her charade. "It's unkind of you to remind me, sir."

After a moment came the dry comment, "My apologies, my dear, but you don't appear to be a grieving widow."

She made the mistake of glancing at him.

He caught her gaze, held it.

After a moment, she narrowed her eyes, then, deliberately, looked away.

Fought to ignore the soft, very masculine chuckle that fell, a distractingly warm caress over her senses.

"Tell me." He'd lowered his voice and shifted closer; the deep rumble teased her ear. "Why aren't you joining your sister in hunting for a husband?"

"I have other matters in hand, other responsibilities. I don't need to add a husband to the list."

She refused to look at him, but sensed she'd said something to make him pause.

Not for long. "Most ladies in your position would look to a husband to shoulder their responsibilities for them."

"Indeed?" Still surveying the crowd, she raised her brows as if considering, then shrugged. "Perhaps, but I have no ambitions for myself in that direction. If I can see my sister comfortably established, married to a gentleman worthy of her, then I'll retire from this Season well pleased."

Glancing at Adriana's court, she noted one particular gentleman who was making every attempt to monopolize her sister's attention. The surprising thing was he appeared to be succeeding.

"Well pleased from a guardian's point of view perhaps, but as a lady of some experience, a widow's lonely existence can hardly be fulfilling."

Distracted, she heard the deep, drawled words, but wasted no wit on divining their meaning. Frowning, she turned to him. "Instead of twitting me, you might attempt to be useful—who is the gentleman with my sister?"

Tony blinked. Thrown entirely off his stride, he looked. "Ah . . . there's at present seven gentlemen surrounding your sister."

She made a frustrated sound—the sort that intimated he was being willfully obtuse. "The one with wavy brown hair speaking with her now. Do you know him?"

He looked, and blinked again. It was several seconds before he replied, "Yes. That's Geoffrey Manningham, Lord Manningham."

An instant later, his prey prodded his arm. "Well? What can you tell me about him?"

He glanced at her. Far from observing the stiff formal distance she'd been working to preserve between them, she'd shifted closer; he could smell the perfume wafting from her throat. If he shifted his head just an inch, he'd be able to touch his cheek to her hair.

She'd been staring, frowning, at Geoffrey; now she glanced up at him, pointedly opened her green eyes wide.

"His estate is in Devon. It shares a partial boundary with mine. If I know anything of Geoffrey, and I've known him since childhood, then his estate, houses, and finances will all be in excellent condition."

Her green eyes narrowed. "You . . ." She glanced at Geoffrey.

"No." It was comforting to be with a woman he could read so easily; she made very little effort to hide her thoughts. "Geoffrey didn't send me to distract you so he could waltz your sister off from beneath your careful nose."

She looked up at him, still suspicious. "And why should I believe that?"

He held her gaze, then caught her hand, lifted it to his lips. Kissed. "Because I told you so." Her eyes flashed; he smiled, and added, "And because Geoffrey and I haven't met in over ten years."

Perfectly aware that with the simple caress he'd fractured her concentration, he gestured to the circle a few feet away. "Shall we join them?"

She gathered herself and managed a regal nod. Delighted, entranced, he tucked her hand in his arm and steered her to Geoffrey's side.

"Manningham?"

Geoffrey looked up from his pursuit of the lovely Adriana. The rivalry that in their youth had never been far beneath their surfaces instantly leapt to his eyes.

Tony smiled. "Allow me to present Mrs. Carrington— Miss Pevensey's sister and guardian."

Geoffrey's gaze deflected, then he threw Tony a speaking glance and made haste to bow and shake Alicia's hand. Others made hay of his distraction and reclaimed Adriana's attention. Tony noted that while she showed no partiality to those anxious to gain her approbation, she did sneak swift glances at Geoffrey, engaged by her sister in the customary social niceties.

Content to observe, he made no attempt to extricate Geoffrey. Instead, he listened to Alicia Carrington craftily confirm all he'd told her, and elicit a few details more. Her protectiveness toward her younger sister, her determination to ensure she was in no way taken advantage of, rang true and clear. Not one of the men gathered about Adriana could doubt it; her sister would always stand as her protector.

With her single-minded focus, she reminded him of a

lioness watching over her cubs; woe betide any who dared threaten them. She was calm, determined, sensible, and strong-willed, mature yet not old; she was as chalk to cheese to the young misses he'd been exposed to over the past weeks—the contrast was a blessed relief.

Via the groom he'd sent to chat in the mews near Waverton Street, he'd learned that Mrs. Carrington hired her carriage from the nearby stables, and also that, as was her habit, she'd sent her evening's instructions to the coachman at midday. Armed with the information, he'd arrived early, much to Lady Mott's delight; he'd been in the ballroom waiting when Alicia Carrington had walked in.

He'd watched her for an hour before he'd approached; in that time, he'd seen her dismiss without a blink three perfectly eligible gentlemen who, as he did, found her quieter beauty, with its suggestion of maturity and a more subtle allure, more attractive than her sister's undeniable charms.

As with all else she'd revealed in response to his probing, her dismissal of marriage rang true. She was truly disinterested, at least at present. She was focused on her task . . . the temptation to distract her, to see if he could . . .

He refocused on her; she was still interrogating Geoffrey who, to Tony's educated eye, was finding the going increasingly grim.

He'd done his duty. He'd convinced himself that his first impression of Mrs. Carrington had been accurate; she hadn't slid a stiletto between Ruskin's ribs, and he could see no reason to doubt her assertion that she had known Ruskin only socially. There was nothing there to interest Dalziel.

Mission accomplished, there was no reason he couldn't retire and leave Geoffrey to his fate. No reason at all to remain by Alicia Carrington's side.

The distant scrape of bow on string heralded the return

of the musicians and an impending waltz. Geoffrey straightened, stiffened, then threw him an unmistakable look of entreaty. Man-to-man. Ex-boyhood-rival-to-rival.

Tony reached for Alicia's hand. "If you would do me the honor, Mrs. Carrington?" He bowed.

Alicia blinked, startled by the sudden clasp of Torrington's hard fingers on hers. As he straightened, she glanced at Lord Manningham only to discover his lordship had grasped her single moment of distraction to turn to Adriana, who, from her smile, had been waiting, having already granted him this dance.

She opened her lips—on what words she didn't know—only to find herself whisked about. "Wait!"

"The dance floor's this way."

"I know, but I wasn't going to accept your offer."

He threw her a black glance, not irritated but curious. "Why?"

"Because I don't want to waltz."

"Why not? You're passably good at it."

"It's got nothing to do with . . . I'm a chaperone. Chaperones don't waltz. We're supposed to keep an eye on our charges even while they're waltzing."

He glanced over her head. "Your sister's with Manningham. Unless he's changed beyond belief in the last ten years, he's no cad—she's as safe as she can be, and you don't need to watch."

They'd reached the floor; the musicians had launched into their theme. He swung her into his arms, then they were whirling down the room.

As before, she found breathing difficult, but was determined not to let it show. "Are you always this dictatorial?"

He met her gaze, then smiled, an easy, warming, simple gesture. "I don't know. I've never been questioned on the subject before."

She threw him a look she hoped conveyed total disbelief.

"But educate me—I've been away from the ton for

more than ten years—should your sister be waltzing at all? Wasn't there some rule or other about permission from the hostesses?"

"She had to get permission from one of the patronesses of Almack's. I spoke to Lady Cowper, and she was kind enough to give her approval." Alicia frowned. "But why have you been away from the ton for ten years—and more? Where were you?"

He looked at her for a moment, as if the answer should be obvious, tattooed on his forehead or some such, then his smile deepened. "I was in the army—the Guards."

"Waterloo?"

The concern in her face was quite genuine. It warmed him. "And the Peninsula."

"Oh."

Tony watched her digest that. Despite the fact he waltzed well—always had—the waltz wasn't his favorite dance; with a woman in his arms, he'd much rather be involved in a romp that heated up the sheets on some bed, rather than a sedate revolution about some tonnish ballroom.

And in this case, the woman in his arms teased and challenged on a level he'd forgotten what it was like to be challenged on. For too many years, women, ladies and all, had come to him easily; generally speaking, he'd only had to crook his finger, and there'd always been more than one willing to slake his lust. He was an accomplished lover, too experienced to be anything other than easy and generous in his ways.

Too experienced not to recognize when his senses were engaged.

Taller than average, supple and svelte, she was less buxom than those ladies who normally caught his eye, yet she hadn't just caught his attention, she'd fixed it— quite why he couldn't say. There seemed a multitude of small attractions that made up the whole—the sheen of the candlelight on her perfect skin, a soft cream tinged with rose, a very English complexion, her eyes and their green gaze—direct, without guile, amazingly open—the lush, heavy locks of her dark mahogany hair, the way her lips set, then eased and lifted.

He wanted to taste them, to taste her. To tempt her to want him. And more. With her in his arms, his appetite, along with his imagination, was definitely inclined toward a bed.

Alicia was conscious of an escalating warmth, one that seemed to rise from within her. It was pleasant, even addictive—her senses responded with a wish to wallow and luxuriate. It was something to do with him, with the way he held her, whirled her so easily down the room, with the reined strength she sensed in him but which triggered her innate defenses not at all—that strength was no threat to her.

His effect on her, however, might be; she wasn't experienced enough to know. Yet it was just a dance—one waltz—and she'd never waltzed like this before, never felt quite like this. Surely it couldn't hurt. And he was a military veteran, an ex-Guardsman, and a viscount.

Quite what that said of him she wasn't sure, but it couldn't all be bad.

He swung her through the turns at the end of the room; her heart leapt as his thigh parted hers. Letting her lids fall, she concentrated on breathing—and on the warmth her senses seemingly craved.

The music slowed, stopped, and they halted. And she realized just how pleasant—how pleasurable—the dance had been. She glanced at him, met his black gaze, and thought she saw a fraction too much understanding in his dark eyes. How black could seem warm she had no idea, but his eyes were never cold . . .

She looked to where Adriana's court waited, and saw Adriana on the arm of Lord Manningham ahead of them, moving that way. Torrington took her arm and steered her in their wake.

As seemed normal for him, he didn't offer his sleeve or ask her permission . . .

And, as was starting to be normal for her, she'd let him.

She frowned. Not once during the waltz had she thought to check on Adriana and Manningham—her distraction had been that complete.

The man on whose arm she was strolling was dangerous.

Seriously dangerous; he'd managed to make her forget her plan for a full five minutes, in the middle of a ton ballroom, no less.

Tony saw the frown form on her face. "What's the matter?"

She glanced up. He looked into her green eyes, watched as she debated, then decided not to tell him the truth—that he was disturbing her, ruffling her senses, undermining her equanimity—as if he didn't know.

Frown deepening, she looked down. "I was just wondering whether my demon brothers had behaved themselves tonight."

He felt his brows rise. "*Demon* brothers?"

She nodded. "Three of them. I'm afraid they're quite a handful. David is a terror—he pretends to be a pirate and falls out of windows. I don't know how many times we've had the doctor to the house. And then Harry, well, he has a tendency to lie —one never knows if the house really is on fire or not. And as for Matthew, he is only eight, you understand, if we could just stop him from locking the doors after people, and slipping around the house at night—we've lost three parlor maids and two housekeepers, and we've only been in town for five weeks."

Tony looked into her face, into her green eyes so determinedly guileless, and struggled not to laugh. She was a terrible liar.

He managed to keep a straight face. "Have you tried beating them?"

"Oh, no! Well, only once. They ran away. We spent the most awful twenty-four hours before they came home again."

"Ah—I see. And do I take it these demons are your responsibility?"

Head rising, she nodded. "My *sole* responsibility."

At that, he grinned.

She saw. Frowned. "What?"

He lifted her hand from his sleeve, raised it to his lips. "If you want to scare gentlemen off, you shouldn't sound so proud of your three imps."

Her frown would have turned to a scowl, but her sister came up on Geoffrey's arm and effectively distracted her. Adriana's court trailed behind; within minutes they were once more part of a fashionable circle, within whose safety Alicia remained, shooting the occasional suspicious glance his way until, deeming his duty on all counts done, he bowed and took his leave.

THREE

He repaired to the Bastion Club.

With a sigh, he sank into a well-stuffed leather armchair in the library. "This place is a godsend."

He exchanged a glance with Jack Warnefleet, ensconced in another chair reading an issue of *The Sporting Life*, savored a sip of his brandy, then settled his head against the padded leather and let his thoughts roam.

To his life—what it used to be, what it now was, most importantly what he wanted it to be. The past was behind him, finished, brought to a close at Waterloo. The present was a bridge, a transition between past and future, nothing more. As for the future. . . .

What did he truly want?

His mind flashed on snippets of memory, a sense of warmth in company, of rare moments of closeness punctuating long years of being alone. Of camaraderie, a sense of shared purpose, a passion for life as well as justice.

Dalziel and his mention of Whitley had brought Jack Hendon to mind. The last he'd seen of Jack he'd been firmly caught in his lovely wife's coils, trooping, gesticulating and protesting, at her dainty heels. A vision of Kit with their elder son in her arms, Jack hovering protectively over them both, swam through his mind. And stuck.

Jack and Kit were coming down to London this Season; they'd be here within a few days. It would be good to see them again, not only to renew old friendships but to refresh his memory, to sense again how a successful marriage worked.

The restlessness that for a few hours had been in abeyance returned. Draining his glass, he set it aside and rose. With a nod to Jack, who returned a salute, he left the library and the club.

At that hour London's streets were quiet, the last stragglers from the balls already at home while the more hardened cases were ensconced in their clubs, hells, and private salons for what was left of the night. Tony walked steadily, his strides long, his cane swinging. Despite his self-absorption, his senses remained alert, yet none of those hanging back in the shadows made any move to accost him.

Reaching his house in Upper Brook Street, he climbed the steps, fishing for his latch key. To his surprise, the door swung open.

Hungerford stood waiting to relieve him of his coat and cane. The hall lights were blazing. A footman stood to the side, still on duty.

"The gentleman who called this morning has returned, my lord. He insisted on waiting for your return. I've put him the library."

"Dalziel?"

"Indeed, my lord."

From Hungerford's tone, it was clear that he, no more than Tony, was certain just who, or more correctly what, Dalziel was, other than someone it was unwise to disobey, let alone cross.

Tony headed for the library.

"The tantalus is well supplied. Do you require anything further, my lord?"

"No." Tony paused and glanced back. "You and the staff can retire. I'll see"—he'd been about to say his lordship; Dalziel was at the very least that—"the gentleman out."

"Very good, my lord."

Tony continued across the green-and-white tiles toward the library door. The hall was paneled in oak, an airy, high-ceilinged space . . . it was a night for memories. He could recall running here as a child, with a fire roaring in the hearth at the end, the dancing flames reflecting off the oak, a sense of warmth enveloping him.

Now the hall seemed . . . not cold, but it no longer held that encompassing warmth. It was empty, waiting for that time to come again, for that phase of life to return.

Hungerford and the footman had disappeared through the green baize door. Alone, Tony paused; with his hand on the knob of the library door, he looked around. Let his senses stretch farther than his eyes could see.

He was alone, and his house was empty. Like it, he was waiting. Waiting for the next phase of life to rush in and fill him, engage him.

Warm him.

For a moment he stood silent and still, then he shook off the mood and opened the door.

Dalziel was in an armchair facing the door, an almost empty brandy balloon in one long-fingered hand. His brows rose faintly; his lips curved, cynical and amused, in welcome.

Tony eyed the entire vision with a misgiving he made no attempt to hide; Dalziel's smile only deepened.

"Well?" Crossing to the tantalus, Tony poured a small measure of brandy, more to have something to do than anything else. He raised the decanter to Dalziel, who shook his head. Replacing the decanter, picking up the glass, he crossed to the other armchair. "To what do I owe this . . . unexpected visit?"

They both knew it wouldn't have anything to do with pleasure.

"We've worked together for a long time."

Tony sat. "Thirteen years. But I work for the government no longer, so what has that to say to anything?"

Dalziel's dark eyes held his. "Simply that there are matters I cannot use less experienced men for, and in this case your peculiar background makes you too ideal a candidate to overlook."

"Bonaparte's on St. Helena. The French are finished."

Dalziel smiled. "Not that peculiar background. I have other half-French agents. I meant that you have experience of Whitley's side of things, and you have a better-than-average grasp of the possibilities involved."

"Involved in what?"

"Ruskin's death." Dalziel studied the amber lights in the glass he turned between his fingers. "Some disturbing items came to light when they started clearing the man's desk. Jottings of shipping information derived from both Revenue and Admiralty documents. They appear to be scribbled notes for more formal communications."

"Nothing in any way associated with his work?"

"No. He organized Customs clearances for merchantmen, hence his access to the internal Revenue and Admiralty notices. His job involved the dates of expected entry to our ports. The information jotted down relates to movement of ships in the Channel, especially its outermost reaches. There is no possible reason his job required such details."

Dalziel paused, then added, "The most disturbing aspect is that these jottings span the years from 1812 to 1815."

"Ah." As Dalziel had prophesied, Tony grasped the implication.

"Indeed. You now perceive why I'm here. Both I and Whitley are now extremely interested in learning who killed Ruskin, and most importantly why."

Tony pondered, then looked at Dalziel, directly met his eyes. "Why me?" He could guess, but he wanted it confirmed.

"Because there is, as you've realized, the possibility that someone in Customs and Revenue, or the Home Office, or any of a multitude of government agencies is involved, in one capacity or another. It's unlikely Ruskin could use the information himself, but someone knew he had access to it, and either made use of him themselves, or put someone else on to him. In either case, this nebulous someone might be in a position to know Whitley's operatives. He won't, however, know you."

Dalziel paused, considering Tony. "The only connection you've had with Whitley's crew was that operation you ran with Jonathon Hendon and George Smeaton. Both are now retired; both are sound. Despite Hendon's background in shipping, he's had no contact with Ruskin—and yes, I've checked. For the past several years, both Hendon and Smeaton have remained buried in Norfolk, and their only links in town are either purely social or purely commercial. Neither is a threat to you—and as I recall, no one else of Whitley's crew ever knew who Antoine Balzac really was."

Tony nodded. Antoine Balzac had been a large part of his past.

"On top of that, you found the body." Dalziel met his gaze. "You are the epitome of an obvious choice."

Tony grimaced and looked down, into his glass. It seemed as if the past was reaching out, trying to draw him back; he didn't want to go. Yet all Dalziel said was true; he *was* the obvious choice . . . and Alicia Carrington was, at least peripherally, involved.

She wasn't part of his past.

"All right." He looked up. "I'll nose around and see what connections I can turn up."

Dalziel nodded and set his glass aside. "Ruskin worked at the main office of Customs and Revenue in Whitehall." He gave details of the building, floor, and room. "I suggested that his papers, indeed, all his office be left as was. I gather that's been done. Naturally, I've asked for no clearances. Let me know if you require any."

Tony's lips curved; he inclined his head. Both he and

Dalziel knew he wouldn't ask for clearances. He'd been an "unofficial agent" for too long.

"Ruskin lived in lodgings in Bury Street—Number 23. His home, Crawton Hall, is near Bledington in Gloucestershire, just over the border of north Oxfordshire, southwest of Chipping Norton, the nearest market town."

Tony frowned, but his knowledge of England was nowhere near as detailed as his knowledge of France.

"Ruskin has a mother living, and an older spinster sister. They reside at Crawton Hall, and haven't left it in decades. Ruskin spent but little time there in recent years. That's what we know of him to date."

"Odd habits?"

"None known—we'll leave that to you. Obviously, we can't afford any overt activity."

"What about manner of death—any word from the surgeon?"

"I called Pringle in. According to him, Ruskin was knifed with the stiletto you found. Very professionally slipped between the ribs. Angle and point of entry suggest a right-handed assailant standing beside and a little behind his left side."

They both could see how it was done.

"So." Tony sipped. "A friend."

"Certainly someone he in no way suspected of murderous intent."

Such as a lady in a pale green silk gown.

Tony looked up. "Did Pringle give any guesses as to the murderer—size, strength, that sort of thing?"

Dalziel's eyes, scanning his face, narrowed. "He did. A man almost certainly as tall as Ruskin and, of course, of reasonable strength."

"How tall was Ruskin?"

"A trifle shorter than me. Half a head shorter than you."

Tony hid his relief behind a grimace. "Not much help there. Any other clues?"

"No." Dalziel stood, fluidly graceful.

Tony did the same, with even more innate flair.

Dalziel hid a grin and led the way to the door. "Let me know what you find. If I hear anything useful, I'll send word."

He paused as they reached the door and met Tony's gaze. "If I do have anything to send, where should I send it?"

Tony considered, then said, "Here. Back door. My butler's reliable, and the staff have been with me for years."

Dalziel nodded. They stepped into the hall.

Tony saw Dalziel out and locked the front door, then returned to the library.

He went straight to one of the bookcases and crouched, scanning the spines, then he pulled out a large tome. Rising, he crossed to where the lamp on the desk threw a circle of stronger light. Opening the book—a collection of maps of England's counties—he flicked through until he came to the pages showing Oxfordshire. He located Chipping Norton, and Banbury in the far north of the county.

It took a few minutes of flicking back and forth, comparing maps of Gloucestershire, Oxfordshire, and Warwickshire, before he had the geography straight. The only bit of Warwickshire "not far from Banbury" was also not far from Chipping Norton, and therefore, in turn, not far from Bledington.

Alicia Carrington's home lay within ten miles of Ruskin's.

Shutting the book, Tony stared across the room.

How likely was it, given the social round of county England that, living in such proximity, Alicia Carrington née Pevensey and Ruskin had never met?

The question suggested the answer. Ruskin hadn't spent much time in Bledington recently, and despite telling him she and her sister hailed from the area, Alicia Carrington could well have meant their home was there now. The home she'd made with her husband; most likely she was referring to his house, not necessarily the area in which she and her family, the Pevenseys, had lived most of their lives. Of course.

He returned the book to the shelf, then headed for the door.

Of course, he'd check.

That, however, would have to come later. The first thing he needed to do, and that as soon as humanly possible, before any whisper of an internal investigation into Ruskin's affairs could find its way to anyone, was search Ruskin's office.

The Customs and Revenue Office in Whitehall was well guarded and externally secure, but for someone who knew how to approach it from within, down the long, intersecting corridors, it was much less impenetrable. Even better, Ruskin's office was on the first floor at the back, and its small window faced a blank wall.

At four o'clock in the morning, the building was cold and silent. The porter was snoring in his office downstairs; lighting a lamp was safe enough.

Tony searched the desk, then the whole office methodically. He collected everything pertinent in the middle of the desk; when there was no more to discover, he transferred all he'd found to the deep pockets of his greatcoat.

Then he turned out the lamp, slipped out of the building, and went home, leaving not a trace of his presence, or anything to alert anyone that Ruskin's office had been searched.

Despite his late night, he was out again at noon, heading for Bury Street. It was a fashionable area for single gentlemen, close to clubs, Mayfair, and the seat of government; Number 23 was a well-kept, narrow, three-story house. He knocked on the door and explained to the land-lady that he worked alongside Mr. Ruskin and had been sent to check his rooms to make sure no Customs Office papers had been left there.

She led him up to a set of rooms on the first floor. He thanked her as she unlocked the door. "I'll return the key when I leave."

With a measuring glance that read the quality of his coat and boots in much the same way as a military pass, she nodded. "I'll leave you to it, then."

He waited until she was heading downstairs, then en-tered Ruskin's parlor and shut the door.

Again, his search was thorough, but in contrast to Ruskin's office, this time he found evidence someone had been before him. He found a pile of old IOUs lying in a concealed drawer in the escritoire atop more recent correspondence.

Dalziel and Whitley would never have permitted any other from either the official or unofficial sides of govern-ment to meddle in an affair they'd handed to him; who-ever had been through Ruskin's papers was from the "other side." Indeed, the fact the rooms had been searched—he found further telltale signs in the bedroom—meant there was, most definitely, an "other side."

Whatever dealings Ruskin had been involved in, some-one had believed there might be evidence they needed to remove from his rooms.

Presumably they'd removed it.

Tony wasn't unduly concerned. There were always threads left lying around in the aftermath of any scheme; he was an expert at finding and following such flimsy but real connections.

Such as those IOUs. He didn't stop to analyze them in detail, but a cursory glance revealed that they'd been paid off regularly. More, the sums involved made it clear

Ruskin had enjoyed an income considerably beyond his earnings as a government clerk.

Stowing the notes in his pockets, Tony concluded that discovering the source of that extra income was logically his next step.

After taking an impression of the key, he let himself out, returned the key to the landlady with typical civil service boredom, admitting to removing "a few papers but nothing major" when she asked.

Back on the street, he headed for Torrington House. He needed a few hours to study and collate all he'd found. However, the day was winging, and there was other information he needed to pursue that would, he suspected, be best pursued in daylight.

He'd been wondering how to approach Alicia Carrington and learn unequivocally all he needed to know. He'd left a corner of his brain wrestling with the problem; an hour ago, it had presented him with the perfect solution.

First, he needed to empty his pockets and let Hungerford feed him. Two o'clock would be the perfect time to essay forth to rattle Mrs. Carrington's defenses.

He found her precisely where his devious mind had predicted—in Green Park with her three brothers and an older man who appeared to be their tutor.

The two older boys were wrestling with a kite; the tutor was assisting. The younger boy had a bat and ball; Alicia was doing her best to entertain him.

He spent a few minutes observing, assessing, before making his move. Recalling Alicia's description of her demons, he grinned. The boys were sturdy, healthy-looking specimens with apples in their cheeks and shining brown hair. They were typical boys, rowdy and physical, yet they were quick to mind their elder sister's strictures.

Obedient demons.

Amused, he walked toward her. The bat in her hands, she had her back to him. The youngest—Matthew?—tossed the ball to her; she swung wildly and missed. The ball bounced past her, giving him the perfect opening.

He stopped the ball with his boot, with a quick flick, tossed it up, and caught it. Strolling forward, he hefted the ball; as he reached Alicia's side, he lobbed it to the boy.

And reached for the bat. "Here, let me."

He twitched the bat from her nerveless fingers.

Alicia stared at him. "What are you doing here?"

Torrington glanced at her. "Playing ball." He waved to the side. "You should stand over there so you can catch me out."

Matthew, blinking at the changes, shook his head. "She's not much good at catching."

Her tormentor smiled at him. "We'll have to give her a bit of practice, then. Ready?"

Alicia found herself stepping back in the direction Torrington had indicated. She was not sure about any of this, but . . .

Matthew pitched the ball to him, and he tapped it back between her and Matthew. Matthew squealed delightedly and pounced on it. A huge grin wreathing his face, he hustled to square up again.

After a few more shrewdly placed shots—one which came straight at her and surprised a shriek out of her—David and Harry left Jenkins with the kite and came hurrying to join in.

Normally, the older boys would have immediately taken over the game; she girded her loins to defend Matthew, but Torrington, bat still in his hand, elected himself director of play. He welcomed the older boys and waved them to fielding positions, leaving Matthew as bowler.

What followed was an education in how boys played, or could play if led by a competent hand. When Jenkins came up, the discarded kite in his hands, she waved him to take over her position. He might be more than twice her age, but he was better at catching.

The kite in her arms, she retreated to lean against a tree. Given the focus of the game, she naturally found herself gazing at Torrington.

Not a calming sight.

He literally made her pulse skitter and race. She was far enough away to appreciate his perfect male proportions, the wide shoulders and tapering chest, slim hips and long, lean legs. She'd yet to see him make an ungraceful move; she wasn't sure he'd know how. His reflexes were excellent.

She saw the laughing humor in his face as he skied a ball to Harry, who with a rowdy whoop caught it. Torrington's black locks, thick and lightly wavy, hugged his head; one fell forward across his broad brow as he goodnaturedly surrendered the bat to Harry. He took the ball and bowled for a while, then tossed it to David.

And came strolling over the lawn to take up a fielding position near her. He grinned at her. "Coward."

She tipped up her nose. "As you've been informed, I'm hopeless at catching."

The look he gave her was enigmatic, but a ball hit his way recalled him to his duty.

She tried to watch the play and call encouragement as a good sister should, but having Torrington so close, watching him move and stretch and stand, hands on hips, then wave, directing her brothers, was distracting.

His occasional glances did nothing to slow her pulse.

What really worried her was why he was there.

As soon as David and Matthew had had a turn at batting, she called a halt. "Come along—we have to get back for tea."

Her brothers, flushed and glowing with happiness, ran up.

"I say." David tugged her hand. "Can Tony come home with us for tea?"

Alicia looked down into David's bright eyes. Tony—Torrington was *Tony* to them. That seemed dangerous. But David, even more than the other two, was lonely here in London, and what, after all, could Torrington do? She smiled. "If he wishes."

"Will you come? Will you come?" The chorus was instantaneous.

Joining them, Tony—Torrington—glanced at her. "If your sister doesn't mind."

She wasn't at all sure it was a good idea, and he knew it; she met his gaze, but kept her expression easy. "If you have no objection to sitting down to a nursery tea, then by all means do join us."

He smiled, not just with his lips but with those coal black eyes; if she'd had a fan, she would have deployed it. He bowed. "Thank you. I'd be delighted."

Thrilled, thoroughly pleased with their new acquaintance, the boys took his hands; surrounding him, they danced by his side all the way back to Waverton Street, peppering him with questions.

At first, following behind with Jenkins, she merely listened, learning that Tony was an only child and had grown up mostly in Devon, but also in part in London. He knew all the childhood haunts. But when Harry, military mad, asked if he'd served overseas, and he replied he had, her protective instincts flared.

Quickly lengthening her stride, she came up beside Matthew, tripping along, Tony's hand in his, gazing adoringly up at his new friend.

"So which were you in—the navy or the army?"

"The army—the Guards."

"And you were at Waterloo?"

"Yes."

"Did you lead a charge?"

She jumped in. "Boys, I really don't think we need to hear about charges and fighting over tea."

Torrington glanced at her briefly, a swift, penetrating look, then he turned back to her brothers. "Your sister's right—war is not fun. It's horrible, and frightening, and dreadful to be involved in."

David's eyes grew round. Harry's face fell.

Alicia only just managed to keep her own jaw from falling.

"But . . ." Harry blinked at Torrington. "I want to be a major in the Guards when I grow up. Or the cavalry."

"I was a major in both, and I'd suggest you rethink. Aside from all else, there are no more enemies to fight. Being in the cavalry in peacetime might not be the exciting life you imagine."

They'd reached the front steps of the house. Torrington waved the boys ahead of him, then waited for Alicia to precede him. She went quickly up the steps and opened the door, then stood back, and the three boys filed in.

Gracefully, Torrington waved her on, then followed.

"Upstairs and wash your hands, please." She shooed her brothers to the stairs. "Then you may join us in the parlor."

They flashed swift smiles at Torrington, then clattered up the stairs. Jenkins shut the door. She turned to him. "If you could order tea, Jenkins?"

"Indeed, ma'am." Jenkins bowed and left them.

She turned to Torrington. "Thank you." She met his black eyes. "That was just the right thing to say."

He studied her for a moment, then one black brow arched. "It's no more than the truth."

But one few ex-majors in the Guards would admit. Inclining her head, she led him to the parlor. Located at the back of the house, it was the room she and Adriana used most, when they were alone or with the boys, *en famille*. A comfortable room in which the boys could relax without worrying overmuch about the furniture, it was a trifle shabby, but she didn't care as she led Torrington in; she'd warned him it was to be a nursery tea.

Adriana was there, poring over the latest fashion plates. She glanced up, saw Torrington, and rose, smiling.

After Adriana and Torrington exchanged greetings, they all sat. Even though the room was decently sized, Alicia was aware of his physical presence, his strength. Adriana asked how he had come to join them; he related the story of the game in the park. Every now and then, his gaze would touch Alicia's, and a teasing smile would flirt about his lips. She was relieved when the boys rejoined them, bursting upon them in a noisy, albeit well-behaved wave, and the talk became more general.

Jenkins appeared with the tray; if Torrington noticed the oddity in that, he gave no sign.

She poured; on their best behavior, the boys offered Torrington the plate of crumpets first. He went up in their estimation—and hers—when he accepted one and smeared it with globs of jam, just as the boys did with theirs. All were soon munching happily.

Crumpet dealt with in three bites, Torrington wiped his fingers on his napkin, then reached for his teacup. He looked at her brothers. "Your sister told me you live in Warwickshire—is there much sport up that way? Shooting? Hunting?"

David wrinkled his nose. "Some fishing, some shooting, not much hunting just where we are. That's south Warwickshire."

Harry waved his remaining crumpet. "There's hunting around Banbury, but not down near us."

"Well," David temporized. "There's a small, really *tiny* pack runs out of Chipping Norton, but it's not what you'd call a real hunt."

From the corner of his eye, Tony saw Alicia and Adriana exchange a swift glance; the instant the boys had started mentioning towns, Alicia had tensed. He pressed harder. "Chipping Norton? Is that your nearest town? I've a friend who lives up that way."

Alicia leaned forward. "Harry! Be careful. You're about to drip jam."

Adriana grabbed his napkin and wiped Harry's fingers. Neither Tony nor Harry could see any physical reason for his sisters' sudden action.

"There." Adriana sat back. "Now why don't you tell Lord Torrington about that huge trout you caught last year?"

Instead, the boys fixed Tony with round eyes.

"Are you really a lord?" Matthew asked.

Tony grinned. "Yes."

"What sort of lord?" David asked.

"A viscount." Tony could see from their faces they were trying to recall the order of precedence. "It's a small lordship. The second smallest."

They weren't deterred. "Does that mean you get to wear a coronet at a coronation?"

"What sort of cloak do you get to wear?"

"Do you have a castle?"

He laughed, and answered as best he could, noting the relieved look Alicia threw Adriana; his presence in her parlor was making her skittish, and on more than one front.

Interrogating her brothers was not a gentlemanly act, yet he'd learned long ago that when it came to matters of treason, and that was what he and Dalziel and Whitley were dealing with in one guise or another, one couldn't adhere to gentlemanly scruples. In that particular theater, adhering to such scruples was a fast way to die, failing one's country in the process.

He felt no remorse for having used the three boys; they'd come to no harm, and he'd learned what he needed. Now he had to interrogate their elder sister. Again.

"Time for your afternoon lessons, boys. Come along, now." Alicia stood, waving her brothers to their feet.

They rose, casting glances at Tony; knowing on which side his bread was buttered, he gave them no encouragement to defy their sister, but rose, too, and gravely shook hands.

With resigned polite farewells, the boys trooped out; Alicia followed them into the hall, consigning them into Jenkins's care.

Seizing the moment, Tony turned to Adriana.

She'd risen, too, and now smiled. "I believe you're acquainted with Lord Manningham, my lord."

"Yes. He's an old friend."

Amusement flashed through her brown eyes, suggesting Geoffrey had painted their association with greater color.

He didn't have much time. "I wanted to speak with you. Your sister will have mentioned the matter of Mr. Ruskin." Adriana's face immediately clouded; like Alicia, she possessed little by way of a social mask. "I gather you hadn't met him in the country."

"No." Adriana met his gaze; her eyes were clear, but troubled. "He appeared a week or so after we arrived in town. We only met him a handful of times in the ballrooms, never anywhere else."

She hesitated, then added, "He was not a man either of us could like. He was . . . oh, what is the word . . . 'importuning'. That's it. He hovered about Alicia even though she discouraged him."

From her expression, it was clear that while Alicia was mother lion, Adriana would be fierce in her sister's defense. He inclined his head. "It's perhaps as well, then, that he's gone."

Adriana muttered a guiltily fervent assent.

Alicia reentered; he turned to her and smiled. "Thank you for an entertaining afternoon."

Her look said she wasn't sure how to interpret that. He

took his leave of Adriana, then, as he'd hoped, Alicia accompanied him to the door.

Following him into the hall, she shut the parlor door. He glanced about; fate had smiled—they were alone.

He gave her no time to regroup, but struck immediately. "Ruskin lived at Bledington, close to Chipping Norton. Are you *sure* you never met him in the country?"

She blinked at him. "Yes—I told you. We only met recently, socially in London." Her eyes, searching his, suddenly widened. "Oh, was he a friend of your friend? The one you mentioned?"

He held her gaze; he could detect not the slightest hint of prevarication in the clear green, only puzzlement, and a hint of concern. "No," he eventually said. "Ruskin's friends are no friends of mine."

The reply, especially his tone, further confused her.

"I understand he'd been bothering you—in what way?"

She frowned, clearly wishing he hadn't known to ask; when he simply waited, she lifted her head and stiffly stated, "He was . . . attracted."

He kept his eyes on hers. "And you?"

Irritation flashed in her eyes. "I was not."

He felt his lips ease. "I see."

They remained, gazes locked, for two heartbeats, then he reached out and took her hand. Still holding her gaze, he raised her fingers to his lips. Kissed, and felt the tremor that raced through her. Watched her eyes widen, darken.

She drew in a quick breath, tensed to step back.

He reacted. Tightening his grip on her fingers, he drew her nearer. Bent his head and touched his lips to hers in the lightest, most fleeting kiss.

Just a brushing of lips, more promise than caress.

He intended it to be that, not a real kiss but a tantalizing temptation.

Raising his head, he watched her lids rise, saw surprise, shock, and curiosity fill her eyes. Then she realized, stiffened, drew back.

Releasing her, he caught her gaze. "I meant what I said. I truly enjoyed the afternoon."

He wondered if she understood what he was saying.

Before she could question him—before he could be tempted to say or do anything more—he bowed and turned to the door.

She saw him out and shut the door.

Gaining the pavement, he paused, letting the last moments fade from his mind, turning instead to running through all he'd learned thus far.

His instincts were pricking. Something was afoot, but just what he'd yet to divine. Turning on his heel, he headed for home and his library. There was a great deal he had to digest.

FOUR

HE SPENT THE REST OF THAT DAY AND THE ENTIRE EVE-
ning analyzing all he'd retrieved from Ruskin's office and
lodgings. Ruskin's scribbled notes and the receipts of his
debts appeared to be the only clues, the only items war-
ranting further investigation.

After assembling a schedule of the dates on which the
debts, in groups, had been paid, along with the sums involved, Tony called it a night. At least working for
Dalziel gave him an excuse not to attend the ton's balls.

The next day, just after noon, he girded his loins and
dutifully presented himself at Amery House for one of his
godmother's at-homes, to which he'd been summoned.
He knew better than to ignore the dictate. Strolling into
her drawing room, he bowed over her hand, resignedly
noting he was one of only four gentlemen present.

Felicité beamed up at him. *"Bon!* You will please me
and your *maman* by talking and paying attention to the
demoiselles here, will you not?"

Despite the words, there was an ingenuous appeal in
her eyes. He felt his lips quirk. Hand over heart, he declared, "I live to serve."

She only just managed to suppress a snort. She rapped
his knuckles with her fan, then used it to gesture to the
knots of young ladies gathered by the windows. *"Viens!"*
She shooed. "Go—go!"

He went.

It was a cynical exercise; none of the young things to whom the matrons prayed he'd fall victim had any chance of fixing his interest. Why they thought he might be susceptible escaped him, but he behaved as required, pausing by first one group, then another, chatting easily before moving on. He did not remain by any lady's side for long; no one could accuse him of being the least encouraging.

He'd scanned the room on entering; Alicia Carrington had not been present. As he moved from group to group, he resurveyed the guests, but she didn't appear.

While moving to the fifth knot of conversationalists, he caught Felicité's eye, noted her puzzled expression. Realized he was giving the impression he was searching for someone, waiting for someone.

Mentally shrugging, he strolled on.

He was with the sixth group, inwardly debating whether he'd dallied long enough, when he heard two matrons standing a little apart exchanging the latest gossip—the items they considered too titillating for their charges' delicate ears.

His instincts flickered; he'd noticed there was some flutter—some piece of avid interest—doing the rounds among the older ladies.

The two biddies a yard behind him put their heads together and lowered their voices, but his hearing was acute.

"I had it this morning from Celia Chiswick. We met at Lady Montacute's morning tea. You've heard about that fellow Ruskin being murdered—stabbed—just along the path there?"

From the corner of his eye, Tony saw the lady point into the garden.

"*Well!* It seems he was blackmailing some lady—a widow."

"No! Who?"

"Well, of course no one knows, do they?"

"But someone must have some idea, surely."

"One hardly likes to speculate, but . . . you do know who he was speaking with just before he left this room and walked to his death, don't you?"

"No." The second woman's voice dropped to a strained whisper. "Who was it?"

Tony shifted and saw the first lady lean close to her companion and whisper the answer in her ear.

The second lady's eyes widened; her jaw dropped. Then she looked at the first. "*No!* Truly?"

Lips thinning, the first lady nodded.

The second flicked open her fan and waved it. "Great heavens! And she with that ravishing sister of hers in tow. *Well!*"

Tony fought to keep his expression from hardening, from revealing anything of the maelstrom of emotions that rose up and buffeted his mind—and him. Inwardly grim, he spent a few more minutes with the sweet young things, then excused himself and headed for the door.

Only to have Felicité step into his path. "You're not leaving so soon?" She put a hand on his arm; immediately concern flared in her eyes. She lowered her voice. "What is it?"

He hesitated, then said, "I'm engaged on some business. I have to go."

Her concern only deepened. "I thought you'd finished with such things."

His short laugh was harsh. "So did I. But not yet." He eased her hand from his sleeve and bowed over it. "I must go—there's someone I have to see."

Her gaze had flicked to where he'd been, then to the garden. He could see the connections forming in her mind. He stepped away.

She looked back at him. "If you must go, you must, but take care. And you must tell me later."

With a curt nod, he left. For once, he didn't stop to consider his plan.

* * *

Alicia strolled the clipped lawns of the park in the wake of Adriana and her swains. A morning promenade was becoming a regular event in their schedule. The gentlemen preferred the less-structured, less-cramped encounters such a stroll allowed; it gave them more time to worship at her sister's feet unfettered by any need to pay attention to any other young lady.

She'd countered that by inviting Miss Tiverton to walk with them. Adriana now strolled beside that young lady while five perfectly eligible gentlemen vied for their attention.

The most prominent, and most assiduous, was Lord Manningham. Alicia studied the undeniably attractive figure he cut in his morning coat, pale, tightly fitting breeches, and black Hessians. His address was polished without being oversmooth, his features were handsome rather than beautiful.

He was turning Adriana's head, and her sister knew it.

It was time, perhaps, to learn more of Geoffrey Manningham.

Especially as he was apparently a friend of Lord Torrington's. He who had almost-kissed her, who without provocation let alone permission had deliberately teased her in her own front hall.

The moment flared in her mind; her nerves tensed . . .

Ruthlessly, she bundled the memory aside—he probably did such things all the time. She refocused on Adriana and her court. Adjusting her parasol, she strolled on.

She had no warning, no premonition of danger, until she heard herself hailed in a voice that cut like a whip.

She whirled, but Torrington was already upon her. Hard fingers closing manacle-like about her elbow, he swung her around and marched her down the lawn, away from the carriageway.

"What—?" She tried to free her arm, but couldn't. She glared at him. "Unhand me, sir!"

He ignored her. He strode on, forcing her with him; she

either had to keep up, or stumble and fall. His face was set like stone, his expression unforgivingly grim. Thunderclouds would have looked more comforting.

She glanced back at the others, strolling on unaware. "Stop! I have to watch over my sister."

He glanced briefly at her—too briefly for her to read his eyes—then lifted his gaze and looked back at the others. "She's with Manningham. She's safe." Looking forward, he growled, "You aren't."

He'd lost his senses. She tugged against his hold, then dragged in a breath. "If you don't stop this instant and let me go—"

Abruptly, he did both. She'd been strolling along the periphery of the fashionable throng; they were now in an area where no others were walking. They were out of earshot of everyone, too far from the carriageway for any to discern even the tenor of their exchange.

On top of that, he stood squarely between her and the rest of the ton. Cutting her off from the world. Stunned, she raised her eyes to his face.

His black gaze impaled her. "What was Ruskin blackmailing you about?"

She blinked; her eyes grew wide. The world lurched and fell away. "Wh—what?"

He gritted his teeth. "Ruskin was blackmailing you. About *what*?" His eyes narrowed to obsidian shards. "What was the hold he had over you?"

When she didn't answer, couldn't get her wits to stop whirling quickly enough—dear God, how had he found out?—his jaw set even harder. From the corner of her eye, she saw his hands clench; locking eyes, she sensed he wanted to seize her, shake her, but was exercising quite amazing restraint.

"Was. He. Blackmailing you?"

The words were uttered with such force they dragged the answer from her. "Yes—*no*! That is . . ." She stopped.

"Which?" He took a half step nearer, towering over

her, menacing, intimidating. Aggression poured from him.

And ignited her temper. She straightened to her full height, tipped back her head, met his piercing black gaze. "Whichever, it is *no* concern of yours."

"Think again."

The low growl skittered over her nerves; she dug her heels in even deeper. "I beg your pardon?" Outraged, she held his gaze, absolutely determined not to quail. "You, my lord, are skating on thin ice. Don't *think* to browbeat me!"

For an instant, they stood, all but toe to toe, certainly will against will, then, to her surprise and immense relief, he eased back. Reined in the sheer male power that beat against her senses.

Yet he didn't shift back; his eyes didn't leave hers. When he spoke, his tone was dark, definite, but harnessed, fractionally more civilized.

"I've been asked to investigate Ruskin's death. I want to know what your connection with him was."

She stared. "Why? *Who*—?"

"Just answer the question. What was your connection with Ruskin?"

She felt the blood drain from her face. "We didn't have any—I told you!"

"Yet he was blackmailing you."

"No—at least, not in the way you mean."

He opened his eyes wide. "What other way is there?"

She had to reply; there was clearly no option. "It wasn't about money. He wanted me to marry him."

He blinked. His tone lost a little of it sureness. "He was blackmailing you to marry him?"

Lips tight, she nodded. "He . . . offered me a *carte blanche*. I refused, and he offered marriage. When I refused that . . . he thought to pressure me into agreeing."

"With what?"

She searched his eyes; his demand was precise, implacable. Who was he?—she didn't really know. "He'd learned something about us—about me—that if it became common knowledge, would make establishing Adriana . . . very difficult. It's nothing nefarious or terrible, but you know what the gossipmongers are like."

"Indeed." The word was clipped, imbued with meaning. "You spoke with him immediately before he left Lady Amery's drawing room. I want to know what was said, and exactly what happened to result in you going into the garden and finding his body."

Whoever he was, he knew far too much. The thought chilled her. He also knew how to interrogate; even restrained, there was a threat in his manner—avoiding his questions wasn't going to be possible. She had absolutely no doubt his claim of being asked to investigate was true.

"I . . ." Her mind slid back to that moment in the drawing room, when Ruskin had threatened to pull the rug from under their future. "As I said, I'd declined his offer of marriage. That evening, he came up and requested a private interview. I refused—I was watching Adriana. He insisted, so we retreated to the side of the room. He told me he lived near Bledington, and had seen us last Christmas, in the square at Chipping Norton."

She refocused on the black eyes fixed so intently on her face. "He'd seen us—we hadn't seen or met him. Not then. Only after we came to London."

"What was it he knew of you?"

Feeling compelled to keep her eyes on his, she considered, eventually moistened her lips. "It's not anything to do with his death. It can't be. It doesn't concern anyone but me."

Tony held her gaze for a full minute; she didn't waver, didn't offer anything more. She was no longer so defiant, but on that one point intractable; she wasn't going to tell him. He forced himself to look away, over her head, forced himself to take a deep breath and think. Eventually, he looked down at her. "Does anyone else in London know of this *thing* that Ruskin knew?"

She blinked, thought. "No." Her voice strengthened. "No one."

He digested that, accepted it. "So he propositioned you—threatened you with exposure." He forced himself to say the words, ignoring the violence the thought evoked. "What then?"

"I asked for time, and he agreed to twenty-four hours. He said he'd call on me the next evening." Remembered horror flitted through her eyes; he wondered what she wasn't telling him. "Then he walked away."

When she said nothing more, he prompted, "What then?"

"I was upset." She seemed not to notice the hand she raised to her throat. "I asked for a glass of water, sat, then I started to think again, and realized he . . . that it might be possible to buy him off. I stood and saw him slip out of the terrace doors. I decided to follow and speak with him—at least convince him to give me more time."

Remembered fear tinged her voice. Swallowing an oath, he suppressed the urge to haul her into his arms; she'd probably struggle. "So you followed him out?"

She nodded. "But first I crossed the room to Adriana. I told her where I was going."

"Then you went onto the terrace?"

"Yes, but he wasn't there. It was chilly—I looked around and saw movement beneath that huge tree. I assumed it was he, so I went down. Then I found him . . ." She paused. "You know the rest."

"Did you see anyone else go out on the terrace before you did—or before Ruskin did?"

"No. But I wasn't watching the doors."

Regardless, it was unlikely a gentleman wearing a coat and hat would leave Amery House via the drawing room and the terrace doors. Fitting her information with his, it seemed clear what had happened.

She'd taken advantage of his silence to regroup.

He met her gaze. "I take it Ruskin made no mention of going to meet anyone."

"No. Why? Oh . . . I suppose he must have met some-one."

"He did. As I came up Park Street, I saw a gentleman in a coat and hat leave by the garden gate. He was too far away for me to identify, but he definitely came out of that gate. Allowing time for you to walk to the tree, and for me to walk to the gate, it must have been he—that man— you saw moving beneath the tree."

She paled. Looked at him, stared at him. After a long moment, she asked, "Who are you?"

He let two heartbeats pass, then replied, "You know my name."

"I know I have only your word that there was another man, that it wasn't you who stabbed Ruskin."

The accusation pricked; holding her gaze, he softly said, "You might want to consider that I'm all that stands between you and a charge of murder."

The instant he uttered the words, he wished them un-said.

Her head snapped up. She stepped back. "I do not un-derstand what right you have to question me—interrogate me—*or my family*." Her eyes blazed; her tone was scathing. "In future, please leave us alone."

She turned.

He caught her hand. "Alicia—"

She swung on him; fury lit her eyes. "*Don't* presume to call me that! I have *not* given you leave—and I won't." She looked down at his fingers circling her wrist. "Please release me immediately."

He had to force his fingers to do it, to slide from her skin; she snatched her hand away, backed two steps, watching him—as if she suddenly saw him for what he truly was.

Her eyes had widened; for an instant, he glimpsed a vulnerability he couldn't place.

Alicia fought to subdue the emotions roiling inside her. Her stomach was knotted, her lungs tight. He'd played with her brothers, interrogated them and Adriana, flirted quite deliberately with her. All because . . . and she'd thought he was honest, that he was trustworthy, genuine . . . how foolish she'd been.

When he said nothing, she dragged in a breath. "I've told you all I know. Please"—for the first time, her voice quavered—"don't come near me again."

With that, she whirled and walked quickly away.

Tony watched her go. Then he swore comprehensively in French and strode off in the opposite direction.

He hailed a hackney and headed into the city. Resting his head against the squabs, he closed his eyes and concentrated on getting his temper under control and his thoughts straight; it had been years since they'd been so tangled.

He'd stalked into the park furious with her for concealing from him such a potentially dangerous connection. Not because that concealment interfered with his investigation, but purely because the damned woman hadn't availed herself of his abilities—his protection.

Because she deliberately hadn't trusted him.

Stalking out of the park, he'd been furious with himself. She'd questioned who he was, his integrity, and he'd reacted by taking a high hand, which any fool could have predicted would fail miserably—in his case, spectacularly.

He hadn't meant it to sound as it had, hadn't in the least meant to threaten her.

Eyes still closed, he sighed. In thirteen years of operations, he'd never let his personal life interfere with his duty. Now the two were inextricably entwined. She hadn't killed Ruskin, but courtesy of whoever had started the rumors, she was now involved. Worse, he had a nasty suspicion that the person who had started the rumors would prove to be Ruskin's killer. If threatened, he might kill again.

He spent the rest of the day in the city, using his erstwhile talents to gain access to Ruskin's banking records. A combination of suggestion and implied threat, together with his title and the supercilious arrogance he'd learned long ago worked so well with those whose status depended on patronage, got him what he wanted.

His first stop was Daviot & Sons, the bank Ruskin had favored, exclusively as far as the notes in his rooms went. Ten minutes, and he'd gained access to all documents relating to Ruskin's dealings. The records revealed no major sums credited to Ruskin's account, only a trickle of income the bank verified came from Gloucestershire, believed to be derived from Ruskin's estate. There were no large deposits, nor any large withdrawals. Wherever the wealth Ruskin had used to pay off his considerable debts hailed from, it had not passed through the hands of the Messrs Daviot.

He proceeded to check all the likely banks; they were located in close proximity, scattered about the Bank of England and the Corn Exchange. Using his success at Daviots to pave the way, he encountered no resistance; by afternoon's end, he'd established that the city's legitimate financiers had not facilitated the flow of pounds to Ruskin's gaming acquaintances.

Hailing a hackney, he headed back to Mayfair. On the evidence of Ruskin's IOUs, the man had been not only a poor gambler but an addicted one. He'd lost steadily for years, yet there was no indication of any panic in his dealings. He'd paid off every debt *regularly* . . .

Muttering a curse, Tony tapped on the roof; when the

jarvey inquired his pleasure, he replied, "Bury Street—Number 23."

There had to be—*had to be*—some record somewhere. Ruskin was a clerk by nature; the contents of his desks, both in his office and his rooms, testified to his compulsive neatness. He'd even kept those old IOUs in chronological order.

The hackney halted in Bury Street; Tony swung down to the pavement, tossed a coin to the jarvey, and strode quickly up the steps of Number 23. This time, an old man let him in.

"I'm from Customs and Revenue—I have to check Mr. Ruskin's rooms for something I might have missed when I checked yesterday."

"Oh, aye." The old man stood back. "You'll know the way, then."

"Indeed. I have his key. I'll be a few minutes —I can see myself out."

The old man merely nodded and shuffled back into the downstairs front room. Tony climbed the stairs.

Once in Ruskin's rooms with the door shut and relocked, he stood in the center of the rug and looked around. He imagined himself in Ruskin's shoes; assuming he'd kept a record of his illicit dealings and had wanted to keep that record secret, where would he have hidden it?

The room was clean, neat, dusted; the furniture was polished and well cared for. Someone came in to clean. Whatever secret hole Ruskin had, it would be somewhere not likely to be found by a busy char woman.

Behind the solid skirting boards was unlikely; the cleared floor space, even under the rugs, would be too risky. Working as silently as he could, Tony shifted the heavy furniture and checked beneath and behind, but found only solid walls and solid floorboards, and dust.

Undeterred, he checked inside the small closet, shifting the items he'd searched before. He pressed, prodded, gently tapped, but there was no hint of any secret place. Next, he examined the door and window frames, searching for any crevice opening into a useful gap within the walls. There wasn't one.

Which left the fireplaces and their chimneys.

There were two—one in the parlor and a smaller one in the bedroom. The mantelpieces and hearths were easily examined; no luck there. With a resigned sigh, Tony stripped off his coat and rolled up his shirtsleeves before tackling the chimneys.

He saw the place as soon as he crouched down, ducked his head, and looked into the parlor chimney. Enough light seeped past his shoulders for him to discern the single brick, up on the side well above the flames' reach, that was considerably less grimed than its fellows. Its edges were free of soot and the detritus of years. Reaching in, he pressed one corner; the brick edged out of place. It was easy to grip it and drag it free.

Setting the brick down, he dusted his fingers, then reached into the gaping hole. His fingertips encountered the smooth surface of leather. He felt around, then drew out a small, black leather-bound book.

Grinning, he laid the book on the floor and replaced the brick. That done, he cleaned his hands on his handkerchief, then rolled down his sleeves and shrugged on his coat. Picking up the book, he hefted it— then gave in to temptation and quickly leafed through it.

It was exactly what he'd hoped to find—a miniledger that many gamesters kept, noting their wins and losses. The book was almost full; the entries stretched back to 1810. Each entry comprised a date, the initials of the opponent, and sometimes the name of the game—whist, piquet, hazard—and the sum involved; the latter was placed in one of two columns ruled at the right of the page—either a loss or a win.

In Ruskin's little black book, the losses greatly outnumbered the wins. However, the tally of wins and losses, scrupulously noted at the end of each page, was readjusted every few months, being brought back into balance by an entry, repeated again and again, of a substantial sum, noted as a win.

Tony checked back through the book. The regular "wins" started in early 1812. Although always substantial, the sums varied; the initials noted for each payment did not.

A. C.

Tony felt his face harden. He looked up. His mind in a whirl, he closed the book and slid it into his pocket. A moment later, he stirred, and headed for the door.

He was on his way down the stairs when the old man stuck his head out of the downstairs room. He squinted at Tony, then recognized him, nodded, and moved to retreat.

Tony reacted. "One moment, sir, if you would."

The old man turned back.

Tony assumed a faintly harrassed expression. "Have there been any other visitors to Mr. Ruskin's rooms since he died?"

The old man blinked, thought, then opined, "Well, not since you folk came by, but there was a gentl'man called here the night Mr. Ruskin met his end. It was late, so mayhap that was after he died."

"This gentleman, was he one of Mr. Ruskin's friends? A regular acquaintance?"

"Not that I ever saw. Never seen him before."

"What happened on that night?"

The old man leaned on his cane; he peered up at Tony with eyes that retained a deal of shrewdness. "It was late, as I said. The man rapped politely, and as it wasn't after midnight, I let him in. I was sure Ruskin was out, but the gentleman insisted he'd go up and check . . . didn't seem any harm in that, so I let him. He went up the stairs, and a minute later I heard the door open, so I thought, then, that Ruskin must have slipped in, and I hadn't noticed. I left them to it and went back to my fire."

Tony stirred. "Ruskin hadn't come home. He spent most of the evening at a soirée in Green Street. It was there, in the garden, that he was killed."

"Aye. So we heard the next day. Howsoever, that night, the gentleman that called and went into Ruskin's rooms stayed for more than an hour. I could hear him moving around; he wasn't thumping about, but it's quiet around here at night. One hears things."

"Did you see him when he left?"

"No—I'd put the door on the latch and gone to bed. They can still let themselves out, but the door locks as it closes."

"Can you describe this gentleman?"

Running his eye up Tony, the old man grimaced. "I can't recall much—no reason to, then. But he was decently tall, not so tall as you though, but more heavily built. Well built. He was nicely kitted out, that I do remember—his coat had one of those fancy fur collars, like rippling curls."

Astrakhan. A vision flashed into Tony's mind—the glimpse he'd caught at a distance as the unknown man leaving the Amery House gardens had passed beneath a streetlamp. His thought had been "well rugged up"— prompted by the astrakhan collar of the man's coat.

"And," the old man continued, "he was a toff like you. Spoke well, and had that way about him, the way he walked and carried his cane."

Tony nodded. "How old? What color hair? Was there anything notable about him—a squint, a big nose?"

"He'd be older than you—forties at least, but well kept. His hair was brownish, but as for his face, there was nothing you'd notice. Regular features"—the old man squinted again at Tony—"though not as regular as yours." He shrugged. "He was a well-dressed gentl'man such as you'd find on any street about here."

Tony thanked the man.

Once on the pavement, he paused, then set off for Upper Brook Street; the walk would do him good, perhaps clear his mind. An A. C. had paid Ruskin large sums for the last four years. Be that as it may, he was perfectly certain things were not as they seemed.

A few hours closeted in his library clarified matters, at least as far as identifying his immediate next steps.

Through Ruskin's blackmail and fateful coincidence, Alicia Carrington was being drawn further and further into his investigation. Given his personal interest, he needed to regain lost ground rapidly—needed to regain her trust. Doing so would require an apology, and worse, explanations. All of which necessitated a certain amount of planning, which in turn required a certain amount of reconnoitering. His groom returned from the mews near Waverton Street with the necessary details, by which time he'd formulated his plan.

He began its implementation with a note to his godmother, then sent a different note around to Manningham House.

When the clocks struck nine, he and Geoffrey were propping the wall of Lady Herrington's ballroom, keeping a careful eye on the arrivals.

"I would never have thought of sending around a groom." Eyes on the throng, Geoffrey seemed to be relishing his role.

"Stick with me, and you'll learn all sorts of useful tricks." Tony kept his gaze on the ballroom stairs.

Geoffrey softly snorted.

The strands of old companionship had regrown quickly, somewhat to the surprise of them both. Tony was four years Geoffrey's senior; much of their childhood had been colored by Geoffrey's need to cast himself as Tony's rival. Despite that, there'd been many occasions when they'd combined forces in various devilry; the friendship beneath the rivalry had been strong.

"There they are." Tony straightened. At the top of the

steps, he'd glimpsed a coronet of dark hair above a pale forehead.

Geoffrey craned his head. "Are you sure?"

"Positive." Which was of itself revealing. "Remember—the instant they reach the bottom of the steps. Ready?"

"Right behind you."

They swooped as planned, a perfectly executed attack that separated Alicia and Adriana the instant the sisters set foot on the ballroom floor. Geoffrey took Adriana's hand—offered with a delighted smile—and smoothly cut in, drawing Adriana forward while simultaneously insinuating himself between the sisters, cutting Alicia off from Adriana's immediate view.

Before Alicia could even gather her wits, she was captured, swept aside; Tony propelled her across the front of the ballroom steps and around into their lee, where a small and as yet uncrowded little foyer stood before a closed door.

They'd reached the foyer before she caught her breath.

Then she did. Her eyes swung to his face. They blazed.

He caught that scorching glance, held it. Her breasts swelled; her lips parted—on a scathing denunciation he had not a doubt. "*Don't* fight me." He spoke softly; there was steel in his voice. "Don't look daggers at me, and for God's sake don't rip up at me. I *have* to talk to you."

Her jaw set mulishly. She tugged her right arm, firmly gripped in his right hand; his left arm was around her waist, steering her on. She tried to stop, to dig in her heels, but she was wearing ballroom slippers. "If we must, we can talk here!"

He didn't pause, but looked down at her, leaned closer, drawing her into the shield of his body. "No, we can't. You wouldn't like it, and neither would I."

He released her arm to fling open the door, catching her in his left arm when she tried to step back. He swept her over the threshold and followed, shutting the door behind him, by sheer physical presence forcing her on along the corridor beyond.

She hissed in frustration, took two steps, then swung to face him and glared. "This is ridiculous! You can't simply—"

"Not here." He caught her arm again, propelled her on. "The door on the left at the end is our best bet."

He could sense her temper rising, seething like a volcano. "Our best bet for *what*?" she muttered beneath her breath.

He glanced at her, but held his tongue.

They reached the door in question; he sent it swinging wide. This time, she entered of her own volition, sweeping in like a galleon under full sail. He followed, shutting the door, taking note of her gown—a sleekly draped silk confection in bronzy, autumnal shades that became her extremely well.

She turned on him, faced him; the silk tightened over her breasts as she dragged in a deep breath—

He heard a click as the door at the head of the corridor opened. The noise of the ball washed in, abruptly cut off again as the door was shut. A woman giggled, the sound quickly smothered.

Reaching behind him, he snibbed the lock on the door.

Too far from the corridor to realize the danger, eyes blazing, Alicia opened her mouth to deliver the broadside he undoubtedly deserved.

He stepped forward, jerked her into his arms, and silenced her—saved them—in the only possible way.

FIVE

HE KISSED HER.

Her mouth had been open, her lips parted; he slid between, caressed, claimed—and felt her attention splinter. Her hands had gripped his upper arms; they tensed, but she didn't push him away. She clung, held on.

As a whirlpool of want rose up and engulfed them.

He hadn't intended it, had had no idea how much he wanted, how much hunger he possessed, or how readily it would rise to her lure. Hands framing her face, he angled his head and flagrantly feasted. Asking for no permission, giving no quarter, he plunged them both into the fire. She was a widow, not a skittish virgin; he didn't need to explain things to her.

Such as the nature of his want. His tongue tangling with hers, aggressively plundering, he released her face and gathered her to him. Into his arms, against his hard frame. Glorying in the supple softness that promised to ease his ache, he molded her to him, blatantly shifted his hips against hers. He felt her spine soften as she sank into him.

As her bones melted and her knees gave way.

Alicia struggled to cling to her wits, but time and again he ripped them away. Her breath was long gone; with their mouths melded she could only breathe through him—she'd given up the fight to do otherwise.

Her head spun—pleasurably. Warmth, burgeoning heat,

spread through her veins. Intoxicating. Shocking. She tried to cling to her anger, rekindle her fury, but could not.

She'd had only a second's warning, but she'd expected a kiss—a touching of lips, not this ravenous, flagrantly intimate exchange. Mild kisses she could cope with, but this? It was new territory, unknown and dangerous, yet she couldn't—*could not*—let her innocence, her inexperience show.

No matter how much her senses swam, how much her wits had seized in sheer shock.

She had nothing to guide her but him. In desperation, she mimicked the play of his tongue against hers, and sensed his immediate approval. In seconds, they were engaged in a duel, in a sensual game of thrust and parry.

Of lips and tongues, of heated softness and beguiling aggression, of shared breaths and, amazingly, shared hunger.

It caught her, dragged at her mind. Drew her in. Held her captive.

He urged her closer still, one hand sliding down her back to splay over her hips, her bottom, lifting her and pressing her to him.

Sensation streaked over her skin, prickling, heated; she clung tight, felt the world whirl.

And she was engulfed in his strength, enveloped by it, a potent masculine power that seemed to weaken every bone in her body, that promised heat and flames so dizzyingly pleasurable all she wanted was to wantonly wallow, to give herself up to them and be consumed.

On one level it was frightening, but she couldn't retreat—had wit enough left to know she couldn't panic, couldn't run.

She was supposed to be a widow. She had to stand there, accept all, and respond as if she understood.

Eventually his aggression eased, the tension riding him gradually, step by step, reined in. Gripping his arms, fin-

gers sunk deep, she felt that drawing back; the kiss lightened, became a more gentle if still intimate caress, lips
clinging, teasing, still wanting.

At last he raised his head, but not far.

Her lips felt swollen and hot; from beneath her lashes,
she glanced at his eyes. His black gaze touched her eyes,
held, then he sighed. Bent and touched his lips to the corner of hers.

"I didn't intend this. There were people in the corridor.
A danger . . ."

Deep, gravelly, the words feathered her cheek; sensation, hot and immediate, flashed over her.

"I wanted to apologize . . ." He paused, raised his head.
Again she met his eyes, again found them waiting to capture hers. Something predatory flashed in the rich black-
ness, then he continued, "Not for this. Not for anything
I've done or even said, but for how what I said in the park
sounded."

His tone was still low, slightly rough, teasing something—some response—from her.

Her gaze had drifted to his lips; his hands tightened on
her back, and she looked up, eyes widening as she felt the
heat between them flare again.

He caught her gaze, held it. "I'm not Ruskin. I will
never hurt or harm you. I want to protect you, not
threaten you." He hesitated, then went on, "Even this—I
didn't plan it."

This. He was still holding her close, not as tight as before yet just as flagrantly. Only lovers, she was perfectly
certain, should ever be this close. Yet she didn't dare pull
back, fought instead to ignore the warm flush the embrace sent coursing through her. What had gone before no
longer seemed terribly relevant.

"So—" She broke off, shocked by the sound of her
voice, low, almost sultry. She moistened her lips, tried for
a normal tone. Didn't quite manage it. "What had you
planned?" She met his eyes, clung to her bold front.

He studied her face, then his lips twisted. "I spoke the truth—I do need to speak with you."

He made no move to release her. How would an experienced widow react? She forced herself to remain passive in his arms and raised a haughty brow. "About what? I wasn't aware we had anything to discuss."

One black brow arched—arrogantly; holding her gaze, he deliberately shifted her against him, settling her in his arms—sending her senses reeling again. "Obviously"— he gave the word blatant weight—"there's much we could, and later will, discuss. However . . ."

The room, a small parlor overlooking the gardens, was unlit, but her eyes had adjusted—she could see his face well enough. Although he didn't physically sigh, she sensed his mind lift from them and refocus on something beyond. A frown in his eyes, he looked down at her, studied her face.

"When did you marry Carrington?"

She stared at him. "Marry?"

His frown grew more definite. "Humor me. When was your wedding?"

"Ah." She struggled to remember when it must have been. "Eighteen months—no, more like two years ago, now."

She dragged in a breath, struggled to ignore the way her breasts pressed into his chest, how her nipples tightened, and dragooned her wits into order. He was investigating Ruskin's death; she couldn't afford to prod his suspicions. "It was a very short marriage. Poor Alfred—it was terribly sad."

His brow arched again. "So you've been Alicia Carrington for only two years?"

She checked her calculations. "Yes." She bit her tongue against adding anything more; better to keep her answers short.

He didn't seem to notice; he seemed, not exactly relieved, but pleased. "Good!"

When she looked her surprise, he smiled rather grimly. "So you can't be A. C."

"Who's A. C.?"

"The person who paid Ruskin for his treasonous services."

She stared at him. Her lips formed the word twice before she managed to utter it. *"What?"*

Tony grimaced. He looked around. "Here." Reluctantly releasing her, he steered her to a chaise. "Sit down, and I'll tell you."

It hadn't come easily, his acceptance that if he wanted her trust, he would have to tell her, if not all, then at least most of what was going on, how he was involved, how she was involved—how she was threatened. He needed her cooperation for reasons that struck much deeper than his mission; that mission—his investigation—was a whip he could use to command her, but only one thing would suffice to make her trust him. To lean on him as he wished her to.

Appeasement—a peace offering, some gift on his part—was the only way to nudge her onto the path he'd chosen. The most important element between them right now was the truth; as far as he was able, he would give her that.

He waited while, with a suspicious and wary glance, she sat and settled her skirts, then he sat beside her and took her hand in his. Looked down, played with her fingers as he assembled his words.

Then, keeping his voice low yet clear enough for her to easily hear, he told her simply, without embellishment, all he'd learned of Ruskin.

She listened, increasingly attentive, but made no comment.

But when he came to how and where he'd discovered the initials A. C., her fingers tensed, tightened on his. He glanced at her.

She studied his eyes, searched his face. Then she

breathed in tightly. "You know I didn't kill him—that I'm innocent of all this?"

Not so much a question as a request for a clear statement.

"Yes." He raised her hand to his lips, held her gaze as he kissed. "I know you didn't kill him. I know you're not involved in any treasonous use of shipping information." He lowered their locked hands, then added, "However, you—we—have to face the fact that *someone* started the rumor I heard."

"I can't understand it—*how* could anyone know?"

"Are you sure, absolutely sure, that your secret, whatever it is, was known only by Ruskin?"

Frowning, she met his gaze, then looked away. Her hand remained resting in his. After a moment, she replied, "It might be possible that, in the same way Ruskin had learned what he had, then someone else might have, too. But what I can't understand is how that someone could know Ruskin was using the information as he was."

She looked at him.

"Indeed. Blackmail doesn't work if others know." He paused, then added, "From what I've learned of Ruskin, he wasn't the sort to give away valuable information. He'd have charged for it, and—"

Releasing her hand, he stood; he thought better on his feet. "The dates of payments noted in his black book not only match the dates he paid his debts, but also follow by about a week the dates he noted for certain ships." He paced, caught her eye. "However, there's no other payment— any unaccounted payment —entered. So I think we're on firm ground in assuming he hadn't sold any information other than the shipping directives."

Halting by the fireplace, he considered her. "So the question remains. Who would he have told about you, and why?"

Her brow creased as she looked at him; her gaze grew distant.

"What?"

She flicked him an impatient glance. "I was just wondering . . ."

When he moved toward her, she quickly continued, "When he left me, Ruskin was sure—absolutely confident—that I'd agree to his proposal. He"—she paused, blushed, but lifted her head and went on—"was so certain he expected to call the next evening and . . . receive my acceptance."

After a moment, she met his eyes. "I didn't know him well, but given his nature, he probably couldn't help gloating. About me—I mean, about gaining a wealthy widow as his wife."

Tony could visualize such a scenario readily, but he doubted it was her wealth Ruskin would have gloated about. Nevertheless . . .

"That would fit." He paced again. "If Ruskin, quite unsuspectingly, mentioned his coup—and yes, I agree, he was the type of man to gloat, then . . ." Bits and pieces of the jigsaw slid into place.

"What?"

He glanced at her, and found her glaring at him; he felt his lips ease. "Consider this. If Ruskin was murdered by whoever he'd been selling his information to—"

"By this A. C., you mean?"

He nodded. "Then if he mentioned he was about to marry, quite aside from any risk from the blackmail going wrong—it's always a risky business—the knowledge that Ruskin would soon have a wife would have increased the threat Ruskin posed to A. C."

"In case he told his wife?"

"Or she found out. Ruskin even mentioning knowing A. C., even years from now, might have been dangerous."

Alicia pieced together the picture he was painting. At one level, she could barely believe all that had happened since they'd entered the room. That searing kiss—it was as if it had cindered, felled, and consumed all barriers between them. He was talking to her, treating her, as if she was an accomplice, a partner in his investigation. More, a friend.

Almost a lover.

And she was reacting as if she were.

She was amazed at herself. She didn't—never had— trusted so readily. Yet if she was honest, it was why she'd been so furious with him in the park, when, despite her totally unwarranted trust—one he'd somehow earned in a few short days—it had seemed his interest in her and her family had all been fabricated. False.

That kiss hadn't been false.

It had been a statement, unplanned maybe, but once made, it couldn't be retracted—and he hadn't tried. It had happened, and he'd accepted it.

She had no choice but to do the same.

Especially as she, innocent or not, was being drawn deeper and deeper into the web of intrigue surrounding Ruskin's murder.

"Is this what you think happened?" She didn't look up, but sensed his attention fasten on her. "Presumably the man—let's assume he's A. C.—had arrived in the Amery House gardens via the garden gate. Ruskin went out to meet him—it had to have been an arranged meeting."

Torrington—Tony—drew nearer. "Yes."

"So then Ruskin babbled about his soon-to-be conquest—me—but . . ." Frowning, she glanced up. "Had Ruskin some information to sell, or had A. C. come there with murder on his mind?"

Tony mentally reviewed all Ruskin's notes on shipping. None had been recent. Even more telling . . . "I don't think there could be anything worthwhile for Ruskin to sell. With the war over, the information he had access to wouldn't be all that useful. . . ."

He was aware of her watching him, trying to read his face, follow his thoughts. He glanced at her. "I haven't yet defined how the information Ruskin passed on was used, but it's telling his association with A.C. began in early '12. That was when naval activity once again became critical. From '12 up until Waterloo, shipping was constantly under threat. Now, however, there is no significant danger on the seas."

He was going to have to pursue that angle hard, and soon.

She took up the tale before he could. "If Ruskin no longer had anything of real use to A.C., then . . ." She looked up at him.

He met her gaze. "A.C., assuming he has a position and reputation to protect, would have been threatened by Ruskin's continued existence."

"If Ruskin was not above blackmailing me . . ."

"Indeed. He may not have called it by that name, but given his debts, he would have needed an injection of capital quite soon, and almost certainly would have looked to A.C."

"Who decided to end their association." She nodded. "Very well. So while Ruskin is gloating, A.C. stabs him and leaves him dead. I come down the path—" She paled. "Do you think A.C. saw me?"

He considered, then shook his head. "The timing—when I saw him on the street—makes that unlikely."

"But then how did he know it was me Ruskin was blackmailing? Would Ruskin have told him my name?"

"Unlikely, but A.C.—and I agree, it most likely was he—didn't need your name to start the rumors."

She frowned at him. "These rumors—what exactly do they say?"

"That Ruskin was blackmailing some lady—a widow."

Her frown deepened. "But there are many widows in the ton."

"Indeed, but only one was seen talking to Ruskin immediately before he died."

Her gaze remained locked with his, then, abruptly, all color drained from her face. "Oh, good heavens!"

She sprang to her feet; her eyes flashed fire at him as if he was in some way culpable. "If they've decided I'm the widow in question, then what . . . ? *Good lord!* Adriana!"

Whirling, she raced for the door. He got there before her, closing his hand about the knob. "It's all right—calm down!" He caught her gaze as she paused, impatient before the door. "Manningham's with her."

Her eyes flashed again. "You and he planned this."

He tried to frown her down. "I had to talk to you."

"That's all very well, but what's been happening out there"—she jabbed a finger toward the ballroom—"while we've been talking?"

"Nothing. Most will be waiting, wondering where you are, hoping to catch a glimpse but not surprised given the crush that they haven't yet succeeded." He took in her wide eyes, the tension now gripping her. "There's no need to panic. They don't know it's you, and they only will know if you behave as if it is. As if you're frightened, or watchful. Ready to take flight."

Alicia met his steady gaze. To her surprise, she drew comfort from it. She drew in a breath. "So I have to carry it off with a high head and a high hand?"

"Absolutely. You can't afford to let those hyenas sense fear."

Despite all, her lips twitched. Hyenas? The hard line of his lips eased; she realized he'd deliberately tried to make her smile.

Then his gaze flicked up to her eyes.

He lowered his head—slowly; she sucked in a breath.

Held it as her lids fell and his lips touched hers—not in a tantalizing teasing caress, yet neither with their earlier ravenous hunger.

A definite promise; that's what the kiss was—as simple as that.

Slowly, he raised his head; their lips clung for an instant, then parted.

Lifting her lids, she met his black gaze.

He searched her eyes, then turned the knob and opened the door. "Come. Let's face down the ton."

She returned to the ballroom on his arm, calm, her usual poise to the fore. It was all a sham, but she was now an expert in the art of pulling wool over the ton's collective eyes.

One thing he'd said stuck in her mind: watchful. She had to stop herself from looking around, from searching for signs that people suspected her. She had to appear oblivious; it was the most difficult charade she'd ever performed.

He helped. On his arm, she strolled; he was attentive, charming, chatting inconsequentially as two such as they might. He was a wealthy peer; she was a wealthy, well-born widow. They didn't need to hide a friendship.

They progressed down the room; she smiled, laughed lightly, and let her gaze rest on the dancers but no one else. He distracted her whenever the temptation to scrutinize those watching them burgeoned.

At one point, his lips curved rakishly; he bent his head to whisper, "They're totally confused."

She met his gaze as he straightened. "About what?"

"About which rumor they should spread."

When she looked her question, with a self-deprecatory quirk of his lips he explained, "The one about you and Ruskin, or the one about you and me."

She looked into his black eyes. Blinked. "Oh."

"Indeed. So all we need do is continue on our present tack, and their befuddlement will be complete."

Just which tack he meant she discovered a minute later. She'd expected him to guide her to Adriana's side; her sister wasn't on the dance floor, which surprised and concerned her—she hadn't yet located her among the crowd. Instead, he led her to a chaise midway down the long ballroom. Lady Amery was seated on it, along with an older lady Alicia had previously met.

Nervousness struck; her fingers fluttered on Tony's sleeve. Instantly, his hand closed, warm and comforting, over hers. Steering her to the chaise, he bowed to the two dames. "*Tante* Felicité. Lady Osbaldestone."

Spine poker straight, Lady Osbaldestone nodded regally back.

"I believe you're both acquainted with Mrs. Carrington?"

Alicia curtsied.

"Indeed." Lady Amery reached for her hands; her eyes glowed with welcome. "My dear, I must apologize for this *dreadful* business. I am most distressed that it was your attendance at *my* soirée that has given rise to such unpleasantness. Why, there are any number of widows in the ton, and as we all know, many of those others are much more certain to have secrets to hide. So foolish of these *bourgeoisie*"—with a contemptuous flick of her hand she dismissed them—"to imagine you had any connection with Mr. Ruskin beyond the natural one of living nearby."

Her ladyship paused; bright eyes fixed on Alicia's face, she surreptitiously pressed her fingers. "Tony tells me you spoke with Mr. Ruskin, but it was purely an exchange about mutual acquaintances in the country."

In the corridor just before they'd reentered the ballroom, he'd primed her with that tale. Alicia longed to turn her head and glare at him; he hadn't mentioned this little encounter he'd arranged for her.

"Indeed." To her relief, the glamor she'd perfected over the last weeks didn't waver; she smiled with easy assurance tempered with just the right touch of innocent bewilderment. "We hail from the same area. Although we only met recently, here in town, we shared a number of mutual acquaintances. It was they we discussed in your drawing room that evening."

Lady Osbaldestone humphed, drawing Alicia's attention. The old black eyes assessing her were a great deal sharper and harder than Tony's ever were. "In that case, you'll have to excuse those with nothing better to do than wag their tongues and make mischief. For my money, they've hay for brains.

"I ask you," she continued, "even if Ruskin was black-mailing some widow, what has that to say to anything?" She gave a dismissive snort. "The idea of some lady in evening dress pulling a stiletto from her reticule and stabbing him to death is ludicrous. Aside from the fact he was no weakling, and would hardly have obligingly stood still while she poked him, where would she have carried the blade?" The black eyes flashed, at Tony as well as Alicia. "That's what I'd like to know. Have you ever seen one of those things? *Pshaw!* It's not possible."

Apparently entertained, Tony inclined his head. "As you say. I heard the authorities are looking for a man at least as tall as Ruskin."

"Indeed?" Lady Osbaldestone brightened at the news. "Not perhaps revealing, but interesting nevertheless." She rose; although she carried a cane, she rarely used it.

She was a tall woman, taller than Alicia; her face had never been pretty, but not even age could dim the strength of its aristocratic lines. Her piercing black eyes rested on Alicia, then her lips lifted, and she looked at Tony. "Send my regards to your mother when next you bestir yourself to write. Tell her Helena sends her fondest wishes, too." Lifting her cane, she jabbed it at him. "Don't forget!"

"Naturally not." Eyes on the cane, Tony bowed with a flourish. "I wouldn't dare."

With a glint in her eye, Lady Osbaldestone regally ac-knowledged Alicia's bobbed curtsy and Lady Amery's salute, then glided away.

"Well, there you are!" Lady Amery beamed at Tony and Alicia. "It is done, and Therese will do the rest, you may be sure." She lifted a hand, waved it at Tony; he took it and helped her to her feet.

"*Bien!* So now I am going to enjoy myself, too, and see

what a stir I can cause." She glanced at Alicia, and patted her arm. "And you must go and dance, and pretend not to notice, and it will all blow over, my dear. You'll see."

Alicia looked into Lady Amery's button-bright eyes, then implusively squeezed her hand. "Thank you."

Her ladyship's eyes glowed brighter. "No, no, *chérie*. That is not necessary—indeed, it is I who must thank you." Her gaze shifted to Tony. "I am an old woman, and I have been waiting an age to be asked to help. At last it has happened, and you are the cause. It is good." She patted Alicia's hand and released it. "Now go and dance, and I will go and make mischief."

The first strains of a waltz were percolating through the room; Tony offered his arm. "I suspect your sister will be located most easily on the dance floor."

Alicia narrowed her eyes at him, but consented to place her hand on his arm. He steered her to the floor; seconds later they were whirling.

She took a few minutes to adjust, to regain her breath, realign her wits and subdue her clamorous senses. The physical power with which he so effortlessly swept her along, the shift and sway of their bodies, the subtle repetitive temptation of their limbs brushing, touching, then moving away—the waltz was a seduction in itself, at least the way he danced it.

Surreptitiously clearing her throat, she looked up; she studied his expression, arrogant, latent charm lurking, yet difficult to read. "Why did you ask Lady Amery to help?"

He glanced down at her. "She's my godmother. You heard her—she's been waiting for the bugle call for years." He looked ahead, then added, "It seemed appropriate."

"It's *you* she wanted to help, not me."

His lips quirked. "Actually, no—it's *you* she's been waiting all my life to aid."

She frowned and would have pursued the odd point, but a flash of dark curls caught her eye. Turning, she saw

Adriana whirling down the room in Geoffrey Manning-ham's arms. Her sister was . . . the only fitting word was scintillating. She drew eye after male eye, and a good many female ones, too. Her delight seemed to fill her and overflow.

Alicia looked at Tony, caught his eye. "Please tell me your friend is entirely trustworthy."

He grinned; after whirling her through the turns at the end of the room, he dutifully parroted, "Geoffrey is entirely trustworthy." He paused, then added, "At least where your sister's concerned."

"What does that mean?"

"It means he won't do anything you would disapprove of."

She blinked at him. "Why not?"

"Because if he makes you unhappy, then I'll be unhappy, and Geoffrey and I have been down that road before."

She studied his eyes. A vise slowly tightened about her lungs. Then she forced in a breath, lifted her head, fixed her gaze over his left shoulder, and stated, "If you imagine I'll be grateful . . ."

Her courage failed her; she couldn't go on. But he thought her a widow, and clearly had a certain interest, and just possibly imagined. . . .

He frowned at her; from the corner of her eye she watched . . . it took a moment for him to follow her reasoning, then his eyes flared. His lips set in a thin line. The fingers about her hand tightened; the hand at her back tensed . . . then, very slowly, eased.

Eyes narrow, Tony waited; when she didn't look at him, he looked away, unseeing. After a moment, he exhaled. "You are without doubt the most difficult female I've ever—" He bit the words off, abruptly stopped as his temper threatened to erupt. When he had his fury once more in hand, he drew breath and went on, his voice low, tight, very definitely just for her. "I'm not helping you in the expectation of gaining any specific . . ." He cast about in his mind, but could only come up with, *"Service."*

Her eyes flicked to his face, wide, curious, wanting to know.

He trapped her gaze. "I want you, but not as a result of any damned gratitude!"

Her eyes remained on his, then scanned his features. "Why, then"—her voice, too, was low, intensely private—"are you helping me?"

For an instant, he inwardly rocked, then he found the right words—words he could say. "Because you deserve it. Because you and your sister and your demon brothers *don't* deserve the censure of the ton, let alone being implicated in a murder."

For a long moment, she held his gaze, then her lips gently lifted. "Thank you." She looked away; he only just caught her last words. "You're a good man."

He wasn't quite so good as he would have her believe, but he definitely wasn't expecting her gratitude to stretch as far as an invitation to her bed. He *did* expect to be invited to her bed, but not because of his efforts on her behalf.

The next morning, he was still . . . not so much smarting as ruffled, a disordered sensation he appreciated not at all. A vague disgruntlement that she'd even *imagined* that he might *need* to resort to gratitude—

He cut off the thought and headed for the Bastion Club.

Sanity in a disconcerting world—a world with females in it.

He was looking for advice. In the club's drawing room, he found Christian Allardyce slouched in an armchair, his long legs stretched out, ankles crossed, a news sheet propped before his face. He lowered it as Tony entered.

"Ho! And here I've been wondering about these tales of you stumbling over a dead body."

Tony grimaced. "All true, I'm afraid, and there's a

deadly twist. The game's fallen into Dalziel's lap, and guess who he's tapped on the shoulder?"

Christian's brows rose. "And you agreed?"

Elegantly sitting in another chair, Tony shrugged. "Aside from the fact that refusing Dalziel is marginally more difficult than taking an enemy battery single-handed, there were other aspects that attracted me."

"Quite apart from tripping over the body."

"Indeed. From what we have, the man was a traitor of sorts." Crisply, he outlined what he knew of Ruskin, omitting all mention of one lovely widow. After describing the payments made by A. C., he went on, "I wondered if perhaps, if A. C. was truly wise, he might have channeled the payments through a moneylender."

Christian opened his eyes wide. "Used a moneylender to draw the large sums, then paid them back with numerous smaller amounts much easier to explain from his own accounts?"

"Exactly. Do you think that's possible?"

Christian nodded. "I would say so." He met Tony's gaze. "Certainly worth asking."

"Next question: who do I ask? I've never had any dealings with such gentlemen."

"Ah! You've come to the right source."

It was Tony's turn to open his eyes wide. "I would never have imagined you deep in debt and reduced to dealing with moneylenders."

Christian grinned and laid aside the news sheet. "No, I never was. But I once bailed out a friend, and along the way I made the acquaintance of a good handful of the gentlemen. Enough, certainly, to start you on your way."

Folding his hands across his waistcoat, Christian leaned his head back; eyes on the ceiling, he started re-counting all he knew.

Tony drank it in. At the end of fifteen minutes, he knew exactly who to approach, and even more importantly, how.

Thanking Christian, he left the club and headed into the city.

His interview with Mr. King, the most famous—or infamous depending on one's point of view—usurer in London was an unqualified success. Mr. King's office was a stone's throw from the Bank of England; as Christian had prophesied, Mr. King was perfectly happy to assist the authorities given their investigation in no way threatened him or his trade.

A traitor lost all claim to confidentiality; Mr. King had ascertained that no gentleman with the initials A. C. had borrowed large sums of cash from him. He'd confirmed that the practice of disguising major debts in such a way was not uncommon, and had undertaken to inquire on the government's behalf among the other moneylenders capable of advancing such sums.

Tony parted from Mr. King on genial terms. Hailing a hackney, he headed back to Mayfair. With the money angle in hand, he had two other avenues of inquiry to pursue; as the carriage rocked along, he considered how best to tackle them.

Nearing the fashionable quarter, he glanced out at the pavement. It was a glorious day, ladies walking, children laughing and dancing.

Temptation whispered.

Reaching up, he thumped on the roof, then directed the jarvey to Green Park.

He arrived to an exuberant welcome, and had just enough time to have a quick turn flying the kite before Alicia, feigning primness, gathered them all and herded them back to Waverton Street.

Although he quizzed her with his eyes, she remained spuriously aloof, walking smartly along, the boys skipping about them.

He matched his stride to hers, inwardly amused, not only with her but with himself. It had been a long time—

thirteen years at least—since he'd felt so relaxed, experienced this kind of subtle content. He'd honestly enjoyed his time with her brothers; it was almost as if his military years, especially as he'd lived them, had been taken out of his life, excised, so the youth he'd been at nineteen had more in common with the man he had become.

Or perhaps all he'd seen, all he'd experienced in those thirteen years away, had left him with a deeper appreciation of life's little pleasures.

Reaching their house, she opened the door. The boys tumbled in.

"Blackberry jam today!" Matthew sang, and rushed for the stairs.

The older two raced after him, laughing and calling. Jenkins, the kite in his arms, smiled and trudged after them.

Alicia called after him, "Do make sure they're clean before they come down, Jenkins."

"Aye, ma'am." Jenkins looked back. "And I'll let Cook know about tea."

He nodded deferentially to the presence behind her; suddenly realizing, Alicia whirled. "Oh—yes." She met Tony's black eyes; uncertainty flared. "You . . . er, will stay for tea, won't you?"

They were suddenly alone in the hall. He smiled, slowly, into her eyes, then inclined his head. "Blackberry jam's my favorite."

His gaze dropped to her lips; the image that flashed into her mind was of him licking blackberry jam from them. Heat rising in her cheeks, she quickly turned away. "Adriana will be in the parlor."

She led the way, with some relief saw Adriana look up as they entered. Adriana and Tony exchanged easy greetings; as was her habit, Adriana was studying the latest fashion plates prior to designing their next round of gowns.

They all sat; a companionable, almost familial ease fell over them. From her corner of the chaise, Alicia watched as Adriana asked Tony's opinions on various styles depicted in the latest issue of *La Belle Assemblée*. He responded readily; it was quickly apparent he understood more about ladies' garments than one might suppose a gentleman would. . . .

She broke off the thought. His attention was on the plates Adriana had spread before him; she seized the opportunity to study him.

She wished she could see into his mind.

Since they'd parted the previous evening, she'd been plagued by one question: how did he think of her? How did he see her—what were his intentions, his expectations? What direction did he imagine they were headed in?

Given the circumstances, those were not only valid questions; learning the answers was vital to maintaining her charade and succeeding in their aim of having Adriana marry well.

Tony—*Viscount Torrington*—could easily scupper their plans. If he learned of them, and if he so chose. There was, at present, no reason he should stumble on their—her—crucial secret. That secret, however, was precisely the fact that most complicated her way forward.

Along with all the ton, he thought her a widow.

Last night had been a warning. If she was to maintain her charade long enough to establish Adriana, and then disappear, she was going to have to as far as possible restrict her interaction with Torrington.

And what she couldn't avoid, she was going to have to respond to as if she was indeed a widow; she couldn't risk all they'd done, all their success to date, by succumbing to any missish sentiment.

The thunder of feet on the stairs heralded her brothers' arrival. They burst in, full of chatter and exclamations. Jenkins followed with the tray. In seconds, the parlor was filled with rowdy, boisterous warmth and comfort; if anything was needed to remind her why she was playing the role she was, it was there before her in her brothers' smiling, laughing, happy faces.

Torrington—thinking of him by his title helped to keep a sensible distance between them, at least in her mind—gave his attention to the boys, answering questions, joining in their speculations and wonderings, occasionally teasing in a way the boys not only understood and accepted, but took great delight in.

As the guardian of three males, she'd long known they were incomprehensible beings; watching Tony—Torrington!—slouched on the floor, munching a muffin slathered with blackberry jam only compounded her wonder.

He caught her watching; their gazes touched, locked, then he smiled. A fleeting, wholly personal, even intimate gesture, then he looked again to David, who'd posed the question of when the animals in the zoo were most likely fed.

To the boys' disappointment, Tony admitted he didn't know; to their delight, he promised to find out.

It was time to step in. She leaned forward. "Enough, boys! Time for your lessons."

With artistic groans, they clambered to their feet; eyes alight, each shook hands with Tony. Armed with his promise to let them know what he learned with all speed, they left with remarkable alacrity for their books.

Inwardly frowning, Alicia watched them disappear. Jenkins entered and removed the tray.

As he was leaving, Adriana bounced to her feet. "I want to do some sketching. I'll be up in my room."

Before Alicia could think of a suitably worded protest, given he whose presence occasioned that protest was stretched at her feet looking thoroughly at home, Adriana had blithely taken her leave of him, then, without meeting her eyes, her sister whisked out of the room.

And closed the door behind her.

SIX

ALICIA CONSIDERED THE CLOSED DOOR, THEN LOOKED AT Tony. *Torrington*! He remained on the floor, shoulders against the side of an armchair; his expression gently amused, he raised a brow at her.

She cleared her throat. "Have you learned anything more about Ruskin?" She needed to keep his mind away from her, from his interest in her; his investigation was assuredly her best bet.

His eyes opened a fraction wider. "Yes, and no. I haven't learned anything definite, but I have certain inquiries in train. Whether they bear fruit remains to be seen."

When she waited, pointedly, Tony grinned. "I spent a most illuminating morning learning about money-lenders."

"Moneylenders?" Alarm flared across her face; her hand instinctively rose to her breast.

"Not on my account." He frowned fleetingly at her. "It's not unknown for gentlemen like A. C. to move the large sums they use to pay their informants via money-lenders, thus concealing their part in the transaction. I visited Mr. King this morning, and asked if he knew of any gentleman with the initials A. C. who had borrowed large sums regularly over recent years."

She continued to stare at him; her stillness was

strange. "Any gentleman . . ." She drew breath. "I see. And did he?"

"No." Tony studied her, trying to fathom the cause of her reaction. "He had no such borrower on his books. However, he agreed to check with the other moneylenders. Given he's something of an institution in the field, if A.C. has been using moneylenders to cover his tracks, I believe we can rely on Mr. King to unearth him."

She blinked; some of her tension had faded. "Oh." She searched his face, then abruptly rose; with a swish of skirts, she went to stand before the window. "Ruskin's information must have some bearing on this. Presumably A.C. used it to his benefit, or why seek and pay for it?"

"Indeed." His gaze on her, Tony got to his feet, resettled his coat, then approached. "There are other avenues I'm exploring."

His voice warned her; she glanced over her shoulder as he halted behind her, so close she was to all intents and purposes—certainly his intents and purposes—trapped between him and the wide windowsill.

Her eyes widened; she sucked in a quick breath. "What avenues?"

Standing this close, with the perfume of her hair and skin rising, wreathing his senses, his mind wasn't on his investigation. "The shipping is one." He slid one palm across her waist, then splayed his fingers and urged her back against him.

She hesitated, then permitted it, letting him settle her, warm and alive, against him. "How are you going to investigate that?"

The words were thready, starved of breath. He inwardly grinned, and sent his other hand to join the first, anchoring her before him, savoring the supple strength of her beneath his palms, her warmth and the softness of the feminine curves riding against him. "I have a friend, Jonathon Hendon. He and his wife will be in London in a few days."

Bending his head, he set his lips to cruise the fine skin above her temple. "Jonathon owns one of the major shipping lines. If anyone can indentify the likely use of Ruskin's information, Jonathon will."

There was a nervous tension in her he couldn't place, didn't understand.

"So you'll learn what A.C. used the information for from Jonathon?"

Beneath his hands, she stirred. Her pulse had accelerated; her breathing was shallow.

"Not quite." He bent lower, let his breath caress her ear. "Jonathon will be able to say what the information might have been used for, but proving that someone did use it, then following the trail back to that someone won't be quite so simple."

"But . . . it would work."

"Yes. Regardless of how we identify A.C., we'll still need to piece his scheme together. Eventually." He breathed the last word as he set his lips to her ear, then lightly traced with his tongue.

A telltale shudder racked her spine, then she surrendered and sank back against him. Feeling ludicrously victorious, he changed position so he could minister to her other ear.

Her hands closed over his at her waist, gripped. "What other route . . . you said avenues . . . plural . . ."

Her voice faded as he artfully teased; when he lifted his head, she sighed. He grinned openly—wolfishly—knowing she couldn't see. "There'll be some other connection between Ruskin and A.C. They'll have met somewhere, have known each other, even if only distantly. Their lives will have touched somewhere, at some time."

Sliding his hands from under hers, he ran his palms slowly upward. Heard the swift intake of her breath as his thumbs brushed the undersides of her breasts. She stiffened, stilled. He caressed knowingly, reassuringly; gradually, almost skittishly, she eased back.

"How—" She cleared her throat. "How do you plan to investigate . . . that?"

She was having trouble finding breath enough to speak; he decided to make it harder still. "I have a friend, not exactly up that way, but close enough." Boldly turning his hands, he cupped her breasts.

Alicia thought she might faint. Her lungs seized; her head whirled. Desperate, she clung to her wits. Dragged in a tight breath. "Ah . . . what . . . ?"

"I'll ask him to check in Bledington. See if the initials A. C. mean anything to people there."

She jerked as his hands shifted, frantically fought down all further reaction. She hadn't imagined he would . . .

His voice had grown deeper, darker, more gravelly. Would a widow protest? On what grounds?

Giddiness threatened. She hauled in a breath, briefly closed her eyes, battered by conflicting impulses. Panic that his friend might stumble on more than she would wish. The urge to stiffen—not just in response to that, but to his boldness, to the liberties he was taking . . . her head was spinning. The countering instinct to sink against him, to arch her spine, press her breasts, now aching so strangely, into his hard hands only added to her dizziness.

Then he closed his hands and kneaded.

She lost the last of her breath. Her senses fractured. Her wits fled.

Beyond her control, her spine softened, gave; she had to lean fully against him, her hands dropping helplessly to brace against his muscled thighs.

His fingers shifted, then closed again. Tightened.

Fire lanced through her. She gasped, arched; eyes shut, she let her head fall back as he repeated the torture, then he bent his head to her throat, now exposed. His lips cruised, then settled.

Hot, wet, his mouth covered the spot where her pulse raced. He kissed, licked, laved, all the while massaging her breasts, sending wave after wave of pure sensation rushing through her.

Heat built beneath her skin; the rasp of his tongue over her pulse point shocked and teased her senses. His hands were strong, his grip confident, knowing, his body a wall of hard muscle and bone, holding her there, a captive to delight.

To the pleasure even in her innocence she knew he was orchestrating.

She felt totally at his mercy. And witlessly content to be so.

Madness—but an oh-so-pleasurable insanity.

This had to be lovemaking, a part of it, of the type a nobleman indulged in with his mistress.

Illicit. Exciting. Enthralling . . .

The moment for protest was long past. Her role was set; eyes closed, head back, she gave herself up to it—she couldn't draw back now.

Tony was intrigued by her response, with the ardor he sensed beneath her restrained veneer. As he ministered to her senses, learned the curves of her breasts, their weight, their wonder, he cataloged, analyzed, noted for future reference. She was amazingly responsive; her breasts, now sensitive and swollen, filled his hands. She shifted under them, pressing back against him, sirenlike, openly sensuous.

Despite her reserve, an understandable defense for an attractive well-born widow, she couldn't hide her reactions; she understood what lay between them as well as he. The flames that leapt into being at just a touch were more than strong—they were scorching. They could both feel them licking, beckoning, hungry yet held back.

They couldn't take things much further yet, but their time would come. On the physical plane, the path ahead was straightforward, but there was much about her he'd yet to learn.

"Your parents." Releasing her breasts, he nuzzled her ear, gently blew. "When did they die?"

Eyes still closed, Alicia dragged in a breath—it felt like her first in ten minutes. Then she felt a tug at her neckline; opening her eyes, she looked down—to see his long fingers easing the top button of her bodice free. "Ah . . . Mama died almost two years ago."

Good Lord! She had to stop this—had to call a halt. If he touched her . . .

"And your father? From your brothers, I gather he's been gone a long time."

Her mouth was dry; she nodded. "Years and years." Gaze fixed on his busy fingers, she licked her lips.

"And you have no other family? No one close?"

"Ah . . . no." She dragged in a breath. "I really think—"

"You're not supposed to think."

She blinked, lifted her gaze. "Why not?"

"Because"—his fingers were inexorably descending, leaving her bodice gaping—"at the moment, you're supposed to be enjoying, simply feeling. You don't need to think to do that."

He sounded eminently reasonable, even faintly amused; the idea of a missish protest and consequent retreat seemed unwise.

"Have you always lived near Banbury?"

"Ah . . . yes." Once he'd opened her bodice, what did he plan to do?

He shifted behind her, easing back; the realization that she wasn't the only one affected by his play burst across her mind, stealing what few wits she'd managed to reassemble.

"I assume Carrington hailed from that area, too?"

The words sounded distant, vague, but whether that was due to the drumming in her ears, the titillating panic locking her lungs, or because he was no more interested in the subject than she was, she wasn't sure.

A cool wash of air slipped beneath her gaping bodice;

she quelled a shiver. His hands drifted down, then fastened about her waist.

"Ah . . . y-yes. He came from there, too."

"How old are your brothers?"

She frowned. "Twelve, ten, and eight." His hands had settled; she gulped in a breath. "Why are you asking all this?"

His fingers gripped, then he stepped back, turned her and stepped forward once more, locking her against the windowsill, his hips to hers, his erection rigid against the softness of her stomach.

He trapped her gaze.

She couldn't think—not at all. Could only stare into his black eyes, and wonder if there really were embers glowing in them. The sheer maleness of him engulfed her; his gaze dropped to her lips—she felt them throb.

His lips quirked, wryly humorous. He released her waist; one hand rose to cup her jaw, angling her face upward as he bent his head. "Because I want to know *all* about you."

His lips closed on hers as his other hand slid boldly beneath her bodice, and closed about her breast.

She gasped, tensed; only a fine layer of silk lay between her sensitized skin and his burning palm. Her breasts instantly felt heavy, swelling, tightening, aching anew.

Then he entered her mouth, possessive and demanding, capturing her attention, insistent and commanding; she scrambled to meet him, to remember how, to play the experienced widow she was pretending to be. The hand on her breast shifted, knowingly cupping, then his fingers toyed with the silk, shifting it over the tightly ruched peak, heightening its excruciatingly sensitive state—then he closed his fingers around the pebbled tip, tugged gently, then tightened, tightened . . .

She tried to break from the kiss, but he wouldn't let her; his hand framing her face, he held her captive. Once again lavished delight and sheer sensual pleasure on her through the play of his lips and tongue, and the even more expert play of his fingers.

He captured her totally. Not just with the heat, with the sudden flare of hot desire, but with something simpler, more fundamental.

His hunger—and hers.

He didn't try to hide his want, his wish to have, to know, to take, to explore, to experience; it was there, laid before her, stated more clearly than in words. A hunger of her own rose in reply, not mere curiosity but something more definite—a need she hadn't known she had.

He angled his head, ravaged her mouth, and she consciously met him. Flagrantly urged him on. His fingers closed again and she shuddered, no longer trying to disguise her response. Her hands rose, of their own volition found his shoulders, then pushed on, around, back, then she speared her fingers into his black hair.

The silken touch of the heavy locks didn't distract, but only added to the tactile experience; her greedy senses, awakened and starved, welcomed and wallowed. His hand shifted on her breast, blatantly possessive; his fingers tightened again—hers clenched in response.

He moved closer, into her, deepening the kiss—and suddenly they were somewhere else, in some place they hadn't been before. Somewhere hotter, more fiery, where their needs escalated and their senses grew ravenous. Clamorous.

Urgent.

It was he who broke the kiss, lifted his head and hauled them free of the fire. Drew them back to earth, back to themselves, to their bodies locked close in the parlor.

To their breaths fast and shallow, to their pulses hammering in their veins. Lids lifting, their gazes locked; in his, the flames still smoldered. Her lips throbbed, appeased yet still hungry.

His gaze fell to them, then lower. To where his hand

lay over her breast. He closed that hand, slowly, deliberately. Desire welled and washed down her spine; something inside her clenched tight.

His eyes lifted to hers. "Not here, not now." He bent his head and kissed her, slowly, deeply, intimately, then drew back. "But soon."

His hand left her aching flesh, yet he didn't step back. Instead, his gaze returning to her eyes, trapping her, holding her, he deftly rebuttoned her bodice.

Her head was whirling, but some part of her no longer cared. That part of her that seemed new, different—changed. Or perhaps revealed, called forth. That part of her that thrilled to that decisive "But soon."

She might have thought she was mad, but knew she wasn't. This was a facet of life she'd yet to experience, yet to explore.

As a widow, she couldn't pretend not to understand. The look in his eyes convinced her she'd never succeed in denying what she'd felt, in pretending her hunger didn't exist. He'd seen it, felt it, understood it—almost certainly better than she did.

There was nothing she could say—that she could think of that was safe to say—so she merely held his gaze and, her pulse still thundering, waited to follow his lead.

That seemed an acceptable response. When, stepping back, he quizzed her with his eyes, she merely arched a brow, and saw his lips quirk.

He took her hand, raised it to his lips. "I'll leave you. I'm afraid I won't be attending the Waverleys' ball tonight." He turned to the door; she walked beside him. "I need to consult with some others about the investigation."

He opened the door; she led him into the front hall.

"The rumors concerning you and Ruskin should be fading."

She glanced at him, saw a frown in his eyes. "I'm sure we'll manage."

Her even reply didn't reassure him. "Lady Amery will

be attending, and Lady Osbaldestone, too, should you need any support."

Opening the front door, she held it, and looked at him. "I doubt that will be necessary, but I'll bear it in mind."

Pausing by her side, he looked into her eyes. She got the distinct impression he wanted to say something more, something other, but couldn't find the words.

Then he reached out, with the pad of his thumb caressed her lower lip.

It throbbed.

Swiftly, he bent his head, pressed a kiss, hard and definite, to the spot, then he straightened. "I'll call on you tomorrow."

With a nod, he went down the steps.

She stood at the door, watching him walk away, then shut it. She paused, waiting until her nerves steadied and untensed, then, lips firming, she headed for the stairs.

Alicia tapped on the door of Adriana's bedchamber, then entered.

Sprawled on her bed, her sketchbook before her, Adriana looked up, then smiled. Impishly. "Has he gone?"

"Yes." Alicia frowned as Adriana bounced into a sitting position. "But you shouldn't have left us alone."

"Why ever not?" Adriana grinned. "He was waiting to be alone with you, wasn't he?"

Sitting on the end of the bed, Alicia grimaced. "Probably. Nevertheless, it would be wiser if I didn't spend time alone with him."

"Nonsense! You're a widow—you're *allowed* to be alone with gentlemen." Adriana's eyes sparkled. "*Especially* gentlemen like him."

"But I'm *not* a widow—remember?" Alicia frowned. "And gentlemen like him are dangerous."

Adriana sobered. "Surely not—not him." She frowned. "Geoffrey told me Tony—Torrington—was totally trustworthy. An absolutely to-his-bones honorable gentleman."

Alicia raised her brows. "That may be so, but he thinks I'm a widow. His attitude to me is based on that."

"But . . ." Adriana's puzzlement grew; curling her legs, she shifted closer, studying Alicia's face. "Gentlemen do marry widows, you know."

"Perhaps." Alicia caught her eye. "But how many noblemen marry widows? I don't think that's at all common. And you know what the books said—unless of the nobility herself, a widow is often viewed by gentlemen of the haut ton as a perfect candidate for the position of mistress."

"Yes . . . but the books were warning of the general run of gentlemen, the bucks, the bloods, the—"

"Dangerous blades?" Alicia's lips twisted; reaching out, she squeezed Adriana's hand. "You're not, I hope, going to tell me Tony—Torrington—isn't dangerous."

Adriana pulled a face. "No. But—"

"No buts." Alicia spoke firmly, then stood. "In my estimation, it would be unwise for me to be alone with Torrington in future."

Adriana's eyes, fixed on her face, narrowed. "Did he kiss you?"

Her blush gave her away; she met Adriana's eyes fleetingly. "Yes."

"And?" When she said nothing, Adriana prompted, "How was it? How did it feel?"

The word brought back exactly how it had felt; warmth spread beneath her skin, her nipples tightened. One glance confirmed that Adriana was not going to be deterred. "It was . . . pleasant. But," she quickly added, "indulging in such pleasantness is far too risky."

She could see more questions forming in Adriana's inquisitive mind. "Now that's enough about me." She reverted to her firmest tone. "I intend to avoid Torrington in future. But what about you? You're the reason we're here, after all."

Adriana gazed up at her. After a moment, she said, "I like Geoffrey. He's kind, and funny, and . . ." She drew breath and continued in a rush, "I think he might be the one."

That last was said with an almost stricken look. Alicia sat again. "If you only *think* he might be, perhaps we should cast around a trifle more until you're certain. There are three weeks yet before the Season begins, so you've plenty of time—there's no reason to feel you must reach a decision quickly."

"Indeed." Adriana frowned. "I wouldn't want to make a mistake."

The sisters sat side by side, both staring into space, then Alicia stirred. "Perhaps"—she glanced at Adriana— "to help in deciding, it might be time to ask Mr. King to dine."

Adriana looked at her, then nodded. "Yes." Her chin firmed. "Perhaps we should."

Alicia held her head high, her parasol deployed at precisely the correct angle as the natty barouche she'd hired from the livery stables rolled smoothly onto the gravel of the avenue through the park.

The morning was fine; a light breeze drifted through the branches of the trees, just coming into bud. She and Adriana sat in elegant comfort; on the box before them and clinging behind, the coachman and footman were attired in severe black with bright red ribbons circling the crowns of their hats. That last was Adriana's suggestion, a simple touch to add a hint of exclusivity.

Such things mattered when going about in the ton.

"I still can't get over Lady Jersey being so attentive." Adriana lifted her face to the breeze; her dark curls danced about her heart-shaped face. "She has *such* a reputation, but I thought she was quite nice."

"Indeed." Alicia had her own ideas over what had prompted Lady Jersey's kind words, and those of the other senior hostesses who had found a moment during the Waverleys' ball to stop beside her to admire Adriana and wish them both well. She strongly suspected Lady Amery and her dear friend Lady Osbaldestone had been busy. And she knew at whose behest.

"Oh! There's Lady Cowper." Adriana returned her ladyship's wave.

Alicia leaned forward and directed their coachman to pull up alongside her ladyship's carriage, halted on the verge.

Emily, Lady Cowper, was sweet-tempered and good-natured; she had from the first approved of Mrs Carrington and Miss Pevensey. "I'm so glad to see you both out and about. The sun is so fickle these days one daren't let an opportunity pass."

"Indeed." Alicia touched fingers; Adriana smiled and bowed. "One can only attend a few balls each night, and there's so many one simply cannot find in the crowds."

Lady Cowper's eyes gleamed. "Especially when so many need to have their notions set straight. But that small *contretemps* seems to be sinking quite as quickly as any of us might wish."

Alicia shared a satisfied, understanding smile with her ladyship. They chatted about upcoming events for five minutes, then took their leave; the carriage rolled on.

To Lady Huntingdon, then Lady Marchmont, and finally Lady Elphingstone.

"That color so becomes you, my dear." Lady Elphingstone examined Alicia's maroon twill through her lorgnette, then turned that instrument on Adriana's gown of palest lemon. "I declare you both are forever at the very pinnacle of modishness—always just so, never a step too far. I only wish my niece would take note."

Alicia recognized the hint. "Is your niece in town?"

Lady Elphingstone nodded. "She'll be at Lady Cranbourne's rout tonight. I take it you both will be attending?"

"Indeed." Adriana smiled warmly; she knew her role well. "I would be pleased to make your niece's acquaintance, if that might be possible?"

Lady Elphingstone beamed. "I'll be sure to make her known to you."

Alicia returned her ladyship's smile. "We'll look forward to it." By such little strategems were valuable alliances formed.

They parted from Lady Elphingstone. Alicia glanced ahead, then instructed the coachman to return to Waverton Street. Adriana cast her a questioning glance. Settling back, she murmured, "I've had enough for today."

Adriana accepted the decree with easygoing cheerfulness; Alicia shut her lips on her real reason—she didn't need to burden Adriana with that.

She had had enough—enough of deceiving others. But she'd accepted the role she had to play; any guilt associated with it was hers alone to bear.

As the carriage rolled under the trees, along the drive lined with the conveyances of the fashionable, she and Adriana continued to smile, wave, and exchange nods; the number of ladies with whom they were acquainted had grown dramatically over the past days. Or, more correctly, the number of ladies wishing to make their acquaintance had grown, courtesy of Tony—his lordship—and those he'd asked to look kindly upon them.

The gates of the park loomed; the carriage swept through, and they were free of the necessity of responding to those about them. Alicia couldn't help but wonder what their reception would be if the ton knew the truth.

The prospect increasingly impinged on her mind. Tony—Torrington—had allied himself with them; if her secret became known, he would be involved by implication. Guilt by association, something the ton was quick to indulge in.

That worry dragged at her; only when they turned into Waverton Street and her mind swung to her brothers and her small household did she realize her worry for Torrington was of the same type, that nagging insistent consideration that she felt for her dependents, all those in her care.

The carriage rocked to a halt. Inwardly frowning, she let the footman hand her down. She wasn't wrong in assessing how she felt, yet Tony wasn't a dependent, nor yet in her care. Why, then, was her feeling so strong—so definite? So *real*.

After handing Adriana down, the footman bowed, then left. The carriage rumbled off. Adriana started up the steps. Closing her parasol, Alicia followed more slowly.

Jenkins would be upstairs with the boys; Adriana opened the door and went in, then turned to take Alicia's parasol. "I'll put these in the parlor. I thought of a new design—a variation of that French jacket. I want to sketch it before I forget." With a swish of her skirts, she headed for the parlor.

Alicia paused in the hall, watching her sister . . . just for one instant pausing to give thanks, then she heard a footfall on the stairs.

She looked up—and her heart leapt.

There could be no doubt; as she watched Tony slowly, elegantly descend, his lips set in an easy line but his eyes watchful, intent, she understood what she was feeling, couldn't stop the welling tide of anticipation, the burgeoning of simple happiness.

She was in a very bad way.

With one hand, he indicated the upper floor. "I've been with your brothers." Reaching the bottom stair, he stepped down, walked closer.

With every step he took, she could feel her awareness

come to life, feel her consciousness expand, reaching for him.

He stopped directly in front of her. His eyes met hers, their expression quizzical, faintly amused. Then, before she could stop him, he bent his head and kissed her.

Gently, warmly.

He raised his head, met her gaze. "I need to speak with you privately." He glanced around, then gestured. "Shall we use the drawing room?"

She looked at the closed door. Her lips still tingled; it was an effort to bludgeon her wits into working order. "Yes. If . . ." Had her brothers said something they shouldn't?

That thought and the incipient panic it evoked helped get her mind functioning. Turning, she crossed the hall by Torrington's side, her protective instincts abruptly on full alert. No matter what she felt for him, she shouldn't forget that if he learned the truth, he could pose as big a threat to her and her family as Ruskin had.

Indeed, the threat he could pose was even greater.

Tony opened the door, waited for her to enter, then followed her into the elegantly appointed room. His gaze went first to the windows—two long panes looking onto the street. Shutting the door, he glanced around, but there was nothing of her or her family there, on the mantelpiece or the occasional tables set between the two chaises and the well-padded armchairs.

She stopped in the middle of the richly colored Turkish rug; head up, spine straight, hands clasped before her, she faced him.

"You don't have enough menservants." He had no idea what she'd expected him to say, but it assuredly wasn't that. She blinked, then frowned as her mind shifted to the domestic arena. If he told her he'd discovered a certain delight in throwing her off-balance, in confusing her, she most certainly wouldn't approve, yet such moments revealed an underlying vulnerability, one she didn't normally show, but which he treasured seeing and knew he responded to. As he presently was.

"Menservants?" Her frown was definite. "We have Jenkins, of course."

"One man for a house of this size, with a family of this size?"

Her chin rose as he closed the distance between them. "We've never seen the need for a large staff. We're quite comfortable as we are."

Halting before her, he caught her gaze. "I'm concerned."

She searched his eyes. "About what?"

"About the direction my investigation is taking, and the fact someone started rumors about you. Specifically *you*—the widow Ruskin was blackmailing."

She hesitated, then said, "Adriana and I are always careful."

"Be that as it may, this house is large . . . and you have three young brothers."

He didn't need to say more; he watched alarm flare in her eyes, only to be replaced by consideration, then consternation. He picked his moment to murmur, "I have a very large house with a very large staff, most of whom have very little to do given I'm the only member of the family in residence." Her gaze lifted to his; he held it. "I would feel much happier, less concerned, if you would allow me to lend you a footman, at least until my investigation is successfully concluded."

She returned his regard steadily. A minute ticked by, then she said, "This footman . . . ?"

"I have one in mind who would suit admirably— Maggs. He's been with me for years. He's well trained, and I can assure you he'll know how to deal with your brothers and the rest of the household, Jenkins especially."

Her eyes narrowed; her look stated that she understood his tactics, that she recognized he'd left her little room to maneuver, no real excuse to refuse. "Just for the duration of your investigation?"

"You may have him for as long as you wish, but I'd urge you to allow him to stay at least until we have Ruskin's murderer by the heels."

She pressed her lips together, then nodded. "Very well. I'll warn Jenkins."

They were standing close; he sensed her impulse to step back, away. Instead, she fixed him with a direct look. "It may interest you to know that at the Waverleys' ball last night and in the park this morning, Adriana and I met with, not just a gratifying degree of acceptance, but a quite astonishing level of support."

He raised his brows. "Indeed?"

"Indeed." She held his gaze. "You arranged it, didn't you?"

His face remained impassive, unreadable; his eyes, he knew, gave nothing away while he debated his answer. Eventually, he said, "Although she no longer resides in the capital, my mother has a large circle of friends among the *grandes dames* of the haut ton. I used to find their existence a trial. Now . . . I'm prepared to admit they do have their uses."

She drew a slow, deep breath; although he kept his eyes locked with hers, he was highly conscious of the swelling of her breasts. "Thank you." She hesitated, then added, "I don't know why you're doing this—"

Alicia broke off when something flashed in his eyes—an expression so vibrant, so powerful, even as fleeting as it was, the glimpse distracted her.

In the same moment, he reached for her; hands sliding around her waist, he drew her to him. Against him. Into his arms as he bent his head.

"The reason I'm doing this . . ."

The words washed over her lips, suddenly hungry; for a second, their gazes touched, locked, then his lids fell. She felt his gaze on her lips.

"Ought to be obvious."

Deep, low, the words sank into her brain as his lips covered hers, and he sank into her mouth. Claimed her attention, then sent it spinning, fractured, dispersed. Called her senses, drew them to him, then trapped them, held them enthralled.

She kissed him back, found herself mentally floating as the slow, drugging kisses took their toll. Sinking her fingers into his shoulders, she tried to hang onto her wits, to some degree of control, but steadily, inexorably, implacable and irresistible, he drew it from her grasp.

Then he drew her hard against him, locked her body to his, and the flames and the magic flared.

It had to be magic, that surge of sensation, the giddy delight, the anticipation streaking down her nerves, tingling, tightening so that the need to sate it was suddenly more important than breathing, far more important than any consideration of social strictures.

His hands spread over her back, stroked possessively down the long planes, curving over her hips to close proprietorially over her bottom, provocatively kneading, then boldly caressing. Hot as a flame, heat spread beneath her skin; a deep-seated yearning flowered in its wake.

Then he angled his head and ravaged her mouth, took more, demanded more. Unhesitatingly she followed him deeper into the exchange, encouraging and enjoying the ever more intimate melding of their mouths.

The first inkling she had that he'd opened her bodice was the slithering caress of her silk chemise as, loosened, it slipped down, helped by his long fingers. And then those fingers were on her skin, and she lost touch with the world.

And plunged into another.

Into a realm where sensation and emotions were the only reality, where touches and caresses formed the language, with needs, wants, and desires the only goals. Every slow, possessive caress heightened her need, made her want with an ever greater certainty fueled by escalating, burgeoning desire. Yet that desire seemed entwined with his, with him, with his obvious reason. With what she sensed, in her bones knew, he wanted.

Their lips parted; from under heavy lids, their gazes met, held as his fingers moved on her, upon her, drawing whorls of flame on her skin, tightening her nerves to an excruciating degree. Unable to bear it, she closed her eyes, with a soft gasp let her head fall back. Felt him bend near, felt his lips on her throat, sliding down to fasten over her thudding pulse.

His hands shifted; her gown slid over her shoulders, then cool air caressed her heated skin. The bared skin he set his lips to tracing, with flicking licks and long trailing laves teasing, the hot, wet promise of his mouth withheld . . . as the fever built, as some need within her grew, and grew . . . until she moaned.

The sound, soft, nearly suppressed, surprised her, but through the hands at her waist holding her, supporting her, she sensed his satisfaction. A wholly male triumph that he crowned by closing his mouth—every bit as hot and wet as she'd imagined—over the taut, aching peak of one breast.

She tensed, her nerves clenched, not with rejection but delight. Her hands slid through his hair, tightened on his skull as he swirled his tongue about the ruched peak, then sucked gently. Sensation, pure and elemental, streaked through her, racing through her body to pool deep and low, a warming glow within her.

Cracking open her lids, she looked down. Watched as he feasted on her bounty—and wondered at her reaction. Some part of her was shocked, yet she couldn't, even now, summon any will to refuse him, deny him—to push him away. She couldn't tense her muscles, couldn't break the spell. She didn't want to, couldn't pretend. Could only watch, feel, learn, and experience.

Something new, something novel, something she'd never felt before.

Tony sensed her fascination and was content. For now. He knew her acquiescence was not, yet, freely given; he could draw her into such sensual exchanges, but she did not, yet, seek them of her own accord.

That was what he wanted. Needed. For her to want him as he wanted her.

Overwhelming her natural resistance, taking over, controlling her—for one of his talents, that wasn't all that hard. For him, the challenge lay deeper, in making her come to him, making her desire him enough to set aside her reserve and actively seek to be intimate with him.

Only by that route would he gain the surrender he sought, the complete and conscious giving that, for one of his nature, was the ultimate prize.

He raised his head; their gazes briefly touched, then he covered her lips, and took her mouth again. In a slow, thorough, leisurely engagement that left them both starved of breath.

Gradually, he drew back. Her breasts were swollen, tight beneath his hands; her skin felt like hot satin beneath his fingertips. He kept his lips on hers as he searched for and found the top edge of her chemise, and drew it up, tugging the drawstring so it tightened and held.

She stirred in his arms. He ended the kiss and lifted his head. Their eyes met for an instant, then she looked down; drawing her hands from his shoulders, she resettled and retied the chemise, then, a blush tinting her cheeks, she rapidly did up the buttons of her bodice.

He couldn't keep his lips straight when she glanced at him; his satisfaction was too deep to hide.

She saw it, read it; a frown in her eyes, she waved him to the door.

Smiling, he turned, glancing at her as she fell in beside

him. Before the door, he halted, caught her eye as she looked up. "I'll send Maggs this afternoon."

She blinked at him. "Maggs?"

"The footman."

"Ah." She drew herself up, nodded. "Yes, of course. Thank you."

He grinned, ducked his head, and kissed her—stole one last kiss from her luscious lips—then straightened and met her eyes, green and slightly dazed. "I'll see myself out."

He managed to suppress a smirk; feeling positively virtuous, he opened the door, gracefully saluted her, then closed it.

Alicia stared at the panels. Beyond them, she heard his footsteps recede, then the front door opened, and shut.

He was gone.

Reason and logic returned in a flood; the last minutes—however many minutes it had been—replayed in her mind.

Her increasingly horrified mind.

Her lips still throbbed, her skin still tingled, her breasts . . . she could still feel the sensation of his mouth moving over them . . .

With a groan, she closed her eyes and slumped against the door.

What was she going to do?

SEVEN

"My dear Mrs. Carrington, may I present Sir Freddie Caudel?"

Lady Hertford beamed at Alicia, who divined that gaining Sir Freddie's notice was something of a coup. She extended her hand with a polite murmur.

Sir Freddie took her fingers and bowed gracefully. A gentleman in his middle years, he was handsome in a quiet, patrician way.

Alicia smiled. In a few short minutes, she established that Sir Freddie was a scion of an old and ancient house and consequently socially prominent, held a political post in the government, possessed a degree of polish and address to which younger men could only aspire, and was on the lookout for a wellborn, beautiful, and young bride.

Not surprisingly, Adriana had caught his eye.

Alicia hestitated, wondering if she should, in all compassion, nip Sir Freddie's aspirations in the bud; from all she could see, Adriana was fast losing her heart to Geoffrey Manningham.

Sir Freddie had followed her gaze to where Adriana stood by Lord Manningham's side. "I realize, of course, that youth and beauty go hand in hand, yet often you ladies have a remarkably discerning eye."

Alicia met Sir Freddie's blue eyes, guileless and amused. Geoffrey might be younger, yet Sir Freddie was undeniably distinguished, and his manners, while absolutely correct, had an ease about them, a comfortable confidence deriving from years of moving in the first circles.

Sir Freddie might give Geoffrey a run for his money.

More particularly for Adriana's heart, which her hand would follow.

Lips curving, Alicia inclined her head. "If you wish to join my sister's circle, I have no objection." She seriously doubted Sir Freddie would succeed, but there was no harm in him attempting to upset Manningham's applecart.

"Sir Freddie offered his arm. "If you would introduce me?"

Placing her fingers on his sleeve, Alicia allowed him to lead her to Adriana's side.

Adriana was, as always, polite to anyone who sought her attention. Introduction completed, Alicia withdrew, rejoining Lady Hertford at the side of the room.

"He's very highly thought of," her ladyship whispered. "Marcus tells me he can be quite stiff-rumped on occasion, but always the true gentleman." Adriana drew Miss Tiverton into the conversation with Sir Freddie; Lady Hertford smiled delightedly. "Such a sweet girl, your sister. Who knows? If Sir Freddie doesn't fix her interest, perhaps he'll look at Helen. Of course, there's his age, but when men of his stamp look to take a wife, one can at least be sure they're in earnest. And his estates are quite respectable, I believe—they've been in the family for generations."

Alicia smiled easily; she let Lady Hertford's chatter wash over her, nodding here and there. Eventually, her ladyship departed, leaving Miss Tiverton along with Adriana under Alicia's watchful eye.

She did keep her gaze on her sister's circle, some yards away, but the instant Lady Hertford's distraction disappeared, Alicia's thoughts focused on her own distraction.

Anthony Blake, Viscount Torrington.

Her reaction to his practiced seduction surprised her;

she'd assumed she'd be uninterested, disinterested, that repulsing any gentleman's advances, especially those of a predatory nobleman, would be instinctive, a natural response she wouldn't have to pause to consider, let alone battle to achieve.

It was a battle she was losing; she'd already lost significant ground. Quite why, she didn't understand.

When she was with him, in his arms or even simply alone with him, the world seemed to shift, the frame of reference by which she'd lived her life thus far to alter. It swung to focus on him, to accommodate him, to center, not just on him, not just on his wishes, but on hers—those wishes she hadn't known she had.

When with him, her attention shifted to a different landscape, one encompassing all that was growing between them. That change was unprecedented, unsettling, yet fascinating. Even addictive.

Something in him called to something in her; from the coalescing of those somethings grew the power she sensed, the power that was strong enough to suborn her wits, shackle her senses . . . and seduce her.

She shivered, and refocused on Adriana's circle, and saw Sir Freddie successfully solicit her sister's hand for a waltz. Noting Geoffrey Manningham's studiously impassive countenance, she smiled.

Hard fingers, a hard palm, closed about her hand.

She turned as Tony—Torrington!—raised it; eyes capturing hers, he pressed a kiss to her fingers. Faintly smiled.

"Come and dance."

Within seconds, she was whirling down the floor. She didn't bother trying to resist; instead, she turned her mind to her most urgent need—trying to understand what was going on.

He seemed content simply to dance, to hold her in his arms and revolve about the ballroom, his gaze resting on her face, on her eyes.

Drinking her in.

She lowered her lids, screening her eyes, shifted her gaze to look over his shoulder. Smoothly, he drew her closer as they went through the turns, and didn't ease his hold; abruptly she was aware of their bodies, the subtle brushing of their hips, of his thigh parting hers as they turned . . . as if he'd reached for her and enveloped her in a flagrantly intimate embrace. The memory leapt to her mind, instantly impinged on her wanton senses.

Instantly stirred her hunger.

She looked up, met his gaze. "This is madness."

The words were low, breathy. He smiled, but his eyes remained on hers, his gaze intent. "If it is, we're both infected."

Beyond recall. She drew breath, read his eyes; their expression was openly predatory—his intent could not have been clearer. Realization, as inescapable as the dawn, burst upon her.

Deep within her, something quivered.

Tony looked up, over her head, wishing for once that she possessed a more definite mask, a countenance less easy to read. One long look into her eyes, and he was aching. If Cranbourne House had boasted any suitable room, he'd have whisked her off to it, there to pursue, however impulsively, the connection growing between them. Unfortunately, Cranbourne House was small, pokey, a totally unsuitable venue. Added to that, her sister was present, which meant she'd be distracted. When he finally had her beneath him, he didn't want her thinking of anything else.

He noticed Geoffrey standing by the side of the room, not exactly scowling, yet clearly not happy. A quick glance about the floor located Adriana waltzing in the arms of a somewhat older man.

"The gentleman waltzing with your sister—who is he?"

Alicia had been studying his face; she answered

evenly, "Sir Freddie Caudel." After a moment, she asked, "Do you know him?"

One distraction was as good as another. Resigning himself to yet another night of escalating frustration, he glanced down at her. "No, but I've heard of him. Very old family. Why? Is he interested in your sister?"

Alicia nodded. "How interested, I'm not sure, and I doubt his interest, at whatever level, will be reciprocated, nevertheless . . ."

His lips quirked; he glanced again at Geoffrey. "Another iron in the fire?"

Alicia narrowed her eyes. "Precisely." One with which she might prod things along.

"I take it the footman met with your approval?"

"Maggs?" Bearing a written introduction, the man had presented himself at the back door in Waverton Street. She met Torrington's gaze, let a moment pass; Maggs, as he had to be aware, was the most unprepossessing specimen. His features were irregular, his face appeared pushed in, yet he seemed possessed of an easy disposition and had already, in just a few hours, gained acceptance from Cook, Fitchett, and, most importantly, Jenkins. For which she was grateful. "I daresay he'll suit well enough. As I pointed out, we really have little use for a footman."

"Nevertheless." Torrington's black eyes quizzed her. "Just so that I can rest easy."

She suppressed a humph.

The waltz ended. Without instruction, Torrington led her back to her position not far from Adriana's court. He remained by her side, chatting inconsequentially on this and that, the customary exchanges of tonnish life. Others joined them, remained for a time, then moved on; she tried not to dwell on the fact that she preferred having him near, that his easy, in many ways undemanding presence made her evening distinctly more enjoyable.

More relaxing on one level, more unnerving on another.

It was the minor moments that tripped her up, that set her nerves jangling. That brought what was between them flooding back into her mind, blocking out all else, even Adriana.

Like the moment when having remained by her side, her cavalier through the rest of the evening, Torrington parted from them in the Cranbournes' front hall. They were among a small crowd of departing guests; to gain her attention, he touched her shoulder.

His fingertips brushed lightly. Despite being decently sheathed in ruby silk, her skin reacted. Goosebumps rose and spread in a wave; her nipples tightened.

Her eyes flew to his, wide, aware; he read them, his lips thinned, and she knew he knew, too.

Then he met her gaze fully. The expression in his eyes nearly slew her; the heat was so open, so intense, it was a wonder it didn't melt her bones.

His lashes swept down; he grasped her hand and very correctly took his leave of her.

She mumbled some response, then watched his back as he walked away through the crowd; only when he disappeared through the front door did she manage to breathe again. Manage to give her attention to the footman waiting to be told which carriage to summon. Thankfully, Adriana hadn't noticed; her sister seemed as distracted as she.

The journey back through the night-shrouded streets provided a welcome respite, a quiet moment all but alone when she could gather her wits, review what had happened, all she'd felt, how she'd reacted, without worrying about her betraying blush.

Finally to make some attempt at defining where she stood. And whither she was heading.

The first seemed all too clear; she stood teetering on the horns of a dilemma. As for the second, the possibilities were varied but uniformly unsettling.

Her dilemma was clear enough. She had to play the part of a tonnish widow, an experienced lady aware of, indeed personally acquainted with, all aspects of intimacy. The question now facing her was simple: how far should she go in preserving her charade?

To her perturbation, the answer was not at all simple.

Dedication to their cause argued the answer should be as far as she needed to go to see Adriana through her Season and secure their family's relief. But that immediately raised another highly pertinent question: how far *could* she go without Torrington realizing?

He was not just experienced; he was an expert. She'd been scrambling to keep up with him thus far; at some point she would falter, and he'd realize. . . .

The social strictures at least were clear. Regardless of her charade, she wasn't a widow, but a virtuous spinster—she shouldn't permit him even the liberties he'd already taken. Unfortunately, her inner voice was quick to argue, to speak in support of those wishes and needs she was only just realizing she possessed; where, that inner voice asked, was the harm?

She'd accepted over a year ago that she'd missed her chance at marriage; she was twenty-four—not unmarriageable by ton standards, yet in reality the likelihood had faded. Once Adriana was established, she, Alicia, would disappear from society; she'd imagined she'd retire to the country to watch over the boys, to keep home for them whether with Adriana and her husband or otherwise.

That plan still stood; nothing had happened to alter her path. Any liaison with Torrington would be, as such things generally were, temporary, fleeting. A liaison with him might, however, be her only chance to experience all she was presently pretending to know.

He was the only gentleman who had ever engaged her on that level; even now, she wasn't sure how he'd done it, how it had happened. Yet it had; the possibility now existed where it hadn't before. If she wanted to know more, wanted to experience all that could be between a man and a woman, all she had to do was let Torrington teach her.

The carriage rocked along, heading into Mayfair, pausing here and there as other carriages crowded the streets. She barely noticed the delays, indeed was grateful for the opportunity to let her mind range ahead, examining, imagining.

If she did indulge in a liaison with Torrington . . .

He would realize she was a virgin, would guess she'd never been married. However, she doubted he would expose her to the ton; there was no reason he should, not once she'd explained.

There was, however, another danger. One her instincts, uneducated though they were, had detected. Just how real that danger was she couldn't be certain, yet Tony— Torrington—was a nobleman to his toes. Arrogant, yes, with a definite streak of ruthlessness behind his charming facade, and . . . she searched for the word to describe what she sensed when he looked at her, held her, kissed her, caressed her.

Possessive.

If she gave herself to him, trusted him that far, would he agree to let her go?

She wasn't foolish enough to overlook the point; if she became his mistress, allowed him to become privy to her secret, he'd be in a position much as Ruskin had been, able to dictate her behavior. She recognized the possibility, viewed it clearly, yet she couldn't, despite all, see it happening. Adriana had mentioned Geoffrey's assessment of Torrington; it concurred with her own reading of the man. He was simply not the sort to hold a woman against her will. Regardless of all else, he was an honorable man.

If she did become his mistress, for whatever length of time, he would, in the end, let her go.

All of which left her precisely where she'd started, fac-

ing the question of what she should do and no nearer to
finding an answer.

The only alternative to making a decision was to stave
it off. Somehow to hold him off, to avoid the culmination
he was clearly steering them toward. If she could hold to
a line just short of surrender, then the instant Adriana was
established, disappear . . .

With a creak, the carriage turned into Waverton Street.
Adriana stirred, stretched. Alicia straightened, and gathered her shawl and reticule. The carriage halted; looking
out, she saw the light burning above their door.

Thought of her brothers innocently asleep in their
beds.

Resist Torrington. The problem with that strategy was
that in order to implement it, she'd have to fight not only
him, an experienced campaigner, but her own, largely unknown, desires.

She let the footman hand her down, then led the way
up the steps. Their reckless but straightforward plan had
developed serious complications.

The next morning, Tony headed for the Bastion Club. On
foot. He needed the exercise.

Needed the physical activity to ease the building frustration of a type he'd rarely had to endure. Indeed, he
couldn't remember ever wanting a woman so much, and
not having her. Worse, in this instance, he recognized the
need to go slowly, carefully; his relationship with Alicia
was forever, not for a few weeks or a few months. It
would be the most important relationship of his life; it
demanded and deserved a degree of care, of respect, of
attention.

He'd noticed her occasional hesitations, the sudden
tensing, almost a skittishness that sometimes gripped her.
He'd always succeeded in soothing it, in getting her to set
it aside and relax, to trust him. To open her eyes, see and
accept all that could be and would be between them.

Although he hadn't foreseen it, her reserve didn't surprise him; she might be a widow, but that wouldn't change the underlying truth of her nature—she was a virtuous lady, and as such would not easily be seduced. And in her case, there was yet more—a complicating factor. She was responsible for her family, and she took that responsibility seriously.

He hadn't imagined that in gaining his bride, he'd have to compete with her family for her attention. While the fact was a difficulty, and clearly would continue to raise hurdles, he didn't, as it happened, disapprove.

He enjoyed her family—enjoyed spending time with her brothers, even enjoyed watching Adriana make her choice, especially given Geoffrey was involved. But more, he found the circumstance of her family reassuring.

As an only child, he'd never experienced the relationships Alicia and her siblings took for granted. The warmth, the closeness that was simply there, the support it never occurred to them to question . . . all that was not only attractive, but spoke strongly of Alicia's ability to create for him, with him, the sort of home and family he wanted. And needed. How much he hadn't realized until he'd met her and her brood.

Regardless of his frustration, he wouldn't have her change, didn't wish she was otherwise. He valued her for what she was, as she was, and was fully prepared to accommodate that, to woo her as she needed to be wooed.

And pray he didn't do himself an injury in the meantime.

With a wrench, he hauled his mind away from that moment in the Cranbournes' front hall. Just thinking of that made him ache. Determinedly, he focused on the meeting he was heading for, with Gervase Tregarth and Jack Warnefleet.

They were waiting in the club's meeting room, comfortably slouched about the mahogany table. Christian Allardyce was also there; when he raised his brows, Tony waved him to stay. "You've already heard part of this affair—the more help the better."

Christian grinned. "And Dalziel is involved."

"Indeed." Tony sat and quickly, concisely, told them all he'd learned of Ruskin, his death, and his dealings with A. C. "This is a list of the ships mentioned in Ruskin's notes, and the associated dates, and these"—he handed over a second sheet—"are the dates on which Ruskin received large cash donations to his gambling fund."

Gervase studied the list of ships and dates, then compared them with the dates of the payments. Shifting to sit beside him, Jack perused the lists, too.

Christian, beside Tony, looked across the table at them. "I take it the payments in some way coincide with the shipping dates?"

Checking back and forth, Gervase nodded. "About a week in between, but not for every ship listed."

Tony sat back. "It appears Ruskin provided the information, it was used or in some way confirmed, and then he received payment."

"Whoever A. C. is, he ran a tight operation. No payment unless . . ." Jack stopped, looked up.

Grimly, Tony nodded. "Presumably no payment unless the information was useful."

"Which," Christian murmured, "suggests it was used for something."

"And if it was," Gervase was still studying the lists, "it wasn't for anything good."

"That," Tony agreed, "is the inescapable conclusion. What we need to determine is exactly how it was used."

Gervase nodded. "And trace it back to whoever that use benefited."

"Precisely." Tony paused, then asked, "Can you help?"

Gervase looked up, grinned. "I was intending to slip home for a few days. I can easily ask around in Plymouth, and along the coast there." He met Tony's gaze. "But you've more extensive contacts in the Ísles and on the French side, and to the southeast on this side, I'd imagine."

"Yes, but my problem—our problem at present—is that that information"—Tony nodded at the lists in Gervase's hands—"is all we have. I compiled the list of ships from scattered jottings, more like reminders. Presumably the information Ruskin passed contained more detail."

"But what detail we don't know?" Jack asked.

"Exactly. Via the Revenue and Admiralty dispatches that passed through his hands, Ruskin had what amounted to each ship's sailing orders, at least for their approach to our shores." Tony looked at Gervase. "If you can find any hint of what was going on—how the information was used—I can put out feelers more widely. But given the nature of my contacts, if I ask general questions, rather than specific ones, I won't get any answers. Worse, I might alert whoever it is that's behind this."

They all understood how the informant system worked; he didn't need to explain further.

"Can I keep these?" Gervase held up the lists.

Tony nodded. "Those are copies."

Folding the lists, Gervase slipped them into his pocket. "I'll ask around and see if I can find any whisper of any action involving these ships on or about those dates. If I find anything, I'll bring it back immediately."

"Once we have a clue what we're dealing with, I'll follow up more widely."

Jack frowned. "Have you thought of inquiring via the shipping lines? If these ships are merchantmen . . ."

"I've a friend who'll be in town in a day or so—he has a similar background to ours. He's been out of the service for some years, but knows the game well. He also owns Hendon Shipping, one of the largest of the local lines. He has the contacts and will know how to make such inquiries without raising a dust."

Jack nodded. "So—what did you want me to pursue?"

"Ruskin himself, and how A.C. knew him. Ruskin lived at Bledington when he was in the country. Not often, admittedly, but it's an area we shouldn't overlook. Given you're the closest of us countywise, your inquisitive presence is least likely to attract attention. Our ultimate aim is to identify A.C. It's possible he's someone who lives out that way, and that's how he knew Ruskin, and most importantly where Ruskin worked."

"Right." Jack's gaze had grown distant. "I'll check into Ruskin's background and see if I can turn up anyone with the initials A.C. connected in however vague a fashion with our boy."

"While you're up there . . ." Tony hesitated, then went on, "You might check on a Mrs. Carrington and her family, the Pevenseys. Their connection with Ruskin appears to be via Chipping Norton. It seems Mrs. Carrington and the Pevenseys didn't know Ruskin, but he knew them."

"Carrington." Christian murmured. "That's a C."

"Indeed. More confusing, she's Alicia Carrington, so she is A.C., but she married Carrington about two years ago, so wasn't A.C. four years ago, when Ruskin first started receiving large sums from A.C. More to the point, her husband, deceased for two years, was Alfred Carrington. Although he can't be the A.C. involved either, given the way names run in families there may be a connection with Ruskin of which Mrs. Carrington is unaware."

"Oh, yes." Jack nodded; for one instant, the dangerous man behind his hail-fellow-well-met cheerily handsome facade showed through. "Second cousin, third cousin, whatever. I'll check."

They all exchanged glances, then, as one, pushed back their chairs. They stood, stretched, resettled their coats; as they turned to the door, Christian murmured, "That shipping business sounds decidedly nasty." He caught Tony's eye, then glanced at the others. They were all thinking the same thing—that someone had been using the war for their own ends.

"We definitely need to learn what the information was used for, and how," Gervase said.

"And, most importantly"—Tony followed Christian from the room—"by whom." That, indeed, was their primary interest.

Tony returned to Upper Brook Street and spent the next few hours attending to numerous matters of business. Under his father's hand, the Blake estates had grown considerably; he was determined that during his tenure, the family's fortunes would continue to expand.

The activity naturally brought to mind the family—the people—that fortune was intended to support. When the clock struck two, he set aside his papers and strolled around to Green Park.

David, Harry, and Matthew were delighted to see him. Alicia was rather more circumspect; she greeted him with a polite smile and suspicious eyes. The wind was brisk, perfect for kites; together with the boys, he spent a thoroughly satisfactory hour making theirs soar higher than anyone else's.

"It'll get trapped in the trees," Alicia grimly prophesied.

"Nonsense." Halting before her, he looked into her eyes. Fought down the urge to see how she would respond if he kissed her there, in the middle of the park with all the nursemaids and Maggs looking on. He forced himself to turn and look at the boys. All three were hanging on to the kite strings, shrieking and whooping as the kite, courtesy of his maneuvering now high above the treetops, swooped and tugged in the wind. "I assure you I manage the reins better than that."

An instant's pause ensued, then she replied, "You might. They won't."

She was right, but before the kite could come to grief in the leafless branches, he stepped in and took control again, and gradually brought the flapping creation with its long tail safely back to earth.

The boys were ecstatic, their eyes shining, cheeks rosy, glowing with happiness. Walking to join the group, Alicia studied the man about whom her brothers danced; no matter her suspicions, she could not doubt that he, too, had enjoyed the play. His black eyes gleamed as he shared the moment with her brothers; his lips were curved, the normally austere lines of his face relaxed.

As usual, he was dressed with consummate elegance in a perfectly cut dark blue coat over a white shirt, his long legs encased in tight buckskin breeches that disappeared into glossy black Hessians. The wind ruffled the black locks of his hair as he helped her brothers gather the long tail of the kite.

He was sophisticated, worldly, a gentleman of the ton, yet at moments like this she could almost believe she could see the boy he must have been, the boyishly open soul still lurking behind his adult glamor.

When she stopped beside the group, he looked up and grinned, still very much the boy. She smiled spontaneously in return. "Tea?"

The boys instantly raised a chorus of entreaty, but he didn't take his gaze from her; his grin eased into a smile of quite devastating charm. "Thank you. I'd like that."

With the boys about them and Maggs following with the kite in his arms, they headed back to Waverton Street.

Teatime was the usual relaxed and comfortable interlude. Maggs brought in the tray. The boys peppered Tony with questions on their latest interest—horses, curricles, and phaetons, and racing the same, while devouring their usual quota of crumpets and jam.

Alicia exchanged a smiling glance with Adriana and sat back, content to let Tony—Torrington!—manage as he would; although his knowledge of such male subjects was patently wide, she now trusted him to know what was appropriate to tell her brothers, and what was not.

It wasn't them he was intent on seducing; he was more than wise enough to know he'd have more chance with her—

She broke off that thought and looked at Adriana. Busy as usual with sketches of gowns, hats, and accessories, her sister seemed quieter than usual. She seemed to be thinking, mulling—over what Alicia could easily guess.

She leaned closer; under cover of a rowdy conversation about swan-necked phaetons and their propensity to overturn, she murmured, "Mr. King sent a reply. He'll gather his information and dine with us the day after tomorrow."

Adriana looked up, held her gaze for a moment, then, lips firming, nodded. "Good." After a moment, she added, "If there's any difficulty . . . I need to know now."

Alicia patted her hand, then drew back.

Although courtesy of her brothers' eager opinions Tony hadn't heard what was said, he noted the sisters' exchange and made a mental note to ascertain just how serious Geoffrey was. The last thing he wanted was for Alicia to become anxious over her sister's budding romance. He wanted her attention, as much of it as he could get, for himself.

Maggs reappeared to remove the tea tray, bending a glance on Tony that he read with ease: nothing to report. At Alicia's command, the boys stood and took their leave, resigned to returning to their lessons. As they trooped to the door, Tony looked at Adriana.

She met his gaze, then fleetingly, conspiratorially smiled. Gathering her papers and sketchbook, she stood; directing an airy, "I'll be in my room if you need me," to Alicia, she followed her brothers out of the door, shutting it behind her.

The instant the door closed, Tony rose and sank onto the chaise where Adriana had been. Alongside Alicia.

She directed a wide-eyed look his way. "Ah—have you learned anything more about Ruskin, about what he was up to?"

Habit prompted him to answer with a simple "No," and then distract her from the subject, but his decision not to conceal such matters from her weighed against such a tack. "Nothing specific—as I said, I've various inquiries under way."

Reaching into his coat pocket, he drew out the originals of the lists he'd made of ships' names, dates, and Ruskin's payments. "This"—stretching out his legs, crossing his ankles, he settled back. Straightening the lists, he held them up before him—"are all we have to work with at present."

She hesitated, but had to lean closer to look.

Her shoulder brushing his arm, Alicia read the entries; she was determined to keep their conversation focused on the safe and highly pertinent subject of his investigation. Relatively safe; clearly, he was not above using every opportunity that came his way to ruffle her senses, even this. His writing was neat, precise, but quite small; she had to press closer still to make out the dates—her senses flared with awareness, of him, of his strength, of the promise of sensual delight her wanton wits now associated with him.

She waved at the lists. "These dates. They seem to be related in some way—not exactly, but . . ."

He nodded. "We think—"

Without further prompting, he explained what the lists were, what he believed they meant. To her surprise, he even told her what his assumptions regarding the lists' significance were, what he hoped to learn from the shipping companies, the ports, and the mariners, and how that might indicate further avenues to explore . . . it was intriguing.

She found herself enthused with a zeal to in some way assist in working out the puzzle of what Ruskin's information was used for, and why. She'd intended to do something—pushing the investigation to a rapid conclusion would remove the most compelling excuse Torrington had to call on her, to be close to her.

About to ask how she could help, she stopped; why ask? Reaching for the lists, she drew them from his fingers. "May I make copies of these?"

His brows rose, but he nodded. "If you like."

Tony watched as she stood and crossed to the escritoire standing against the wall between the windows. She sat, drew out a sheet of paper, then settled to copy his lists. A slanting beam of sunlight struck coppery red glints from her dark hair. In the evenings, she wore it coiled high; during the day, the heavy loops were neatly constrained at her nape, the dark silk lustrous against her pale skin.

A fleeting notion of releasing that restrained abundance, of spreading it in a sheening mahogany veil over her bare shoulders, a distracting screen about her charms, filled him. Caught him. Momentarily held him.

She glanced at him, alerted, suspicious, but not knowing why.

He frowned, surreptitiously shifted. "What do you intend to do with those?"

Laying aside her pen, she blotted the lists, then rose and turned to him. "I don't know. If I have them, then when I think of something . . ." She shrugged. His originals in her hand, she walked back to the chaise.

His frown wasn't feigned. "If you do think of anything, or learn anything, promise me you'll tell me immediately."

Alicia halted before him, met his eyes. After a moment's consideration, she nodded. "I promise." What else was she to do with anything she learned?

She held out the lists. For one moment, his gaze didn't leave her face, then it slowly lowered, eventually fastening on the sheets in her hand.

He reached out—reached farther than the sheets and grasped her wrist. Long fingers locking, he tugged.

Before she could catch her breath, she was on his lap, in his arms. In a flurry of skirt and petticoats, she tried to right herself, tried to push back.

She heard a deep chuckle, felt it reverberate through her palms, braced on his chest. "We have a few moments . . ." His tone was pure temptation.

Resist, resist, resist.

She drew breath, looked up. And his lips came down on hers.

He captured them, captured her mouth, bewitched her senses. She was kissing him back, flagrantly participating in the exchange before her wits caught up with her actions. He shifted; she felt him pluck his lists from her nerveless fingers, fold them, and tuck them into his pocket.

Then his arms rose and closed about her, his head angled, and he parted her lips wider, his tongue evocatively thrusting deep, then settling to a typical, devastatingly intimate game. Of exploration, of enticement.

Soon her mind was whirling, senses locked with his as together they fed their mutual hunger, created and assuaged a mutual desire. Fingers tangled in his hair, she clung, savored, appeased, and demanded.

How long they indulged in the heated sensations she had no idea, but her wits returned with a jolt when she felt his hands between them, opening the buttons down the front of her walking dress.

It took a huge effort but she broke from the kiss, he was distracted, so let her go. On a gasp, she looked down, then glanced wildly around. "Ah . . ."

"Don't worry." From under his heavy lids, his black eyes caught hers. He searched, read, then his lips twisted wryly. "Your brothers are safe upstairs, so is your sister. Jenkins is with your brothers, and the rest are in the kitchens. No one is going to come through the door, not in the next half hour."

Half hour? What might he do in half an hour?

"That's—" She had to stop and moisten her lips, had to whip her wits into order. She was supposed to resist, or at least . . . she looked down, saw his fingers dark against the skin he was swiftly uncovering, couldn't quite suppress a tense, expectant shiver. "This is . . . really too . . . that is . . ."

Good Lord! Her words died along with her wits when he slipped a hand between the gaping halves of her bodice, with a flick of his fingers dispensed with her chemise, and boldly set his hand to her skin.

The touch was a sensual shock, not muted in the least by the fact she'd expected it, knew what his hand felt like there, cupping her breast, taking its weight, fingers gently kneading, then artfully teasing the already tightly ruched peak. Her lids drifted down, eyes closing as the sensations swept her—then she remembered and jerked her eyes open. Half-open. Enough to look into his face.

He was watching her. "Stop fighting it—just enjoy."

His hand moved on her, her wits started to slide . . .

"No! That is . . ." She drew a determined breath, only to discover she couldn't; her lungs had locked. Her nerves had tensed, not in rejection but in pleasured delight. The urge to press her breast into his warm hand was compelling, almost overwhelming. She held it at bay.

Fingers sinking into his shoulders, lids closing, she managed to shake her head. "I—you . . . this. We *can't*—"

She broke off with a sound very close to a moan.

His hand shifted, fingers closing more definitely about the aching peak he'd so effectively tortured, with expert ministrations soothed the pain, but that somehow only escalated the ache.

"I told you not to worry."

His words, deep and gravelly, reached through the fog of her whirling senses. "If you need to go slowly, we will. We have no need to rush."

On the words, his hand left her, fingers trailing upward, then she felt him ease her gown over the peak of her left shoulder. Baring her breast. His hand returned to its seductive play; she knew he was watching as he caressed her swollen flesh. As he knowingly tightened every nerve she possessed.

"We can take the long road." His voice had deepened, darkened, weaving a sorcerous spell. "And spend as much time as we wish enjoying every sight, every experience along the way."

Her breasts ached; her whole body seemed to throb.

He leaned nearer; his lips brushed hers. "Is that what you want?"

She nodded. "Yes." The word was a whisper between their lips.

"So be it," he whispered back. Then sealed the pact with a kiss.

A kiss that ripped her wits away and sent them spinning. That sent heat and flame pouring through her, down every nerve, down every vein. His hand left her and he gathered her closer; holding her in one arm, he sent his hand exploring again.

Caressing her through her clothes. Not just her breasts, but everywhere. His hand traced her shoulders, her back, her spine, delineated the muscles on either side, then spanned the back of her waist. His palm, hot and hard, passed over her hip, then boldly caressed her bottom. He traced the globes, over and around, all the while holding her to their kiss, to the slow, steady dizzying rhythm of thrust and retreat he'd established.

Her senses spun as he cupped the back of her thigh, then moved down, found her knee, then swept upward. Inward.

She gasped, would have stiffened in his arms, but he didn't allow it. His other hand shifted, gripping her bottom, holding her still. Then his questing hand splayed over her stomach; he pressed, kneaded, then held her tight, not just in his arms but sensually, too, as he reached lower, traced the tops of her thighs, then stroked, through the fine fabric of her walking dress gently probed the hollow between, caressed the soft curls beneath chemise and gown.

Teased her to life.

Until every nerve in her body was tingling, until heat pulsed just beneath her skin.

Eventually, gradually, he drew back. Eased her back.

Eventually he lifted his head, looked into her face, then brushed her lips once more with his. "If you want it slow, we'll go slowly. Very, *very* slowly."

From beneath her heavy lids, she caught the fire in his eyes.

The reassurance was what she'd wanted.

She wasn't sure she'd survive.

EIGHT

Afternoon tea in Waverton Street was a social engagement Tony felt he could easily grow fond of. In contrast, balls, routs, and soirées held far less appeal; there he had to share Alicia's attention with anyone else who thought to claim it.

However, she'd asked to go slowly, to rein in their progress, and if he was honest and viewed the whole dispassionately, there was much to be said in support of her request.

He was engaged in a serious and difficult investigation, one in which she was involved; it made sense to conclude the matter, to identify, locate, and nullify A. C. before addressing what lay between them. Before formally mentioning marriage and precipitating the associated hullabaloo.

She was right; they should take the long road. Entering Lady Cumberland's ballroom, he tried to tell himself he accepted the decree.

He found Alicia in her usual position by the wall near Adriana's circle. As more families returned to town, that circle grew; the quality of its members was also increasing. Adriana now had two earl's sons dancing attendance, along with six of lesser standing, including Sir Freddie Caudel and Geoffrey, who looked somewhat tense.

Recognizing in his childhood friend some of the impatience he himself was feeling, Tony inwardly raised his brows. Luckily in his case, Alicia seemed impervious to the frequent advances made by numerous gentlemen; she consistently dismissed them with an almost absent-minded air. He was the only one she'd allowed to draw close, to impinge on her personal world. Unlike Geoffrey, he didn't need to worry that some rake would appear and turn her head.

Reaching Alicia, all thoughts of Adriana and her swains disappeared; taking Alicia's hand—the hand she now freely offered—he bowed, then placed her fingers on his sleeve, covering them with his.

She looked up at him, faintly arched a brow.

He simply smiled at her.

With a haughty look, she returned to her watching brief.

He studied her. Her gown of apricot silk, a warm and subtle shade, deepened the rich mahogany of her hair and made her creamy complexion glow. The gown hugged her curves, the silk flowing over her hips and down the long line of her legs. For the moment, he was content simply to stand and let his senses drink her in.

Two days had passed since he'd last had her to himself. He'd spent those days and the intervening evening pursuing a whisper Dalziel had heard of a possible link between Ruskin and someone in the War Office. Nothing, however, had come of it; while there might be someone in the War Office interested in things that were no business of theirs, there was no hint of a connection between Ruskin and anyone bar the mysterious A. C.

He'd caught up with Alicia at a ball yesterday evening; he'd had to content himself with a waltz before leaving to spend the rest of the night trawling through gentlemen's clubs and exclusive hells.

Jack Warnefleet was busy, Gervase likewise in Devon, and Jack Hendon would arrive in town late tomorrow. Jack had conveyed his willingness to place his time and contacts at Tony's disposal, an offer he intended to take up with all speed.

Tonight, however, the single question nagging him was: how slow was slow?

Cumberland House was a massive old mansion, one with numerous useful little rooms; he'd explored it years ago with some amorous young matron who had known more of its amenities than he. Such knowledge, however, was never wasted.

The musicians were resting; he wondered at his chances of convincing Alicia that Adriana would be perfectly safe for a time.

He glanced at her; she straightened, coming alert. He followed her gaze and saw Adriana looking questioningly Alicia's way.

Alicia responded; he moved with her as she glided to Adriana's side.

Adriana looked uncertain. "Sir Freddie was wondering . . ."

Smoothly urbane, Sir Freddie stepped in. "I was wondering, Mrs. Carrington, if you would permit me to take Miss Pevensey for a stroll in the conservatory. It's been opened for the evening, and many others are enjoying the cooler air. I thought perhaps you and"—Sir Freddie's gaze flicked, man-to-man, to Tony—"Lord Torrington might accompany us?"

Alicia smiled regally. "A stroll in the conservatory sounds an excellent idea—it's quite stuffy in here." She nodded encouragingly to Adriana, who smiled and accepted Sir Freddie's arm. "You go ahead, we'll follow." Alicia glanced at Tony as Adriana and Sir Freddie turned away. "If you're willing . . . ?"

He looked down at her, then slowly arched a brow. She blushed lightly and glanced away.

Ignoring Geoffrey and his suppressed displeasure—an emotion Tony had no difficulty interpreting—he tucked

Alicia's hand more definitely in his arm and steered her in her sister's wake.

While crossing the crowded ballroom, they chatted of this and that, but once inside the long conservatory, with its glass doors latched open and a wide corridor down the center cleared for promenading, there was space enough to ask, "How lies the wind in that quarter?" With a nod, he indicated Adriana, conversing animatedly with Sir Freddie.

Alicia humphed. "Much as I feared. Your friend Manningham has stolen a march on all others. However, as the saying goes, true love never runs smoothly."

"Oh? How so?"

"Adriana believes she should be certain of her feelings before she bestows her hand on any gentleman. And how is she to be sure other than by testing the waters?"

"Ah. I take it Geoffrey isn't taking well to her testing program?"

"Indeed."

He glanced down; a distinctly satisfied expression was stamped on Alicia's fine features.

"It's only sensible that a lady should be sure of her choice before declaring it, and if a gentleman has problems with that, well . . ."

Her gaze was fixed on Adriana and Sir Freddie; Tony told himself she wasn't speaking of herself. Their conversation drifted to other things, yet as they returned to the ballroom, he couldn't quite rid himself of the suggestion.

If she needed assistance making up her mind, he was only too ready—and willing—to supply it. How slowly could slowly be, after all?

The musicians had resumed; Lord Montacute was waiting to claim Adriana's hand in a country dance. Sir Freddie nobly requested Alicia do him the honor; to Tony's irritation, she granted Sir Freddie's wish.

Deserted, he went searching for the refreshment room.

Geoffrey found him there. He eyed the glass in Tony's hand. "Don't tell me you've been given your congé, too?"

Tony humphed; through the arch, he was observing the dancers. "Just for this dance." He sipped, then said, "Incidentally, I was informed you're being tested."

It was Geoffrey's turn to humph. "So I'd supposed."

Shoulder to shoulder, they watched the couples swirl about the floor.

Geoffrey shifted, lifted his glass, and sipped. He glanced at Tony. "I don't suppose you'd consider staging a diversion?"

Tony's gaze was on Alicia, twirling down the set. "Divert the lioness while you whisk away her cub?"

Geoffrey swallowed a laugh, nodded. "Precisely."

Watching Alicia's body sway as, hand high, she turned beneath Sir Freddie's arm, Tony asked, "What's your interest there?"

Geoffrey's tone—insulted, a touch vulnerable—gave him his answer more than the words, "What do you think?"

Tony nodded. "Done." He set down his glass. "But I'll have to move first. If she gets any inkling of your intention, I'll never get her away."

"The field's yours." Setting down his glass, Geoffrey followed him into the ballroom. "Just make sure I get at least half an hour."

Tony glanced at him, then looked back at his prey. And smiled. "Half an hour won't be any problem."

Getting Alicia out of the ballroom and into the tiny withdrawing room at the end of the east corridor—a room Tony remembered from that long-ago exploration—was the principal difficulty. He managed it by the simple expedient of talking fast.

His topic was guaranteed to fix her interest—the contrast between sophisticated gentlemen such as Sir Fred-

die Caudel and backbone-of-the-country types epito-
mized by Geoffrey Manningham.

"I didn't know he'd been in the navy." Alicia looked
thoughtful. "I don't think Adriana knows that."

"Understandably he doesn't speak much of it, but he
served with distinction. And then, of course—"

He rattled on, borrowing from his knowledge of Geoffrey, inventing shamelessly with regard to Sir Freddie.
Her eyes on his face, her mind on his words, Alicia barely
registered entering the corridor running alongside the
ballroom; when she went to look around, he mentioned
Geoffrey's mother—her gaze immediately swung back to
his face. His fingers firmly over hers, resting on his
sleeve, he steered her on.

When he opened the door to the withdrawing room,
she swept over the threshold of her own volition, held by
the vision he'd painted of Geoffrey's manor house and
the surrounding countryside, the rolling fields leading
down to the river with the blue hills in the distance, the
lowering plateau of Exmoor stretching to the horizon.

Gesturing, she turned to face him. "It sounds an almost
idyllic place."

Much of what he'd described was his own land, his
boyhood memories of home; his smile was genuine. "It
is."

He closed the door; without taking his gaze from her
face, he snibbed the lock. The sound broke the spell.

She blinked, glanced around. A three-armed candelabrum threw a warm glow through the small room.
Aside from a chaise and a single armchair, the only furniture was a small table and a heavy sideboard. She looked
at him. Directly. "Why are we here?"

He raised his brows, approached. "Guess."

Suspicion burgeoned in her eyes; as usual, she made
no effort to hide it. He watched her cast about in her mind
for some deflecting comment, yet as he neared . . . her

eyes widened, darkened—he could almost see her senses awakening, stretching. Reaching for him. Could almost see her wits start to slow . . .

He reached for her, gently drew her to him.

She came without resistance, her hands rising to rest on his chest. Her gaze dropped to his lips. "I . . . ah . . . I thought we'd agreed to slow down."

"We did." He urged her closer, settled her against him, bent his head. "We are." He kissed her, made her lips cling. "Progressing step by small step."

He took her mouth again; she gave it freely, met him, parted her lips, welcomed him in. Her hands clenched, clutched as he captured her senses and drew her deeper into the exchange, into the sensual game they both so enjoyed.

Lips caressed, pressed, tongues tangled, stroked, probed, mouths melded. Both took, gave, delighted, then explored.

Sensation streaked through Alicia; warmth welled, pooled, and dragged her senses down to wallow, to luxuriate, to expand and experience a world of sensual delight, of wanton, illicit, addictive pleasure.

No matter how much a small part of her mind tried to warn her, tried to make her see how dangerous it could be, her body, her nerves, her skin and her senses, and the greater part of her whirling wits, were eager to go forward, to follow the path he opened before her, to seize the moment to learn and feel.

To learn of herself, of what could be, of all she could be. To feel the welling tide of compulsive emotions—the hunger, the need, the flagrant desire, and most especially the triumph.

A simple and pure triumph she hadn't known existed, the confidence, delight, and sheer pleasure of knowing he found her desirable, that he wanted her in the most blatantly sexual way, and the satisfaction that flowed from knowing not only that she could evoke his hunger, but also from the innate womanly knowledge that she could, indeed, sate it.

He'd drawn her close, fitting her body against his, but once they reached that plateau of more urgent, definite need—one she now recognized—his arms eased, then his hands, hard and demanding, slid over her silk-encased form. Over her back, over her sides, around over her already aching breasts.

Through the fog of desire flooding her mind, she inwardly smiled. She eased back from the kiss enough to murmur against his lips, "I'm afraid this gown has no buttons down the front." She'd worn her topaz silk for that very reason.

"I'd noticed," he murmured back.

His lips brushed hers, then settled, drawing her into a long, increasingly intimate exchange . . . as it ended her awareness slowly returned. And she realized the pressure about her breasts had eased.

Her bodice was loose.

She drew back from the kiss as he did. Looked down as he raised his hands to her shoulders. Slowly, very slowly, he pushed her now gaping gown off her shoulders, sliding the small puff sleeves down her arms.

He'd undone the laces.

Her mind seized; she stopped breathing. She hadn't thought . . .

The neckline caught across the peaks of her breasts. Leaving the sleeves at her elbows, he ran his fingers up, then slipped them beneath the neckline and eased it over and down.

She shuddered, told herself it was due to the cool caress of the air. Knew it wasn't. Desperate, she hauled in a breath. Ignored the sudden lifting of her breasts. "Wait—"

"Lift your arms." The words were half entreaty, half command. They were reinforced by his touch, fingertips running over her bared shoulders, down the sensitive skin of her arms to her elbows. He gripped lightly, urged.

She freed her arms from the clinging sleeves. "This—"

"Is the smallest step I could think of." His black gaze touched hers; the emberlike glow in the dark depths only heated her more.

She sucked in a tight breath. "But—"

"Going slowly isn't stopping." He held her gaze, his fingers lightly caressing—so lightly they barely touched the heavy, swelling curves of her breasts. "You don't want to stop."

Not a question, a statement, one verified by the shiver that streaked through her, a silvery sensation that brought every nerve alive.

His lips curved, openly predatory, entirely undisguised. He bent his head. His lips cruised over hers as his fingers drifted, as his hands followed, then firmed, taking possession as they had before. But before she hadn't been as aware, as blatantly near-naked. As heated.

Her breath caught.

One hand kneaded, the other slid away. His arm slipped about her waist; holding her, he backed her, step by slow, easy step until she felt the sideboard behind her.

Lifting his head, he fastened both hands about her waist and lifted her to the sideboard's top. He sat her there; hands clutching his shoulders, she glanced down. Her gown had slid to her hips. Before she could react, he bunched the skirts and raised them to her knees, allowing him to part them and step between.

Her mind was whirling, wits totally scattered.

He met her eyes; his lips curved, but it wasn't exactly in a smile. "For us . . . the only way to slow our inevitable progression is to indulge in more intensive play."

She searched his eyes, instinctively accepted that as truth. Yet . . .

He leaned closer, lips swooping, nearing as his hands rose, fingers reaching for the tiny ribbon bows securing her silk chemise. The last flimsy barrier screening her from his sight.

Dizzy desperation gripped her; she sank her fingers into his shoulders. "I—"

He hesitated, but when she couldn't find the words—any words that made sense—he closed the inch between their lips, kissed. Drew back enough to breathe, "You know where we're headed, don't you? You know what lies at the end of our road."

Her lips were dry, yearning, hungry. She forced herself to nod. "Yes."

"Then there's no reason I shouldn't see you, bare you, and look my fill. No reason I shouldn't take what pleasure I wish with you, in you—and you shouldn't take all you wish of me."

His lips closed on hers, warm and beguiling; he didn't rip her wits away, didn't send them spinning, but left her aware, attuned, every nerve tight and flickering.

So she knew when his fingers closed on the ribbon ties, so she felt the tugs as he unraveled the bows, then slowly, gently, inexorably eased the fine fabric down. Exposing her breasts.

And then his hands were on her, hot skin to hot skin. He caressed, fondled, kneaded, squeezed. Her senses filled, overflowed; sensation rushed through her, down her nerves, down her veins.

She couldn't think, no longer had space in her mind for that activity, swept away, consumed by the dizzying splendor, the bone-melting pleasure he pressed on her. His lips left hers; he nudged her head back, skated his lips down the taut tendon to settle over her pulse point, heating her blood still further. Her fingers, until then gripping his shoulders, eased; she sent her hands sliding over and back, found and caressed his nape.

His lips left her throat and slid lower. Splaying her fingers, she speared them through his thick locks, then clutched. Eyes closed, she held tight as his burning lips cruised the upper swells of her breasts. Then dipped lower still.

Her world stopped when his lips found one aching peak.

Splintered when he took it into his mouth.

Hot, wet, he caressed, laved, licked, than gently rasped.

Her breasts felt on fire, tight, taut; head tilting back, she gasped, spine tensing as he artfully teased, then openly feasted. Then he shifted, drew the aching, tormented peak deep, and suckled.

The jolt of sensation rocked her, shocked her, surprised a small cry from her. Her fingers spasmed on his skull. Eyes shut, she struggled to cope, to cling to sanity as with mouth, lips, and tongue, hard fingers and palms, he pressed sensation after sensation upon her.

Through her fingers, through the tension gripping her, Tony read her increasing desperation. Every sense he possessed was locked on her, watching, gauging . . . he eased back.

Heard in her tortured breathing a return from the brink of panic.

He didn't take his lips from her skin, but traced, kissed lightly, soothed with gentle caresses. When she'd calmed enough to be lucid, he cupped both breasts in his palms, straightened slightly, shifting between her spread thighs. Bent again to touch his lips to the hot satin skin of the now swollen mounds. "Didn't your husband caress you like this?"

Her lids cracked open. From behind the screen of her lashes, her eyes met his. A moment passed, then she licked her lips. Tried to speak, ended by shaking her head.

When he waited, she dragged in a breath. "No. He . . ."

Primitive joy streaked through him. He waited; when she remained silent, he prompted, "Wasn't inclined to see to your pleasure?" A common enough failing, after all.

She shuddered. Beneath his hand, he could feel her heart still pounding, but slower. Her skin was still heated; he kept it that way, idly kneading, caressing.

Again she drew breath, again met his eyes. "I . . . don't know all that much about . . . pleasure."

The word came out on a soft exhalation; she closed her eyes as he again bent and savored one tightly budded nipple. He released it, blew gently on it, then soothed it again.

Lifting his head to examine the effect, he murmured, "It'll be my pleasure to teach you." Shifting his hands, he set his thumbs to circle her nipples.

"I—that's why . . ." She broke off, drew in a hissed breath. "Why it must be slow . . ."

On his shoulders, her fingers tensed again, but not, this time, with any sense of desperation. He watched her face as he caressed. "Forget about your husband. Forget all you ever knew." Keeping one hand on her breast, he slid the other to the small of her back and eased her to the sideboard's edge. His hand still at her breast, he bent his head to take her mouth.

Before he did, he murmured, his voice low, gravelly, decided. "Start again. With me. I'll teach you all you should know, all you need to know."

Her fingers slid to his nape, cupped as he covered her lips, held tight as he plunged into her mouth and took possession. Plundered, ravished, devoured as he wished; she met him, went with him, followed him deeper. Until the exchange became a flagrant echo of that other intimacy, until hot and heated she clung to the rhythm, matching him, sating his hunger as it rose, learning of her own.

He'd pressed her thighs wide; her silk skirts lay in a spill covering her knees, but beneath . . . he knew precisely what he would find when he released her breast and slid his hand beneath the folds of silk.

The skin of her inner thighs was as fine as the silk, as delicate, but far warmer. She was too deep in the kiss to do more than vaguely register as he stroked, caressed. Deliberately, he let her surface, step by step until he sensed her sudden awareness, felt the gasp smothered between their lips as she realized.

She started to tense; he deepened the kiss, just enough to distract her, to fracture her attention long enough to let him explore further. To reach higher and find her, swollen and fever-damp, hot enough to scald.

Slow. Step by step.

He forced himself to do no more than touch her, to find the tiny nubbin within the folds and caress, but go no further.

Tiny shivers of sensation coursed through her as he stroked, gently pressed. He knew what he might do, knew the potential, but sensed she wasn't ready for that yet.

Alfred Carrington must have been an insensitive clod.

He continued to touch her gently, undemandingly exploring, letting her grow accustomed to him touching her there, to the intimacy, mild to his mind though it was.

Step by step.

He let her surface by degrees, let her awareness rise free from the drugging kisses, until at the last he could raise his head and watch her face. Watch her lips, parted and swollen as he circled, then pressed lightly. Catch her eyes as he stroked, and she shuddered.

Then softly sighed.

She dropped her forehead to his shoulder. After a moment, said, "This is all so—"

She broke off. He stroked again, felt her shiver. "More than you expected?"

Against his shoulder, she nodded. "Much, much more."

Satisfied with the way events were proceeding not just with Alicia but also with his investigation, Tony felt distinctly mellow, a prey to pleasurable anticipation as the next evening he went upstairs to change.

He'd reached the landing when a heavy knock fell on the front door.

He recognized the knock. Halting, he waited, one hand on the balustrade as Hungerford strode majestically to the door. He'd recognized the knock, too. He pulled open the door, revealing Maggs.

Hungerford looked down his nose. "I believe you know where the back entrance is?"

"'Course I do. Live here, don't I?" Maggs lumbered in, his hat in his hands. "But I'm supposed to be Mrs. Carrington's footman. If I came with a message, I wouldn't come to the back door, would I?"

Turning back down the stairs, Tony straightened his lips. "What is it, Maggs?"

Maggs looked up. "Oh, there you be." He hesitated, frown growing as Tony descended. As he gained the front hall, Maggs suggested, "You might want to hear this in private."

Brows rising, Tony looked at Hungerford. "Thank you, Hungerford. I'm sure Maggs can see himself out."

That last was said with a hint of understanding. Hungerford bowed stiffly. "Indeed, my lord. If you have need of anything, you have only to ring."

"Thank you." Tony turned to Maggs and waved to the study. Hungerford departed; Maggs opened the study door. Tony entered and went to sit behind his desk; closing the door, Maggs came to stand before it.

Maggs had been a stable lad at Torrington Chase when Tony had been a boy; he'd attached himself to the son of the house and followed him into the army. Whenever Tony had had need of a batman, Maggs had filled the position. He'd been a part of Tony's life for longer than he could remember, and continued as his most trusted servant. Despite Maggs's bruiser's countenance, the man was intelligent, capable, and effective.

"What is it?" Tony asked.

Maggs's frown hadn't eased. "I don't know as you'll

believe this, but the ladies, Mrs. Carrington and Miss Pevensey, are sitting down to dinner—well, they'd be near to finished by now—with a gentleman goes by the name of Mr. King. Wouldn't've thought much of it 'cept I've seen him before, and I'd swear on my mother's grave he's Mr. King, the moneylender."

Tony blinked. After a long moment of staring at Maggs, he nodded. "You're right—I find that very hard to believe."

Maggs sighed heavily. "Well, there you are. But Collier's on watch at the corner, so you needn't think I've deserted my post and left the lady unguarded."

"Good." Tony was finding it hard to focus his thoughts. Mr. King? As a *dinner guest*? He refocused on Maggs. "What's the relationship between Mr. King and the ladies? How did they react to him?"

"Friendly." Maggs shrugged. "Nothing heavy-handed, if that's what you're thinking. They treated him like he was an old friend of the family."

Tony inwardly goggled. He stood. "Come on. I'll know Mr. King if I see him." He shook his head as he rounded the desk. "I can't believe this."

"Aye, well." Maggs lumbered after him. "I did warn you."

Half an hour later, from the shadows of his town carriage pulled up by the curb close to the end of Waverton Street, Tony watched a large, burly gentleman take his leave of Alicia and Adriana. The sisters remained just inside the front hall, but the hall and porch lights were lit; it was easy to make out the genuineness of their smiles as the three shook hands.

Then Mr. King turned and descended to the unmarked black carriage that awaited him.

Maggs had returned to his duties. Collier, the man Tony had set to watch the street, was in his accustomed place. Tony sat back and waited until Mr. King's carriage

rumbled past. He didn't bother to glance again at the occupant; it was definitely London's most famous moneylender.

He remembered Alicia's odd reaction when he'd mentioned he'd visited the man.

The door of the Carrington abode shut. Slumped
against the cushions, Tony waited, totally unable to for-
mulate any possible scenario to account for what he'd
seen. Five minutes later, he tapped on the roof and directed his coachman to return to Upper Brook Street.

Courtesy of Maggs, these days he always knew where
Alicia would be. That evening, she was attending Lady
Magnuson's ball; as usual, he found her by the side of the
room, watching over Adriana.

Who, he inwardly admitted, now needed to be
watched. The Season was nearly upon them; the wolves
of the ton were back in force, actively hunting in their favorite ground. As he approached, he saw Alicia step forward and engage one of the younger brethren who, until
then, had remained unwisely oblivious of her presence.

It was instantly apparent from the young buck's face
that a few words had sufficed for her to draw blood; his
face hardened, lips thinning. After one last look at Adriana, he sloped off to find easier—less well guarded—prey.

A flicker of unease tickled Tony's shoulder blades.
Adriana and her beauty posed a danger. She was too
young to fix the interest of the truly dangerous blades, yet
she nevertheless drew their eyes, which then passed on—
to her sister. Who was much more the sort to attract a
connoisseur's attention.

Reaching Alicia, gowned in a pale bronze creation
edged with tiny pearls, he took the hand she offered, almost absentmindedly raised it to his lips, then met her
eyes as he kissed.

He watched a light blush rise to her cheeks.

She tugged; placing her hand on his sleeve, he covered it with his.

"I need to speak with you." He glanced at Adriana's court. "And before you tell me you need to remain here and protect your sister, regardless of your recent intervention, you don't."

She frowned. "That doesn't make sense."

"It does if you consider." Casting a last glance at Adriana's circle, he turned her, steering her down the long room. "If you hadn't stepped in, either Sir Freddie or Geoffrey would have. Or even Montacute. They've been dancing at your sister's feet for weeks—none of them will take kindly to any rakish interloper thinking to poach their prize."

She still frowned, more in puzzlement than irritation, but continued strolling beside him. "You make it sound like a competition. A sport."

"It's a game no matter which side you're on." He spotted an opening between two groups of potted palms; deftly, he whisked them into it. "Now, quite aside from that . . ."

He stopped, unsure how to proceed. How to ask what he had to. He glanced at her; she was studying him, not suspiciously but directly. "I was passing along Waverton Street earlier this evening and saw Mr. King leaving your house."

Her gaze didn't waver; she continued to regard him attentively.

"I mentioned meeting Mr. King in the course of my investigations. Is he . . . an acquaintance?"

Without hesitation, she nodded, then looked out at the room. "Yes—he's just that, an acquaintance."

Alicia let a moment elapse, then, her gaze still on the crowd, asked, "Do you want to know why he called?"

She heard a hiss, an exhalation through his teeth.

"Yes."

She'd assumed he would hear of King's visit; she'd rehearsed her explanation. "We made his acquaintance some months ago through matters arising from my late husband's estate. Mr. King knew of our wish to establish Adriana creditably." She glanced up, and found Tony watching her closely. "He offered to give us the benefit of his knowledge regarding the financial status of any gentleman Adriana was seriously considering."

The look in his eyes was priceless; he was astounded, could barely believe his ears . . . she sensed it the moment he did.

His gaze sharpened. "What did Mr. King say about Geoffrey?"

She grimaced, let her uncertainty show. "That he's perfectly sound. He's never had dealings with any moneylenders, but they would be happy to have him on their books. His credit is excellent, his estates are in exemplary order. Financially, he passed with flying colors."

"So why aren't you thrilled?" Two matrons took up position on the other side of one set of palms. Grasping Alicia's elbow, Tony guided her out of their nook. A waltz was just starting; the dance floor seemed the next safest place.

He drew her into his arms, looked down at her face as he started them revolving, noted the frown in her eyes. "It's obvious your sister favors Geoffrey, and he's intent on her. You've received reports from all and sundry that his character and situation are beyond reproach. Why, therefore, your hesitation?"

They revolved twice before she met his eyes. Her gaze was level and serious. "Money, title, and estate are all well and good, and character to date as well. But who can foresee the future?" She blew out a breath and looked away. "If I could be certain he's all Adriana *deserves*, I'd feel happier."

Tony steered her around the tight turn at the end of the

room; she remained relaxed in his arms, warm, at ease, yet as so often was the case, focused on her family, in this case, Adriana. He studied her face as they precessed up the room; he could read her abstraction clearly.

What a lady deserved.

He'd never heard that advanced as a criterion for marriage, yet for the sort of marriage Alicia wished for her sister it was perhaps more pertinent, more relevant. And she was right; such a stipulation was much harder to guarantee—that a gentleman could and would provide what a lady deserved.

The waltz ended, but her concept remained, inhabiting his mind, directing his thoughts as they strolled through the glittering throng. Lady Magnuson was old but wealthy and well connected; all those of the haut ton already in town were certain to attend, to look in for at least an hour and show their faces. Many stopped them, most trying their hand at divining just what their relationship was; neither he nor Alicia gave them any joy. Which only fed the whispers.

He glanced at her. She was frowning, trying to catch a glimpse of her sister's court. Lifting his head, he looked over the crowd. "Adriana appears hale and whole." He glanced at Alicia. "She's managing perfectly well."

She frowned at him. "I should return to her—"

"No, you shouldn't." He anchored her hand more firmly on his sleeve. "She's too sensible to go out of the ballroom without your permission, and with both Geoffrey and Sir Freddie standing guard, no bounder will have any chance of whisking her off undetected."

"Yes, but—" She broke off as he whisked her into a dimly lit corridor. "Where are we going?"

"I don't know." That was the worst of having spent the last decade elsewhere. Taking her hand in his, he strolled on. "I don't know this house."

His hearing was acute; he passed door after door, hearing muffled giggles or grunts from the rooms within.

She tried to slow, but he kept her with him. She tugged at his hand. "We can't just—"

"Of course we can." He stopped outside a door, listened, then hearing nothing opened it silently. Caught a glimpse of a white rump plunging, and swiftly closed it. "Just not there."

He heard the growing frustration in his voice; from the odd glance she threw him, she heard it, too.

They turned a corner; it was instantly apparent they'd reached a wing that was no longer in use. No lights glowed; there was dust on the sidetable farther along. He stepped to the side and opened a door, cautiously. Looking in, he breathed again. "Perfect."

He drew her over the threshold and closed the door, with one finger snibbed the lock. Busy looking around, she didn't hear.

"What a lovely room."

He released her and she headed for the windows; uncurtained, they looked out over a stone-flagged courtyard with a long pond in its center, a fountain, still and silent, rising from the black water. Lily pads were unfurling, spreading across the obsidian surface. Moonlight, stark and ghostly white, poured softly over all, casting black shadows in the lee of the creeper-covered walls, edging each new ivy leaf in silver.

She glanced at him as he joined her. "I wonder why the room's unused."

"The Magnusons were a large family, but there's only Lady Magnuson left now. Her daughters are married and gone." He hesitated, then added, "Both her sons died at Waterloo."

She looked around the room, at the furniture swathed in holland covers. "It seems . . . sad."

After a moment, she glanced up at him.

What a lady deserves.

How unpredictable, how ephemeral, how precious life was.

Slowly, he bent his head and kissed her, despite all gave her the chance to deny him if she chose. She didn't. She lifted her face, met his lips with hers. They touched, caressed, firmed. She raised a hand and gently, tentatively, laid her fingers along his cheek.

He slid an arm around her, smoothly yet more slowly than usual; it seemed important to savor each moment, to draw each instant, each movement, each acceptance, each commitment out. To fully know and appreciate every subtle nuance as they came together, as without words, he steered her to the next step.

Heat blossomed, spread beneath their skins, pooled low, then coalesced. Tightened. Throbbed.

Alicia opened her senses, tried for the first time to deliberately explore the effect of each touch, each caress. Whenever she tried to cling to control, she was swept away, so instead she went forward of her own accord, eyes open, senses aware, ready to learn, to see, to know. To, perhaps, understand what this was, what fed the power he could so easily conjure between them.

And learn to manage it herself.

As he did.

The kiss lengthened, deepened, yet not once did his control even quiver. He knew what he was doing, scripted and directed their play . . . this time she participated without hestitation, eagerly, determinedly following his lead. Waiting to see where it led

She was trapped in his arms, locked against him, flagrantly molded to him when he finally raised his head. He looked down at her face. She could feel their mutual need, a well-stoked furnace seething between them.

He eased his hold on her, held her until she was steady on her feet. His eyes were dark as they held hers, yet she could feel the heat in his gaze.

"Open your bodice for me."

The words were gravelly, deep, and dark. She held his gaze for an instant, then calmly looked down. Lifting her hands, she slipped the tiny pearl buttons free.

She felt him exhale. His arms fell from her. He looked around, then stepped back and lifted the holland cover from a large shape, revealing a big, well-padded armchair. It was set facing the windows so any occupant could enjoy the view.

Dropping the dust sheet to the floor, he looked at her. Met her gaze as she slipped the last button free.

He reached for her, still moving with that measured grace that only heightened her expectations, that gave time for anticipation to well before she felt the next touch as he drew her to stand before him.

She watched him watching her as his hands rose and closed on her shoulders. He pushed the gown down, inch by inch steadily slipped the sleeves down. Without waiting for any instruction, she lifted her arms from the narrow sleeves, then, emboldened, draped them about his shoulders and stepped closer.

Saw the dark flare in his eyes as she did. Felt his hands tense on the folds of silk at her waist, then, holding her gaze, he slowly slid his hands down, tracing the curve of her hips, sliding her gown over them until, with a soft swoosh, it fell to the floor.

She caught her breath, felt the air on her skin, felt panic rise—

He circled her waist, drew her against him, flush against his hard body, and kissed her. Not ravenously but forcefully, then he lifted his head. "Slowly. One step more." He lifted his lids, met her gaze. "Trust me. It'll be as you wish." His gaze dropped to her lips; he lowered his head. "And all you deserve."

The promise feathered over her lips. Then he kissed her.

She stood locked against him in a dark, deserted room clad only in her chemise and her even finer silk stockings.

If she wished, she could retreat—she knew it—yet as he kissed her she could feel the strength of his control, could feel the tight rein he kept on his passions.

Therein lay safety.

Nothing ventured, nothing learned. And she had to learn more. At least his next step, so she could predict the one after.

Tightening her arms about his neck, she kissed him back.

NINE

Her chemise reached to midthigh; in the poor light, he wouldn't be able to see through it. Her stockings covered her legs, the garters hidden beneath the chemise's hem. She was clad, albeit thinly; wrapped in his arms, his lips on hers, his tongue tangling with hers, she certainly wasn't cold.

Committed to playing her part, she set aside all maidenly reserve and gave herself up to it—to his embrace, to the slow-burning embers that glowed between them. No flames yet; he kept them dampened, but she knew the potential was there. It was a measure of his control that he could so easily hold the conflagration at bay, at a safe distance so she could feel the warmth, experience the pleasure, but not be burned by it. Not be consumed.

He held to his slow, measured, almost languid pace. The intimacy deepened; the urgency did not.

His control—the trust she placed in him—was what allowed her to stand within his arms and with simple passion kiss him back. He took her invitation as offered, savored her mouth, her lips; she in turn savored his pleasure.

When he straightened, eased his hold on her, sat in the armchair and urged her onto his lap, her confidence, her need to know, and her trust in him held firm, allowing her to sit across his hard thighs, to let him lift her, arrange her as he would. Then he drew her to him, locking her again in the circle of his arms, and kissed her. She responded willingly, eagerly, waiting to learn.

They were taking the long road; there had to be more steps before they approached the ultimate intimacy. She'd done her homework as well as she could, yet although she'd found two texts purporting to describe the physical aspects of intimacy as indulged in by blue-blooded rakes, said texts were so riddled with euphemisms she'd ended more confused than instructed.

The manuals had, however, demonstrated that the spectrum of activity was wide, that if an experienced gentleman were so inclined, there were indeed a large number of steps between a first kiss and consummation.

From what she'd understood, his attentions to her breasts, even his stroking of her curls, were relatively early in the sequence. Tonight, he wished to take one step further; she wanted to know what that step was. With luck, it would allow her to gauge just how far along their long road they were and how fast they were progressing.

How much more time in his arms she had.

That knowledge—that her time with him was limited—dragged at her mind; he seemed to sense it. He lifted his head. Close, their breaths mingling in the darkness, from beneath his heavy lids, he caught her gaze. After a moment, he murmured, "You're not frightened, are you?"

She thought, then shook her head. "No." She hesitated, then boldly raised her hand, traced a fingertip down his lean cheek. "Just . . . unsure." As far as she could, she'd be honest with him.

His lips curved, but didn't soften. The lines of his face seemed harsher, harder. Swiftly turning his head, he trapped her fingertip between his teeth. Bit gently. Then he drew it into his mouth, sucked . . . she blinked, then shuddered lightly.

He released her finger. His grin was so fleeting she nearly missed it. His arms tightened; he drew her back down, bent over her, paused to whisper in his dark sorcerer's voice, "Slow. As you wish. All you deserve."

Then he kissed her.

Tony pressed deep, let the kiss, not just a meeting of lips but a melding of mouths, sink into realms they'd not previously explored. Let the drugging, absorbing effect take full hold . . . until they were captive, both trapped, held but not tightly within the web of their mutual desire. A desire that glowed, warm, alive, real, not yet red hot but a thing of flame.

She was with him, as committed as he to their road; he read it in her lips, through the way she met each increasingly explicit exchange, in the way her body, lithe and supple, lay lightly tensed, poised and willing in his arms.

Regardless, he held back, held his own desires in a grip of iron and focused solely on hers. On awakening them, coaxing them, stirring them—step by step, as he'd promised—into full-blown life.

She hadn't been down this road before; to one of his experience that was clear. Her husband . . . was dead, of no importance now. He set himself to search out and eradicate any lingering difficulties, any unnecessary hesitations. Any instinctive drawing back. He was committed to teaching her what could be—what should be and would be between them. All the glory he was capable of summoning and laying at her feet.

Her chemise had no straps; a drawstring secured it above her breasts. He caressed, taunted, teased her breasts through the fine layer of silk, then tweaked the tie undone and slipped his hand beneath.

Closed it about one firm mound, and felt something in her, and in him, ease in sensual relief. He drew back from the kiss, lifted his head to look down as he played. As he filled his senses and hers with simple delight, with uncomplicated pleasure.

She—they—had been this far before; despite her harried breathing, despite her racing pulse, she didn't protest, didn't pull away. He could feel her gaze on his face, watching him savor her, watching him fall more deeply under her spell.

He glanced at her, caught the gleam of her eyes from under her weighted lids. His answering smile was tight, dangerous. Shifting his hold, he lifted her, raising her breasts, her spine bowing over his arm as he bent his head to do homage.

In that, he held nothing back. Deliberately sent fire racing through her veins, set desire chasing hard on its heels. Her fingers found his hair, tangled, clung, then clenched as he feasted. He took all he wished, all she wordlessly offered, gave her in return all the delight, all the tight, thrilling, illicitly intense pleasure his expertise could evoke.

Alicia gasped. Her body seemed no longer hers. He suckled more deeply. Taut in his arms, a soft moan escaped her, then the suction eased, and fire flared anew; hot and scalding, it raced through her to flow into the furnace building deep within her.

Her breasts were on fire, but it was the increasingly insistent, increasingly powerful demands of her body that gripped her, shook her. Unknown, as-yet-incomprehensible demands that threatened to overwhelm her, to sweep aside what wits she'd managed to cling to. She struggled against the tide; she wanted to know more, to learn what this and their next step would be. They'd gone no further than before—yet. He hadn't even touched her curls—yet.

This time, she knew, and waited—for that knowing touch, that oh-so-illicit caress. Her whole body was taut, quivering in anticipation. Of that, of what would follow the delight, the almost excruciating pleasure he, with clear intent, lavished upon her.

His mouth was scalding as he tasted her sensitized skin. Her nipples ached with a deep-seated pain that was intensely sweet. Then he placed his hand, large and heavy, over her waist; through the silk, she felt its heat and hardness, felt her muscles leap.

He raised his head. Looked down at her breasts. Even in the dimness, she could see the possessiveness limning his features.

His gaze rose. Black, hot, it searched her face, read her features, then his eyes returned to hers. He held her gaze, held her awareness.

His hand drifted lower.

The silk softly shushed, the last barrier between his hand and her flesh. Flesh that now pulsed hotly, nerves that slowly, slowly tightened with expectation.

Almost negligently, he caressed her stomach, then his hand drifted to the curve of her hip, then followed the line of one thigh.

Tony watched her, watched her senses follow his hand, his fingers. He did nothing to break the spell, held aside his own clamorous instincts and forced himself to keep to the same slow steady pace that had, from the moment they'd entered the room, contributed to the magic.

Orchestrated it, built it.

He needed that magic. He didn't just want to introduce her to passion, to take her and make her his. He wanted— needed—to expand her horizons, to bring her to know, to experience, and ultimately to want to explore the outer reaches of desire with him. To achieve that he needed to show her, to make her see and appreciate that there was a great deal more beyond the simple act.

So he held back his frustration, without compunction sacrificed it to their greater good, closed his mind against the drumming insistence of even deeper instincts, those that had reacted to the thought of other men—other rakes—coveting her as he did, those instincts that still, beneath all else, prowled, prodded to possessive life by the nebulous threat of her involvement with Ruskin.

He pushed them all aside, and concentrated on her. On the tale told by her rapid breathing, the way her nerves leapt as he stroked down her thigh. The armchair was commodious; her legs were a heated weight across his lap. Against one firm thigh, he was hard as rock, rigid and aching, but relief was not in the cards, not tonight. He'd survive, but he was determined in recompense to advance their one small step.

Still holding her gaze, he closed his fingers about one knee and lifted it, shifted it, parting her thighs. She permitted it, but tensed; her breathing tightened. Intent, he kept her with him and stroked his fingers, his palm, up the sensitive inner face of her thigh.

All the way to where her tight curls brushed his fingertips. He smoothed them aside, in the same movement boldly cupped her. Set his hand to her softness and covered it. Claimed it.

She caught her breath, stopped breathing entirely. His gaze locked with hers, he held still, then, adhering to that same slow steady beat, he eased his palm back, and with his thumb and one finger began to explore her.

Alicia quivered, and followed his every move. She couldn't do otherwise; he had her locked to him in some heightened state where she was shockingly aware of their flagrantly sexual play, where they were in some way connected so she both felt the sensations of his touch and simultaneously experienced something of his reaction.

Of what he felt as he learned her, caressed and boldly explored the soft, swollen folds between her thighs. She'd never known that part of her body to feel so hot, so wet, so achingly wanting. Pulsing, almost throbbing; her hips stirred, of their own volition lifted to his caress as if seeking more.

A glimmer of satisfaction flashed across his hard face. That he understood her body better than she did she didn't doubt; his caresses changed, became subtly more deliberate, more potent.

More satisfying to both of them.

He was showing her, teaching her. She remembered his

words as his thumb swirled knowingly about the tight pearl of sensation he'd found, that exquisitively sensitive spot that seemed pleasurably connected to every nerve she possessed. He swirled again and her whole body reacted; she arched lightly, heard herself gasp, let her lids fall.

"Stay with me."

The deep words were an outright command. She forced her lids up, met his gaze. Tried to read it and failed. "Why?"

To her surprise, the single word was all sultry temptation. Not like her at all, or so she had thought, yet it was. Emboldened, she shifted her hands, until then slack on his shoulders, let her fingers stroke his nape.

In response, his fingers stroked, but more slowly, as if savoring the wetness they'd drawn forth.

"Because I want you to know this, and I want to know you—all of you. All that you feel, all that you enjoy."

On the words, as if to demonstrate, his wicked fingers shifted, parting her folds, this time gently probing.

The action captured her attention. Completely. She moistened her lips; her gaze once again locked with his, she felt him ease one blunt fingertip between the slick folds.

Her body reacted, flushed, heated. She dragged in a tight breath. "One step."

He held her gaze, his eyes black, intent. "Just one step."

Slowly, he slid his finger into her.

Into the heated softness of her body, into the scalding furnace of her desire. Mentally gritting his teeth, Tony held tight to his reins and watched her outward attention splinter. Watched her focus inward, on the steady penetration of his finger into her tight sheath.

Her breathing was labored; she struggled to do as he'd asked and cling to the contact, to keep her eyes open, locked albeit unseeing on his.

Still keeping to their slow, steady rhythm, he reached as far as he could, gently pressed, then equally slowly reversed, until his fingertip reached the tight constriction that guarded her entrance. Then he reversed direction, deliberately pressing in, stroking the soft tissues, teasing the nerves and muscles beneath.

She lay in his arms, not passive but accepting, following, letting him learn her body even more intimately. Aware, as her widening eyes testified, of the building beat in her own body, of the heat, the burgeoning need.

Relentlessly, he built the rhythm until, with a small cry, she lifted against his hand. He pressed deeper, faster, clung to their visual contact as she climbed the peak, as her nails sank into his shoulders, her body bowing as the tension tightened. Heightened.

Then broke.

She came apart in his arms. The shocked awareness on her face, the stunned expression that was washed away as rapture took her, was a revelation—she'd never known the pleasure before.

As her lids drifted down, fierce satisfaction broke over him. His innate possessiveness roared, pleased beyond measure that it had been he who had brought her her first taste of sexual bliss.

He kept his hand between her thighs, one finger buried deep within her, savoring her contractions, the telltale ripples as her muscles relaxed into satiation. All her tension melted; as it did, he slid another finger in alongside the first, gently worked both deep. Stroked as she floated; she was so tight . . . Alfred Carrington had clearly been inadequate in more ways than one. When their time finally came, she'd need help stretching to accommodate him. Perhaps it was as well their time was not yet. Would likely be some while yet.

Eventually withdrawing his fingers from her softness, smoothing her chemise down, he settled back in the chair. And tried to ignore the musky scent that teased his senses, compounded by the warm weight of well-pleasured woman in his arms. Not an easy task.

Only one topic held the power to distract him; he turned his mind to scripting their next step.

Alicia reached home in the small hours, her wits in disarray. Her body . . . felt glorious. The former was a direct consequence of the latter.

She now understood something she never had before—why ladies allowed themselves to be seduced. If that evening's sample of what a noble lover could produce was in any way indicative, it was a wonder any lady remained a virgin by choice.

A gloating whisper in her brain suggested only those ignorant of the possibilities did.

Leaving her cloak in Jenkins's arms, leaving him and Maggs to lock up the house, she headed for the stairs.

Adriana joined her, glanced at her face. "What's wrong?"

Alicia looked briefly her way. Wondered that her experience hadn't left some tangible evidence in her face. She felt different from her head to her toes, yet no one in the ballroom, whence they'd eventually returned, had seemed to notice. Apparently not even her perceptive sister could see the change in her. "Nothing."

Looking forward, she remembered the two texts on lovemaking she'd consulted. Remembered their shortcomings. "I wonder if there are *advanced* manuals?"

She'd mumbled—grumbled—the comment aloud. Adriana, passing on her way to her bedchamber, cast her a puzzled look. "What was that?"

She tightened her lips. "Never mind."

Opening the door to her bedchamber, the one nearest the stairhead, she nodded a good night to Adriana and went in.

Closing the door, she stood for a moment staring into space, then she moved into the room, dropping her reticule on the dressing table, quickly unpinning her hair. She undressed and donned her nightgown—then couldn't remember doing it. Finding herself ready for bed, standing beside the bed, she climbed in and lay down. Drew the sheet and coverlet over her.

Lay flat on her back and stared at the canopy.

Every nerve she possessed was still humming; warm pleasure still coursed her veins. Yet there was an expectation, an underlying anticipation that the evening's small step had done nothing to assuage.

Instead, that nebulous but definite anticipation had grown.

She didn't truly know what it was, could only guess for she'd never felt it before. But then she'd never indulged as she had that evening, never let any man touch her intimately at all, let alone as he had.

And now . . . having learned what she'd wanted to know, she found herself facing an even bigger unknown. An even more frightening unknown.

Knowledge, it seemed, was a two-edged sword.

By the next morning, she'd talked herself around. Her analysis of her situation, her decision on her best way forward, had been right; there was nothing in the events of the past evening sufficient to deflect her from her path.

It would, however, clearly behoove her to make a serious effort to push Torrington's investigation along. The investigation provided his major excuse to spend time in her company, seducing her, being kind to her brothers, helping her with Adriana . . .

Pushing aside such thoughts, she rose from the breakfast table and went in search of the lists she'd made.

Tony sat comfortably slumped in a leather armchair in the library of Hendon House. Idly swirling a glass of brandy, he recited the story of Ruskin's death, the subsequent revelations, and the ongoing investigation to Jack—

otherwise Jonathon, Lord Hendon—who was similarly comfortable in another chair, and his strikingly beautiful wife Kit, presently perched at Jack's elbow.

"So," he concluded, "Ruskin's been selling information on ships and dates to someone, who presumably used the information for their own gain—they certainly paid Ruskin well for it. However, we have no idea of the precise nature of the information Ruskin passed, so we don't know how it might have been used—"

"And therefore can't trace said user of same." Jack met his gaze, his expression hard.

"That"—Tony saluted him with his glass—"sums it up nicely."

Kit straightened. "Well, Jack will just have to help you learn what was important about those ships, but meanwhile, what about this widow? What was her name?"

Tony met Kit's violet gaze. The first time he'd met her, he'd thought she was a boy—understandable given he was half-dead courtesy of a brig full of smugglers, and she'd been traipsing about in breeches at the time. Now her glorious red hair was longer, elegantly cut to frame her piquant face. Her figure, previously slender and slim, had filled out a trifle, but that only made it all the more womanly. Two children had done little to curb her fire; she was one of the most disconcertingly active women Tony knew.

He was supremely thankful she was Jack's wife. "The widow isn't involved, other than by the unfortunate act of stumbling on Ruskin's body."

Kit frowned. "Why, then, are you being so careful not to use her name? You've mentioned her at least six times, but always as 'the widow.'"

Jack had turned to study his wife; now he turned, and studied Tony. "She's right. What going on with this widow?"

"Nothing." Tony sat forward, then froze. To Jack and Kit, who knew him well, both his tone and that movement had betrayed him. "Oh, all right." He slumped back. "The widow is Mrs. Alicia Carrington, and she is, as you've guessed, of more than passable charms, and . . ."

When he didn't go on, Jack pointedly prompted, "*And* . . . ?"

Kit was grinning.

Tony grimaced at them both. "And it's possible, perhaps, that . . ." He waved the question aside. "That's beside the point. The first thing"—he fixed Kit with a narrow-eyed look—"indeed, the *only* thing I need from you both is help with this shipping business. We need to make some headway on how the ships were involved."

Kit continued grinning. "And later?"

She wasn't going to give up. Tony closed his eyes. "And later you can dance at my wedding." Opening his eyes, he glared at her. "Good enough?"

She beamed. "Excellent." She looked at Jack. "Now what could be the crucial *thing* about those ships?"

Jack studied the list Tony had given him. "If I had information like this . . ." He looked up, met Tony's gaze. "These are all merchant ships. If the dates are convoy dates, the dates on which these ships were due to join convoys to come up the Channel, or alternatively the dates on which they left the protection of the convoy to turn aside to their respective home ports . . ."

"You think the information might have been used to take the ships?"

"As prizes?" Jack thought, then grimaced. "That's one possibility. Another is deliberate sinking to lay hands on the insurance—I won't tell you how frequent that is. Wrecking is another option."

Tony pointed at the list. "All those ships are still registered." That was the first thing he'd checked.

"That makes sinking or wrecking unlikely." Jack looked again at the list. "The next thing to determine is who owns these vessels and from where they were coming."

"Can you do that?"

"Easily." Jack looked at Tony. "It'll take a few days."

"Is there anything else we can pursue in the meantime?"

Jack pulled a face. "I can ask, quietly, as to whether there's anything noteworthy about one particular ship, and perhaps put out feelers about a few others, but until we know something more specific . . ." He grimaced. "We don't want to tip our quarry the wink."

"Indeed not. Anything I can do?"

Jack shook his head. "Lloyd's Coffee House is the obvious place to ask, but it's a closed group. I'm one of them, so I can ask nosy questions, but the instant you walk in . . ." He looked at Tony. "You'd have to make it official to get any word out of anyone there."

Tony grimaced, then drained his glass. "Very well, I'll leave it to you."

Kit rose in a rustle of skirts. "I'll tell Minchin you'll stay to luncheon."

"Ah—no." With a charming smile, Tony stood. "Much as I would love to grace any board presided over by your fair self, I've other engagements I must keep."

Taking Kit's hand, he bowed with consummate grace.

As he straightened, she arched a brow at him. "I must be sure to make Mrs. Carrington's acquaintance."

He grinned and tapped her nose. "I'll warn her to keep a weather eye out for you."

Coming up behind Kit, Jack wrapped his arms around her waist. "Well, you've one night's grace—we're staying in tonight."

Kit leaned back against her husband's broad chest. "It was a wrench to part from the boys. It's the first time we've left them."

Tony noted her misty-eyed expression as she thought of her two sons. Last time he'd seen them, they were robust and active—the sort to run their keepers ragged.

Jack snorted and glanced down at her face. "God knows, by the time we get home, they'll have exhausted everyone and be lording it over all and sundry."

Tony saw the pride in Jack's face, heard it in his voice. He smiled, kissed Kit's hand, saluted Jack, and left them.

TEN

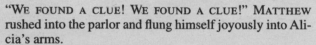

"We found a clue! We found a clue!" Matthew rushed into the parlor and flung himself joyously into Alicia's arms.

"Well, we think it's a clue," David temporized, following Matthew in.

"We had a wonderful time!" Harry's eyes were shining as he plonked himself down on the chaise beside Alicia. "Are there any crumpets left?"

"Of course." Smiling, Alicia hugged Matthew, relieved as well as pleased. Five minutes of studying Tony's lists that morning had convinced her that she, personally, had no hope of making any sense of them. Adriana, too, had had no idea, but had suggested Alicia ask Jenkins and the boys, pointing out that their frequent excursions often took them to the docks.

She'd harbored reservations over the wisdom of such a course, but Jenkins had welcomed the challenge for himself and his charges. The boys, naturally, had been thrilled to assist Tony in any way. Soothing her sisterly concern by sending Maggs with them, she'd consented to an afternoon excursion.

Releasing Matthew, she signaled Adriana, who rose and tugged the bellpull. A moment later, Maggs and Jenkins both looked in. Alicia beckoned. "Come and tell us your news, but first we need to order tea to celebrate."

She wasn't sure how much credence to place in her brothers' "clue," but they undoubtedly deserved a reward for doing as she'd asked and looking.

Matthew and Harry told her which wharves they'd visited, glibly naming various seagoing vessels and their likely destinations. Then Maggs opened the door, Jenkins carried in the tea tray, and everyone settled to hear the news. Both Matthew and Harry were busy with their crumpets, today dripping with honey; by unspoken consensus, everyone looked at David.

He asked for the list; Jenkins handed it over. David smoothed the sheet. "There are thirty-five ships listed, and for many, there's nothing odd or unusual to report." He glanced at Alicia. "We asked lots of stevedores, and we found at least one who could tell us about each of these ships. So we know that for nineteen of them nothing odd has happened, nothing anyone knows to tell or talk about. *But*." He paused, making the most of the dramatic moment, checking to see that both his sisters had recognized its import. "We learned that the other sixteen ships were all lost—on or around those dates!"

David's eyes gleamed as he glanced from Alicia's face to Adriana's; hardly surprising, they were both agog.

"Sunk?" Alicia asked. "All sixteen were sunk?"

"No!" Harry's tone indicated she'd missed the whole point. "Taken as prizes during the war!"

"Prizes?" Puzzled, she looked to Jenkins.

He nodded. "During all wars, merchantmen are targeted by opposing navies. It's a customary tactic to deny the country one is at war with vital supplies. Even a shortage of, for instance, cabbages, could cause internal civil unrest and pressure an enemy's government. It's a very old tactic indeed."

Alicia tried to put the information into perspective. "So you're saying that sixteen ships"—she reached for the list David held; little 'P's had been written in the margin beside nearly half the names—"these sixteen ships were taken as prizes of war by . . ." She looked up. "By whom?"

"That we didn't learn," Maggs replied. "But those we asked thought it was most likely foreign privateers, or the French or Spanish navies." He nodded to the boys. "Your brothers hit the nail on the head over who to ask—it was their idea to approach the navvies. They unload the cargoes, so they remember the ships they've been hired to unload that don't come in, because then they don't get paid."

Alicia sat and absorbed all they'd told her while they consumed their tea and crumpets. When, finished, the boys eyed her hopefully, she smiled. "Very well. You've done an excellent job, and doubtless learned a great deal this afternoon, so you're excused from lessons for the rest of the day."

"Yayyyy!"

"Can we go and play in the park?"

She glanced out; it was still light, but night would soon start falling.

"I'll take 'em if you like, ma'am." Maggs rose. "Just for half an hour or so—let 'em run the fidgets out."

She smiled at him. "Thank you, Maggs." Then she looked at her brothers. "If you promise to attend Maggs, you may go."

With a chorus of assurances, they jumped up, jostling as they raced from the room. With an understanding grin, Maggs followed.

Alicia watched him go. She owed Torrington a debt for sending him. Maggs was as careful of her brothers as she could wish.

Jenkins cleared the tea things and removed the tray; Adriana returned to her sketching. Alicia sat with the list in her hand, and wished Tony—Torrington—was there.

* * *

That evening, Alicia had elected to attend Lady Carmichael's ball. Thus advised by Maggs, Tony saw no reason to arrive early; better to let the first rush ebb before making his way up the Carmichaels' stairs.

He'd spent the best part of his afternoon with Mr. King, learning more about Alicia, specifically about her finances. As he'd suspected, she had had a contract with King, but to his surprise, the man hadn't jumped at his offer to buy out said contract.

A degree of verbal fencing had ensued, until both he and King had agreed to show their hands. Once he'd made the nature of his interest clear, King had been much more accommodating; he'd agreed to burn Alicia's contract in Tony's presence in return for a bank draft for the appropriate amount. As King's goal was to ensure that no one, not even he, could hold the contract over Alicia's head, and as *his* only aim was to lift the financial burden from her shoulders, he'd been happy to agree.

The amount he'd paid had been another revelation. He knew how much it cost to run his various houses and to meet his mother's milliners' and dressmakers' bills; how Alicia was managing on the frugal sum she'd borrowed was beyond his comprehension. Her gowns alone would cost more.

Yet King had assured him Alicia was not in debt to anyone else. Understanding what had occasioned his query, he'd added that he, too, had thought the amount far too small, but when recently he'd dined with them, he'd detected not the slightest frugality or lack.

Tony now understood that the face the Carrington household presented to the world was a facade—a superbly crafted one with no cracks. Behind the facade, however . . . he'd recalled the lack of servants and the simple but hearty fare Maggs had described.

Like crumpets and jam for tea.

Alicia's payment to King, capital plus interest, would

fall due in July. Her life would have changed dramatically by then, but if she recalled the debt and inquired, as both he and King fully expected she would, King had agreed to simply say that an anonymous benefactor had paid the sum. She would guess it was he; he was looking forward to her attempts to make him admit it.

Lips curving as he entered Lady Carmichael's ballroom, Tony inwardly basked in a self-satisfied glow.

He made his bow to her ladyship, then joined the throng. The ball was in full swing, the ballroom a collage of silks and satins of every hue swirling about the black splashes of gentlemen's evening coats. He looked around, expecting to locate Adriana's court somewhere along the side of the room.

Instead, he saw Geoffrey Manningham, shoulders propped against the wall, his gaze, distinctly black, fixed on him.

Instincts pricking, he strolled the short distance to Geoffrey's side. Met his scowl with a questioning frown.

"Where are they?" Geoffrey growled. "Do you know?"

Tony blinked. Satisfaction fled. He turned to survey the room, but didn't see the crowd. "My information was that they'd be here."

"You can take it from me they aren't."

The tension in Geoffrey's voice, in his stance, had effectively communicated itself to him. Tony's mind raced; he tried to imagine what might have happened. Could Maggs have been wrong? He looked at Geoffrey. "How did you know they'd be here?"

Geoffrey looked at him as if that was a supremely silly question. "Adriana told me, of course."

That raised the stakes. The sisters had expected to be there, and were now seriously late.

A contained commotion by the door drew their attention. A footman was whispering urgently to the butler, proffering a note. The butler took it, straightened magisterially, then turned and surveyed the guests.

His gaze stopped on Tony.

The butler swept forward, not running, yet as fast as one such as he might go. He bowed before Tony. "My lord, this message was just delivered by one of your lordship's footmen. I understand the matter is urgent."

Tony lifted the folded note from the salver. "Thank you."

Flicking it open, he rapidly scanned the contents, then glanced at the butler. "Please summon my carriage immediately."

The butler bowed. "Of course, my lord." He withdrew.

Tony opened the note again, held it so Geoffrey, looking over his shoulder, could read it, too.

The writing was a feminine scrawl, the hand holding the pen clearly agitated. Adriana had been too overset even to bother with any salutation.

> *My lord, I don't know who else might help us and Maggs assures me this is the right thing to do. Just as we were about to set out for the Carmichaels', officers from the Watch arrived, along with a Bow Street Runner. They've taken Alicia away.*

The writing broke off; a blob of ink was smeared across the page. Then Adriana continued: *Please help! We don't know what to do.*

She'd signed it simply Adriana.

Geoffrey swore. "What the devil's going on?"

Tony stuffed the note into his pocket. "I've no idea." He glanced at Geoffrey. "Coming?"

Geoffrey sent him a grim look. "As if you need ask."

They went quickly down the stairs and reached the portico just as Tony's town carriage rattled up.

Tony reached for the door, opened it, and waved Geoffrey in. "Waverton Street! As fast as you can." With that, he followed Geoffrey, slamming the door behind him.

His coachman took him at his word. They rocketed along the streets, swinging about corners at a criminal pace. In five minutes, the coach was slowing; it lurched to a halt outside Alicia's front door.

Tony and Geoffrey were on the pavement before the carriage stopped rocking. Maggs opened the front door to Tony's peremptory knock.

"What's going on?" Tony shot at him.

"Buggered if I know," Maggs growled back. "Strangest bit of work I've ever seen. Nice thing it is when a lady getting ready to go to a ball is set on in her own front hall. What's the world coming to, I ask you?"

"Indeed. Where's Adriana—and do the boys know about this?"

"They're all in the parlor. Couldn't keep the boys from hearing—there was a right to-do. Mrs. Carrington gave the blighters what for, but they weren't about to go away, nor yet let her go out and wait until later. I'm thinking she went with them just to get them out of the house, what with the boys and Miss Adriana being so upset."

Tony's face hardened. He led the way to the parlor. The instant he opened the door, four pairs of eyes fixed on him.

A second later, Matthew flung himself at him, arms clutching limpetlike about his waist. "You'll get her back, won't you?"

The words, not entirely steady, were muffled by Tony's coat.

David and Harry were only steps behind. Harry caught Tony's arm and simply clung, the same question in his upturned face. David, older, tugged at Tony's sleeve. When Tony looked at him, he swallowed and met his gaze. "They've made some mistake. Alicia would never do anything wrong."

Tony smiled. "Of course not." Putting a hand on Matthew's head, he tousled his soft hair; laying an arm around Harry's shoulders, he hugged him, then urged the trio back into the room. "I'll go straightaway and bring her back. But first . . ."

One glance at Adriana's white face told him she was as upset as her brothers, but having to comfort the boys and contain their panic had forced her to master her own. Despite the shock, despite the way her fingers clutched and twisted, she was lucid, not hysterical.

Her eyes were wider than he'd ever seen them. "They said they were taking her to the local Watch House."

"South of Curzon Street, it is," Maggs put in.

Tony nodded. Urging the boys ahead of him, he made his way deeper into the room. Geoffrey followed on his heels. While Tony sat in the armchair, the boys scrambling to perch close on the padded arms, Geoffrey sat beside Adriana. He took her hand and squeezed it reassuringly. She smiled weakly, rather wanly, at him.

"Now," Tony commanded, "tell me exactly what happened."

Adriana and the boys all started talking at once; he held up his hand. "Adriana first—listen carefully so you can tell me anything she forgets."

The boys dutifully settled to listen; Adriana drew a deep breath, then, her voice only occasionally quavering, she described how, just as she and Alicia were about to leave for the ball, a heavy knock on the door had heralded the Watch, accompanied by a Bow Street Runner.

"There were two from the Watch, and the Runner. He was the one in charge. They insisted Alicia had—" She broke off, then dragged in a breath and continued, "That she had killed Ruskin. Stabbed him to death. It was ludicrous!"

"I presume she told them they were fools?"

"Not in those precise words, but of course she denied it."

"The men wouldn't believe her," Matthew said.

Tony smiled at him. "Fools, as I said."

Matthew nodded and settled back against Tony's shoulder.

Tony looked at Adriana. She continued, "We tried to reason with them—Alicia even used your name. She told them you were investigating the matter, but they wouldn't even wait while we sent for you. They were totally certain—absolutely—that Alicia was a . . . a *murderess*!"

Eyes huge, Adriana looked at him imploringly. "They were very rough men—they won't hurt her, will they?"

Tony bit back a curse, exchanged a swift glance with Geoffrey, and stood. "I'll go there now—I'll bring her back straightaway. Geoffrey will stay and keep you company. If I'm an hour or so, don't worry." Resettling his sleeves, he flashed the boys a reassuring smile. "I'll need to have a word with this Bow Street Runner, and make sure the gentlemen of the Watch don't make such a silly mistake again."

Five minutes later, he strode up the steps of the Watch House. Two stalwart members of the Watch were heading out on their rounds; they glanced at him—and rapidly got out of his way.

Tony's heels struck the tiles of the foyer; glancing swiftly around, he fixed his gaze on the supervisor behind the narrow desk, who was already eyeing him with increasing unease. This Watch House was situated on the edge of Mayfair; the hapless supervisor would know Trouble when he saw it. His expression as he hurriedly got to his feet suggested he recognized it bearing down on him now.

"Can I help you, sir—m'lord?"

I believe you have something of mine.

Tony bit back the words, reined in his temper, and quite softly said, "I believe there's been a mistake."

The sergeant paled. "A mistake, m'lord?"

"Indeed." Tony drew out his card case, withdrew a card and flipped it on the desk. "I'm Lord Torrington, and according to Whitehall I'm in charge of the investigation into the murder of William Ruskin, lately of the Office of

Customs and Revenue. I understand two of your men in company with a Bow Street Runner visited a private residence in Waverton Street an hour ago and removed, *by force*, a lady—Mrs. Alicia Carrington. The taradiddle I've been told—no doubt you and your men can explain it—is that Mrs. Carrington is accused of having stabbed Ruskin to death."

At no point did he raise his voice; he'd long ago learned the knack of making subordinates quake with a quiet and steely tone.

With his gaze, he pinned the supervisor, who was now holding on to his desk as if he needed its support. "I should perhaps mention that it was *I* who discovered Ruskin's body. In the circumstances, I would like an explanation and I would like it now, but first, before all else, you will release Mrs. Carrington into my care." He smiled, and the supervisor visibly quailed. "I do hope you've taken exceptionally good care of her."

The man could barely draw breath. He bowed, bobbed. "Indeed, m'lord—she did mention . . . we've put the lady in the magistrate's office." He hurried around the desk, almost stumbling in his haste to conduct Tony thither. "I'll just show you, then I'll get ahold of Smiggins—he's the Runner, m'lord. We was acting under his orders."

"Very well." Tony followed the bobbing supervisor. "What's your name?"

"Elcott, sir—m'lord, begging your pardon." Elcott stopped outside a door, and gestured. "The lady's in here, m'lord"

"Thank you. Please send Smiggins here immediately. I wish to attend to this business and remove Mrs. Carrington as soon as possible. This is no place for a lady."

Elcott kept bobbing. "Indeed, m'lord. Immediately, m'lord."

With a curt nod, Tony dismissed him. Opening the door, he walked in.

Alicia was standing by the window, dressed in all her finery for the ball. She swung around as he entered; the pinched look in her face dissolved as she recognized him. "Thank God!"

She didn't exactly fly to him, but she crossed the room quickly, her hands rising; shutting the door, he grasped them, and pulled her into his arms.

He held her tight, his cheek against her hair. "I came as soon as I could. You needn't worry about Adriana and the boys—they know I'm here, and Geoffrey's with them."

A large part of her tension dissipated; she looked up, pushing back to look into his face. "Thank you. I didn't know what to do—and I've no idea what's going on. For some reason they think I stabbed Ruskin."

"I know." Tony heard footsteps approaching. Reluctantly releasing her, he urged her to the chair behind the desk. "Sit down—try not to say anything. Just listen and watch."

A hesitant tap sounded on the door.

Resuming his previous, grim expression, he took up a stance beside Alicia's chair. "Come."

The door opened; a heavily built man in the distinctive red coat of a Bow Street Runner looked around the edge. He saw Tony; his eyes widened. He cleared his throat. "Smiggins, m'lord. You sent for me?"

"Indeed, Smiggins. Come in."

Smiggins looked like he'd rather do anything else, however, opening the door wider, he entered, then ponderously shut the door. He turned to face them; meeting Tony's eyes, he stiffened to attention. "Sir?"

"I understand you saw fit to apprehend Mrs. Carrington this evening. Why?"

Smiggins swallowed. "I had orders to bring the lady in to answer questions seeing as she was said to have stabbed some gentleman called Ruskin. To death, m'lord."

"I see. I take it Elcott informed you that I have been

placed in charge of the investigation into Ruskin's murder by Whitehall?"

Hesitantly, Smiggins nodded. "That were a surprise, m'lord. We hadn't been told that."

"Indeed. Who gave you your orders?"

"Supervisor at Bow Street, m'lord. Mr. Bagget."

Tony frowned. "I assume a warrant has been issued—who was the magistrate?"

Smiggins shifted; all color fled his cheeks. "Ah—I don't know about any warrant, m'lord."

Gaze fixed on the hapless Runner, Tony let the silence stretch, then quietly asked, "Are you telling me you seized a lady from her own house *without* a warrant?"

Smiggins looked green. Spine poker stiff, he stared straight ahead. "Information came in latish, about six, m'lord. Sir Phineas Colby—the magistrate on duty—he'd already left. It was thought . . . well, the information was that the lady was looking to leave the country, so . . ."

"So someone had the bright idea to send you, along with two ruffians, to take matters into your own hands and forcibly remove the lady from her home?"

Smiggins trembled and said nothing.

Again, Tony let silence work for him, then softly asked, "Who laid the information?"

It was abundantly clear that Smiggins wished himself anywhere but there. He hesitated, but knew he had to answer. "From what I heard, m'lord, the information came anonymous-like."

"Anonymous?" Tony let his incredulity show. "On the basis of anonymous information, you acted to remove a lady from her home?"

Smiggins shifted. "We didn't know—"

"You didn't think!"

The sudden roar made Alicia jump; she stared at Tony. He glanced briefly at her, but immediately turned back to the now quaking Runner. "What exactly did this anonymous information say?"

"That Mrs. Alicia Carrington presently residing in Waverton Street had stabbed Mr. Ruskin to death and was likely to do a flit any minute."

His gaze on the Runner, Tony shook his head. "We already know that whoever stabbed Ruskin was taller than he was and had to have possessed the strength of a man, not a woman. Ruskin was nearly as tall as me—taller than Mrs. Carrington. She could not have stabbed Ruskin."

The Runner glanced at Alicia, then quickly looked forward.

Tony continued unrelenting, his tone lethally quiet. "You, Smiggins, and your supervisor have acted completely outside the law—the law you are supposed to uphold."

"Yes, m'lord."

"In a moment, I will be taking Mrs. Carrington from here and returning her to her home. Henceforth as far as Bow Street are concerned, she is to be considered as being under my legal protection in this matter—is that clear?"

"Perfectly clear, m'lord."

"And in recompense to Mrs. Carrington for causing her distress, and to me for disrupting my evening, you will undertake, with your supervisor's full support, to track down the source of your 'anonymous information.' You will do nothing else, take part in no other duty, until you have accomplished that and made a full report to me. Do I make myself clear, Smiggins?"

"Yes, m'lord. Very clear."

"Good." Tony waited, then quietly said, "You may go. Report to me the instant you learn anything—Torrington House, Upper Brook Street."

Bowing, Smiggins backed to the door. "Yes, m'lord. At once."

The instant the door shut behind him, Tony reached for Alicia's hand. "Come. I'll take you home."

She rose with alacrity, more than ready to leave; as he led her to the door, she glanced at his face, at the hard, set planes, heard again his tone as he'd dealt with the Runner.

As she walked beside him out of the Watch House, her hand tucked possessively in his arm, she absorbed the other side of him she'd just seen.

It wasn't until the carriage moved off from the curb and she relaxed against the well-padded seat that the shock and panic hit her. Until then, she'd been thinking of her brothers, of Adriana, worrying about them; until then, she'd taken everything in, but hadn't spared any real thought for herself.

She shivered and twitched her cloak closer, huddled into its warmth. If he hadn't come . . . a chill washed through her veins.

He glanced at her, then his arm came around her; he hugged her to him, against his warmth.

"Are you truly all right?" He whispered the words against her temple.

Her teeth were threatening to chatter, so she nodded.

Even through their clothes, the solid warmth of him reached her; as the carriage rolled on, negotiating the swell of evening traffic along Piccadilly, her chill slowly faded. His strength, the decisive and effective way he'd dealt with the entire episode, the simple fact of his presence beside her, seeped into her mind, into her consciousness, and reassured.

Eventually, she drew breath, glanced at him. "Thank you. It was just . . ." She gestured.

"Shock." He looked out at the passing facades. "We'll be back in Waverton Street soon."

Silence descended. A minute passed, then she broke it. "I didn't stab Ruskin." She studied his face as he looked at her, but in the dimness couldn't read his expression. She drew a determined breath. "Do you believe me?"

"Yes."

Tony gave the word, simple, straightforward, uninflected, and unadorned, its moment, let it sink into her mind. Then he looked down; taking her hand, he played with her fingers. "You heard me tell the Runner, and *Tante* Félicité and Lady Osbaldestone before that. Physically, you couldn't have killed Ruskin. I—we—knew that from the day after his death."

Her fingers twined with his. He could almost hear her mind working, hear the questions forming, sense her searching for the words.

"I. We. You told me you'd been asked to investigate, but until this evening, in the Watch House, I didn't truly comprehend what that meant, that you were investigating at the behest of Whitehall."

He felt her gaze trace his features. Waited for the next question, wondered how she'd phrase it.

"Who are you?"

When he didn't immediately react, she drew breath, straightened within his arm. "You're not just a nobleman the authorities—even less the gentlemen in Whitehall— just happened to ask to look into a matter because you stumbled over a body." Turning her head, she studied him. "Are you?"

He let a moment pass, then met her gaze. "No. That isn't how Whitehall operates."

She didn't respond, but simply waited.

He looked away, rapidly sorted through his impulses. He shouldn't expect her to accept him as her husband without knowing who he was, all he truly was. Ingrained instincts urged continued and total secrecy, yet he recalled the trouble Jack Hendon had landed himself in when he'd failed to tell Kit the whole truth. He'd thought he was protecting her; instead, he'd hurt her, nearly driven her away . . .

He glanced at Alicia, then reached up and rapped on the roof. His coachman opened the trap. "Drive around the park." The gates would be locked, but the streets around the perimeter wouldn't be crowded at this time of night.

The trap fell shut; the carriage rolled on. The flare from a passing streetlamp briefly lit the carriage's interior. He glanced at Alicia; she met his eyes, and raised a brow. The light faded; the shadows closed in.

Fittingly, perhaps.

He leaned back, resettling his arm so she could rest more comfortably, curving his palm about her shoulder both to steady her and keep her close. He tightened his other hand about hers, locking their fingers; in the dimness he needed the contact to help gauge her reactions.

Telling her all was a risk, but a risk he had to take.

"I told your brothers I was a major in the Guards, in a cavalry regiment." Her fingers shifted; he squeezed them gently. "I was, but after the first few months, I didn't serve in either the Guards or the cavalry."

She'd turned her head and was watching his face, but he couldn't make out her expression. He drew breath and went on, "There was this gentleman named Dalziel who has an office in Whitehall—" He continued, telling her what he'd never told anyone, not Felcité, not even his mother; quietly, steadily, he told her the truth of the past thirteen years of his life.

His voice remained cool, steady, his tone dispassionate, almost as if his dark and murky past was at a great distance. The carriage rolled on; she didn't interrupt, didn't exclaim or ask questions. Didn't pass judgment, but he couldn't tell if that was because she was shocked speechless or hadn't yet taken in enough to believe and react.

He didn't know how she would react. A surprising number of those whose lives and privileges he and his colleagues had risked their lives repeatedly to protect held that such services as those he'd performed, predicated first to last on deceit, fell outside the bounds of all decency and branded him forever less than a gentleman.

The knowledge that some who welcomed him into their homes would respond to the truth of his life, if they ever learned of it, in such a way had never bothered him. But how she reacted . . .

It was tempting, oh-so-tempting, to gloss over the dark facts, to paint the details of his life in brighter colors, to lighten them. To hide and disguise their true nature. He forced himself to resist, to speak nothing more than the unvarnished truth.

To his surprise, his chest felt tight, his throat not as clear as he liked. At one point, when recounting in bleak black-and-white terms the cold facts of his existence among the seedier elements in the northern French ports, he realized he'd tensed, that he was gripping her hand too tightly; he paused and forced himself to ease his hold.

She tightened hers. Shifted on the seat, then her other hand touched the back of his, and settled, warmly clasping. "It must have been dreadful."

Quiet acceptance, quiet empathy.

Both flowed around him like liquid gold.

His fingers curled, gripping hers again; warmth blossomed in his chest. After a moment, he went on, "But that's all in the past. Along with most others, I got out last year." He glanced at her, sensed the contact when she met his gaze. "However . . ."

She tilted her head. "When Ruskin was stabbed, and *you* reported the body . . . ?"

"Indeed. Dalziel reappeared in my life." He grimaced. "If I'd been in his place, I'd have done the same. Whatever the business Ruskin was involved in, it's almost certainly treasonous."

They'd circled the park; ahead, the flickering streetlamps played over the stately mansions of Mayfair. He reached up, and instructed the coachman to head for Waverton Street. Once they were within the fashionable, well-lighted streets, he looked at her and found her watching him, not judgmentally, not even curiously, but as if she could finally see him clearly—and what she saw was something of a relief.

Her gaze shifted past him, then her lips eased and she sat back. "So that's why Whitehall—this Dalziel person—chose you for the investigation. Because you've proved beyond question to be true to the country's cause."

No one had ever described him like that, but . . . he inclined his head. "It's important that whoever is pursuing the investigation is beyond question true, because with Ruskin being within the bureacracy, it's likely whoever he was dealing with is in some way connected either with a relevant department, or the government."

Waverton Street was approaching; Alicia spoke quickly. Her mind was racing, thoughts tumbling. "So is your investigation supposed to be secret?"

His reply was wry. "It was."

She glanced at him. "But now you've had to step in and rescue me—I *am* sorry. I shouldn't have—"

"Yes, you should have." His hand tightened about hers. "Indeed, if you hadn't, I'd have been . . . displeased."

She frowned at him. "Are you sure?"

"Perfectly. Neither the Watch nor Bow Street will be falling over themselves to say anything about what occurred tonight. Unless whoever was behind this evening's events was actually watching the Watch House, they won't be any the wiser."

"Whoever was behind . . ." She stared at him. "You mean the person who laid the information . . . that was deliberate? I assumed it was just a mistake. . . ." Hearing the words brought home the unlikelihood of such a supposition. She faced forward. "Oh."

"Indeed." His tone had hardened.

She glanced at him as the carriage rocked to a stop; his face had hardened, too.

He shifted forward; reaching for the door latch, he met her gaze. "We need to consider how to react—how best to meet this new development."

"She's back!" Harry reached Alicia first, wrapping his arms around her waist and hugging her tightly.

"I'm all right." She hugged him back, then opened her arms to Matthew, who clutched and wriggled until, with an effort, she lifted him into her arms. David hung back, feeling his age, yet clearly wanting reassurance; she smiled, freed a hand, and drew him to her for a quick kiss. "Truly," she whispered, then let him go.

His somber expression eased; turning, he led the way to the chaise.

Having followed Alicia into the parlor, Tony pressed a hand to her back, worried about Matthew's weight. She flashed him a smile, then glanced down at Harry's head.

Transferring his hand to Harry's shoulder, he gripped lightly. "Come on—let's get her to sit down."

Harry glanced at him, then released Alicia; tucking his hand in Tony's, he went with him to the armchair and perched on the arm. Still carrying Matthew, Alicia walked more slowly to the chaise. Matthew slid down and she sat, then he crawled into her lap.

Beside her, Adriana laid a hand on her arm. "It must have been awful—you must have been so afraid."

Alicia smiled reassuringly. "I wasn't there long enough to get into a state." She glanced at Tony, then looked down at Matthew, snuggling close. She ruffled his hair. "Sweetheart, it's long past your bedtime."

He looked up at her, for a minute said nothing, then, smothering a yawn, mumbled, "Have you told Tony about the ships?"

She looked at Tony. Everyone looked at him.

He stared back. "What about the ships?"

Three pairs of eyes focused in brotherly admonition on Alicia. She waved in exculpation. "There's been so much happening"—she exchanged a glance with Tony, the memory of their drive around the park and all it had revealed high in her mind—"I haven't had a chance. But now you can tell him yourselves."

They did, in a chorus of statements and explanations that left him dazed. "Prizes? Sixteen of them? You're sure?"

Tony studied the list Alicia had fetched from her escritoire. The boys had gathered about him, David leaning over his shoulder, Matthew and Harry balancing one on each chair arm. Scanning the list and the inscribed "P"s, he listened as they explained how they'd gleaned their information.

All the ships were still registered, therefore presumably still afloat, as they would be if they'd been taken as prizes and subsequently ransomed by their owners.

Alicia sank back on the chaise. "Jenkins can tell you more if need be. And Maggs—he went, too."

He glanced at her, then looked around at the boys, meeting their eyes. "This is excellent." He didn't have to fabricate his enthusiasm, the sincerity of his thanks. "You've shown us which direction to pursue. Thank you." Solemnly, he shook each boy's hand.

They grinned, and continued pelting him with information about the ships. One part of his mind listened, cataloging useful details; most of his mind was racing, assessing, formulating.

When the boys' observations slowed, then stopped, Alicia rose, clearly intending to gather them and send them upstairs. He stayed her with an upraised hand. "One moment."

One glance at Geoffrey's face, and Adriana's, assured him neither would let him leave without a comprehensive explanation of what was going on; they were merely biding their time. His professional habits urged secrecy—information shared only with those who needed to know—yet this time other instincts, deeper instincts, were increasingly suggesting that sharing knowledge was a wiser, infinitely safer way to proceed.

His gaze came to rest on Alicia's brothers, on the three tousled, silky brown heads, currently bent close as they again examined the list of ships.

If he were on the "other side" in this affair . . .

They'd already targeted Alicia, not once, but twice. They knew where she lived. Anyone watching the house and her would quickly realize what her strongest instinct was—and therein lay her greatest weakness. It would be remarkably easy to engineer, and her reaction would be one hundred percent predictable . . .

Raising his gaze to her face, he waved her to sit. Puzzled, she sank down on the edge of the chaise. He glanced at Geoffrey and Adriana, then looked back at her. "This household—Adriana and Geoffrey, and the boys, too, and Jenkins, Maggs, and any other servants you have—all need to know the basic elements of what's going on."

Concern filled her eyes. She frowned. Before she could voice any protest, he glanced at her brothers; all three had come alert at his words and were now looking expectantly at him.

He smiled slightly, then raised his gaze and met Alicia's eyes. "It's the best way to protect everyone. They all need to know."

Geoffrey and Adriana were quick to voice their agreement.

Alicia glanced at them, then looked again at the boys. A moment passed, then she lifted her gaze to meet his, and nodded. "Yes. You're right. The basic facts so they understand why they need to take care."

He inclined his head. "If you'll summon the others?"

She rose. He watched her, inwardly acknowledging his

ulterior—ultimately his primary—motive: keeping her safe. Keeping her brothers safe was part of that, but it was she who stood in the line of fire. Conscripting her household in her defense was clearly in everyone's best interests; each of them needed her in their own way.

Within a few minutes, the entire household had assembled. He hadn't previously met the cook and their old nursemaid, Fitchett; both women bobbed deferentially, then retreated to sit on the straight-backed chairs Maggs and Jenkins fetched for them. Maggs had warned him of the small number of staff, so that came as no surprise; given what he now knew of the family's finances, the fact even made sense.

When everyone had settled, the boys seated in a semicircle before his chair, despite the hour alert and eager to hear of his investigation, he told them, simply and concisely, all they needed to know.

ELEVEN

He started by telling them of finding Ruskin's body, omitting to mention that Alicia had been there. Her gaze touched his face; he met it, held it, continued explaining who Ruskin had been, and what they now believed he'd been engaged in—selling information on ship movements that had led to at least sixteen ships being taken as prizes by the enemy.

The boys exchanged significant—excited—glances. Tony noted it; he bore their reaction in mind as he admitted to being an agent for the government, stressing that he was in charge of the investigation regardless of the Watch's and Bow Street's imaginings. The boys were, predictably, even more impressed, their approbation edging into awe.

From there, it was a small step to explaining that the investigation, while no longer strictly secret, would progress more surely if pursued with discretion to avoid alerting the mysterious A.C. He asked that they all continue as usual, but if anyone noticed anything out of place, no matter how small or mundane, they should tell Maggs or, if that wasn't possible, send word immediately to him or, failing that, to Geoffrey.

Able to read behind his careful words, Geoffrey, his expression impassive, nodded, accepting the unstated commission.

Finally, he came to his peroration, specifically intended to impress on his audience, especially the three boys, that the matter was serious—deadly serious. It required tact to walk the line between frightening the boys and fixing it in everyone's heads that in no circumstance were they to court any risk whatever. He alluded to Alicia's recent trauma—a trauma her siblings and the household had shared—as an example of how A. C. might play his game, but he also cautioned that whoever he was, A. C. would not balk at more violent deeds—it was assuredly he who had murdered Ruskin.

From the looks on the boys' faces, worry, concern, but also determination all present in their expressions, he succeeded in his aim.

He glanced at Alicia, faintly raised a brow; she met his gaze, read his question, nodded almost imperceptibly.

Glancing around, surveying the faces, he said, "So now you all know what the problem is, and that there's a need to keep alert at all times."

"Aye." Maggs pushed away from the wall. He looked to the other servants, getting to their feet. "We'll keep our eyes peeled, you can count on that."

"Thank you." With a nod, Tony dismissed them.

Alicia flashed them a grateful smile as they filed out of the room, then turned to her brothers. "Bed for you three, now. It's been a very long evening, and you have lessons tomorrow."

They looked at her, then, somewhat to her surprise, quickly rose. They came to hug her; she kissed their cheeks, then they hugged Adriana and, without any argument, headed for the door. Alicia turned. Maggs and Jenkins had dallied in the doorway; they took the boys under their wings and herded them upstairs.

She sat back on the chaise, hugely relieved, amazed, given the events of the evening, to feel so. Then Geoffrey was bowing before her. She gave him her hand, smiled in gratitude. "I can't thank you enough for coming to stay with Adriana and the boys."

He looked faintly irritated; he frowned at her, reminding her of Tony. "Nonsense. Any gentleman would have done the same." He glanced at Adriana, who'd risen, too.

She beamed at him. "But you did." She squeezed his arm. "Come—I'll see you out."

With a tired but genuine smile for Alicia, Adriana led Geoffrey to the door; he closed it behind them.

Alicia turned to Tony. He'd been watching the door close; now he looked at her.

His gaze rested on her face for a long moment, then he said, "My apologies. I should have asked before I spoke—do you expect any trouble with your staff?"

She blinked. "You mean because of . . ." She let her words trail away, uncomfortable with their direction.

He refused to mince words. "Because despite the fact I avoided using the term, a threat clearly exists toward this household, and, consequently, there has to be a certain if unspecified danger. Household staff aren't partial to getting caught in any cross fire."

She smiled at the military allusion. "In this case, you needn't worry. Cook, Fitchett, and Jenkins have been with us for longer than even I can remember—they won't give notice. They're part of the family."

He looked at her—studied her—then inclined his head and rose.

Quickly, she rose, too. In the distance, she heard the front door shut; she paused, waiting, then the sound of Adriana's light footsteps on the stairs came clearly to her ears.

And Tony's. One glance at him—at the black eyes that were watching her—was enough to assure her of that. But he made no move, simply watched her.

There was a great deal she wanted, indeed felt compelled to say. Quite aside from her rescue, aside from his revelations, his taking the lead in dealing with the matter, here, within her household, had given her time to calm, to reassess and catch her mental breath. She felt infinitely more confident, more assured, than she had two hours earlier. Her latent panic had disappeared; she could face the immediate future sure in her ability to cope.

He didn't move, just watched, waited.

She drew breath, lifted her chin, and closed the distance between them. She stopped directly before him—or would have, but he reached out and smoothly drew her on, into his arms. Her heart leapt; her senses stirred, came alive. His arms settled about her, a loose cradle; her hands coming to rest on his chest, she looked into his face.

A face that gave little away; she couldn't guess what he was thinking.

"I wanted to thank you." Without his intervention, she couldn't imagine what might have happened, how matters might have developed.

He said nothing; instead, he slowly raised a brow. His black gaze touched hers, then swept down to her lips.

She knew exactly what he was thinking. She didn't stop to consider, to assess the wisdom of her response. Drawing in a quick breath, she gripped his arms, stretched up against him, and touched her lips to his.

It was an invitation rather than a kiss; when he didn't immediately respond, she eased back.

His arms tightened, locking her more definitely to him. Her lashes fluttered up; his dark gaze met hers for an instant, then he bent his head.

His lips touched her cheek, a light, insubstantial caress. He paused, then closed again; this time, his lips found the corner of hers, and slowly teased.

As he drew back, just an inch, she turned her head, fleetingly met his eyes. Then she raised one hand, laid her palm along his cheek, and guided his lips to hers.

He closed them over hers and took what she offered. Her mouth, herself. He drew her deeper into his arms, parted her lips, and sank deeper into the kiss. Into the explicit exchange she now knew well.

She responded, more than willing. It seemed very right that she should thank him this way, that she should give and appease the hunger she sensed in him, that elusive desire she exulted in evoking, equally exulted in sating.

As far as she dared.

The warning sounded in her mind—there could not be that many milestones left in the long road they'd agreed to travel. All but instantly, that small voice of caution was drowned out by the memory of his assurance that instead they would dally longer, more intensely, more intimately at every stage.

His mouth feasted on hers; his hands roamed, pleasuring her while feasting on her curves. He molded her to him, explicitly rocked the hard ridge of his erection against her.

Heat erupted inside her, spread through her veins, suffused beneath her skin. Raising her hands, she framed his face, then ran her fingers back, spearing them through his hair. She opened her mouth wider beneath his, with her tongue boldly taunted, deliberately incited him to take, and take more. Never had she felt so alive, so blatantly desirable.

So wanted.

They were standing locked together in her family's parlor; she was sure he wouldn't forget. Felt sure she could leave the decision on what was appropriate to him.

She knew, in her heart, in her soul, that he wouldn't let her down.

Tony had no intention of doing so, yet the demands of the moment were many. A wild and primitive emotion was burgeoning within him; he didn't recognize it, but he knew what it demanded.

Her. Not just her giving but his taking. A claiming, yet . . . this, he accepted, was neither the time nor place.

Not yet, not here. Soon, yes, but tonight . . .

He didn't question the instincts that told him what to do; he'd been their captive for too many years. Experience analyzed, instructed, informed; he fell in with its directives.

Breaking from the kiss, he murmured, unsurprised his tone was low, almost harsh, "Jenkins?"

Courtesy of their kisses, she was close to breathless. "Upstairs. He locks up the front of the house early, all except the front door."

Thank God. He kissed her again, ravenously, arms locking her against him, lifting her as he backed her toward the chaise. Stopping before it, he lifted his head and let her slide down until her feet touched the floor. "So we're alone?"

"Um-hmm." Her hand pressed under his collar and curled around his nape; she lifted her lips to his.

"Good." He took them, kissed her hungrily, in no way disguising his need. She met him, flagrantly urged him on—didn't so much as catch her breath when he eased her gown over her shoulders, then pushed it down to pool about her feet.

Still he held her to the kiss. Shifting to trap her between the chaise and him, he closed his hands about her breasts. Through the fine silk of her chemise, he teased the sensitive mounds, stroked and kneaded until they were full, until her breathing was tight, threatening to fracture.

Swiftly, he undid the ribbon ties and eased the fine fabric down; it fell in folds about her waist. Deciding his control didn't need further strain, he left the flimsy garment there. It was so fine, it was barely a sop to modesty, but having her completely naked on the chaise beneath him might be that one step too far.

At the first touch of his hands on her bare breasts, she murmured incoherently, the words trapped between their lips, and pressed closer.

He held her, for long moments simply savored the sensations—of her mouth freely offered, all his, of her tongue slowly tangling, caressing his, of the way she

softened as he explored, claiming at will, then artfully
stoking her fires. A deep pleasure coursed through him,
part victory, part desire, at the tactile confirmation his
hands reported; he had her in his arms all but naked, her
breasts bare, pressed to his chest, her hips, the cradle in
which he ached to lie, screened by nothing more than a
thin barrier of silk.

Now she was his, it was time to feast.

His hands shifted over her body, then he lifted her,
knelt on the chaise and laid her on the damask, following
her down so their lips didn't part, settling beside her, his
longer, harder frame trapping hers on the cushions. One
hand rising to cradle her face, he plunged once more into
her mouth.

Plunged them both back into the building flames.

Alicia went willingly, eager to know, to experience
whatever and wherever he led. She knew it was dangerous, yet when he finally lifted his head and released her
lips, and she struggled to breathe, to fill her starved lungs,
there was no thought in her mind of drawing back.

Not when he looked at her with desire, hot and glowing, behind his black eyes. His gaze had dropped to her
breasts; they were swollen and aching. Nerves tightening,
she waited for his touch, waited for the burning delight of
his mouth, for the sharp, addictive pleasure.

His gaze flicked up to meet hers, briefly locked, then
his lips curved, knowing and sure. He looked down, bent
his head, and gave her all she'd wanted, all her tight
nerves craved, the intoxicating play of lips and tongue,
the hot, wet suction of his mouth.

He orchestrated the whole until her gasps filled the
room, until her fingers were clenched on his skull, her
body bowing under the hand he'd splayed across her
midriff.

A deep rumble of satisfaction reached her; he shifted
lower, leaning over her. One hand still massaged her
breasts, stroking, tweaking, caressing as his lips trailed

down between, down over the centerline of her body. With one finger he drew the silk folds of her chemise aside, so he could continue his line of openmouthed kisses to her navel.

Raising his head slightly, he circled the indentation with one fingertip, then lowered his head and boldly probed with his tongue, an echo of their kisses, of the plunder, the claiming.

Dazed, her limp fingers retensing on his skull, she watched him minister to her body as if it was a thing worthy of his worship.

Finally lifting his head, his eyes met hers; they were dark and fathomless, hot yet unreadable. Watching her, he shifted, parted her legs and settled between, ran his hand up her thigh, sliding it under the layer of silk to lay it over her stomach, hard possessive palm to her hot, soft skin.

She couldn't take her eyes from his, from the intent, burning look burnished in the black, didn't dare shift her gaze even when she felt his hand move, felt his fingertips brush her curls, then slide further to caress her as he had before.

Her breath strangled, her lungs slowly seizing as he artfully, deliberately explored, then stroked, caressed, finally probed. One large finger slid a little way in, just enough to tantalize, to freeze her mind, and send her frenzied senses searching. Reaching.

He caressed and her body came to life, muscles tensing, flickering, her hips lifting in anticipation. Slowly, he slid one long finger into her, pressed steadily deeper, deeper.

Her lungs locked; her hips lifted, but he held her down, moving lower, his shoulders sliding from her weakened grasp.

He looked down, watched as he worked his hand between her spread thighs, as he worked his finger within her, then he glanced up at her face, with his thumb circled that critical spot he'd discovered before, simultaneously reaching deeper still.

On a moan, she closed her eyes, let her head fall back. This had to be wicked; it was too glorious to be right.

A wave of sheer sensual delight swept through her, caught her wits, trapped her mind in sensations. Wild, wanton, indescribable pleasure flooded her; this time, he seemed content to let the wave lap at her, lap at her, rather than build.

The deliberate, flagrantly intimate repetitive penetration encouraged her to wallow in the warmth, to let her body simply enjoy every moment.

She was hardly relaxed, yet with every minute the landscape grew more familiar, less threatening. The urgency hadn't infected her yet, but she knew it would. Before it did . . .

She managed to catch her breath and look down at him. Reach for him, with her fingers brush his shoulders. He looked up; his eyes were so black she could read nothing of his thoughts, but his face was a graven mask etched with a desire she comprehended instinctively.

"You . . ." She moistened her dry lips. "I'm the one who's grateful. I want to give to you, not . . ."

Her gesture encompassed her body, thrumming with warmth and pleasure, and him, now propped between her knees, one shoulder cushioned against one of her thighs.

His hot black gaze didn't flicker. He glanced briefly down to where his hand steadily pandered to her senses, then he looked up and met her eyes.

"Then lie back, close your eyes, and let me take this, at least." His thumb swirled about the tight nub nestled within the now slick and swollen folds.

She tensed, but he held her with his eyes.

His words reached her, gravelly, low, primitively dark. "If you can't be mine yet, give me this instead. Let me claim this much."

Caught in his eyes, captured by the sheer need she

could feel pouring from him, she tried to think, couldn't—didn't care. "Take—whatever you wish." Caution reared. "But . . ."

His gaze seemed almost blank. "Just one more step." He shifted further back. "Do as I asked—lie back and close your eyes."

He waited; she could feel her pulse hammering in the soft flesh his fingers were tracing. She had no real idea . . . couldn't imagine . . .

She closed her eyes, let her head fall back.

"Just like that—try not to move."

She didn't get a chance to reply. At the first touch of his lips, she lost all capacity even to think. Sensations buffeted her, rose and crashed through her. The intimacy all but slew her.

She heard her gasp, followed by a long moan as his fingers slipped from her sheath and blatantly, holding her thighs wide, he settled to feast.

His mouth worked, and she thought she might die. Of their own accord her hips lifted, twisted, but his hands had closed about them and he held her down, held her in position so he could, as he'd wished, claim her in this way.

A brutally explicit, intensely intimate claiming.

As she squirmed helplessly, struggled to breathe, the fact he knew of no reason to hold back, to withhold from her any degree of his transparently well-educated expertise, was forcefully borne in on her. He knew just what he was doing, to her, to her nerves, to her senses, to her mind.

To, in some way she didn't comprehend, her heart.

She might be giving, he might be taking, yet he gave selflessly, too. If she'd harbored any doubts that lovemaking was in essence a sharing, the long, heated moments she spent under his hands, under his mouth, with his tongue stroking, probing, lapping at her softness, burned every shred of doubt away.

The flames built, expertly stoked, until the conflagration simply became too much. Too much for her to resist, to hold back from the beckoning delight. She would have warned him if she'd been able, but he didn't look up, didn't pause in his increasingly potent ministrations even when she tugged his hair.

And then she was there, at the heart of the firestorm, and for one blinding moment nothing else mattered but the intense, golden glory. It held her tight, a vise of his making, then she fractured, and the glory shattered, sharp shards streaking down her veins to melt deep within her, beneath her fingertips, under her skin.

Exulting, Tony savored the powerful contractions, savored her release, then licked, lapped. Eventually, he eased back and lifted his head.

Ignoring the fiery pressure in his loins, he looked at her, spent, dazed, gloriously sated. Gloriously exposed. He let his gaze travel slowly down her body, seeing and claiming anew, then he bent and placed a kiss on her damp curls, pushed up her chemise, and dropped a gentle, lingering kiss on her belly.

Next time. He promised himself that.

Lifting away, he shifted higher and lay down once more beside her. Propping on one elbow, he laid a hand on her breast, and settled to watch her return to earth and welcome her back.

An hour later, lying in her bed with the house silent about her, Alicia tried to take in, to understand, all that had happened. Not physically; shocking though that had been, stunning beyond her wildest imaginings—or, apparently, those of the authors of both sexual texts she'd consulted—she knew, to her bones, exactly what had happened, what part of him had touched what part of her, and how.

That was a problem in its own right, but what consumed her, what mystified her, was the connection she sensed, the link that steadily, day by day, interlude by in-

terlude, seemed to be growing, forged in the fires between them.

That was something else. Something beyond the facts
she'd considered when she'd decided to adhere to her
widow's role, to pretend to be as experienced as she was
not.

He'd agreed to go slowly; by his standards, he probably had. Even though it was now patently clear that
they'd all but arrived at their final destination, it wasn't
panic over that that filled her mind.

From the first, she'd responded to his practiced caresses instinctively, had been forced to rely on instinct to
guide her. It seemed instinct had, but in a way she hadn't
foreseen, in a direction she hadn't intended to take.

She hadn't foreseen the danger. Not at all.

Rolling over on her side, she clutched a pillow to her
and tried not to think about him, tried not to feel . . . tried
not to be aware of the compulsion that had grown to give
him more than she at any stage had contemplated.

Yet the more she fought it, the more she tried to turn
her mind from the prospect, tried to deny it, the more it
grew.

Fascination had turned into something more.

Something a great deal more powerful.

At an unusually early hour the next evening, Tony entered Lady Arbuthnot's ballroom. Without glancing at
anyone else, he made his way to Alicia's side.

Truth be told, he didn't truly register anyone else's
presence; his mind, all of his awareness, was centered on
her.

Not by choice. He felt driven, whipped along at the
mercy of emotions he'd never before had to conquer.
Mild possessiveness was one thing, but this?

There was so much in her life he wanted to spare her—
more, that some part of him felt driven to fix, almost as if
his very self—his honor, his name, his self-respect—

depended on it. Taking care of her, protecting her, keeping her safe, ensuring her happiness, had become that important.

How, he wasn't sure, but to his mind reasons were by the by. He knew how he felt; he knew what he wanted. He knew how he needed to act.

Reaching her side, he took the hand she smilingly offered, raised it, and placed a kiss on her fingers, then without pause, pressed another to her palm.

Startled, she searched his eyes. "Are you all right?"

He hesitated, then nodded. "Perfectly."

A lie, but he didn't want her asking questions he couldn't answer.

Tucking her hand into his elbow, he pretended to survey the other guests. The dancing had not yet commenced. "Has anyone behaved oddly toward you or Adriana today—here, or in the park?"

She glanced at him. "No." After a moment, she went on, her voice lowered, "Are you expecting rumors about me being taken up by the Watch?"

"Possibly. I want to know if any surface."

He could feel her gaze on his face, studying; he glanced at her, arched a brow.

She held his gaze. "What have you done? Tell me."

He debated whether to inform her he wasn't one of her brothers, but couldn't see it stopping her interrogation. "I've asked *Tante* Felicité and her bosom-bows to keep their ears open. I told her the bare bones of what happened yesterday—she and the few other *grandes dames* who were present were shocked and suitably outraged." He squeezed her fingers before she could protest. "This is the sort of thing that in different circumstances might happen to them. They have a vested interest in ensuring the customs of the ton aren't manipulated for subversive purposes."

Alicia frowned, then nodded, conceding the point. "I'll tell you if Adriana or I encounter any difficulties."

She continued to study his face; he seemed more tense, more on edge than he usually was. "What else did you do today?"

He paused, to her now-informed eye deciding where to start rather than deciding whether to speak.

"I passed the information about the ships on to Jack Hendon."

"The friend who owns a shipping line?"

"Yes. Now he knows what to look for, we'll get along faster. I also sent word to another friend who's checking along the southwest coast. With luck, we'll have a clearer idea of what's been happening soon, then we can start following the trail back to the perpetrator."

"A. C." Remembering the fright of the day before, she shivered. Feeling Tony's gaze on her face, she met it. "He must be someone quite knowledgeable, mustn't he? He knew how to start those first rumors, knew how to trick Bow Street into seizing me."

Lips set, he nodded. "He's intelligent, and cold-blooded."

He hesitated, then went on, his fingers absentmindedly stroking the back of her hand. "I heard back from Smiggins. It seems his 'anonymous information' came via a flower seller who'd been paid by a well-to-do gentleman, one expensively dressed, to take the information to the Watch. She can't describe the man beyond that."

The vision of a gentleman wrapped in an expensive coat with an astrakhan collar, viewed through the mists of a chilly night, slid through Tony's mind. For him, A. C. was no phantom, but a dangerous adversary, one he'd yet to put a name to.

Which, of course, only made it harder to protect Alicia from the danger. He let his gaze drift to Adriana's circle; through her connection with Alicia, she, too, was in danger. There were six gentlemen gathered about her; Sir Freddie Caudel was, as usual, one of the crew. He was engaged in describing some play to Adriana; prettily, she hung on his words, her attention politely all his, at least for the moment. Tony was not at all surprised to see Geoffrey hovering even more determinedly, more definitely possessive.

From beside him came a small humph. "I daresay, if Lord Manningham is all you and Mr. King tell me he is, then I'll shortly be entertaining an offer from him."

He glanced at Alicia, caught her eye. "I should think that's a foregone conclusion." He paused, then asked, "Will she, and you, accept Geoffrey's suit?"

She looked at Geoffrey and Adriana, hesitated, then nodded. "If she's happy, and if he wishes to hold to his offer once he's fully informed of the family's circumstances."

He arched a brow. "Circumstances?" He knew precisely what she meant—the fact she and her brood were as poor as church mice. She, however, didn't know he knew; he wondered when she'd tell him.

She met his gaze, her expression open. "There's the boys, of course, and myself—not every gentleman wants to marry into such a close family."

More fool them. He raised his brows noncommittally, and let the matter slide. Time enough to see how she reacted to his proposal once he'd made it. With her and her family in A.C.'s sights, eliminating A.C. had to be his top priority; there would be time aplenty to speak of marriage once they were safe.

More guests were arriving; her ladyship's rooms were fast filling. He remained by Alicia's side; with only two weeks to go before the start of the Season, tonnish entertainments once more resembled the melee he recalled, one through which wolves of various hues prowled.

Felicité waved from across the room, then Lady Holland stopped by to compliment Alicia on her and Adriana's gowns. The comment drew his notice; as usual, the sisters were superbly turned out . . . again he wondered

how they managed it. Then he recalled Adriana's preoc-
cupation with fashion; she was forever sketching the latest designs, or similar designs artfully modified.

He looked again at their stylish attire. Understanding
dawned; he saw Adriana in a new light.

"Good evening, Torrington—I trust you will introduce
me to your lovely companion. I do not believe I have yet
had the pleasure of making her acquaintance."

The perfectly modulated tones, still distinctly ac-
cented, jolted him from his thoughts. Lowering his gaze,
he smiled easily and bowed. "Your Grace." His gaze
passed on to the lady—yet another *grande dame* if ap-
pearances spoke true—by Her Grace of St. Ives's side.
The lady smiled with charm, and a hint of determination.

"Allow me to present my sister-in-law, Lady Horatia
Cynster." The Duchess of St. Ives smiled at him, pale
eyes alight. She waited while he bowed over Lady Horatia's hand, then continued, "*Bon*! And now you may introduce us both to this lady, if you please."

He nearly laughed; one of his mother's oldest and
dearest friends, Helena, Duchess of St. Ives, was both in-
corrigible and unstoppable. She was a petite force of nature, and woe betide any who thought to say her nay. He
turned to Alicia. She met his eyes; he smiled encouragingly. "Ladies—Mrs. Alicia Carrington, allow me to
present Helena, Duchess of St. Ives, and Lady Horatia
Cynster."

Alicia dipped into a curtsy of precisely the right degree.

Impulsively, Helena took her hand and waved her up.
"Your sister is *ravissante*, as all the ton now knows, but
you, too, will do very well I believe."

Alicia smiled, but demurred. "I seek only to establish
my sister."

Helena bent on her a look of patent incomprehension,
then glanced at her sister-in-law.

Whose lips were not straight. "My dear, a word of

advice—*you* may not seek, but the gentlemen assuredly will. Indeed"—her gaze slid teasingly to Tony—"I'm quite sure they already are."

The only way to deal with such females was to meet their jibes with polite impassivity; Tony did so. They stayed by Alicia's side, chatting about this and that, for nearly ten minutes, then moved on.

Before Alicia had time to draw breath, two other haughty matrons stopped to speak kindly. He stood by her side, suavely urbane, and thought cynical thoughts along the lines of: where Cynsters led, others followed.

He was grateful for Helena's support; he knew her well enough to know the gesture had been intentional. To be seen to be accepted by the elite of the haut ton provided a social cachet which was of itself a protection. Rumors were simply much less likely to be credited. Socially, Alicia and Adriana were gaining a status it would require a major public indiscretion to shake.

As more of the ladies on whose opinion the ton turned made a point of acknowledging Alicia, either by stopping for a few words or by exchanging nods across the room, he felt increasingly reassured on the social front.

Other fronts, however, were not so secure.

"Good evening, Mrs. Carrington."

The deep timbre of the voice sent Tony's hackles rising. He turned to see a dashingly handsome gentleman with unruly blond curls bowing over Alicia's hand; from the look on her face, she hadn't meant to surrender it. The gentleman had approached from the rear, escaping Tony's watchful eye, which endeared him to Tony even less.

The gentleman straightened and smiled at Tony. "Your servant, Torrington." Exchanging a brief nod, he looked back at Alicia. "My mama chatted with you earlier—she told me your name. I'm Harry Cynster."

His smile thawed Alicia; she returned it, relaxing. "It's a pleasure to make your acquaintance, sir."

It took Tony a few seconds to make the connections.

Harry Cynster, he of the guileless blue eyes and a distinctly predatory streak. Horses—he was a renowned whip, a legendary rider, in more than one sense, appropriately nicknamed Demon.

He was chatting with Alicia, his voice a deep, fashionable drawl, deploying the charm for which the Cynsters were notorious. "My mama dragged me along. Now we're all of us back from the wars, it seems our mothers and aunts are determined to marry us all off."

"Indeed?" Alicia returned his innocent look with one of polite scepticism. "And what of you? Doesn't marriage figure among your ambitions?"

His eyes met hers, their expression rather less innocent. "Not just yet."

The undercurrent beneath the words registered as a warning.

Harry raised a brow. "I believe that's a waltz starting up."

To her surprise, Tony reached across; his fingers closed about her hand. "Ah, yes. Thank you for reminding me, Cynster." He smiled urbanely, and drew her to him. "Mrs. Carrington has promised me this dance."

Over her head, blue eyes met black. There was something—some form of masculine challenge—behind Tony's polite mask. She glanced from one to the other, then Harry Cynster raised both brows, faint surprise in his face. "Well, well. I see." Then he grinned and saluted her. "A pity, but I wish you good riding, my dear."

Before she could reply to the strange comment, Tony whisked her away.

"Mrs. Carrington doesn't often dance at all," she informed him as he drew her into his arms.

He met her eyes. "Except with me."

With that, he whirled her into the revolving circle of dancers. The floor was crowded; he had to hold her close. So close his strength and that fascinating power he wielded, a potent blend of physical confidence and sexual prowess, wrapped about her, a seductive spell she wasn't even sure he knew he was weaving.

Then he guided her through the turns; his thigh parted hers, and all she could think of was . . .

She looked away, cleared her throat. Desperate to cool her thoughts, she struggled to find some distraction . . . "What did he mean?" Glancing up, she caught Tony's black gaze. "Harry Cynster—why wish me 'good riding'? He doesn't even know if I ride."

For an instant, Tony stared down at her; she couldn't interpret his expression. "He assumed," he eventually said. His tone seemed flat. "He's an exceptional rider himself . . ." He shrugged lightly. "Probably all he thinks of."

His lips tightened, as if he didn't want to say anything more. He looked up, steering her on; she wasn't sufficiently interested to pursue the point—whatever it was.

But that left her mind free, and her senses susceptible. Left her nerves leaping when they were jostled and he drew her protectively close, into the safe harbor of his arms. For a moment, their hips and thighs touched, brushed; when they moved on, she felt heated. She glanced up at him, praying the heat hadn't reached her cheeks, afraid it had, afraid that her eyes, too, would give her away, would hold some impression of her thoughts, reveal her sudden, unexpectedly flaring need.

His eyes met hers; darkly burning, they reflected thoughts that mirrored hers.

Abruptly, it seemed they were the only couple on the floor, the sole focus of their senses. They moved in a social vacuum charged with sensual heat, wracked with restrained passion. It flowed about them, caressed their skins. Teased, taunted, and left them yearning.

The music ended. It was a wrench to stop, to part, to step back even though both recognized they must. It was harder yet to pull back onto that other plane, to deny any expression to what was beating inside them, burgeoning between them, especially when each knew the other felt it, too. That the other wanted just as passionately, just as hungrily.

The need was there in his eyes; the answering tug was very real within her. But they had to play their parts, had to stroll easily, apparently nonchalantly back up the room, returning to take up her usual position near Adriana's circle, with him by her side.

Tony settled her hand on his sleeve, but didn't dare leave his hand over hers. He wanted her close, closer than she was; such unsatisfying skin-to-skin contact was almost painful.

Dragging in a breath, he glanced around, unseeing. How he would survive . . . one thing was certain—no more waltzes. Not until they'd danced to a different tune in a much more private setting.

Not until he'd felt her skin against his, naked body to naked body.

After . . . he assumed—fervently prayed—that the pressures that seemed to be building inside him, seething volcano-like from somewhere deep within, those emotions he accepted but didn't wish to examine, would ease. That he wouldn't feel like snarling when men like Harry Cynster hove near, that he'd be able to waltz with her without remembering . . . and imagining . . .

Without wanting to behave like some primitive caveman and toss her over his shoulder, seize her, and cart her away. And . . .

He had to stop thinking about it, or he'd go mad.

At the end of the ball, he and Geoffrey accompanied the sisters into the front hall. Adriana gave Geoffrey her hand; he bowed over it, whispered something Tony didn't catch, then took his leave of Alicia, who, distracted, had missed that little interaction entirely. With a nod to him, Geoffrey left.

Alicia turned to him, held out her hand. "Thank you for your company."

He looked at her, took her hand, and tucked it in his arm. "I'll escort you home."

She blinked, but allowed him to draw her close. "You don't need to do that."

He looked down at her, then softly stated, "I do." After a moment, his chest swelled; he looked ahead. "Aside from all else, you're in my custody."

She frowned. "I thought you just said that for the benefit of the Watch."

A footman came to tell them their carriage was waiting. Tony steered her onto the steps, then leaned close, and murmured, "I said it for my benefit, not theirs."

TWELVE

AFTER THAT COMMENT . . . ALICIA SPENT THE ENTIRE journey home in a fever of speculation. The waltz had left her nerves, her senses, primed and flickering; rocking over the cobbles in the dark with Tony beside her, his hard thigh riding alongside hers, did nothing to calm them.

Last night—or had it been this morning? Whichever, there was no doubt in her mind that there were no further halts along their road. Yet she hadn't until now seriously considered, hadn't asked herself the fateful question.

If it came to that, would she?

If the moment arose and she had the chance, would she take it? Or try to the last to avoid it?

A small voice whispered . . . how did one avoid the inevitable?

By the time they reached Waverton Street, and he handed her down, she felt as tense as a bowstring. Adriana followed her up the steps. Tony brought up the rear. Maggs opened the door and held it wide; Alicia stepped back and let Adriana precede her. Tony, she noticed, cast comprehensive glances up and down the street as he climbed to the door.

She entered; he followed.

Adriana, no doubt thinking thoughts of Geoffrey Manningham, drifted upstairs without so much as a good night. Uncertain if she should be grateful or irritated, Alicia nodded to Maggs. "Thank you. You may retire. I'll see his lordship out."

Maggs bowed and lumbered away.

She watched the green baize door swing shut behind him.

Leaving her alone with the man who would be her lover.

Slowly, she turned . . . and found herself alone.

Tony had gone. The drawing-room door stood open.

Frowning, she went to the threshold; a dark shadow in the unlighted room, he was standing before the long windows. Puzzled, she went in. "What are you doing?"

"Checking these locks."

The windows gave onto the narrow area separating the house from the street. "Jenkins checks the locks every night, and I suspect Maggs does, too."

"Very likely."

Halting in the middle of the floor, she folded her arms beneath her breasts. "Do you approve?"

"No." Tony turned from the windows, through the dimness studied her. "But they'll do." For now.

Until he could think of some way to improve the defenses he felt compelled to erect about her. He needed to know she was safe. He wanted her his. In the circumstances, satisfaction would—indeed needed to—come in that order.

The reality had come crashing down on him as he'd sat beside her in the carriage and sensed the flickering and skittering of her nerves, her growing agitation. After all she'd been through in the last two days, what woman wouldn't be on edge?

This was not the time to press his suit, regardless of the strength of their passions. Aside from all else, he hadn't forgotten her earlier mistake over him expecting her to be grateful. Hadn't forgotten Ruskin's diabolical scheme—"gratitude" demanded as payment for protection.

Now *he* was her protector, in more ways, more arenas,

more effectively established than Ruskin had ever stood to be.

No. He wanted her safe, wanted her to know she was safe, and had no need to thank him further. No need to come to him out of gratitude.

He didn't want her in that way, didn't want her to come to him with any complicating emotions between them. He wanted much more from her.

When she came to him, it had to be because she wanted to, because she wanted him as he wanted her.

That simple—that powerful.

To gain all he wanted, to achieve all his goals, that point was critical. He didn't question why that was so, but knew absolutely that it was.

She was watching him, puzzled, increasingly tense.

He crossed the room to her. She watched him approach, but didn't move. Either toward him, or away.

Halting in front of her, through the shadows he looked down on her upturned face. Slowly raising both hands, he feathered his fingers along her delicate jaw, then cupped her face, framed it as he tipped it up, bent his head, and set his lips to hers.

She opened to him readily; she kissed him back, not urging him on, yet not denying their mutual hunger. Her hands rose, her soft palms lightly clasping the backs of his, a subtle, accepting, very feminine caress.

For long moments, they stood in the cool dark, their bodies inches apart and, mouths melding, giving and taking, drank each other in.

The distant chiming of a clock broke the silence, reminding him of time passing. Reluctantly, he drew back; equally reluctantly, or so it seemed, she let him.

Lifting his head, he looked into her face, into the soft pools of her eyes. He couldn't read their expression, but he didn't need visual cues to know that she was as aware as he, as achingly, tormentingly conscious of the sensual whirlpool that was swirling about them, of the sheer strength of the attraction that had grown into so much more between them.

He lowered his hands, had to clear his throat to find his voice. "I'll leave you then." Despite his determination, there was the tiniest hint of a question in the words.

She drew a deep breath, breasts rising, and nodded. "Yes. And . . . thank you for all you've done."

No words could have better convinced him he should go. He turned to the door. She followed. He stood back to let her step over the threshold; as she did, a heavy knock fell on the front door.

They both froze, then he reached forward and moved her to the side. "Let me see who it is."

She made no demur but stood quietly where he'd set her while he crossed the hall and opened the door.

One of his footmen looked up at him. The man smiled in relief. "My lord." He bowed and offered a letter. "This came from the Bastion Club with instructions it be delivered to your hand as soon as possible."

Tony took the missive. "Thank you, Cox." A quick glance at the seal informed him it was from Jack Warnefleet. "Good work. I'll take care of this. You may go."

Cox bowed and retreated. His footsteps faded along the street as Tony shut the door.

"What is it? News?" Alicia came to his side.

"Very likely." Breaking the seal, Tony spread the single sheet. Took in the single sentence with a glance.

"What? Who is it from?"

"Jack Warnefleet. He's been digging into Ruskin's county connections." Folding the note, Tony slipped it into his pocket. "He's returned with some news he thinks I should hear immediately."

Jack had written that he'd uncovered something significant and suggested Tony meet him at the Bastion Club "pdq." Pretty damn quick. Between such as they, that meant with all speed—urgent.

The possibility that they'd finally got some handle on

A. C. sent anticipation, a keen sense of the hunt, rising through him. "He's at the club—I'll go there now."

He glanced at Alicia. His welling excitement had communicated itself to her; eyes wide, she reached for the doorknob. "You will tell me if you learn anything major, won't you? Like who A. C. is?"

Already speculating on what avenues the new information might open up, he nodded as she opened the door. "Yes, of course."

The words were vague, the nod absentminded; Alicia stifled an oath. She caught his arm and tugged until he looked at her, actually focused on her. "Promise me you'll come and tell me the instant you learn anything significant."

She held his gaze, prepared to be belligerent if he turned evasive.

Instead, he looked into her eyes, then smiled. "I promise."

He ducked his head, kissed her swiftly, then slipped out of the door she was holding half-open. "Lock it—shoot the bolts. Now."

Grimacing at him, she shut the door, dutifully reached up, and shot the bolt above her head, then bent and slid home the other near the floor. Straightening, she listened. An instant later, she heard his footsteps descending the steps, then he strode away down the street.

Half an hour later, in the shrouded darkness of her bed, she sat up, pummeled her pillow, then flung herself down on it again.

She hadn't wanted to take the final step.

She reminded herself of that fact in inwardly strident tones—to no avail. They didn't impinge on her restless moodiness in the slightest, didn't alleviate the deflated feeling dragging at her—as if she'd been on the brink of receiving some wonderful gift, but it had been delayed at the last moment.

The feeling was nonsensical. Illogical. But very real.

She'd spent the entire evening on tenterhooks, increasingly sharp ones, worrying over what would unfold between them next, worrying that she knew all too well, that Tony would press ahead, engineer the moment, and . . .

That she felt so ungrateful for his forebearance was damning indeed.

He'd clearly decided to hold back; she should grasp the time he'd granted her to concentrate on those things that were most important—Adriana and their plan and the boys. Closing her eyes, settling her head on the down-filled pillow, she willed herself to keep her mind on such matters, on the things that had always dominated her life.

Determinedly, she relaxed.

Within seconds her mind had roamed, to a pair of hot black eyes, to the feel of his lips, firm and pliant on hers, to the sensations of his hands stroking, caressing, to the intimate probing of his tongue . . .

Sleep crept into her mind and swept her into her dreams.

She woke sometime later to a preemptory knock on her bedchamber door. She couldn't imagine . . . she stared through the shadows at the door.

It opened. Tony walked—stalked—in. He scanned the room and located her in the bed; even through the dark his gaze pinned her. Then he turned and quietly closed the door.

She struggled up onto her elbows, struggled to shake off the cobwebs of sleep and make her mind work. What? Why? Had something serious occurred?

Tony's calmly deliberate movements made that last seem unlikely. He'd crossed the room. Without meeting her eyes, he turned and sat on the end of her bed. It bowed beneath his weight.

She stared at his back, then wriggled and sat up, hugging the coverlet to her breasts. She'd caught only a glimpse of his face, but her eyes were adjusted to the darkness; it had seemed somewhat harder than usual, the harsh features sharply delineated, the angular planes set like granite.

He didn't turn around, but bent forward.

She frowned. "What's going on?"

Her whisper floated out through the room.

He didn't immediately answer; instead, she heard a thud.

Realized with a sudden clenching of nerves that he'd pulled off one shoe.

He shifted and reached for the other. "You made me promise to come and tell you the instant I learned anything significant."

Those had been her exact words. She shifted, wondering . . . "Yes? So what—" A sudden thought took precedence over everything else. She stared at the back of his head. "How did you get in?"

His second shoe hit the floor. "I slipped the lock on the drawing-room window. But you needn't worry." He stood and faced the bed. "I locked it again."

That wasn't what was worrying her.

Eyes widening, mouth drying, she watched as he shrugged out of his coat, glanced around, then flung it over her dressing table stool. Then his fingers rose to his cravat, smoothly tugging the ends free.

"Ah . . ." Good heavens! She had to . . . had to . . . she swallowed. "Did you learn something from your friend?"

She had to distract him.

"From Jack?" His tone was flat, his accents clipped. "Yes. As it happened, I learned quite a lot."

He had the cravat undone; dragging it free, he flung it on his coat, then his fingers went to the buttons of his shirt.

It was getting harder and harder to think, to swallow,

even to breathe. Had the moment really come? Just like that, without warning?

Panic inched higher and higher.

She clutched the edge of the coverlet. "So . . . what did you learn?" She tried to recall what had passed between them earlier—had she inadvertently issued some sexual invitation?

"Jack investigated Ruskin's background. In Bledington." Tony followed the line of buttons down, then glanced at her, yanked the tails from his waistband and stripped off the shirt. His eyes had adjusted; he could see how wide hers were. Wondered, cynically, intently, just how far she'd go before she broke.

He tossed the shirt aside, set his hands to his waistband, his fingers on the buttons of the flap. "Ruskin's estate amounts to little more than a few fields—he inherited his liking for gambling from his father. The income he enjoyed could not in any way derive from his ancestral acres." He slipped the buttons free. "If anything, the upkeep of the house in which his mother and sister live was a drain on his purse."

She didn't shift, made absolutely no sound as he removed his trousers and sent them to join the rest of his clothes. His determination hardened; it was an effort to keep his emotions—the mix of incredulity, anger, and hurt, and so much more he didn't want to examine—from his face.

Clothed only in shadows, he turned to the bed. Silent-footed, he prowled down its side; it was a large, canopied affair. He was aroused but, apparently stunned, she was following his face; she'd yet to look down.

She moistened her already parted lips. "Ah . . . so . . . what does that . . ." She made a valiant and quite visible attempt to focus her mind. "I mean, why is that important?"

"It's not." He heard the harshness in his tone. Watching her closely, primed to smother a shriek, he reached for the covers. "But there were other facts Jack discovered that were far more startling."

Her knuckles turned white as he grasped the covers, but when, jaw setting, he lifted them, her grip eased; the silky quilt slid through her fingers as he raised the sheets.

"Oh. I see . . ."

She was looking straight at him, but he would have sworn she wasn't seeing him. Her tone seemed distant, as if she was thinking of other things.

His temper, held in tight check until then, flared. He slid onto the bed, dropped the covers, and turned to her.

His plan—what plan he had—was to force her into admitting the truth, the truth Jack had uncovered. The truth she'd so artfully kept from him, her protector and would-be husband. He'd intended to shock her, to use that truth itself to chastise her, to embarrass her into admitting all; he'd imagined she'd succumb to virginal fluster long before now.

Still convinced she would, that at any second she'd panic, call a halt, and admit all, he reached for her. Closing his hands about her slender shoulders, feeling the fine silk of her nightgown slide over the soft skin beneath, he drew her to him.

Slowly, steadily, totally deliberately.

He looked into her face.

No hint of fear, of panic—of anything remotely resembling the frantic, embarrassed fluster he expected—showed in her features.

Quite the opposite. She was finally looking at him, studying his eyes, his face; her expression seemed almost serene, almost glowing.

Her eyes searched; her hands slid up to frame his face, then slid farther, her arms twining about his neck.

Abruptly losing patience, he pulled her to him.

Fully against him, body to body with only a fine layer of silk between.

He hadn't counted on the shock affecting him.

For one instant, the world about them rocked, quaked, then settled not quite as it had been before. His lungs seized; every muscle tensed; every nerve came alive.

Impulses—powerful, primitive, and sure—rose and rushed through him; his head spun.

He heard her breath catch. He looked into her eyes. Saw something like wonder in her expression.

Their gazes touched, held.

For three long heartbeats, time stood still.

Between them, heat welled. Flames ignited, greedily grew.

Her gaze dropped to his lips.

Beyond his control, his dropped to hers.

Who made the first move he didn't know. She lifted her head as he bent his. Their lips met.

And the fires leapt, then raged.

She pressed against him and he was lost. She opened her mouth to him, and he drowned in her bounty.

He sank against her, into her. In no way passive, she met him, her body firm and supple against his, her hands in his hair, her tongue dueling with his, inciting, inviting.

Wanting.

His control was gone before he even saw the threat. Vaporized by a need the like of which he'd never known. She was with him in want, in desire, in passion; her flagrant encouragement left no room for doubt.

Instinct claimed him, primal and unfettered. Unchained after being so long denied. He had to have her, all of her, had to have her beneath him, claimed and incontrovertibly his. It wasn't lust that drove him, but something deeper, more powerful, something that dwelled in his heart and his soul and paid scant attention to the dictates of his brain.

Within a minute, the kiss turned ravenous; his hands hardened, fingers kneading possessively.

Alicia sensed the change in him and exulted. Her own needs unleashed for the first time in her life, she wanted all he did, wanted to experience all he and she together could be.

She'd made her decision. Or had had it made for her; she wasn't sure, but either way she felt certain, confident beyond doubt, that this was meant to be.

The moment he'd turned to her, naked, aroused, yet somehow to her senses still unthreatening, she'd known. To her eyes, he was beautiful, incomparably male yet totally safe; never would she find another man she could trust as she trusted him—never with another would she feel the same certainty that she could go forward without fear, that she could surrender to him yet not lose herself.

That his victory would also be hers. That in his arms she would always be safe. Protected. Cared for.

Worshipped.

Despite the urgency that coursed through him, that hardened his body and shredded the veil of elegance that usually disguised his strength, that last was still apparent. His every touch was blatantly sexual, not rough but driven, forceful, demanding, even predatory, yet still each caress had only one aim, to awaken her senses and heighten their delight.

Pleasure was his currency, first and last.

She accepted it, and made it hers.

She sent her hands roaming, fingers flexing over his bare shoulders, glorying in the sculpted strength tensing beneath her fingertips, in the heavy resilence of his flesh, so unlike her own. He had her locked to him, lips devouring as his hands evocatively kneaded her bottom, his erection a hot heavy ridge impressed against her belly. She couldn't push back enough to press her hands between them; denied the chance of exploring his chest, she ran one hand down his back, reaching boldly for his waist, his hip, the subtle flare of his buttock. That was all she could reach, yet she sensed his pleasure in her touch; his lips clung to hers, distracted, then his attention returned to her in full measure, hotter, harder, more urgent.

Encouraged, determined, she pushed back, and he let her, shifting over her so his weight pinned her to the bed. His legs tangling with hers, he released her bottom; his hands rose to her breasts.

Their kiss continued unabated, mouths melding in a feast of mutual need, their hunger steadily growing, the heat between them swelling, escalating, this time out of control. Neither sought to rein it in; neither even considered it. By mutual accord, they let it rage, and rage it did.

He'd touched all of her before, had had her naked beneath his hands before, yet this was different. Her senses splintered, avidly trying to take in every new sensation. From the crisp, crinkly rasp of his hair-dusted legs against the fine skin of hers, to the unexpected weight of him above her, to the promise in the hard hot length now pressed to her hip, all was new, fascinating and enthralling.

As was the compulsion within her, building and swelling with every beat of her heart, with every knowing sweep of his hard hands. Without pause, he pushed her on and she went gladly, matching him, meeting him, even, when she sensed him struggling to regain control, goading him.

Her hands had been resting on his shoulders; she swept them down, pressing her palms to his hot flesh, fingers searching, exploring, as wantonly sensual as he in learning him, in tracing the muscle bands, letting her fingers tangle in the mat of hair across them, finding a flat nipple beneath the pelt and tweaking it to a tight bud.

His hips shifted against her. Emboldened, she sent her hands lower, caressing the taut, ribbed muscles of his abdomen, then reaching lower yet.

Until she found him, hot, heavy, velvet over steel.

He'd taken his weight on his arms, allowing her her way. She took full advantage and traced, caressed, then took him between her palms almost reverently, amazed, enthralled by the feel of him, the weight, the length and thickness, the baby-fine skin so obviously shatteringly sensitive. She could feel his reaction to her every touch, feel the flickering of his locked muscles, the heat that flowed through their kiss, welling and swelling with every sweep of her fingertips, every gentle squeeze.

Abruptly he broke from the kiss, and rolled onto his back, taking her with him. The sudden change in position momentarily distracted her; while she was reassessing, her attention deflected by the feel of his body now beneath hers, he reached down.

He caught her nightgown, gathered the skirts until he held them bunched at her thighs.

What he intended burst into her mind. She looked down, met his black eyes.

And suddenly they were themselves again, sane, rational—yet no longer who they had been. They'd moved on, traveled the very last stage of their road, and arrived at their destination.

It was different from what she'd imagined.

He said nothing, simply waited, his need in his eyes, in his body taut and tense beneath her.

Within her, she felt her own need swell, recognized it as similar yet subtly different from his. Knew in her soul that their needs were complementary—they would be assuaged by the one act, sated and fulfilled in the same moment.

Their gazes remained locked, their lips mere inches apart, their breaths, panting and ragged, softly filling the silence between them.

She found it was impossible to smile. Instead, she shifted; fingers tangling in the silk, she twitched it. Upward.

He didn't wait for more, but drew the gown up, past her hips, past her waist, tugging it up over her breasts, waiting while she disentangled her arms before dragging it free and flinging it away.

And she was naked in his arms.

He reached for her; giving her no time to think, to dwell on the intimacy, the vulnerability, he drew her lips down, took them, took her mouth, and dragged her back into the flames, into the furnace of their mutual need.

His hands were everywhere, claiming anew, drowning her in glorious sensation.

The flames roared; heat engulfed them.

She was suddenly sure her skin was on fire; as for him, he burned. His hands felt like brands, spreading liquid flame as he caressed, boldly possessed. Then he rolled again and pinned her beneath him.

He spread her thighs and settled between; braced on one arm, he hovered above her, his lips feeding from hers, his hips holding her down as with his other hand he reached between them, and found her.

She was swollen, wet and wanting, all but aching with the need to feel him within her. She knew it, didn't try to deny it, hide from it.

His fingers briefly played, then penetrated her. Once, twice, delved deep, then withdrew.

He shifted, his hips pressing between hers, then she felt the broad head of his erection part her swollen flesh, sliding easily between the folds to press in.

He stopped. Bracing both arms he lifted above her, simultaneously breaking their kiss.

With an effort, she managed to lift her lids; panting, barely sentient, she raised her eyes to his.

He trapped her gaze. Held it.

Desire wrapped them in a cocoon of flames; her body felt molten, yet achingly empty. The need to have him fill that emptiness thrummed, a steady, compulsive beat in her blood. Eyes locked with his, her every sense was focused on where they would join, on the soft swollen flesh between her thighs, on the hard heavy rod of his erection.

He pressed in. He kept his eyes on hers, holding her with him as slowly, steadily, he thrust in, and filled her. Not in a rush, but inch by slow inch. She felt her body give, stretch, felt every inch of his thickness as he pressed deeper, as her body struggled to adjust to the invasion.

The difficult moment came, as she'd known it would. She tried to cling to calm, tried to find some ease by breathing yet more rapidly, but the pressure and the pain steadily built, built . . . she would have shut her eyes, turned her head away, but his black gaze held her trapped.

Held her through it all, steady as a rock, a primitive promise beckoning as fraction by fraction he pressed her farther . . .

Her body tensed, arching under his, and still he held her with his eyes. And sank deeper.

The pressure gave.

In one sharp flash of pain it was gone, leaving her gasping, breasts rising and falling, yet still locked in his black gaze.

She sensed rather than saw his satisfaction. He halted, held still for some moments as she struggled to recover, to assimilate the change; he watched her, waiting. He seemed to know the exact moment the burning sensation faded, and the vise about her lungs eased and fear left her; he resumed his invasion, still slow, yet more assured.

Tony watched her, held her eyes, drank in every nuance of her response as he claimed her, filled her, and made her his. He'd surrendered to instinct long ago, in that first heated moment when his need had broadsided him. Subsequently, no thought had been required. He knew what he wanted, what he needed. Ruthlessly he took it—and her.

And part of that taking was this, this slow, excruciatingly complete first invasion. A branding, a declaration, an acceptance.

A sharing.

He'd needed to know, to be with her, to appreciate what she felt, know how she reacted. He'd always noted the responses of the women he bedded, yet this time he was not simply cataloging, gauging a reaction in order to capitalize on it. This time, he was immersed in the moment, experiencing both her pain and that glorious rush of release, of sexual interlocking, with her.

Experiencing, through it all, a deeper sense of connection, a deeper meaning beneath the sensations, beneath the physical pleasure.

He continued to press in; her body continued to give, to enclose him, until finally he was fully seated within her. Still holding her gaze, he withdrew halfway, then pressed in again, watching for any sign of discomfort.

Seeing none, feeling her body ease beneath him, her scalding sheath clasping tightly about him, he bent his head.

She raised hers, offered her lips.

He took them, claimed them. Without further direction, let his body do as it wished, as it had to do, and claim her.

The tiny fragment of his mind that remained lucid fully expected a fast and furious engagement. Instead, he rode her slowly; even now, even freed from all restraint, his body remained attuned to hers, gauging without conscious direction, responding to each quickening clasp of her sheath, to each restless shifting of her thighs, ultimately to the tentative rocking of her hips as she learned to match him and meet him.

Their progression was slow, measured, deliberate— and all-consuming. As she took him in, and his body followed hers, it occurred to him to wonder who had claimed whom. Who was leading, who was in charge . . .

Not him, and it couldn't be her.

Never had he been so totally absorbed, so totally submerged in the moment, so totally aware. Not just of the woman beneath him, but of his own body, his own pleasure. Hers heightened his; like a series of mirrors, reflecting back over and again, each tiny gasp, each soft moan, every sudden tensing of her fingers on his skin, washed over him and welled, swelled the exquisite tightness in his groin, fueled the tension driving him.

She'd tugged him down so his body met hers; her breasts were trapped beneath the heavy muscles of his chest, the rough hair abrading their sensitive skin, her nipples tight crests, their arousing pressure shifting with every deep thrust. Their skins were aflame, sheened, slick; her hands roamed his back, sweeping over the long planes, increasingly urgent. Their stomachs met, his hips locked in the cradle of hers, her thighs widespread, knees clasping his flanks, calves tangling with his.

Their mouths had fused, lips still greedily clinging, a connection that completed some circuit, that kept them immersed, locked in the compulsion that drove them, wholly given over to it.

Surrender came with a sudden quickening, first of her body, then of his. He was so deeply buried inside her, she took him with her; release swept them both in a long, glorious golden wave. Locked together, they rode it, let it take them and fling them high into the heavens, into the realms of pleasured bliss.

He emptied himself into her, felt her womb contract powerfully, holding him, accepting, taking.

The wave receded.

They drifted slowly to earth, their bodies eased, all tension gone, boneless in the aftermath. Their lips parted; breaths mingling, they clung, eyes still closed, savoring the closeness.

He felt her arms steal around him, then rest, lax. With the last of his strength, he slumped to the side, trying not to crush her as oblivion, deeper than he'd ever known it, caught him and drew him down.

THIRTEEN

REMARKABLE.

It had been that and more; an hour later, Tony still couldn't rationalize how very different the interlude had been, that she, a rank novice, had been the one woman in all his years to shatter his control, capture him utterly, forcing him to rely wholly on instinct, thus taking him to . . . wherever they had been.

A plane on which the pleasure defied all description, in which the physical had been a golden echo of something else.

An unworldly, unearthly, otherworldly place.

In all his years, through all his experience, he'd never even imagined such an exchange could be, or that such a place existed.

On rousing, he'd disengaged and lifted from her. Lying on his back, he'd gathered her to him; unresisting, she'd let him settle her against him, within the circle of his arms, her head on his shoulder.

The covers lay warm about them. Night lay like a blanket over the house; the moonlight had strengthened. He glanced at her face; she still seemed sunk in pleasured oblivion. Lifting his hand, he tentatively touched her hair. When she didn't stir, he set his palm to the silky tresses, smoothing them, drinking in the feel of their warm softness.

Lying back, he looked up at the canopy; slowly stroking, he tried to think.

The gentle, rhythmic comforting caress gradually drew Alicia back into the world. Warmth held her; pleasure still lay heavy in her veins. A sense of safety she'd never before known, so deep, so solid its existence was beyond question, wrapped her about, supporting, reassuring.

She sighed, and her wits returned.

And she remembered. Everything. All of it.

Every moment that had passed since he'd drawn her into his arms, every touch, every blissful second.

His arms remained around her, steel bands cradling her, gently enough, yet still overtly possessive.

The stroking slowed; his hand stilled. He knew she was awake.

Opening her eyes, she shifted her head and looked up. Met his gaze. Excruciatingly aware that she lay naked in his arms, that he was naked, too. Aware that their limbs were tangled, that they lay slumped together in a warm cocoon of rumpled sheets.

His black eyes held hers; it was impossible to read anything from them or his face. "When did you intend to tell me?" His tone was even, uninflected.

She searched his face, remembered . . . refocused on his eyes. "You knew."

He'd known she was—had been—a virgin; he'd watched for every second as he'd taken her virginity, as she'd willingly yielded it to him.

He looked down, at her hand spread on his bare chest. He took it in his; his long fingers toyed with hers. "There wasn't any trace of any Carrington anywhere near Chipping Norton. No entry in the parish records. No one of that name known at any of the stables or inns. Yet many knew the Misses Pevensey—*both* Misses Pevensey."

He glanced up; his eyes were sharp as they found hers. "I would have stopped if you'd wanted me to."

A statement, but there was a question buried in it. She held his gaze steadily. "I know."

She let the two words stand alone, a simple acknowledgment of the decision she'd made. She'd gone to him willingly; she wasn't about to pretend otherwise.

What was done was done; she was his mistress now.

She frowned. "How did you learn . . . ?" The truth struck her, left her horrified. "Your friend?"

Incipient panic flared in her eyes; Tony closed his hand over hers. "There's no need to worry." He hesitated, then explained, "Jack Warnefleet—Lord Warnefleet—investigated Ruskin for me. He also asked after your supposed husband, Alfred Carrington. Another A. C."

Understanding lit her eyes; he added, "We can rely on Jack's absolute discretion."

She studied his face, his eyes; a long moment passed, then she asked, "That was the urgent information he sent you the note about last night?"

He felt his jaw set. "He knew I'd want to know."

She blinked, then her lashes veiled her eyes. "I couldn't tell you." A heartbeat passed, then she added, "I couldn't risk it."

There was no hint of excuse in her tone; she was stating a fact, at least as she'd seen it.

He drew in a breath, lifted his gaze to look, unseeing, across the room. Given all he now knew of her, of the plan she and, he assumed, Adriana had concocted, of her commitment to her sister and even more to her brothers, he couldn't fault her; any hint that she wasn't the widow the ton thought her would, even now, result in complete and unmitigated disaster. Any chance of Adriana making a good match would disappear. They'd be social pariahs, expelled from society, forced to retreat to their cottage in the country to scrape a precarious existence for themselves and their brothers.

Trusting him with the truth . . .

He suddenly realized she had. She just hadn't told him in words.

His silence had bothered her; she tried to edge away. Even before he'd thought, his arms were tightening, holding her to him. "No—I know." She stilled; he drew in another breath, glanced down at her bent head. "I understand."

When she didn't look up, he bent close, placed a kiss on her crown, hesitated, then gently nudged her head.

Alicia looked up, into black eyes that promised far more than understanding. Safety, protection from both the finite and the nebulous dangers of the world, but more precious, at least to her, was the strange and novel relief of having someone with whom she could share her thoughts, her concerns, her schemes. Someone who did indeed understand.

His eyes searched hers; as if to confirm her reading, he asked, "Tell me how this all came about—you, your sister, your plan."

It wasn't a command, but a request, one she saw no reason to refuse; better he know all than half the story. She settled against him, felt his arms close tighter. "It started when Papa died."

She told him everything, even explaining her connection with Mr. King. Although he said not a word, she could tell he didn't approve, yet still he accepted, and made no protest. She was surprised when he questioned her about their gowns, and gave mute thanks not everyone was so acute.

When she in turn questioned why he'd investigated her supposed husband, he explained his thoughts of some other Carrington being involved. The comment led them deeper into the possibilities surrounding Ruskin; they discussed, tossed thoughts back and forth, argued likelihoods—the sort of exchange she'd never indulged in with anyone else.

Gradually, the silences lengthened. Blissfully warm, totally comfortable, she lay in his arms and listened to his heart beat steadily beneath her cheek. The covers lay over them; she still lay half-atop him, stretched alongside, her legs tangled with his, her hand spread over his chest. One muscled arm was wrapped around her, his hand heavy over her waist.

She should, she felt sure, feel some degree of fluster, of maidenly, feminine embarrassment over their naked state, let alone all that had led to it. Instead, the intimacy was addictive, a strange sense of closeness, of inexpressible comfort, of a simple rightness she was loath to shake.

He glanced down at her, then she felt his lips brush her hair.

"Go to sleep."

The whisper floated down to her. Turning her head, she looked up, met his eyes. Then she lifted her head, and touched her lips to his. He met them, returned her kiss, but gently. Briefly. Softly sighing, she drew back. Settling more definitely on his chest, spreading her hand over his side, she relaxed, and closed her eyes.

He merged with her dreams in the darkness before dawn. For long moments as he caressed her, sending sensation after sensation spiraling through her, each exquisite touch driving her higher into the clouds, she wasn't certain where her dreams ended and reality began.

Then he moved over her, spread her thighs wide, and slowly filled her.

She woke as he thrust deep and embedded himself within her, to the sensation of him hard and strong and rigid within her, of her body clamping tightly, joyously, about him, her arms reaching out to embrace him—and knew her life would never return to what it had been.

That was her first and last lucid thought; the instant he started to move within her, her wits deserted her, submerged beneath her clamorous senses, greedy for him, for what was to come.

He stayed close this time, his body moving over hers, murmuring gruff encouragement as she shifted beneath him, tilting her hips, adjusting to the rhythm and the depth of his penetration.

Her body seemed to know what to do; she let herself flow with the tide, gave herself up to the powerful surging rhythm, let it sweep her away into a whirlpool of shattering sensation. He kept them there, held them there, each rocking thrust swirling the vortex higher, tighter. Their lips found each other's without conscious direction, and then they were there again, in the heart of the flames, the center of the furnace.

The heat cindered all barriers, locked them together, desire flowing molten through them, between them. For one glorious instant, she lost touch with the world, couldn't tell where she ended and he began, knew only that they were together, one in thought, in mind, in deed.

Their lips clung, their hands grasped, slipped, gripped; their bodies strove to reach the elusive peak, just beyond their reach.

Then they broke through the clouds and the sunburst took them. The glory fractured, shattered, and poured through them. Rained down on them. Drove them at the last, gasping and shuddering, onto some far-distant shore.

They lay tangled, entwined, struggling for breath, the last shards of ecstasy still shivering through them. Heated, swollen, their lips touched, brushed, then parted. In the instant before she surrendered to beckoning oblivion, one simple truth floated through her mind.

Each time he came to her, each time they joined, left her one step further from the woman she had been.

Tony woke as dawn began to streak the sky. Satiation lay heavy upon him; he didn't want to move.

Eyes closed, he lay still, savoring the sensation of Alicia's soft curves pressed to his side; he consciously considered leaping a few steps and simply staying where he was.

Reluctantly, he accepted that might be going too far, too fast. Although where they were headed was perfectly clear, taking women for granted was never wise.

Stifling a sigh, he disengaged, trying not to disturb her. She murmured sleepily and clutched at his chest, but then slid back into slumber. Gently lifting her hand from him, he slid out of the bed. She snuggled down in the warm depression where he'd lain. The sight of her burrowed there made him smile.

Quickly, he dressed, dropped a light, fleeting kiss on her forehead, then slipped out of her room, and out of the house.

"Are you all right, Miss Alicia?"

Alicia woke with a start, realized it was Fitchett who had spoken. "Ah . . . yes." A lie, but she could hardly explain. "I, ah, overslept."

Struggling to sit up, her gaze fell on the rumpled disaster of her bed. Thank heavens Fitchett was outside the door.

"Aye, well, we was wondering, seeing as you hadn't rung. I'll bring up your water if you're ready for it."

Alicia glanced at the window. A shaft of bright sunlight lanced into the room. Dear God, what was the time? "Yes, thank you. I'm getting up now."

Fitchett lumbered off. Dragooning her wits and her still too-lax muscles into action, Alicia flung back the covers and got out of bed.

By the time Fitchett arrived with her water, she'd stripped the bed; there'd been no possibility of putting things right enough to pass muster. When Fitchett stared at the pile of bedclothes, she airily waved. "I decided to change the sheets. It's only a day or so early."

To her relief, Fitchett merely humphed.

She washed and dressed quickly, then hurried downstairs to discover bedlam reigning at the breakfast table. Adriana had done her best, but she lacked Alicia's authority; called to order, the boys assumed their most angelic expressions and innocently resumed a more civilized rapport.

"I slept in," she replied to Adriana's questioning look. It wasn't a good excuse—she never slept in—but it was all she could think of. Reaching for the teapot, she poured herself a cup. She sipped, relaxed, then realized how hungry she was. Ravenous, in fact.

Jenkins came in, and they discussed the boys' lessons for the coming week while she polished off a mound of kedgeree.

When Jenkins departed, the boys in tow, Adriana frowned at her. "Well, you're obviously not ailing—there's nothing wrong with your appetite."

She waved the piece of toast she'd started nibbling and reached for her cup. "I just slept longer than usual."

Adriana pushed back her chair and rose. "You must have been dreaming."

Recollection flashed across Alicia's mind; she nearly choked on her tea.

"Are we still going to Mr. Pennecuik's warehouse today?"

She nodded. "Yes—we must if we're to make those new gowns." Setting down her cup, she picked up her toast. "In twenty minutes—I have to check with Cook before we go."

The rest of the day passed in the usual busy fashion; she hadn't before noticed how little personal time she had, private time alone in which to think. If she and Adriana weren't out, attending some function or event, then some member of the household would want to speak with her, or her brothers needed supervising, or . . .

She needed to think—she knew she did, knew she

ought to stop and consider, and get her mind in order for
when next she met Tony. She'd taken a major step, turned
a hugely significant corner—one she definitely shouldn't
have turned, perhaps, but she'd willingly taken that road;
it was clearly imperative she stop and take stock.

All that seemed obvious, yet when she finally found
herself alone in her room, bathing, then dressing for the
evening, she discovered her mind had a will of its own.

When it came to all that had passed in the night, and in
the small hours of the morning, while she could recall
and relive every moment, every detail, her mind flatly refused to go any further. It was as if some dominant part of
her brain had decided those events were in some way
sacrosant, that they stood as they were and needed no further examination. No dissection, no analysis, no clarifica-
tion. They simply were.

It was, indeed, as if she'd stood at a crossroads, and
now she'd gone around the corner, she couldn't see where
she'd been. Which left her facing forward along a road
she'd never imagined traveling.

Putting the last touches to her coiffure, she paused and
studied herself in the mirror. She still looked the same,
yet . . . was it something in her eyes, or maybe in her pos-
ture, the way she stood, that assured her, at least, that she
was no longer the same woman?

She had changed, and she didn't regret it. There was
little in this world for which she'd trade so much as a
minute of the time she'd spent in Tony's arms.

Indeed, there was no point looking back. She was his
mistress now.

And if she didn't know what that new status would
bring, or how to cope, she'd just have to learn.

She looked into her eyes for a moment longer, then let
her gaze run down the sleek lines of the deep purple silk
gown Adriana had designed and she and Fitchett had created. The heart-shaped neckline showcased her breasts

without being obvious; the cut below the high waist made the most of her slim hips and long legs, while the small off-the-shoulder sleeves left the graceful curves of her shoulders quite bare.

Turning, she picked up her shawl and reticule, then headed for the door. Luckily, she learned quickly.

The cacophonous sound of the ton in full flight rose to greet Tony as he paused at the top of the steps leading down into Lady Hamilton's ballroom. Her ladyship's rout was one of the events traditionally held in the week before the Season began; society's elite were almost to a man foregathered in town—everyone who was anyone would be present.

Looking down on the sea of bright gowns, of sheening curls, of jewels winking in the light thrown by the chandeliers, he scanned the throng, relieved when he located Alicia standing by the side of the room, Adriana's court, some steps in front of her, partially screening her. Relief died, however, when closer inspection revealed that three of the gentlemen between Alicia and Adriana were not conversing with Adriana.

Jaw setting, he strolled with feigned nonchalance down the steps; cutting through the crowd, he made his way directly to Alicia's side.

She welcomed him with a smile that went some way toward easing his temper. "Good evening, my lord."

He took the hand she offered, raised it brazenly to his lips, simultaneously stepping close. "Good evening, my dear."

Her green-gold eyes widened a fraction. His easy, languid smile took on an edge as, setting her hand in the crook of his arm, he took up a stance—a clearly possessive stance—by her side.

With every evidence of well-bred boredom, he glanced at the gentlemen who had been speaking with her. "Morecombe. Everton." He exchanged the usual nods. The last man he didn't know.

"Allow me to present Lord Charteris."

The tall, fair-haired dandy bowed. "Torrington."

Tony returned the bow with an elegant nod.

Straightening, Charteris puffed out his narrow chest. "I was just describing to Mrs. Carrington the latest offering at the Theatre Royal."

Tony allowed Charteris, who appeared to fancy himself a peacock of sorts, to entertain them with his anecdote; he judged the man safe enough. Morecombe was another matter; although married, he was a gazetted womanizer, a rake and profligate gambler. As for Everton, he was the sort no gentleman would trust with his sister. Not even with his maiden aunt.

Both clearly had their eyes on Alicia.

Behind his polite mask, he took note of the undercurrents in the small group; focused on the men, it was some minutes before he noticed the swift glances Alicia surreptitiously cast him. Only then realized she was, if not precisely skittish, then at least uncertain.

It took a minute more before he realized her uncertainty was occasioned not by any of the three gentlemen before her, but by him.

He waited only until the notes of a waltz filled the room. Glancing at her, he covered her hand on his sleeve. "My dance, I believe?"

His tone made it clear there was no doubt about the fact; as he hadn't previously spoken, it should be patently clear that her hand being his to claim was an arrangement of some standing.

Fleetingly meeting his eyes, she acquiesced with a gracious inclination of her head.

The glances he noticed Morecombe and Everton exchange as, with a polite nod, he led her away gave him some satisfaction. With any luck, they would move on to likelier prey before the waltz ended.

Reaching the dance floor, he drew Alicia into his arms, started them revolving, then turned his full attention on her. He studied her eyes, then raised a brow. "What is it?"

Alicia looked into his eyes; she felt her lips firm, but managed not to glare. *I haven't been a nobleman's mistress before* hardly seemed worth stating. And now she was in his arms, sensing again the familiar reactions—the physical leap of her senses soothed by the feeling of comfort and safety—her earlier worries over how she should react—how he would behave and how he would expect her to respond to him—no longer seemed relevant. "Have you made any progress with your investigations?"

That, at least, was something she could ask.

"Yes." For a moment, he looked down at her as if waiting for her to say something else, then he looked up for the turn, and went on, "I heard from Jack Hendon this morning—he's confirmed all that your brothers learned." Glancing down, he met her gaze. "Incidentally, he was impressed—you might tell them."

"They don't need any encouragement."

His lips twitched. "Perhaps not." He looked up again, drawing her fractionally closer as they came out of the turn and headed up the long room. "Jack's pursuing the matter, trying to find a pattern to the ships that were taken versus those that were not. With luck, that might shine some light on who benefited from the losses."

He met her gaze. "I haven't yet heard back from the friend scouting down in Devon—he has contacts with smugglers and wreckers along that coast. As for myself, now I've got something specific to ask, I'll start putting out feelers among my own contacts."

He'd kept his voice low; she did the same. "Does that mean you'll be leaving London?"

The prospect filled her with a curious disquiet. An odd, novel, uncomfortable feeling; she'd never relied on others before—she'd always been self-sufficient. Yet the thought of coping with the unfolding events stemming from Ruskin's death by herself . . .

His arm around her tightened, drawing her attention and her gaze back to him.

"No—my contacts are primarily along the southeastern coast, from Southampton to Ramsgate, all within half a day from town. I can cover them in single-day journeys. Aside from all else, I need to be here to assess what the others discover, Jack Hendon from Lloyd's and the shipping lines, and Gervase Tregarth in Devon."

She nodded, aware of relief, but they were now *too* close, her bodice brushing his coat, her silk-sheathed thighs shushing against his . . . yet with the press of other couples about them, it was unlikely any would notice. And to the ton, she was still a widow after all.

Tony hesitated, debating, then murmured, "Incidentally, I've arranged for some men to keep a watch on your house. They'll be in the street—you won't know they're there, but . . . just in case you have need, there'll always be someone watching your front door."

She stared up at him; he could see her thoughts whirling behind the green-gold of her eyes. First Maggs, now . . . "Why?"

He had his argument ready. "First the rumor, then the Watch. I want to make sure whoever A. C. is, he gets no chance to do anything more to implicate you. Or your family."

He felt confident those last words would see her accept his arrangements without further question.

She frowned at him, but proved him right. "If you really think there's a need . . ."

Whether there was or not, he would feel much happier knowing that when he journeyed out of the capital, more of his trusted minions had her and her brood under their eye. The three men he'd set to keep a constant watch on the Waverton Street house were one hundred percent reliable; nothing suspicious would escape them.

The music slowed, then ended; they whirled to a halt. Reluctantly releasing her, he tucked her hand in his arm and turned her away from Adriana's court. "I'll go down to Southampton tomorrow."

Looking at him, she nodded, then cast a glance back up the room. "We should—"

"Behave as if we're lovers."

Her gaze snapped back to his face. "What?"

He resisted the urge to narrow his eyes at her; he opened them wide instead. "No one will find anything odd in that—it's what they're expecting." Given he'd laid the appropriate groundwork over the past several weeks.

She frowned. "Yes, but—" Again she glanced back toward Adriana.

"Stop worrying about Adriana. Geoffrey's beside her, and even if he's distracted, there's always Sir Freddie." He paused. "Has he made an offer yet?"

"Sir Freddie? No, thank heavens." She turned and settled to stroll by his side.

"Why so relieved? I thought you wanted Adriana to be able to choose among many?"

She narrowed her eyes at him. "I did. But as you very well know, she's already made her choice, so Sir Freddie making an offer will simply be an unnecessary complication."

He grinned, making a mental note to prod Geoffrey when next he had a chance. "Actually, I'm surprised you haven't been inundated with offers."

"I daresay I would have been if Adriana hadn't hinted many of them away." She shot him a severe glance. "Strange to tell, she seems to feel that avoiding trying Geoffrey's temper unnecessarily is a sound idea."

He looked down at her—and hoped she read the message in his eyes; he concurred with her sister's judgment and sincerely hoped she herself would exercise similar restraint.

The way she looked away, the hoity angle to which she

elevated her nose, suggested she understood him well enough. Hiding an inward grimace at his own susceptibility, he steered her to where his godmother waited, surrounded by a number of her extremely interested friends.

Despite their interest and that shown by any number of the ton's matrons in the relationship between them, the rest of the evening passed well enough. Through a combination of exemplary scouting and good management, he kept Alicia to himself throughout, avoiding the other gentlemen who, prowling through the crowd and attracted by the faintly exotic, definitely sensual picture she presented in her deep purple gown—something he fully intended to enjoy removing later—continually hove on her horizon.

They indulged in another waltz, after which she insisted on returning to check on Adriana and her court. Instead of permitting her to hang back as she usually did, he led her to join the circle of gentlemen and two other enterprising young ladies gathered about Adriana.

Alicia shot him a suspicious glance, which he met with a bland, wholly deceptive smile, but she consented to do as he wished. Thus protected from further incursions— the gentlemen who looked her way were not the sort to dance attendance among the younger crew—they saw out the end of the evening.

As soon as guests started to leave, Alicia turned to him; he got the impression she was tired, then recalled . . . hiding a smug smile, he gathered Adriana and Geoffrey; together with Sir Freddie, they joined the exodus. In the foyer downstairs, they parted. Sir Freddie bowed easily over Adriana's hand, bowed courteously to Alicia, nodded to Tony, and lastly Geoffrey, then left. Geoffrey scowled after him, then turned to farewell Adriana and Alicia.

Tony exchanged a nod and a glance. Geoffrey returned both, an acknowledgment that Tony would see both ladies safe home.

When he accompanied them to their carriage, Alicia shot him a wary frown. He ignored it, handed first Adriana, then her up, and followed.

Adriana accepted his presence without the slightest question. Alicia glanced at him, then gave her attention to the facades they rolled past. He leaned back, content to feel her soft warmth beside him, perfectly aware of what was going through her mind.

When the carriage rocked to a halt in Waverton Street, he stepped down, and handed both sisters down. He shut the carriage door; the carriage lurched, then rumbled off. He turned to find Alicia standing on the pavement, eyeing him uncertainly. Suppressing a smile, he took her arm and guided her up the steps. Adriana had already knocked; Maggs opened the door, and she swept in. He steered Alicia in her wake.

"Good night." Adriana headed for the stairs with barely a backward glance.

Maggs shot the bolts on the front door, then bowed to them both and took himself off.

Alicia watched him go and wished she knew what would happen next. She shouldn't encourage any illicit interlude; she steeled herself to bid Tony good night. Determinedly ignoring the twitching of her senses, the skittering anticipation afflicting her nerves, she tensed to swing about—

His long fingers slid around her wrist. "Come into the drawing room."

She turned, tried to read his face, but he was already moving, drawing her with him. He opened the door; leaving it ajar, he led her into the dimness beyond the shaft of light shed by the candle left burning in the hall.

Halting, he faced her, smoothly drew her into his arms—and kissed her.

Stormed her senses.

She was kissing him back, fully participating in an increasingly heated exchange before she caught her mental breath. Even when she did, it was impossible to draw back, to pull away from the engagement and the spiraling escalation of hunger and need it fueled.

Whose hunger, whose need, she couldn't have said; they were both greedy, ravenous, both wanting.

Her hands were sunk in his hair, holding him to her as their tongues dueled, as their lips feasted. One of his hands had closed about her breast, kneading, leaving it swollen and aching; the other was wrapped about one globe of her bottom, crushing the silk as he held her to him.

He rocked against her, deliberately evocative; heat pulsed within her—she heard a soft moan.

Holding her tight, her body molded to his, he broke from the kiss, raised his head, but not far. With an effort she lifted her heavy lids, and found his black gaze on her eyes.

"There's no reason to step back."

She knew he didn't mean from their kiss.

His gaze fell to her lips, then returned to her eyes. "And don't think to deny this."

She couldn't; given what was so manifestly flaring between them . . . he was right—there was no point.

He bent his head again. She was lifting her lips to meet his when she heard his soft murmur, "Or me."

She set her hand to his cheek as he took her mouth again; he was all heat and fire, tempting and familiar. This, she accepted, was the way it would be; if he wanted her, she was willing.

A minute later, he broke from the kiss to murmur, his voice dark and gravelly, "Upstairs."

He turned her. His hand remained on her bottom as he guided her into the hall, then up the stairs to her bedchamber; her skin didn't cool in the least.

Then they were in her room, and he closed the door. She'd halted in the middle of the floor, the candle in her hand. The flame wavered, but was enough to shed a golden pool of light into the general gloom.

He glanced at her, then at her dressing table; he waved. "Put it down there."

She moved to do so. Leaning over the stool, she set the candlestick down on the polished top, straightened—and saw in the mirror that he'd followed her.

His hands slid around her waist. He shifted her slightly so that she stood directly in front of the three-paneled mirror with its wide central panel flanked by two narrower wings. The rectangular stool stood before her knees. She glanced down at it, then looked up as his hands slid farther and gripped, anchoring her as he stepped closer, trapping her before him.

She caught her breath as, in the shadowy mirror, she watched his dark head bend beside hers; releasing her waist, one hand rose, gliding upward over the purple silk, now deep as the midnight sky, to close possessively over one breast. His other hand splayed down, covering her stomach, pressing in, gently kneading, pressing her hips back against his hard thighs.

Turning her head, she glanced over her shoulder at his face; inches away, she saw his teeth gleam in a fleeting smile.

"Bear with me," he murmured, then his lips touched the corner of hers, then cruised back along her jaw to trace her ear. "I want to see you naked."

He whispered the words, dark and erotic, into her ear.

It took a moment before she realized what he meant— he wanted to see her naked in the mirror.

Her nerves seized; before she could think of any protest—even decide if she wished to protest—he nudged her head back. She complied without thought; his lips traced downward along the column of her throat, then fastened over the spot where her pulse leapt.

His lips moved on her skin; his hands moved over her

silk-clad body, roaming, caressing, then his fingers found her laces.

She closed her eyes, leaned back against him as he loosened her gown, then his hands rose to her shoulders and pressed the soft fabric down.

"Lift your arms."

Opening her eyes just enough to see beneath her lashes, she watched her reflection in the mirror as she obeyed, sliding her arms free of the tiny sleeves. His palms swept down, over her breasts; the gown slithered down to her waist. His hands followed, pressed the folds past her hips; with a soft swoosh, the dress pooled at her feet.

For an instant, he paused, surveying what he'd uncovered. She caught the gleam of his eyes from beneath his heavy lids, felt his gaze briefly roam. In the flickering candlelight her chemise was opaque, the shadowy valleys and contours it hid mysterious.

He looked down. His hands rose and gripped her waist. "Kneel on the stool." He lifted her, and she did; with his knees he nudged her ankles wide and stepped between, so his chest was again a warm wall at her back, his erection a promise against the swell of her bottom.

The candlelight reached her, but didn't light him well; he was a dark presence behind her, his tanned hands contrasting starkly against the whiteness of her skin, the ivory of her chemise. He was a phantom lover, come to claim her, to lavish pleasure on her and take his own.

Her breath caught. He looked up, in the mirror trapped her gaze—as his hands slipped beneath the front hem of her chemise. She steeled herself, anticipating his touch, the fiery delight of his hands on her flesh, skin to bare skin. Instead, he turned his hands, caught the fine fabric and lifted it. Without touching her at all, he raised the diaphanous garment; lungs seizing, she lifted her arms and he drew it off over her head.

She put out a hand to steady herself as the cool air caressed her skin—the only firm purchase she could reach was his thigh behind her. Sinking her fingers into the hard muscle, giddy, she stared at the vision in the mirror—that of a slim, slender woman, her dark hair elegantly high, totally naked but for her silk stockings and the ruched satin garters that held them in place, circling her thighs.

Lifting her gaze to his face, she sensed rather than saw his satisfaction; it was a tangible thing, filling the air, surrounding her. She realized she still had on her ballroom slippers; even as the thought occurred, she saw him glance down, then his fingers caressed each ankle, and he slipped the shoes from her feet and let them fall.

He moved close again, and reached around to her garters. But instead of easing them down, as she'd expected, he ran his fingertips around the upper edge of each. And smiled. "They can stay. For now."

The timbre of his voice sent a shiver down her spine. It took effort to remain upright, yet pride dictated she keep her spine erect; she could feel the fabric of his coat and trousers gently abrading her bare skin.

His gaze had returned, slowly, to her face. He studied it, then shifted back a fraction, just enough to shrug off his coat. Seconds later, his waistcoat joined it on the floor.

He had to step back to deal with his cravat and shirt; she had to let go of him. She watched as he flung the shirt aside, then looked down, his hands going to his waist. His trousers hit the floor, and he stepped out of them, returning to her, his hands sliding over her hips, over her waist, drawing her back against him, against the heat of his skin, the rock-hard wall of his chest and abdomen, the hard columns of his thighs.

"Lean back. Let me love you."

The words were an erotic whisper in the darkness.

"Let me see you. Watch you."

She did as he asked, leaning back against him, eyes almost closed, committed to following his lead, only later, as his hands made free with her body, with her senses, fully understanding what he meant.

At first, his hands simply roved her body, a basic pleasure, heating her skin, teasing her senses to even greater awareness, evoking a deeper, persistent hunger. Flaring need grew as he weighed and caressed her breasts, taunting the tight, aching peaks, then tracing the lines of her body, sculpting the curves with his palms before gliding his fingertips down her thighs, then nudging her knees farther apart.

She watched, immersed in the sensations as he stroked the quivering inner faces of her thighs, then laid his hand over her stomach, the other sliding across her waist, holding her, surrounding her with his strength, giving her a moment to assimilate the heated, raspy reality of his skin, his muscled body pressed to her, locked about her.

In the mirror, she could see his shoulders above hers; his chest was wider than her back, his arms a cage in which she willingly waited.

He murmured something in French—she didn't catch the words but let her head rest back against his shoulder, watching, watching as he shifted, then the hand at her stomach slid lower, long fingers gliding over, then through the dark curls at the apex of her thighs. He reached farther; the breath strangled in her throat, her lungs seized. The vise about her chest locked tight as he stroked, caressed, then deliberately probed.

Farther, then yet farther, until his hand was pressed between her thighs, until her body was awash with flame. Her hands fastened on the arm locked about her waist, fingers sinking into the hard muscle as she watched him watching her—watched his hand, so much darker than her skin, rhythmically lavish fiery delight upon her senses.

She gasped, felt her body tighten, arching, reaching for the beckoning peak. He didn't stop but steadily pushed her on, on, on—until she fractured.

Her soft cry hung in the air; he wrapped her in his arms, in his strength, held her safe as she slowly drifted back from the crest.

She turned her head, glanced at him. He met her gaze, but briefly. His lips curving in what wasn't quite a smile, he glanced down at her body, soft, pliant, still locked against the hard aroused length of his. Then he bent his head and pressed a kiss to the point where her neck met her shoulder.

"First course."

His tone made it clear he intended to feast.

Reaching out, he moved the single candle, still burning bright, across and back on the dressing table, positioning it near the central pane of the mirror, at the very center. Reaching farther, he tugged first one side panel, then the other forward, angling them so they reflected the candlelight back at them. At her—it was her smooth, white skin the light illuminated; in contrast, his darker, tanned, and haired limbs seemed to disperse the light. Yet she could now see him clearly. The new position of the side panels let her see beyond her shoulders.

His hands returned to her body; they circled her breasts, gently kneaded, then slid down, tracing her sides, then he gripped her hips. Bent his head and murmured, his breath a heated promise, "Lean forward—hold on to the edge of the dressing table."

She did, and felt his hand caress the globes of her bottom. He traced the backs of her thighs, then reached between. Touched, stroked.

On a shuddering sigh, she closed her eyes; she had only an instant's warning—an inkling of what he would do—before he shifted, pressed close, and entered her.

Instinctively she locked her thighs, braced her arms, held still as he sank in, gasped when, with a last thrust, he filled her completely. His hands gripped her hips, anchored her as he withdrew, returned, then settled to a slow, steady plundering.

Her senses shook; her wits had long gone. Her breathing sounded ragged in her ears. Beneath her skin, her pulse throbbed, her body aflame as she rode the increasingly powerful thrusts.

The tempo escalated, degree by degree, until she was barely clinging to sanity, wrapped in heat, driven by desire.

"Watch."

The command reached through the flames fogging her mind. She dragged in a breath, forced her lids up. Looked.

And saw.

Him, behind her, his face etched with passion, set, his whole being focused completely on her, on the pleasure he found in her heated body. A body aglow with desire, softly sheened, his hands curved over her hips, his fingers locked on her skin.

She moved with him, not by thought but in instinctive concert, taking, giving, wanting more. Glancing to the side, into the side mirror, she watched their hips move, locked together in their sensual dance.

Her lungs seized; she glanced back at his face, saw the gleam of his eyes beneath his lashes as he watched her.

Then he shifted, thrust deeper, harder, higher. She gasped, let her lids fall; he was impossibly high inside her.

Faster, faster—and the flames roared. Took them, consumed them in an orgy of feeling, of sensations too sharp, too bright, too excruciatingly powerful to survive. And they were whirling, trapped in a whirlpool of delight, passion still driving, ecstasy beckoning . . . until it broke over them, drenched them, washed through them.

Leaving them shuddering, locked tight together, his arms wrapped around her, hers wrapped over them.

The tide faded, and left them.

The bed was close. He lifted her, staggered the few steps, then they collapsed amid the covers. It was a long time before either could summon the will or the strength to move.

FOURTEEN

THE FOLLOWING DAYS WERE AMONG THE STRANGEST Alicia had known. And quite the fullest.

With the Season about to commence, the social pace approached the frenetic; not only were there three or more major balls every night, but the days, too, were crammed with activities—driving in the park, at-homes, teas, luncheons, picnics, and all manner of diversions. So established were they now among the ton that their absence at such events would have been remarked; people expected to see them—they needed to be there.

She'd schemed, hoped, worked for, plotted so that at the start of the Season she and Adriana would be accepted members, indeed fixtures on the social scene. Fate had granted her wish, and they were dancing every night.

Those who had only recently come to town cast covetous eyes at their now-combined circle, with Tony, Geoffrey, Sir Freddie, and a bevy of others regularly forming part of that select company. But most, certainly the major hostesses and the matrons on whose opinion tonnish acceptance hung, had grown used to them; they merely smiled, nodded graciously, and moved on through the crush.

Of course, given Adriana's clear preference for Geoffrey's company, and his for hers, such social prominence was no longer necessary, yet Alicia would have managed society's demands easily enough—if it hadn't been for the distraction of all else in her suddenly and unexpectedly full life.

Tony left her bed every morning before dawn; through the day, he traveled—to the coast, to various towns and hamlets, over the Downs, to Southampton and Dover—speaking with his mysterious "contacts," constantly seeking information that might shed light on A. C.'s nefarious activities.

In the evening, he'd return, not to Waverton Street but his own house; later still, he'd join her at whichever ball or soirée, musicale or rout they had chosen to attend.

Each evening, she'd wait, chatting with those about her but with her thoughts elsewhere, wondering, circling . . . until he arrived. Every time he appeared to bow over her hand, then set it on his sleeve and take his place by her side, her heart leapt. Quelling it, she'd wait still further, impatient yet resigned, for the ballrooms were now too crowded to risk talking of his findings.

Only later when he'd escorted them home, then followed her to her bedchamber would they talk. He'd tell her all he'd done that day, all he'd learned. Snippets of information verified their suspicions that A. C. had somehow profiteered by ensuring certain ships had been taken by the enemy, yet nothing they'd discovered so far had shed enough light to show them how.

Later yet . . . they'd come together in her bed, and the day would fall away, and nothing else—nothing beyond the cocoon of the coverlets and the circle of each other's arms—seemed real, of any consequence.

Later still, she'd lie wrapped in his arms, surrounded by his strength, listening to his steady heartbeat, and wonder . . . at herself, at where she was, where she was heading . . . but those moments were fleeting, too brief to reach any conclusion.

And then the sun would rise, and there'd be another day of frantic activity, of ensuring her brothers' lives and their lessons stayed on track, that Adriana and Geoffrey's romance continued to prosper, and that all else—the façade of her making—continued as it needed to.

Beneath the social bustle, she was conscious of an undercurrent of action. Things *were* happening; Tony and his friends were steadily, quietly, chipping away at A. C.'s walls—at some point they'd break through. Twice, she glimpsed a watchful face in the street; the sight reminded her of the potential danger, kept her on her mental toes.

She tried, once, to find time alone to think, but Adriana burst in in a panic over a new gown that wouldn't drape straight, and she put aside her nebulous concerns. Time enough when the Season had run at least a few weeks, enough to take the edge from society's appetite, and A. C. had been exposed and her family was safe again, and Geoffrey had proposed . . . time enough, then, to think of herself.

That evening, she nearly suggested they stay home—perhaps send a note to Torrington House, and another to Geoffrey Manningham, inviting them to a quiet dinner . . . then she sighed and climbed into the fabulous apple green silk gown Adriana had fashioned. It was the Duchess of Richmond's ball tonight.

The traditional, recognized, start of the Season.

Even before they reached the duchess's door, it was clear the crowd would be horrendous; their carriage took forty minutes just to travel up the drive and deposit them beneath the awning erected to protect the ladies' delicate toilettes from the light showers sweeping past. Once inside, the noise of a thousand chattering tongues engulfed them; friends called greetings through the throng—it was impossible not to be infected with the gaiety.

Geoffrey was the first to find them. "Let me." He took Adriana's arm, offered Alicia the other, then steered them to where a trio of potted palms gave some respite from the packed and shifting bodies.

They stopped, caught their breaths. Alicia snapped open her fan and waved it. "Now I see why they refer to such events as 'crushes.'"

Geoffrey threw her a commiserating look. "Luckily, it doesn't get much worse than this."

"Thank heaven for that," Adriana murmured.

Gradually, the others with whom they'd become most friendly found them; it was a comfortable circle that formed by the side of the room, Miss Carmichael and Miss Pontefract, both sensible and well-bred young ladies, helping to balance the genders. They exchanged the latest stories they'd heard during the day; the gentlemen, most of whom kept to their clubs during the daytime, often had not heard what the ladies had, and vice versa.

Occasionally, a matron would stop by and engage Alicia; some brought their daughters to be introduced. Lady Horatia Cynster smiled and nodded; later, the Duchess of St. Ives stopped by Alicia's side and complimented her on her gown.

"You have become as *ravissante* as your sister." The duchess's pale green eyes quizzed her. "I confess I am surprised Torrington is not here. Do you expect him?"

She wasn't sure how to answer, in the end admitted, "I believe he'll arrive shortly."

"Indeed, and no doubt he will see you home." The duchess's smile deepened. She laid a hand on Alicia's wrist. "*Bien*. It is good. I am most pleased that he has had the sense to act, rather than prevaricate—it is pleasing to see that he takes such excellent care of you." Her pale gaze fell on Geoffrey. "And this one, if my eyes do not lie, will take good care of your sister, *hein*?"

Alicia raised her brows. "It appears he wishes to, certainly, although she has yet to tell him he may do so."

The duchess laughed. "*Bon!* It is wise to keep such as he wondering, at least for a little time."

With a nod to Adriana, and to Sir Freddie Caudel, who

had noticed her and bowed low, the duchess patted Alicia's hand, then moved on into the crowd.

The dance floor was in the next salon, separated by an archway. Alicia refused all offers to lead her thence, remaining by the palms chatting with whichever gentlemen were not engaged with the ladies on the floor.

Such was the crowd, she was almost surprised that Tony managed to find them. It was late when he did.

His fingers slid around her wrist; she looked up, smiling in welcome, aware as usual of faint but definite relief. A relief that turned to concern when she met his eyes and saw her weariness mirrored there.

He raised her hand to his lips, using the gesture to mask his grimace. "I'd forgotten how bad these affairs could be."

She smiled, and let him draw her close. "The dance floor is unnavigable, I've heard."

He raised a brow at her. "There's always the terrace."

"Is there a terrace?"

He nodded. "Through the drawing room."

She considered the question in his eyes, then faintly smiled. "I'd rather go home."

His black eyes held hers. After a moment, he murmured, "Are you sure?"

"Yes."

He held her gaze for an instant, then nodded. With a look and a quiet word, he gathered Adriana; not surprisingly, Geoffrey came, too. Sir Freddie bade them a suavely courteous good night, remaining to chat with Miss Pontefract and Sir Reginald Blaze. Leaving the group, they made their way through the still dense crowd to the foyer.

Tony sent a footman for their carriage. Richmond was a long way from Mayfair; in response to a pointed look from Adriana, Alicia invited Geoffrey to share their carriage. He accepted; minutes later, the carriage arrived, and they set off on the long rocking ride back to town.

Once they were free of the gate and bowling along the main road, Geoffrey looked at Tony. "Have you learned anything yet?"

Tony felt Alicia's glance, shook his head. "Nothing definite. Corroboration, yes, but nothing that defines the game A. C. was playing."

"Was playing? You're sure of that? That it's all in the past?"

He wasn't surprised to find Geoffrey interrogating him; if he'd been in his shoes, enamored of the lovely Adriana, he, too, would want to know. "That much seems certain. Indeed, that's why Ruskin was no longer valuable—why he became an expendable liability."

Geoffrey thought, then nodded.

Conversation lapsed, then Adriana asked Geoffrey something; he looked down at her, and replied. They continued talking, their voices low.

Tony wasn't in the mood to chat; he was in truth tired—he'd traveled down to Rye and spent much of the day chasing men who rarely ventured forth in sunshine. Nevertheless, he'd found them, and learned all he'd needed to know.

He looked at Alicia; shifting his hand, he found hers and wrapped his fingers about it. She glanced at him; in the weak light he saw her smile gently, then she looked forward, leaned her head against his shoulder, her other hand finding and covering their clasped hands. He sensed she was as tired as he; he was tempted to put his arm around her and gather her against him, but in light of the pair on the opposite seat, refrained.

It took nearly an hour to reach Waverton Street.

Geoffrey jumped down; Tony followed. They handed their ladies down, then Geoffrey took his leave of Adriana and Alicia, and walked off.

Tony followed Alicia up the steps of the house, glancing as always to left and right. He'd caught a glimpse of his man on the corner, recalled the report that had been on his desk when he'd returned home that evening.

In the front hall, he waited with Alicia while Adriana went upstairs, and Maggs retreated to the nether regions; he was perfectly sure their charade wasn't fooling Maggs, but he suspected it was important to Alicia, at least at that point, to preserve her facade as a virtuous widow.

Once Maggs's footsteps had faded and Adriana had disappeared down the corridor to her room, he turned back to the front door and slid both bolts home. Alicia had picked up the candle from the hall table; on the lowest tread of the stair, she glanced back at him. He joined her; together they climbed the stairs to her room.

Her bedchamber was the largest, closest to the stairs. Adriana's room lay along the corridor, two dressing rooms and a linen press separating the rooms. He had no idea whether Adriana knew he spent the nights in her elder sister's bed; given the distance between their rooms, there was no reason she would have guessed.

The boys' rooms were on the next floor, the servants' rooms in the attics above. Following Alicia into her bedchamber and shutting the door, he reflected that thus far, her reputation remained safe.

If there was any reason to imagine it threatened, he would make his intentions public, but as things stood, with the ton believing her a widow and thus according her the associated license, there was no compelling urgency to declare his hand.

Indeed, he prayed the necessity wouldn't arise, that once A. C. was unmasked and they were free of his threat, he would have time to woo her, to ask for her hand with all due ceremony. That was, to his mind, the least she deserved, regardless of their established intimacy.

He hadn't intended that, but having once spent the night in her bed, the notion of not continuing to do so hadn't even entered his head. The fact he'd simply assumed her agreement occurred to him. He glanced at her. She'd crossed the room to set the candlestick on the dressing table; seated on the stool, she was calmly letting down her long hair.

The simple, domestic sight never failed to soothe him—to soothe that part of him that was not, even at the best of times, all that civilized.

She had not at any time drawn back, either from him or from their relationship; her quiet, calm acceptance was both balm to his possessive soul and a wordless reassurance that they understood each other perfectly.

Indeed, words had never featured much between them. Aside from all else, he'd always believed actions spoke louder.

Sitting on the bed, he removed his shoes, then shrugged out of his coat. He stripped off his waistcoat, untied his cravat, all the while watching her brush the long, mahogany tresses that spilled down her back, a silken river reaching nearly to her waist.

When she laid down the brush and stood, he crossed to her. Bending his head, murmuring an endearment, he set his fingers to her laces, and his lips to the sensitive spot where her white shoulder and throat met. When her gown was loose, he forced himself to move away, allowing her to remove the gown, shake it out, and hang it up.

Unbuttoning his shirt, he inwardly frowned, returning to a thought that frequently nagged; it would be nice to give her more servants, a maid at least to take care of her clothes and see to her jewels . . . frowning, he pulled his shirt from his waistband. As far as he'd seen, she didn't have any jewelry.

"Oh." At her armoire, she turned, through the shadows looked at him. "I meant to tell you—something rather strange happened today."

Clad in her chemise, she headed for the bed. He started unbuttoning his cuffs. "What?"

Picking up a silk robe, she slipped it over her shoulders. "A solicitor's clerk called this morning." Sinking onto the bed, she met his eyes. "Adriana and I were in the park. The man—"

"A weasely-looking fellow in black?" The description had been in Collier's report; he'd read it before setting out for Richmond.

She blinked, then nodded. "Yes—that sounds like him. He insisted on waiting to see me even though Jenkins told him I'd be a while. Maggs and Jenkins discussed it, then left him in the parlor, but when I arrived home with Adriana and Geoffrey, the man wasn't there." She shrugged. "He must have got tried of waiting and left by the front door, but it seems strange that he left no message."

He'd slowed, stopped undressing, giving her his undivided attention. He considered, then said, "The parlor?"

She nodded.

Biting back a curse, he swung on his heel and headed for the door.

"Tony?"

He heard her whisper, but didn't answer. Glancing back as he went down the stairs, he saw her following, belting the silk robe as she came, her bare feet almost as silent as his.

Reaching the parlor, he opened the door. The fire was still glowing; picking up a three-armed candelabrum, he lit each candle from the embers, then, rising, set the candelabrum on the table beside the chaise.

Alicia silently closed the door. Her eyes felt huge. "What is it?"

Slowly swiveling, he studied the room, the window seat beneath the bow window, the bookselves flanking the fireplace and one corner of the room, the escritoire against one wall, and a high table with two drawers. "How long was he here—do you have any idea?"

Drawing the robe close, she considered. "It could have been half an hour. Probably not more."

He waved to the armchair by the fire. "Sit down. This might take a while."

Sinking into the chair, she drew her legs up, covering her cold toes with the hem of her robe, and watched him search the room. He was thorough—very thorough. He looked in places she'd never have thought of—like the undersides of the drawers of the table against the wall. He found nothing there, and moved on to the escritoire.

"Does this have a secret drawer?"

"No."

He checked every possible nook and cranny, then shifted to the bookshelves. She quelled a shiver. Barefoot on the cold boards, he hunkered down; his shirt flapped loose about his chest, but he didn't seem to feel the chill. He ran his hand along the spines, then started pulling out individual books, reaching into the gaps to check behind.

Tony had no idea what he was looking for, but instinct told him there would be something to find. He pulled out a slim volume; the title caught his eye. *"A Young Lady's Guide to Etiquette in the Ton."* Briefly, he raised his brows. Setting it aside, he pulled out a few more. They, too, dealt with similar subjects; clearly Alicia and Adriana had done considerable research before embarking on their scheme.

Making sure he missed no section of the shelves, he worked his way along.

He found what he was searching for behind a set of books on the lowest shelf, close by the room's corner. A sheaf of papers had been jammed behind the books; drawing them out, he turned to Alicia. One look at her face, her eyes, assured him they weren't hers.

"What are they?"

Rising, he moved closer to the candelabrum, and flicked through the sheaf. "Old letters." He straightened them out, laying each on the table. "Five of them." Sinking down on the chaise, he picked one up.

In a rustle of silk, Alicia left the armchair and came to

join him. Sitting close beside him, she reached for one of the letters—he forestalled her, passing her the one he'd already scanned; she took it and he lifted the next.

When he laid down the fifth missive, she was still picking her way through the second. The letters were in French.

For a long moment, he sat, elbows on his thighs, and stared across the room, then he leaned back, reached for her, and drew her, letters and all, into his arms.

She shivered, and looked up at him. "I've only read one. Are they all similar?"

He nodded. "All to A. C. from French captains acknowledging ships taken on information supplied." Three of the letters were from French naval captains; he could personally verify two of the names. He could also identify from his own knowledge the other two correspondents, both captains of French privateers.

The letters were extremely incriminating. For A. C.

Alicia had never been A. C., and indeed, the letters all dated from before her fictitous marriage had supposedly taken place. The name wasn't what was worrying him.

She frowned at the letter she held, then shuffled the sheaf. "These are all addressed to A. C. at the Sign of the Barking Dog."

Her tone alerted him; he glanced at her. "Do you know it?"

She nodded. "It's not far from Chipping Norton."

He sat forward. "An inn?" Getting to his feet, he drew her with him.

She shook her head. "No, a hedge tavern. Barely even that. It caters to a very rough crowd—most of the locals avoid it."

He hid a grimace. The Barking Dog sounded like the perfect address for a villain. He doubted he would get any help from the innkeeper as to who had picked up the letters, but he'd send someone to inquire tomorrow.

Meanwhile . . . "Let's go upstairs. You're freezing."

He drew her out of the room; she went unresisting, frowning, refolding the letters. Closing the parlor door, he saw her tiptoeing awkwardly to the stairs. Shutting his lips on a query regarding the whereabouts of her slippers, he strode after her, bent, and hefted her into his arms.

She looked into his face, then settled back and let him carry her upstairs. She'd left the door to her bedchamber open; he entered and nudged it closed. The lock clicked shut. She shifted, expecting to be put down.

He strode to the bed and dropped her on it. Filched the letters from her grasp when she bounced. "I'll need those."

She struggled up, watched as he crossed to his coat and slipped the sheaf into a pocket. "That clerk put them there, didn't he? Why?"

"To confuse things."

She swung her legs off the bed, stood, shrugged out of her robe and laid it aside. "How?" Turning back to the bed, she frowned at him. "What do you think will happen?"

"I think"—he stripped off his shirt and dropped it on his coat—"that you can expect a visit from someone in authority within the next few days. They'll be looking for the letters, but"—he smiled evilly—"they won't find them."

Still clad in her chemise, she slipped under the covers. He looked down as he stripped off his trousers, hiding his smile, pretending not to notice as, once safely covered, she wriggled out of the fine chemise and tossed it to the floor. Once he joined her in the bed, it wouldn't stay on her; better she remove it than risk him tearing it, or so he had given her to understand.

She was still frowning. "What should we do?"

Naked, he crossed to the dressing table and doused the candle. "We'll talk about it in the morning. There's nothing to be done tonight."

He returned to the bed and slid under the covers beside her.

She was shivering, still frowning, but accepting his edict, turned into his arms as she always did, as ardent and as needy as he. Her openness was a blessing for which he would remain forever grateful; the instant their limbs met, and their lips found each other's, there was only one thought between them, only one goal, one aim, one desire.

Her chill, her concern over the letters—and his—faded as that simple reality took control, claimed them, heart, minds, and souls fused them. Slumped, exhausted, and thoroughly heated, in each other's arms, they surrendered, and slept. And left tomorrow's problems for tomorrow.

Again, Alicia slept in. Lecturing herself that she couldn't let the practice become habit, she climbed into a new morning gown of forest green, quickly coiled her hair, then hurried downstairs, expecting mayhem.

She came to a teetering halt on the threshold of the dining room. Alerted by the deep rumble of Tony's voice, she looked in—stared.

He was seated at the foot of the table, keeping order, clearly in charge. Her brothers, of course, were on their best behavior; expressions angelic, they hung on his every word. Adriana . . . one glance at her sister as she slowly entered was enough to inform her that Adriana was intrigued.

The boys noticed her, and smiled.

Picking up her pace, as nonchalantly as she could she went to her accustomed place at the head of the table. "Good morning." Sitting, she met Tony's gaze. Inclined her head briefly. "My lord. To what do we owe this pleasure?"

A smile flashed behind his eyes; she prayed Adriana didn't catch it, or if she had, wouldn't be able to interpret it.

"I came to enjoy your company"—he smiled briefly at the boys; he was clearly their hero—"and also to discuss the most recent developments and remind you all to take care." His gaze returned to her face. "It seems matters are progressing, just not as I'd thought, or hoped. You"—his gaze swept the table—"all of you, need to stay alert."

"Why?" Eyes wide, David waited.

Alicia felt Adriana's glance, then her sister leaned forward and looked down the table at Tony. "That odd man who called yesterday but didn't wait—is it something to do with him?"

Looking straight down the table, Alicia met Tony's eyes and read the question therein. Briefly, she nodded.

"Yes." Assembling their collective interest with a glance, he went on to explain about the letters.

She listened, on one level monitoring his words and her brothers' reactions, on another, thinking rather more personally.

At least he'd changed out of his evening clothes; he was wearing a morning coat of rich, dark brown over ivory inexpressibles reaching into gleaming black Hessians. His waistcoat was striped in ivory and browns, his cravat starched white, severely simple. On the little finger of his right hand the gold-and-onyx signet ring he always wore gleamed; his gold watch chain and the gold pin in his cravat completed the picture, one of simple yet formidable elegance.

He'd left her bed at dawn, as usual; he must have gone home, then returned. She hoped he'd rung the doorbell, and hadn't simply waltzed in . . . then again, would anyone have deemed it odd if he had?

Was this a taste of things to come—a guide to how their relationship would develop? That gradually he would become more than just a frequent visitor, over time gaining the status of accepted member of the household, moreover a member whose edicts carried weight.

As they clearly already did with her brothers. Yet he

was impressing on them the need to take care, more, to avoid taking any risks; she wasn't about to complain. They paid his warnings far greater heed than they would any from her.

Deep down, she was conscious of a small, very small, degree of irritation that he'd been able so easily to assume a role that for a decade had been hers, that her family—even Adriana—accepted his usurpation without question . . . yet as, with a glance, he extended his edicts to Adriana, too, who just as avidly as the boys had been drawn in by his glib, truthful but not unnecessarily revealing, or worrying, account of the planted letters and what he thought they would mean, she couldn't find it in her actively to oppose him.

Nevertheless, some part of her, the most private side of her, felt almost exposed. Most definitely uncertain, both of the rightness of the present and what next might come. Until this morning, what had grown between them had remained between them alone, yet now . . . perhaps this was how things were done in his world?

She honestly didn't know; she'd traveled far beyond the limits of the books in the parlor. Not one gave any description of the normal pattern of behavior, the day-to-day arrangements that might exist between a member of the nobility and his mistress.

Presumably he knew how things should be; she would have to, as she'd had to so often thus far, follow his lead.

"I don't know exactly what will happen, or when." Tony met the boys' eyes, then glanced briefly at Adriana. "It's possible nothing at all might occur—we might catch whoever it is before he takes the next step."

He didn't believe that for a moment; Alicia's slight frown suggested she didn't either.

Returning his attention to the boys, he reiterated, "But you can't be too careful—I want you all to be on guard, and not panic if there is some development. I, and others, won't be far away."

The boys, eyes wide, nodded solemnly.

Jenkins came in at that moment; Alicia forced a smile and spoke with him regarding the boys' lessons, then looked at her brothers. "Up you go."

Tony reinforced her command with a look. The boys finished their milk; he inclined his head as they bobbed bows before taking themselves off.

Letting his gaze drift past Adriana, he looked at Alicia. "If I could speak with you for a moment?"

She blinked, glanced at Adriana, and rose. "Yes, of course. If you'll come into the drawing room?"

Rising, he took his leave of Adriana, who seemed totally at ease over his unorthodox presence, then followed her across the front hall. She paused by the drawing room door; he waved her in and followed, closing the door behind them.

She stopped and faced him; halting before her, he met her gaze. "Regardless of what I just said, I fully expect something to happen." He grimaced, let her see his unease. "I just don't know what, or exactly when."

She studied his face, then said, "Thank you for speaking with them. We'll be on guard now."

"My men outside gave me a decent description of this clerk, but there must be thousands like him in London—I don't expect to be able to trace him, let alone his employer." He paused, wondered if she'd see his next maneuver for the revelation it was—decided he didn't care. "With your leave, I'll send another footman—he'll arrive within the hour. Maggs tells me there's room in the attics—I want him—Maggs—free to follow any other strange visitors who come to call."

She blinked. A frown grew in her eyes. "We have Jenkins. I'm sure he can cope—"

"Your brothers." Ruthlessly he fell back on the one argument he knew would overcome her resistance. "I'd rather Jenkins concentrated on keeping watch over them, and I don't want you and Adriana left without some degree of male support."

She held his gaze, evaluating, realizing he'd left her no option. Her lips tightened, but only fractionally. "Very well. If you truly think it necessary."

"I do." Absolutely, definitely necessary; if he thought he could get her to agree, he'd have half a dozen men about her. "I'll be staying in London—Gervase should be back from Devon, and with luck Jack Hendon might have something to report."

"If you learn anything, you will send word, won't you?"

He smiled, a flash of teeth and resolution. "I'll bring any news myself." He studied her eyes. "If anything happens, Scully, the new footman, or Maggs, will get word to those watching—they'll find me. I'll come as soon as I can."

For an instant, her expression remained serious, sober, the reality of the threat, the potential but unknown difficulty she and her family might have to face—that he and she both felt sure they would face—dulling the gold and green, then a smile softened her eyes. "Thank you." Putting a reassuring hand on his arm, she held his gaze. "We'll manage."

Her "we" included him; that was clear in her eyes, in her inclusive smile.

His expression eased. He hesitated, then bent his head. Cradling her face in one palm, he kissed her, briefly yet . . . the link between them was now so strong, even that brief caress communicated volumes.

Raising his head, he stepped back. Saluted her. *"Au revoir."*

Tony returned to Upper Brook Street to discover messages from Jack Hendon and Gervase Tregarth awaiting him. Both expected to have firm information by noon;

Gervase suggested they meet at the Bastion Club. Tony sat at his desk and dashed off a note to Jack, giving him directions and a brief explanation—enough to whet his appetite.

After that he sat and mentally reviewed all he knew thus far. Action was clearly imminent; why plant incriminating evidence if not to expose it? How, by whom, and precisely when he didn't know, but he could and did clear everything on his desk, all matters that might need his attention over the next few days.

Summoning Hungerford, he gave orders that would ensure, not only that his houses and estate would continue on an even keel were he to be otherwise engaged for a week or so, but also that the various members of his extended staff, some of whom did not fit any common description, were apprised of his intentions, and thus would hold themselves ready to act on whatever orders he flung their way.

At a quarter to twelve, he headed for the Bastion Club.

Climbing the stairs to the first floor, he heard Jack, already in the meeting room, questioning, clearly intrigued by the club and its genesis. He pricked up his ears as other voices answered—Christian, Charles, and Tristan were there, regaling Jack with the benefits of the club, especially as applied to unmarried gentlemen of their ilk.

"I'm already leg-shackled," Jack confessed, as Tony appeared in the doorway.

"To a spitfire, what's more." Tony entered, smiling.

Jack raised his wineglass. "I'll tell her you said that."

"Do." Unperturbed, Tony took a seat opposite and grinned at Jack. "She'll forgive me."

Jack mock-scowled. "I'm not so silly as to encourage her."

Quick footsteps on the stairs heralded Gervase. He strode in quickly, brown curls windblown, the light of the hunt in his eyes. Every man about the table recognized the signs.

Christian, Charles, and Tristan exchanged glances. Christian made as if to rise. "We'll leave you . . ."

Tony waved him back. "If you have the time, I'd value any insight you might have on these matters. For our sins, we're all sufficiently connected with Dalziel, and Jack worked for Whitley."

Gervase drew out a chair and sat. "Right, then." He looked at Tony. "Who do you want to hear from first?"

"Jack's been checking the specific ships." Tony looked across the table. "Let's start there."

Jack nodded. "I concentrated on the sixteen vessels listed in Ruskin's notes that we know were taken. Thus far, I've only been able to get a general picture of their cargoes—asking too many specific questions would attract too much interest."

"Were they carrying anything in common?" Christian asked.

"Yes, and no. I've got word on six of the sixteen, and each was carrying general cargo—furniture, foodstuffs, raw products. No evidence of any peculiar item common to all ships."

"Six," Tony mused. "If there's nothing in common between six, then chances are that's not the distinguishing factor."

Jack hesitated, then went on, "All the ships are still registered—there's no hint of any insurance fraud. On top of that, all the ships I've got information on were owned by various lines, their cargoes by a variety of merchants. There's no common link."

Tony frowned. "But if you think of what's lost when a ship is taken as a prize, rather than sunk . . ." He met Jack's eyes. "The lines buy back their ships—it's the cargo that's lost irretrievably."

"To this side of the Channel." Charles looked at Jack. "But aren't cargoes insured?"

His gaze locked with Tony's, Jack shook his head. "Not in such circumstances. Cargoes are insured against loss through the vessel being lost, but they aren't covered if the goods are seized during wartime."

"So it's considered a loss through an act of war?" Tristan asked.

Jack nodded. "The cargoes would be lost, but there'd be no claim to worry the denizens of Lloyd's Coffee House, no fuss perturbing any of the major guilds like the shipowners."

"And if the merchants were unconnected individuals, and the losses varied and apparently random . . ." Tony paused, frowning. "Who would that benefit?"

None of them could offer an answer.

"We need more information." Tony looked at Gervase.

Who smiled grimly. "It took a bit of persuasion, but I heard three separate tales from three unconnected individuals of 'special commissions' being offered in the Channel Isles. The contacts were all English, and all were miffed that these 'commissions' were being offered solely to, not specifically French, but only to non-English captains."

Gervase exchanged a glance with Tony. "You know what the sailors in and about the Isles are like—they consider themselves a law unto themselves, and largely that's true. It never was clear where they stood in recent times."

Tony humphed. "My reading is that they're for themselves, regardless."

"Indeed," Charles put in. "But I assume the links between our shores and the Isles, and the Isles and Brittany and Normandy continued to operate throughout the war?"

"Oh, yes." Both Tony and Gervase nodded; Jack, too.

"Located as they are . . ." Jack shrugged. "It would be wonderful were they not the haunt of 'independent captains.' "

Tony turned to Gervase. "Did you get any confirmation on those particular ships?"

Gervase shook his head. "None of my contacts had information on specific ships—they'd never been in the running for those 'special commissions' and it seems whoever was making the offer played his cards very close to his chest."

Tony grimaced. "I could go over and scout about, but . . ."

Jack shook his head. "Aside from all else, there'd be more than a few who might remember one Antoine Balzac, and that not fondly."

Tony raised his brows fleetingly. "There is that." He reached into his pocket. "Which brings us to my discovery, which makes me even less inclined to go fossicking on foreign shores."

He tossed the bundle of letters on the table; the others' eyes locked on them. "Yesterday, a greasy-looking clerk in dusty black called at Mrs. Alicia Carrington's house in Waverton Street while she and her sister were in the park, as might have been predicted, the hour being what it was. Said clerk insisted on waiting, and was shown into the parlor, but when Mrs. Carrington returned home, no sign of this clerk could be found.

"Later, when I searched the parlor, I found these, wedged behind books in a corner bookshelf."

The others all glanced at him, then reached for the letters. Their faces grew more and more impassive as they read each, passing them around the table. Finally, when all five letters had been tossed back on the table, Christian leaned forward and looked at Tony. "Tell me why Mrs. Alicia Carrington cannot be A. C."

Tony didn't bridle; Christian was playing devil's advocate. "She's been married just less than two years—before that, she was Alicia Pevensey, and that's been checked." He gestured at the letters. "All five of these were written while she would still have been A. P."

Christian nodded. "Her husband—what was his name?"

"Alfred." Tony didn't like pretending Alfred Carrington had ever existed, but life would be easier if he stuck to Alicia's fabrication. "But he died nearly two years ago, so he wasn't the A.C. who was continuing to seek and buy information from Ruskin. Further, the Carrington family have no connections through which they might have used such information, nor wealth enough to have played A.C.'s game. The payments, the system, are consistent throughout—we're looking for one man, A.C., who's very much alive."

"And up to no good, what's more." Charles flicked one of the letters. "I don't like this."

Tony let a moment elapse, then softly said, "No more do I."

After a moment, he went on, "However, the letters confirm that the track we're pursuing is correct. They show A.C. did engage French naval captains and French privateers to capture ships, presumably using information Ruskin supplied." He added his knowledge of the Frenchmen involved.

"Stop a minute." Tristan said. "What have we got so far? How could a scheme based on what we've surmised work?"

They tossed around scenarios, pooling their experience to approve some suggestions as possible, discounting others.

"All right," Tony eventually said. "This seems the most likely then: Ruskin supplied information on convoys, especially when and where certain ships would leave a convoy to turn aside to their home ports."

Charles nodded. "That, and also when frigates were called off convoy duty to serve with the fleets—in other words when merchantmen would be sailing essentially unprotected."

"The merchantmen would have made a good show"—Jack looked increasingly grim—"but against an enemy frigate, they'd stand little chance."

"So, armed with said knowledge, A. C. arranges for a foreign captain to pick off a specific merchantman. Once the deed was done, and Ruskin's information proved good, A. C. paid him, and both he and A. C. went home happy." Tony grimaced. "We need to work out why A. C. was so keen on removing specific merchantmen, thus preventing their cargoes from reaching London."

He looked at Jack, who nodded. "We need the specifics of the cargoes, not just the general description. The only way to access those details after all this time is via Lloyd's—they always keep records."

"Can you learn what we need without alerting anyone?" Tony held Jack's gaze. "We have no idea who A. C. might be, nor yet what contacts he might have."

Jack shrugged. "I wasn't planning on asking anyone—I know where the records are kept. No reason I can't drop by late one night and take a look."

Charles grinned. "A man after our collective heart—are you sure you don't want to join the club?"

Jack answered with a brief grin. "I have my hands full just at present."

"How long will it take you to gather what we need?" Tony asked.

Jack considered. "Two days. I'll need to scout things out before I go in. Wouldn't do to get caught."

"No, indeed." Christian looked at Tony. "This business of those letters planted in Mrs. Carrington's parlor more than worries me. Whoever A. C. is, he's blackguard enough to happily deflect blame onto an innocent lady, without regard for the damage to her—"

Heavy thuds fell on the front door, reverberating up to the meeting room.

They all froze, waited . . .

The door downstairs opened; voices were heard, then footsteps, not precisely running but hurrying, came up the stairs.

Gasthorpe, the club's majordomo, appeared in the doorway. "Your pardon, my lords." He looked at Tony. "My lord, a footman has arrived with an urgent summons."

Tony was already rising. "Waverton Street?"

"Indeed, my lord. The authorities have descended."

FIFTEEN

THEY'D ANTICIPATED SOMETHING OF THE SORT, BUT Tony was nonetheless surprised and made uneasy by how swiftly the expected had arrived.

Jack demanded the number of Alicia's house, then parted from him on the pavement outside the club, saying he'd meet him there. Together with Christian and Charles, Tony piled into a hackney; Tristan intended to join them, but just at that moment Leonora, his wife, emerged from the garden next door—her uncle's house where she'd been visiting. She saw them, and instantly wanted to know what was going on.

Tristan stopped to talk to her; behind his back, he waved to them to go on without him. They did.

In Waverton Street, Tony jumped down from the hackney. Collier, masquerading as a street sweeper, was lounging on the railings close by the Carrington residence.

The heavily built man tipped his cap as Tony paused beside him. "Five redbreasts, m'lord. Never seen the like in all my born days—they pushed in like it was a thieves' den. Pompous little sort leading from the rear."

Tony murmured his thanks. "Keep watching."

"Aye." Collier eased upright. "I will that."

Christian had paid off the hackney; he and Charles followed as, jaw set, Tony strode up the steps. He didn't knock, but flung the front door wide and stalked in.

A young Runner standing before the drawing room

door started, instinctively snapping to attention, then pausing, confusion in his face.

From the direction of the parlor, a stocky sergeant barreled forward, belligerence in every line. "Here, then! Who'd you think you are? You can't just barge in 'ere."

Tony reached into his coat pocket, and withdrew a card. "Viscount Torrington." Face impassive, he handed the card to the sergeant, gestured to Christian and Charles. "The Marquess of Dearne and the Earl of Lostwithiel. Where are Mrs. Carrington and her family?"

The sergeant fingered the expensive card, tracing the embossed printing. "Ah . . ." His belligerence fled. He glanced at his junior barring the drawing-room door. "The inspector placed the lady and her household under guard, m'lord. Took 'em all into custody, like."

"Your inspector seems to have overlooked the point that Mrs. Carrington is already in *my* custody, a fact of which the local office of the Watch is well aware." Tony let his fury ripple beneath his words, subtly scathing.

Yielding to instinct, the sergeant came to attention, eyes fixed forward. "We're not local, m'lord. We came directly from headquarters—Bow Street."

"That's no excuse. Who's in charge here? What's your inspector's name?"

"Sprigs, m'lord."

"Fetch him." Tony caught the hapless sergeant's eye. "I'm going to check on Mrs. Carrington, to make sure neither she nor any member of her household has suffered any ill effects from your inspector's reckless action. Your inspector better pray they haven't. When I return here, I expect to find him waiting, along with every member of your force currently within this house. Is that clear?"

The sergeant swallowed. Nodded. "Yessir."

Tony turned on his heel and made for the drawing-room door. The young Runner gave way, hurriedly stepping back. Tony opened the door; pausing, he scanned the room, then released the knob and walked in.

Relief flooded Alicia; she jumped up from the chaise and went quickly to meet Tony. Two other gentlemen followed him in; from their appearance and actions, they were friends. The one with black curling hair moved to intercept their guard, struggling out of the armchair he'd commandeered with a weak "Hey!"

Tony turned his head and looked at the man.

Suddenly the object of two unnerving gazes, he stopped, apparently paralyzed by caution.

She reached Tony; his gaze returned to her, searched her face. He took her hands, squeezed lightly. "Are you all right?"

His gaze had gone past her to the boys, Adriana, and all their staff gathered about the chaise.

"Yes." She glanced back to see them all on their feet. "Just a trifle shocked." In truth, she was furious, still seething; the inspector's insinuations had made her blood boil. Looking back at Tony, she lowered her voice. "Is this about the letters?"

He squeezed her fingers again; instead of answering— an answer in itself—he kept his attention on the others. "This is all a mistake—we're here to sort it out. I want all of you to stay here quietly. There's nothing to fear."

Adriana nodded; forcing her lips to curve, she sat down again. The boys glanced at her, uncertain, then looked again at Tony.

He nodded. "Stay here with Adriana. Alicia and I will be back in a few minutes." She was close enough to sense the tension that held him, yet he smiled with beguiling charm at her brothers. "I promise I'll explain all later."

The smile and that promise reassured them; with fleeting if brittle smiles, they went to cluster around Adriana.

Alicia noted the look Tony exchanged with Maggs, and more briefly with the new footman, Scully, both of whom had refused to be shifted from her and her family's sides, then he took her arm and turned her to the door.

The other two gentlemen flanked them. Beside her, the larger smiled, as charming in his way as Tony, and half bowed. "Dearne. A pleasure to meet you, Mrs. Carrington, even in such trying circumstances. Rest assured we'll have this settled in short order."

She bobbed a brief curtsy.

"Indeed," the second gentleman said. He saluted her. "Lostwithiel, for my sins." His grin was unrepentant. "We can deal with the introductions later."

Tony shot him a glance as he opened the door.

They emerged into the front hall just as the inspector, a short, red-haired man of uncertain temper with an aggressive attitude and an abrasive tongue, came charging up from the direction of the parlor. "What the *devil's* going on here?" The demand fell just short of a raging bellow.

Fixing on their company, his eyes momentarily widened, then he recovered. "Scrugs! Dammit, man—don't you know better than to allow visitors in?"

He rounded on the sergeant, who held his ground. Scrugs nodded at Tony. "This here's his lordship, what I told you about, sir. And the marquess and the earl." There was enough emphasis in Scrugs's tone to convey the fact that if his superior didn't know when to back off, Scrugs certainly did.

"Inspector . . . Sprigs, is it?" The words were mild, Tony's tone was not. It cut.

Sprigs swung to face him, glaring belligerently. "Aye. And I'll have you know—"

"I assume you checked with the local Watch supervisor before barging onto his patch? Elcott, that would be."

Sprigs blinked; faint wariness crept into his piggy eyes. "Aye, but—"

"I'm surprised Elcott didn't inform you that Mrs. Carrington is already in my custody."

Sprigs cleared his throat. "He did mention it—"

"Indeed?" Tony raised his brows. "And did he also happen to mention that my orders in this matter come from Whitehall?"

Sprigs drew himself up. "Be that as it may, my lord, the information we've received—'deed, the people we received it from—well, we couldn't hardly ignore such, Whitehall or no."

"What information?"

Sprigs pressed his lips together, glanced at Alicia, then ventured, "That Mrs. Carrington here had hired some villains to do away with this man Ruskin, on account of she was in league with the French. Word had it that if we searched this house thoroughly, we'd find evidence enough to prove it."

"From whom did this information come?"

Again Sprigs hesitated; again the stretching silence forced him to answer. "Brought to us indirect, it was." He saw Tony's welling contempt and rushed on, "From the gentlemen's clubs. Seems a number of the high-and-mighty heard the story—wanted to know what we were doing about it. Questions were asked. They even had the commissioner himself in to explain."

Sprigs glanced at Charles and Christian, then looked at Tony. "It's treason we're talking about here. Don't suppose toffs like you care all that much, but if you'd served in the recent wars—"

"I wouldn't suppose quite so readily, Inspector."

The voice, languid, even soft, chilled. Everyone looked toward the front door. They'd left it partially open. A gentleman stood just inside; he walked forward as they stared.

His dark eyes remained fixed on Sprigs. Alicia had grown used to Tony's elegance—this man was equally impressive, moving with innate grace, slim, dark-haired, dressed in dark clothes that exuded that same austere style, a reflection of bone-deep confidence, of their assurance in who they were.

There was one difference. While Tony's tones could cut, whiplike, this man's voice projected a patently lethal threat, quietly efficient, like a scimitar slicing, unhindered, into flesh.

Suppressing a shiver, she glanced at Tony, then at his friends, and realized the newcomer was both known to them and accepted by them. An ally, definitely, yet she sensed he was someone around whom even they trod carefully.

Sprigs swallowed. He glanced at Tony. Behind him, the sergeant and his other two men were rigidly at attention.

"Dalziel." The newcomer answered Sprigs's unvoiced question. "From Whitehall." He halted at Tony's side and looked the unfortunate Sprigs in the eye. "I've already spoken with your superiors. You are to report back to Bow Street immediately, taking all your men, leaving this house in precisely the same state as it was when you, so unwisely, entered. You will not remove so much as a pin."

He paused, then continued, "Your superiors have been somewhat forcefully reminded that, together with Lord Whitley, I am handling this matter, and that contrary to their suppositions, Bow Street's mandate does not extend to countermanding or interfering with Whitehall's actions."

Sprigs, now all but at attention himself, nodded. "Yes, sir." He sounded strangled.

Dalziel let a moment pass, then murmured, "You may go."

They went with alacrity. At a nod from Sprigs, the junior stuck his head into the drawing room and summoned his companion; in short order, the five men from Bow Street were clattering down the steps, routed by a superior force.

All four gentlemen—Tony, Dalziel, Dearne, and Lostwithiel—stood in and about the front door and saw them off, watched them go. Trapped behind, screened from the sight by their broad shoulders, Alicia waited, somewhat impatiently. She knew the instant they all let down their guards.

Tony and Dearne visibly relaxed.

"Importunate devils," Lostwithiel quipped.

"Indeed," Dalziel replied.

They all started to turn inside—

Then paused.

Along with the others, Tony watched two carriages come clattering up, one from each end of the street. Both carriages pulled up before the house. The carriage doors swung open. Tristan sprang down from one carriage; from the other, Jack Hendon stepped down to the pavement. Both turned back to their respective carriages; each handed a lady down.

Kit, Jack's wife, and Leonora, Tristan's wife.

Barely pausing to shake out their skirts, both ladies swept toward the house—and saw each other. At the bottom of the steps, they met, exchanged names, shook hands, then, as one, turned and, beautiful faces decidedly set, swept up the steps.

On the pavement, Jack and Tristan exchanged long-suffering glances, and followed in their wakes.

All four men at the door gave way.

With barely a glance at them the ladies swept in. They saw Alicia, and pounced.

"Kit Hendon, my dear." Taking Alicia's hand, Kit waved toward Jack. "Jack's wife. How terribly distressing for you."

"Leonora Wemyss—I'm Trentham's wife." Leonora waved vaguely at her husband, too, and pressed Alicia's hand. "Are your family quite all right?"

Alicia found a smile. "Yes—I believe so." She gestured to the drawing room.

"It's quite insupportable," Kit declared. "We've come to help."

"Indeed." Leonora turned to the drawing room. "This is going to need action to set right."

Together, the three entered the drawing room. The door shut behind them.

All six men in the front hall stared at the door, then glanced, briefly, at each other.

Dalziel sighed, pityingly or so they all took it, and turned to Tony. "I take it you have whatever Bow Street's minions were sent to find?"

"Yes." Succinctly, Tony described the letters, and how they fitted the scenario they now thought most likely, confirming that A. C. had used Ruskin's information to arrange for merchantmen to be captured by the enemy.

At the end of his explanation, Dalziel, still and silent, stared out, unseeing, through the open door. Then, quietly, he said, "I want him."

He glanced at Tony, then at the others. "I don't care what you have to do—I want to know who A. C. is. As soon as possible. You have my full authority, and as for Whitley, suffice to say he's ropeable. If you have need of his name, you have permission to use that, too."

Briefly, he glanced at them again, then nodded. "I'll leave you to it."

He walked to the door. On the threshold he paused, and looked back. At Tony. "Incidentally, the information against Mrs. Carrington—there's no way to trace it. I've tried. Whoever this man is, he's extremely well connected—he knew exactly in whose ears to plant his seeds. When asked, every concerned soul said they heard it from someone else. I'll continue to keep my ears open, but don't expect any breakthrough on that front."

Tony inclined his head.

Dalziel left, going lightly down the steps, then striding away along the street.

The five men in the front hall remained where they were until his footsteps had faded, then all dragged in a breath and glanced at each other.

"I'm suddenly very grateful I only had to deal with Whitley," Jack said.

"Indeed, you should be." Tony stepped forward and shut the door.

Charles met Tony's gaze as he rejoined them, then glanced at Christian and Tristan. "How did he know?"

Christian raised his brows, openly resigned. "I suspect he knows one of our staff at the club rather well, don't you?"

"Our club?" Charles looked pained. After a moment, he shook his head. "I don't even want to think about that."

Tristan clapped him on the shoulder.

They turned to the drawing room. The door opened; Maggs, Scully, Jenkins, Cook, and Fitchett all slipped out, bobbing before disappearing through the green baize door.

With a glance, Tony halted Maggs. "Check the parlor—I doubt the good inspector's men had time to put their mess right."

Maggs nodded and headed down the corridor.

Tristan opened the drawing-room door and led the gentlemen in.

Kit and Leonora were seated in armchairs facing Alicia and Adriana on the chaise. All four heads were together; they glanced up as the men entered, but the comments that clearly hovered on their tongues had to wait—the three boys had been crowding around the front window; seeing Tony, they flung themselves at him.

"Are they gone?"

"What did they want?"

"Who was that man? The one who just left."

Tony looked down into three pairs of hazel eyes, all very like Alicia's. When he didn't immediately reply, Matthew tugged at his sleeve.

"You promised to tell us."

He smiled and hunkered down to be more on their level. "Yes, they've gone, and they won't be coming back. They'd been given false information, and thought there were documents hidden here—those letters I found. That's what they were searching for. And that man who just left was from the government—he came to tell them they'd made a big mistake, and that they weren't to bother you or your sisters anymore."

Three pairs of eyes searched his, then all three boys smiled.

"Good!" Harry said. "It might be exciting, but they weren't nice."

"And they worry Alicia and Adriana," David whispered.

Both his younger brothers nodded solemnly.

Smiling, Tony rose, ruffling Matthew's hair. "You'll do." He exchanged a fleeting glance with Alicia; with her eyes, she indicated upstairs. He looked back at the boys. "Now you'd better go and see if they searched your rooms." He lowered his voice. "You could help Jenkins and Maggs make sure there's nothing around to upset your sisters."

The boys exchanged glances. Solemnly nodded again.

They looked at Alicia. "We're going upstairs," David said.

She smiled encouragingly. "You can come down for tea."

Everyone waited while the three boys filed out and closed the door behind them.

"Thank heavens," Kit said. She looked at the men, still standing in a loose gathering in the center of the room. "Now! We need to move quickly on this. The damage has to be contained—better yet, turned around."

Jack and Tristan strolled forward.

Tristan shrugged. "I don't know that it's all that serious." He glanced at the other men. "I can't see that A. C. is likely to gain much from this—"

"*Not* your investigation!" Leonora glared at him. "That isn't what we're concerned about."

Tristan blinked at her. "What, then?"

"Why the potential social disaster, of course!"

They were right—that was the most urgent threat arising from Sprigs's visit; this time, Bow Street had come calling in daylight, and there'd been considerable activity visible from the street. Luckily, their counterstrategy was easy to devise and quickly set in train. Aside from Alicia and Adriana, there were seven of them in the room; each had multiple contacts among the *grandes dames*, contacts they normally avoided, yet contacts who, in this instance, once they were apprised of the situation, were very ready to come to their collective aid.

By the time that evening's entertainments commenced, all was in place, the cannons primed.

Tony, accompanied by Geoffrey, made privy to the latest developments, escorted the ravishing Mrs. Carrington and her even more ravishing sister to a formal dinner, followed by three major balls.

They'd barely entered the first ballroom, Lady Selwyn's, when he overheard his godmother spreading the word.

"It is *quite* beyond the pale!" Lady Amery's tones were hushed yet outraged. "This secretive gentleman seeks to manipulate us, those of the haut ton, with rumors and sly tricks, to make us turn on Mrs. Carrington and drive her from town so that her fleeing our wrath will appear an admission of guilt, and so confuse the authorities and hide his infamous deeds."

Lady Amery twitched her shawl straight, both the action and her expression indicating absolute disgust. "It is beyond anything that a gentleman should seek to use us thus."

Wide-eyed, the Countess of Hereford had been drinking in her eloquence. "So none of the rumors is true?"

"Pshaw!" Lady Amery flicked her fingers. "Nothing

more than artful lies. The reason he has focused on Mrs. Carrington is purely because she had the ill fortune to be the last person poor Ruskin spoke with before going to his death—at this very man's hands, no less! She was attending a soirée—I ask you, what is one supposed to do at a soirée if not talk to other guests? But now the devil seeks to deceive and deflect the authorities, and to use us to accomplish his evil ends."

"How diabolical!" The countess looked shocked.

"Indeed." Lady Amery nodded significantly. "You can see why we—those of us who know the truth—must be vigilant in ensuring these lies are quashed."

"Unquestionably." Transparently horrified, Lady Hereford laid a hand on Lady Amery's arm. "Why, if the ton could be used so easily as an instrument of harm . . ."

Her thoughts were easy to follow: no one would be safe.

Lifting her head, the countess patted Lady Amery's arm. "You may rest assured, Félicité, that I'll correct any idle talk I hear." She gathered her skirts. "Poor Mrs. Carrington—she must be quite prostrate."

Lady Amery waved. "As to that, she is one of us and knows how to behave—she will be here this evening, I make no doubt, and with her head high."

"I sincerely wish her well." Lady Hereford stood. "And will do all I can to aid her and bring this dastardly plot to nought."

With a regal nod, which Lady Amery graciously returned, Lady Hereford stepped into the crowd.

From where he'd halted, two paces behind the chaise where his godmother sat, Tony moved quickly forward, drawing Alicia, another fascinated observer, with him. Courtesy of the dense crowd, neither recent occupant of the chaise had noticed them. Now he rounded the chaise and bowed to his godmother, then bent and kissed her cheek.

"You were superb," he murmured as he straightened.

Lady Amery humphed. "It's hardly difficult to act outraged when I am." She held out her hands to Alicia, and when she took them drew her down to the chaise. "But you, *chérie*—I vow it is unconscionable." She looked at Tony. "You will find him soon, yes? And then this nonsense will be over."

"There's a crew of us pursuing him—we'll unmask him, never fear."

"*Bon!*" Lady Amery turned to Alicia. "And now you must tell me how that lovely sister of yours is faring. Has Geoffrey Manningham truly turned her head?"

Standing beside the chaise, Tony scanned the company. A number of senior hostesses had nodded pointedly their way, their acknowledgment marked and openly so. Others less prominent had stopped by to assure Alicia of their support. The tide was already turning.

He saw Leonora and Tristan arrive, and promptly start circulating. Deeming Lady Selwyn's event well covered, he summoned Geoffrey and Adriana with a glance, and they moved on through the crowded streets to the next major event.

The Countess of Gosford's ball was in full swing by the time they arrived. There, they met more hostesses, more *grandes dames*, all supportive. Lady Osbaldestone summoned them with an imperious wave of her cane; she gave them to understand that she hadn't had so much fun in years, and fully intended to make "the blackguard's" attempt to use the ton against Alicia a *cause célèbre*.

"A judgment of sorts on our malicious ways—we'd be fools not to see it." Her black eyes locked on the golden green of Alicia's, she nodded curtly. "So you needn't think to thank us—any of us. Do us the world of good to realize we've created a system so amenable to such dastardly manipulation. Help keep us honest." She grimaced. "Well, more honest."

Switching to Tony, she fixed him with a basilisk gaze. "And how long do you expect to take to lay this villain by the heels?"

"We're doing all we can—some things take time."

She narrowed her eyes at him. "Just as long as you don't at the last seek to sweep this blackguard's name under any rug." Her expression was a warning. "Rest assured we—none of us—will stand for that."

Tony smiled urbanely. "Rest assured," he returned, "no matter who else might think otherwise, I won't be a party to protecting him."

His answer gave Lady Osbaldestone pause; she searched his face, then humphed, apparently appeased. "Very good. You may now take yourselves off. Indeed, I suggest a waltz—that ought to be one starting up now. Last thing you want to appear is too concerned to enjoy yourselves."

Tony bowed; Alicia curtsied, and he led her away. To the dance floor.

She went into his arms readily. After three revolutions, his hand tightened on her back. She dutifully shifted her attention to his face.

"What is it?" There was a frown behind his eyes.

She smiled—more easily than she'd ever imagined she would be able to in such circumstances. "I just . . . find it all a trifle unreal. I've been transported Cinderella-like to an unimagined place. I never expected so many would so readily give me their support." She blushed lightly. "For all that it's you, and Kit and Leonora and the others asking the favor, it's me they have to agree to back."

His smile was slow, genuine and warming. "You take too little credit to yourself." He looked up as they swept into the turn. "Consider this." He drew her closer, bent his head so his words fell by her ear. "You've made few, if any, enemies—you and Adriana have been openly friendly, you've made many real friends over the last weeks. You've been pleasant companions; you've not sought to cut others out, nor to blacken anyone else's name. You've not lent your standing to any less-than-admirable social thrust; you've avoided all scandal."

He caught her eye as they whirled out of the tight turn.

Lips curving, he raised a brow. "Indeed, you're the epitome of a lady of whom society is pleased to approve—one of those the *grandes dames* delight in holding up as an example to others less adept, living proof of the type of lady they are happy to acknowledge."

Except she wasn't. She returned his smile lightly and looked over his shoulder as if accepting his description. Inside, the small kernel of disquiet that had been with her for weeks—ever since he'd first singled her out in some long-ago ballroom—grew, but she didn't have time to dwell on it, not then.

After the waltz, she and Tony strolled the ballroom, eventually rejoining Geoffrey and Adriana; together, they left for their last port of call.

The Marchioness of Huntly was one of the ton's foremost hostesses. When they arrived, Huntly House was ablaze with lights. A theme of white and gilt was repeated throughout the imposing reception rooms; the ballroom was festooned with white silk sprinkled with gilt stars and looped back with gold cords. The light from three brilliant chandeliers winked and glinted in the jewels circling ladies' throats and encrusting the combs in their coiffures.

Born a Cynster, Lady Huntly had been watching for them; she swept forward to greet them, and strolled down the ballroom chatting amiably, then handed them into her sister-in-law's care.

The Duchess of St. Ives positively glowed with social zeal. She smiled brilliantly at Alicia. "He is defeated, you see." Irrepressibly French, she gestured about them. "Oh, it may take a day or so more to complete what we have begun, but there will be no repercussions. He will not succeed in using us in so cowardly a way to attack you, and thus hide his own infamy."

Here, the company were the *crème de la crème*; only those accepted into the most rarefied of tonnish circles were present. The duchess remained with them for some time, introducing them to numerous others. Her generosity and determination added to the weight bearing down on Alicia's conscience.

Then a waltz started up, and Tony swept her onto the floor and into an interlude of pleasant distraction. She knew better than to think of the nebulous worry dogging her, not while in his arms; he was guaranteed to notice, and question, then interrogate further, and that she was not ready for.

So she laughed and smiled at his witticisms, eventually insisting he return her to Adriana's side. They joined her sister's circle. Although in this venue the attractions of those who had gravitated into Adriana's orbit was exceptional, it was clear, at least to Alicia, that her sister's decision to lean on Geoffrey Manningham's arm was not affected in the remotest degree.

Inwardly sighing, she made a mental note to arrange to speak with Geoffrey soon, to explain their financial state. Oddly, the prospect did not fill her with the dread she'd once thought it would.

Brows faintly rising, she realized she now knew Geoffrey too well to imagine mere money, or even their scheme, would weigh overmuch with him. His devotion to Adriana had remained unwaveringly constant throughout the weeks; indeed, it had only strengthened and grown. Adriana, at least, would achieve the goal they'd aimed for.

Her thoughts turned to herself; feeling a stir beside her, she abruptly pushed them aside, away, and turned.

"My dear Mrs. Carrington." Sir Freddie Caudel bowed and shook the hand she offered. He glanced around, then met her gaze. He lowered his voice. "I can't tell you how distressed I am to have learned of the problem besetting you."

Alicia blinked; the phrasing sounded rather strange, but Sir Freddie was one of the old school, somewhat formal in his ways.

"However, it seems the ladies of the ton have rallied to your cause—you must be grateful to have gained the support of such champions."

She'd learned that many gentlemen disapproved of the social power the *grandes dames* wielded; the edge to Sir Freddie's words suggested he was one. "Indeed," she replied, calmly serene. "I can't tell you what a relief it's been. The ladies have been so kind."

He inclined his head, looking away over the crowd. "It's to be hoped this man will be identified soon. Is there any information as to who the blackguard is?"

She hesitated, then murmured, "There are a number of avenues of investigation in hand, I believe. Lord Torrington could tell you more."

Sir Freddie glanced at Tony, on her other side, presently engaged with Miss Pontefract. Sir Freddie's lips curved lightly. "I don't believe I'll disturb him—it was purely an idle question."

Alicia smiled and turned the conversation to the latest play, which she hoped to see during the next week. Sir Freddie remained for several minutes, urbanely chatting, then he excused himself and moved to Adriana's side.

Turning back to Tony, Alicia saw he'd been tracking Sir Freddie. She raised her brows quizzically.

"Has he spoken—or even hinted—yet?"

"No—and don't speak of it. I'm hoping not to tempt fate." On a spurt of decision, she made a silent vow to speak with Geoffrey as soon as possible. There was no need to put Sir Freddie to the trouble of asking for Adriana's hand—no need for her to have to face the ordeal of politely refusing him.

To her relief, the evening rolled on in pleasant vein. Nothing of any great note occurred, no difficult situation arose to challenge her, or them. The small hours of the morning saw them heading back to Waverton Street, tired but content with the way their plans had gone. Geoffrey parted from them at their door. Tony accompanied them in, ultimately accompanying her up the stairs to her bed-chamber, and her bed.

Tony shrugged off his coat, dropped it on the chair, felt very much as if he was shedding some physical restraint along with his social facade.

I don't like this. No more do I.

Charles's words, his answer. A statement that grew more accurate with each passing day. Despite his erst-while occupation, its shadowy nature and often nebulous threats, he and his colleagues had always, ultimately, dealt with foes face-to-face. Once the engagement had commenced, they'd always known the enemy.

Never had he had to cope with a situation like this. The action had commenced with Ruskin's murder; subse-quent acts, strikes at their side, had been mounted and ex-ecuted with impunity, causing damage and difficulty in their camp. A.C. had forced them to respond, to deploy to meet his threats and the actions he'd unleashed, yet even though they'd managed thus far to weather all he'd thrown at them, they'd yet to sight his face.

An unknown enemy, with unassessed capabilities, made the battle that much harder to win.

Yet it was a battle he could not lose.

Glancing across the darkened room, he watched Alicia, sitting at her dressing table, brush out her long hair.

He couldn't even contemplate conceding a minor skir-mish; there was too much here that was now too precious to him.

Yanking his shirt from his waistband, he looked down, started sliding buttons free. Beneath the loosening linen, he shifted his shoulders, aware of muscles subtly easing in one way, tensing in another. A primitive want welling as the civilized screen fell.

I want him.

Dalziel's tone had been lethal, yet no more than an echo of his own resolve. Whatever it took, he would find A.C. and ensure he was brought to justice. The villain had focused on Alicia, struck at her not once but multiple times; for him, there could be no rest until A.C. was caught.

Yet they did not, after weeks of searching, even know his name.

He shrugged off his shirt and felt the last shreds of social restraint fall from him. For a long moment, he stood, his shirt bunched in his hands, staring unseeing at the floor, inwardly watching the volcano of his emotions surge and swell.

The scraping of wood on wood snapped him out of his state. Alicia stood, pushing back her dressing stool.

He dropped his shirt on the chair; unbidden, he padded barefoot across the room to help with her laces.

She glanced at his face, then gave him her back. He could feel his need building; rapidly, with far less than his customary languid sophistication, he unpicked the knots, hooked the laces free.

He glanced up, met her gaze in the mirror.

Saw that she'd sensed the change in him.

She searched his face, then looked down.

Normally, he would have stepped back, given her space to remove her gown . . . he didn't move.

Nor did she. Instead, she looked up, again met his eyes.

Her gaze was direct, questioning, waiting.

He dragged in a slow, deep breath, and reached for her.

Stripped the gown from her, let it and her chemise pool about her feet. Murmured darkly as he stepped close and wrapped his arms about her, locking her silken back to his bare chest, spreading his hands and claiming her glorious bounty. He shifted evocatively against her. Bending his head, he whispered, half in French, half in English, asking her to put her foot on the stool and remove her ruched garters and silk stockings.

Her breath shuddered as she breathed in, and complied.

While she did . . . he let his hands roam. Let them take

and claim as his need willed, set his senses free to wallow and seize all she surrendered to him, would surrender to him, in that moment, and the moments to come.

One arm crossing her body, his palm covering one breast, fingers evocatively kneading, with his other hand, he lightly gripped her nape; as she bent forward to roll the first garter and stocking down, he traced her supple spine, possessively stroking down, over the back of her waist, through the indentation below it, smoothly stroking over the swell of her bottom, down and around to caress the soft, slickly swollen flesh between her thighs.

With one foot on the stool, she was open to him. He parted the soft folds and found her, flagrantly caressed, then worked two fingers deep.

By the time she'd paused, gathered herself, changed legs, when she finally dropped the second stocking to the floor, Alicia was hot, wet and quivering with need.

Her foot still on the stool, her body riding the repetitive probing of his fingers, she looked into the mirror, from under heavy lids met his gaze.

Breasts swollen and full, peaks tight and aching, her skin heated, her breathing already ragged, she waited.

Withdrawing his hand, he grasped her waist; the instant she straightened and her foot touched the floor, he turned her.

She'd expected something else. Instead, he stepped back, drawing her with him, with one hand unbuttoning the flap of his trousers, the only clothing he still wore.

The backs of his thighs hit the bed. He paused only to free his fully engorged staff from the folds of his trousers, then he lifted her. Ignoring her smothered gasp, he sat and brought her slowly down, setting her on her knees astride his hips.

With the broad head of his staff nudging into her body. She could feel him there, throbbing, sense the promise of all that was to come. The hot, aching emptiness within her swelled.

She looked into his face, into his black, fathomless eyes. Raising her hands, she framed his face as his hands closed hard about her hips. Under mutual direction, their lips met. Clung, held.

Beneath his control she sensed all he held back, sensed the power, the desperate need.

She shifted fractionally on him. He caught his breath, broke from the kiss. Screened by their lashes, their eyes met.

He whispered against her lips, his breath a hot flame. "Take me. Give yourself to me." His gaze dropped to her lips. "Be mine."

Gravelly, rough, another seduction, a dark temptation to a deeper level of giving.

She didn't hesitate. Drawing in a breath, tightening her hands about his face to anchor her, she angled her head, set her lips to his, and slowly eased down.

Inch by slow inch, she took him inside her, gloried in the feel of him filling her, stretching her. She'd never before been so aware of how her body closed about him, enclasped him. Took him in.

His hands were hard as iron about her hips as he ruthlessly guided her down; he let her set the pace only until he was fully seated within her, then he took the reins, took control, and the giving began.

Hard, hot, and complete.

Without restrictions, limits, or reservations.

Their bodies merged deeply, compulsively riding a wave of sensual desire higher than any before, a tide of need more desperately urgent, more powerful. More addictive.

Their tongues tangled, their mouths feeding in frenzy. He took her as he would, seizing and claiming every sense she possessed, demanding more even as she gave him all.

In the end, on a gasp, she surrendered completely, opened her body, her soul, her heart, and let him plunder.

Let him capture, take, and make her his.

Beyond all thought. Beyond all denial.

Beyond this world.

She was his. Forever. He would never allow anyone to take her from him.

When he slumped back on the bed, drained, replete, to the very depths of his soul sated, the darker side of his nature for the moment wholly satisfied, as he tumbled her down with him, then kicked off his trousers and wrapped them in the covers, those were the only thoughts to cross Tony's mind.

They were the only thoughts that mattered.

SIXTEEN

IN THE DARKNESS BEFORE DAWN, ALICIA STIRRED.

Awareness slunk into her brain. Her body still thrummed; her hair was a wild tangle, a fine net ensaring them, wrapped about the muscled arm lying protectively about her. Eyes closed, she lay still, safe, secure, warm. Freed by the night, by the silence, her thoughts crept from the corners of her mind, dwelling on the strange twist her life had taken—the deception she'd never intended to practice, not on so many, not to this degree.

The role of her own making now haunted her.

Not in her wildest dreams had she expected to rise to such social prominence, never imagined calling so many of the powerful friend. Yet in her and her family's time of need, they'd come to her aid—how could she now draw back from them, from the protection they'd so generously offered?

Thanks to A. C. and his latest attempt to cast all suspicion on her, she couldn't even slip away, fade from the scene. She had to remain, head high, and face down his rumors, at least for the next weeks.

Had to continue to pretend she was the widow she was not, while parading through the haut ton, the subject of the latest *on-dit*, the central character in the most amazing, attention-getting story.

The idea that someone from her little part of the country might, like Ruskin, pop up and recognize her had assumed the status of a nightmare. No amount of reasoning, of reiterating that there truly were few families of standing near Little Compton, and none who had known her, did anything to lessen its effect; like a dark, louring cloud it hovered, threatening, not breaking but always there, swelling in the back of her mind.

What if the cloud burst and the truth came raining down?

Her heart contracted; she dragged in a breath, conscious of the vise closing about her chest.

Tony had so publicly nailed his flag to her mast, had so openly committed himself to her cause, and brought with him so many of his aristocratic connections . . . if the ton ever learned the truth of her widowhood, how would that reflect on him?

Badly. Very badly. She'd now gone about in society enough to know. Such a revelation would make her an outcast, but it would make him a laughingstock. Or worse, it would cast him as one who had knowingly deceived the entire ton.

They would never forgive him.

And no matter any protestations to the contrary, deep down, in his heart, he would never—could never—forgive her. By making him a party to her deception, she would have ripped from him and put forever beyond his reach the position to which he'd been born, the position she suspected he never even questioned, it was so much a part of him.

She wanted to twist and turn, but with him breathing softly, deeply, beside her, she forced herself to lie still beneath the heavy arm he'd slung across her waist. Dawn was sliding over the rooftops when she finally accepted that she could do nothing to change things—all she could do was move heaven and earth to ensure that no one ever learned her true state.

She glanced at his face on the pillow beside hers. His dark lashes lay, black crescents over his cheekbones; in sleep, his face retained the harsh lines, the austere angularity of nose and jaw. In her mind, she heard his voice dispassionately reciting, describing what the last ten years of his life had been, how they'd been spent, and where; he'd avoided stating in what danger, but she was not so innocent she couldn't read between his lines. When his mask was off, as now, the evidence of that decade still remained, etched in the lines of his face.

Last night—early this morning—he'd needed her. Wanted her. Taken all she'd given, and yet needed more, a more she'd found it possible to give.

His satisfaction was hers, deep, powerful, and complete. She had never imagined such a connection, that a man such as he would have a need like that, and that she would be able so completely to fulfill it.

Her joy in that discovery was profound.

Lifting a hand, she gently brushed back the heavy lock of black hair that lay rakishly across his brow. He didn't wake, but stirred. His hand flexed, lightly gripping her side before easing as, reassured, he sank once more into slumber.

For long moments, she looked, silently wondered.

Faced incontrovertible fact.

He now meant more to her, at a deeper, more intensely emotional level, than all else in her life.

Tony left Waverton Street before the sunshine hit the cobbles. The tide of satisfaction that had swept him last night had receded, revealing, to him all too forcefully, the vulnerability beneath.

He couldn't—wouldn't—lose her; he couldn't even readily stomach the fact she was at risk. Therefore . . .

Over breakfast that morning, as always efficiently served by Hungerford who, despite knowing full well Tony hadn't slept in his own bed for the past week and more, remained remarkably cheerful, he made his plans. Those included Hungerford, but his first act was to repair to his study and pen two summonses. The first, to Geoffrey Manningham, took no more than a few minutes; he dispatched it via a footman, then settled to write the second, a communication requiring far more thought.

He was still engaged in searching for the right approach, the right phrases, when Geoffrey arrived. Waving him to the pair of armchairs before the hearth, he joined him.

"News?" Geoffrey asked as he sat.

"No." Sinking into the other chair, Tony smiled, all teeth. "Plans."

Geoffrey grinned, equally ferally, back. "You perceive me all ears."

Tony outlined the basics of what he intended.

Geoffrey concurred. "If you can get everything into place, including your beloved, that would unquestionably be the wisest course." He met Tony's gaze. "So what do you want me to do? I presume there's something."

"I want you to remove Adriana for the afternoon—or the day, if you prefer."

Geoffrey widened his eyes. "That all?"

Tony nodded. "Do that, and I'll manage the rest."

Just how he would do that last . . . they sat for ten minutes debating various options, then Geoffrey took himself off to accomplish his assigned task.

Tony remained before the fire for a few minutes more, then, struck by inspiration, returned to his desk and completed his second summons, disguised as a letter to his cousin Miranda, inviting her and her two daughters, Margaret and Constance, to visit him in London, to act as chaperone while the lady he intended to make his viscountess spent a week or so under his roof.

If he knew anything of Miranda, that last would ensure her appearance as soon as he could wish—namely, tomorrow.

The letter dispatched in the care of a groom, he rang for Hungerford.

Dealing with his butler was bliss; Hungerford never questioned, never made difficulties, but could be counted on to ensure that, even if difficulties did arise and his orders no longer fitted the situation, that his intent would be accomplished.

Telling Hungerford that he proposed protecting his intended bride from social and even possibly physical attack by installing her under this roof, within the purlieu of Hungerford's overall care, was all it took to get everything in Upper Brook Street ready.

He had little notion of what arrangements would be required to prepare the house to receive not only the widowed Miranda and her daughters, ten and twelve years old, but his prospective bride, her family, and her household, but he was sure his staff under Hungerford's direction would meet the challenge.

Beaming, clearly delighted with his orders, Hungerford retreated. Tony considered the clock; it was not yet noon.

He debated the wisdom of his next act at some length; eventually, he rose, and headed for Hendon House.

At two o'clock, he paused beside Collier, leaning on his street sweeper's broom at the corner of Waverton Street.

The big man nodded in greeting. "Just missed her, you have. She returned from some luncheon, then immediately headed off with the three lads and their tutor to the park. Kites today, if you've a mind to join them."

"And Miss Pevensey?"

"Lord Manningham called 'bout eleven and took her up in his curricle. They haven't returned."

Tony nodded. "I'm going to talk to the staff, then perhaps I'll fly a kite." He paused, then added, "I plan to move Mrs. Carrington and her household to Upper Brook Street, but I'll want you and the others to keep up your watch here. I'll leave Scully and one other in residence, to keep all possibilities covered."

Collier nodded. "When will this move happen?"

Today if Tony had his way. Realistically . . . "At the earliest tomorrow, late in the day."

Leaving Collier, Tony strode on; reaching Alicia's house, he went quickly up the steps. Maggs answered the door.

Tony frowned; Maggs forestalled him. "Scully's with 'em. No need to fret."

His frown darkening at the thought that he was *that* transparent, he crossed the threshold. "I want to speak with the staff—all of you who are here. It might be best if I came down to the kitchens."

From beneath the wide branches of one of the trees in Green Park, Alicia watched, a smile on her lips, as Scully and Jenkins wrestled with the second of the two kites they'd brought out.

The first kite, under Harry's narrow-eyed guidance, was soaring over the treetops. David was watching Scully and Jenkins, a pitying look in his face; Matthew's eyes were glued to the blue-and-white kite swooping and swirling above the trees.

"There you are."

She turned at the words, knowing before she met Tony's eyes that it was he. "As always."

Smiling, she gave him her hand; his eyes locking on hers, he raised it to his lips and pressed kisses first to her fingers, then to her palm. Retaining possession, he lowered his hand, fingers sliding about hers, and looked out at the scene in the clearing before them.

"I wonder . . ." He glanced at her, raised a brow. "Should I rescue Jenkins and Scully from sinking without trace in your brothers' estimation?"

She grinned; leaning back against the tree trunk, she gestured. "By all means. I'll watch and judge your prowess."

Over numerous afternoons, he'd taught the boys the tricks of keeping their kites aloft. He'd transparently enjoyed the moments; something inside her had rejoiced to see him caught again in what must have been a boyhood pleasure.

"Hmm." Studying the kite flyers, he hesitated; she got the impression he was steeling himself to resist the lure of the kites and do something else, something he was reluctant to do.

A moment passed, then he looked at her. "Actually, I wanted to speak with you."

She widened her eyes, inviting him to continue.

Still he hesitated; his eyes searched hers—abruptly she realized he was metaphorically girding his loins.

"I want you to move house."

She frowned at him. "Move? But why? Waverton Street suits us—"

"For safety reasons. Precautions." He trapped her gaze. "I don't want you or your household subjected to any repeat of yesterday."

She had no wish to argue that; no one had enjoyed the experience. But . . . she let her frown grow. "How will a different house avoid . . ." The intentness in his black eyes registered. Her lips parted; she stared, then baldly asked, "To which house do you wish us to move?"

His lips thinned. "Mine."

"No."

"*Before* you say that, just consider—living under my roof you'll have the protection not just of my title, my status, but also of all those allied with me and my family." His eyes pinned her. "So will your sister and brothers."

Folding her arms, she narrowed her eyes back. "For the moment, let's leave Adriana and the boys out of this discussion—it hasn't escaped my notice that you're always quick to drag them into the fray."

He scowled at her. "They're part of it—they're part of you."

"Perhaps. Be that as it may, you can't seriously think—"

He cut her off with a raised hand. "Hear me out. If it's the proprieties that are exercising you, my cousin and her two young daughters—they're ten and twelve—will be arriving tomorrow. With Miranda in residence, there's no reason—social, logical, or otherwise—that you and your household cannot stay at Torrington House. It's a mansion—there's more than enough room."

"But . . ." She stared at him. The words: *I'm your mistress, for heaven's sake*! burned her tongue. Compressing her lips, she fixed him with a strait look, and primly asked, "What will your staff think?"

What she meant was: what will the entire ton think. To be his mistress was one thing; the ton turned a blind eye to affairs between gentlemen such as he and fashionable widows. However, to be his mistress and live openly under his roof was, she was fairly certain, going that one step too far.

His expression had turned bewildered. "My staff?"

"Your servants. Those who would have to adjust to and cope with the invasion."

"As it happens, they're delighted at the prospect." His frown returned. "I can't imagine why you'd think otherwise. My butler's going around with a smile threatening to crack his face, and the staff are buzzing about, getting rooms ready."

She blinked, suddenly uncertain. If his butler thought her living in the Upper Brook Street mansion was acceptable . . . she'd always understood tonnish butlers to be second only to the *grandes dames* in upholding the mores of the ton.

Tony sighed. "I know we haven't properly discussed it, but there isn't time. Just because we've trumped A. C.'s last three tricks doesn't mean he won't try again." His expression resolute, he met her eyes. "That he's tried three times to implicate you suggests he's fixated on the idea of using you to cover his tracks. I'm sure he'll try again."

An inkling of why he was so set on moving her into his

house, having her, at least for the present, under his roof, reached her. She hesitated.

He sensed it. Shifting closer, he pressed his point. "There's a huge schoolroom with bedrooms attached, and rooms for Jenkins and Fitchett nearby. There's a back garden the boys can play in when they're not having their lessons—and the staff truly are looking forward to having boys running up and down the stairs again."

Despite all, that last made her smile.

He squeezed her hand, raised it to his chest. "You and the boys and Adriana will be comfortable and safe at Torrington House. You'll be happy there."

And he'd be happy if she was there, too—that didn't need saying, it was there in his eyes.

"Please." The word was soft. "Come and live with me."

Her heart turned over; her resolution wavered.

"There's no reason at all you can't—no hurdle we can't overcome."

Lost in his eyes, she pressed her lips tight.

Felt a tug on her gown. She looked down.

Matthew stood beside them; neither of them had noticed his approach. Face alight, he stared first at one, then the other, then breathlessly asked, "Are we really going to live at Tony's house?"

By the time they got back to Waverton Street, Alicia had a headache. A frown had taken up permanent residence on her face; she couldn't seem to lose it.

She was seriously annoyed, not specifically but generally—she couldn't blame Tony for involving her brothers, but involved they now were, and determined to convince her of the huge benefits of removing with all speed to Torrington House.

If Tony was ruthless, they were relentless. She went up the steps, shooing them before her, feeling almost battered.

Despite their arguments, she felt very sure she needed

to think long and hard about this latest proposition. She needed to investigate, and make sure that her presence in his house wouldn't harm his standing.

Nor make her own any more perilous.

"Off to wash your hands. No tea until you do."

It was blackberry jam day again, so they rushed off without argument.

With a short sigh, she swung to face Tony.

He was watching her closely. "Come and sit down."

She let him steer her to the parlor. Scully and Jenkins disappeared. Sinking onto the chaise, she fixed Tony with a darkling glance. "I haven't agreed."

He inclined his head and, wisely, made no reply.

Tea should have soothed her temper. Unfortunately, her brothers were not so perspicacious as Tony; although clever enough not to directly argue their case, their artful comments, tossed entirely among themselves, on the possibilities they imagined might accrue should they go to live in Upper Brook Street—possibilities like having suitable banisters to slide down, possibilities they innocently requested advice on from Tony—filled the minutes.

She kept her lips shut and refused to be drawn.

Then she heard the front door open, and Adriana's and Geoffrey's voices. She turned as they came in.

Adriana's face glowed. "We had a lovely drive around Kew. The gardens were well worth the visit."

Alicia sat forward and reached for the spare teacups, wondering how to broach the subject of Tony's proposed move, preferably in a way that would ensure her sister's cooperation in holding back what had started to feel like an inexorable tide.

Adriana tossed her bonnet onto the window seat, took the cup of tea Alicia had poured to Geoffrey, sitting in the second armchair, then sat beside Alicia on the chaise. Taking the cup she handed her, Adriana's gaze went to Geoffrey; he was being served crumpets and jam by Harry and Matthew.

Following her gaze, Alicia watched, noted. Despite their love of crumpets, the boys had readily shared; they'd accepted Geoffrey, not perhaps in the same unquestioning way they'd accepted Tony, yet they clearly counted him one of their small circle and trusted him.

Smiling, Adriana turned to her. "Geoffrey told me about Tony's suggestion that we move to Upper Brook Street." She sipped, then met Alicia's eyes. "It sounds an excellent idea . . ." Her voice trailed away; seeing Alicia's reaction, she blinked. "Isn't it?"

Alicia looked at Tony. He returned her regard steadily, giving not an inch. She glanced at Geoffrey, but he was—quite deliberately she was sure—chatting with her brothers about the merits of blackberry jam.

Slowly, she drew breath, then met Adriana's gaze. "I don't know." The unvarnished truth.

"Well—"

Adriana tried to persuade her all over again; her arguments echoed Tony's, yet were sufficiently different to assure Alicia he hadn't been so foolish as to plot with her sister against her.

He knew the thought crossed her mind; when, recognizing her suspicion was misplaced, she glanced at him, he searched her eyes, then faintly raised a brow. Raising his cup, he calmly sipped. And left her fighting a rearguard action against everyone else in the room.

Her brothers didn't press her directly; instead, they supported and elaborated on Adriana's themes. And then Geoffrey, more quietly but also more seriously and with considerably more weight, threw his support behind Adriana and Tony.

Looking into Geoffrey's steady brown gaze, Alicia felt her resistance waver. She could see why Geoffrey wanted Adriana and the rest of them under Tony's roof. Glancing at Tony, she knew the same reason was a significant part of his motivation, too. Was she being irrational in refusing to agree?

She needed reassurance, but not the sort anyone present could give—

The doorbell pealed. She glanced at the clock; time had flown. Hearing feminine voices in the hall, she rose. She tugged the bellpull to summon Jenkins, and instructed her brothers they could finish the crumpets before returning to their lessons.

Turning, she headed for the door, Adriana behind her. Tony and Geoffrey followed.

"Ah—there you are, Alicia!" In the hall, Kit Hendon beamed at her.

Beside her, Leonora Wemyss smiled. "I hope we haven't called at an inopportune moment, but there's a gathering at Lady Mott's that it would be wise to attend, and we wanted to coordinate which events we'll go to tonight."

Alicia smiled, touched hands, waited while they greeted the others, then ushered both ladies into the drawing room. As they all sat, disposing themselves on the chaise and the chairs, she realized that neither Kit nor Leonora had evinced the slightest surprise at discovering Tony and Geoffrey present.

The middle of the afternoon was not a common time for gentlemen to call.

Leonora plunged immediately into a discussion of the most promising events planned for that evening. "I think Lady Humphries' rout, then the Canthorpes' ball and the Hemmingses', too. What do you think?"

They tossed around the possiblities, eventually replacing the Hemmingses' ball with the Athelstans'. "Much better connected," Tony said, his eyes capturing Alicia's, "and that helps at the end of a long night."

"Yes." Leonora nodded, gaze distant as if reviewing a mental list. "That should do it." She glanced at Alicia. "A very good night's work."

"Now," Kit said, sitting forward, "the reason we think visiting Lady Mott's in the next hour would be wise is that her gatherings invariably attract all the busiest bodies in town. They're of the older, more crotchety crew, and while our story will doubtless have reached some of them, there are others who are highly active but only during the day."

"If we concentrate our activities solely on the evening events, we'll miss them," Leonora put in. "Not only would that leave an avenue open for A. C. to exploit, but those old ladies themselves won't thank us—they hate to be behindhand with gossip."

The observation made them all grin.

Alicia glanced down at her lilac gown; she'd worn it to luncheon at Lady Candlewick's, but courtesy of her sojourn in the park, grass stains now adorned the hem. "I'll have to change my gown."

"So will I." Adriana waved at her carriage dress, quite unsuitable attire for an afternoon call on Lady Mott and company.

"No matter." Sitting back, Kit waved. "Leonora and I will wait."

Alicia looked at Tony and Geoffrey. The opportunity to talk privately to Kit and Leonora, to sound them out over Tony's suggestion, was a godsend—but she didn't want to leave Tony alone with them in case he wooed them to his cause before she'd a chance to assess their true reactions.

As if bowing to her wishes, he uncrossed his long legs and stood. With a glance, he roused Geoffrey, then turned to her. "We'll leave you. I'll call for you at eight, if that's suitable?"

She rose to see them out. "Yes, of course."

He and Geoffrey farewelled Kit and Leonora. Adriana also rose and accompanied them into the hall. Maggs stood ready to open the door.

Alicia gave Tony her hand. He held it, looked into her eyes; reading them, his lips tightened. "You will consider my suggestion, won't you?"

"Yes." She held his gaze. "But I don't know that I'll agree."

The urge to argue welled strong; she could see it in his eyes, feel it in the clasp of his fingers about hers. But he quelled it. Suavely inclined his head.

Releasing her hand, he nodded to Adriana. With Geoffrey following, he went out of the door and down the steps into the street.

Alicia let out the breath she'd been holding and turned.

Saw Adriana's lips open and held up a hand. "Not now. We need to get changed—we can't keep Kit and Leonora waiting."

Adriana, every bit as stubborn as she, pressed her lips tight, but acquiesced. They went quickly up the stairs side by side. Alicia turned into her room—and then hurried like a fiend, selecting a pale green gown of the finest twill and struggling into it, then expertly tweaking and resetting her coiled hair.

She was ready long before Adriana; quickly, shoes pattering, she hurried back down to the drawing room.

Regardless of the fact she'd only made their acquaintance yesterday, with Kit and Leonora she'd felt an instant rapport. Indeed, *they* had only met on her front step, yet the directness, the ready understanding on which friendship and trust were based, were already there between them. She could ask them about Tony's suggestion; they were two of the very few people whose opinion on such an issue she would trust.

Kit was describing one of her eldest son's antics; she smiled as Alicia rejoined them, and quickly brought the story to a close.

Sinking onto the chaise, Alicia clasped her hands in her lap. Both Kit and Leonora looked at her; she drew breath and stated, "In light of the difficulties A. C. seems intent on causing, Torrington has asked me to consider moving this household to Upper Brook Street. To his house."

Leonora opened her eyes wide.

Kit frowned, tapped her fingers on the chair arm. "Who else is resident there?"

"A widowed cousin and her two young daughters—ten and twelve—are expected tomorrow."

Leonora's face cleared; she glanced at Kit. "It would certainly be—" She looked at Alicia and grimaced. "I was going to say an improvement, but by that I mean that while this address is perfectly respectable, Upper Brook Street would place you in the heart of the ton. It would be a statement in itself."

"Indeed," Kit agreed. "And given we suspect A.C. knows the ropes quite well, it's a statement he'll understand." She shifted, her bluey violet eyes studying Alicia. "I know Torrington House—Jack and Tony are old friends. It's a *huge* mansion, and currently only Tony lives there—you can imagine him rattling around like a pea in a cauldron. And it's fully staffed—he's never been able to bring himself to let anyone go, even though there's really no call for three parlormaids when there's only a bachelor to cater for. From what I've seen of his butler, Hungerford, he'll be in alt at the prospect of having a houseful of people to organize for again."

"It sounds like an excellent suggestion." Leonora looked at Alicia. "And it certainly sounds as if your household—boys and all—will fit."

Alicia studied their faces. There was not the slightest hint that either saw anything in any way remotely socially unacceptable in the notion of her living at Torrington House. In the end, she put her question directly. "You don't think it will be seen as scandalous—my living there?"

Leonora opened her eyes wide, clearly surprised by the question. "With his cousin in residence, I really can't see why anyone would disapprove."

She glanced at Kit, who nodded in agreement.

They both looked at Alicia. She summoned a smile. "I see. Thank you."

Adriana came in, a stunning breath of fresh air in a frilled gown of white muslin sprigged with blue. "Ready?"

The three ladies seated smiled and rose. Linking arms, they headed for Lady Mott's.

How he managed to keep his tongue between his teeth Tony didn't know, but he held his peace on the subject of the move for the entire evening.

Kit helped. She swanned up to him in Lady Humphries' ballroom and claimed his arm for a waltz. Alicia laughed and waved them away, remaining chatting with a group of others, all sufficiently harmless. Reluctantly, he let Kit lead him to the floor.

"Mission accomplished," she informed him the instant they were safely revolving. "And I was superbly subtle, I'll have you know. I didn't even have to mention it—she asked, and Leonora and I reassured her. We told her it was an excellent idea."

She smiled at him. "So next time Jack's being difficult about something, remember—you owe me."

He humphed and whirled her about, and forbore to mention that if Jack was being difficult about something, he'd almost certainly agree with him. "How did she take it?" he asked when they were once more precessing sedately up the room.

Kit frowned. "I'm not sure, but the impression I got was that her resistance stemmed primarily from a concern that in accepting your invitation she'd be committing some sort of social solecism." She looked up at him. "She's more or less on her own, with no older lady to guide her. For what it's worth, I don't think her resistance is all that entrenched."

"Good."

They spoke no more of it; at the end of the dance, he returned Kit to Jack's side.

Jack sent a significant glance his way. "I'll be dropping

by that other venue later. I'll catch up with you tomorrow if I learn anything to the point."

He'd lowered his voice, directed his words specifically to Tony, yet Kit caught not only the words, but their subtext. "What point? What other venue?"

Jack looked into her narrowing eyes. "Just a little business matter."

"Oh? Whose business?" Kit sweetly inquired. "A. C.'s?"

"Sssh!" Jack glanced around, but there was no one close enough to hear.

Kit saw her advantage and pressed it, drilling one finger into Jack's chest. "If you imagine you're going out skulking tonight *alone*, then you'll need to promise to inform not just Tony but *all* of us of anything you discover."

Curling his hand around hers, Jack scowled at her. "You'll learn soon enough."

Kit opened her eyes wide. "When you deign to tell us? Thank you, but no—I much prefer to set a time and place for your revelations."

Tony nearly choked; he was privy to the story of what had happened in the early days of their marriage, when Jack had refused to tell Kit what he was involved in. Clearly, Kit had not forgotten. From the look on Jack's face, one of chagrin and uneasy uncertainty, he hadn't either.

When Jack glanced at him, Kit cut in, "And you needn't look to Tony for support." She fixed her violet eyes on him. "He already owes Leonora and me a favor. A very telltale favor."

In her eyes, he read a threat of doom should he fail to capitulate. He sighed and glanced at Jack. "I was going to suggest the club, but let's make it my library. What time?"

Jack humphed. "I'll send word first thing in the morning, once I know what I've managed to find."

Kit beamed at them both. "See? It doesn't hurt."

Jack snorted. Tony fought down a grin. He chatted for a while, then headed back up the ballroom to Alicia, still safe within Adriana's circle.

Which circle was growing less and less intent as more of those aspiring to Adriana's attention *vis à vis* claiming her hand took note of the glances she shared with Geoffrey, and sloped off to pay court to someone else. One gentleman who remained apparently oblivious of the clear firming of Adriana's intention was Sir Freddie Caudel.

As he drew near, Tony wondered if Sir Freddie was biding his time, perhaps thinking to give Adriana more experience of the ton before making his offer, or if he was instead merely using her as a convenient and unthreatening excuse to avoid all other possible candidates. If the man hadn't spoken yet . . . but then, he himself and Geoffrey were of a more direct generation.

Sir Freddie had been conversing with Alicia. He saw Tony approaching, smiled benignly, and excused himself as Tony joined her.

She turned to him, raised a brow. Wariness showed behind the green of her eyes; with an easy smile, he claimed her hand, set it on his sleeve, and inquired if she'd like to stroll.

She agreed, and they did. Because of the many eyes fixed on them courtesy of the story on so many lips, it was impossible to slip away. Resigned, he reminded himself of the true purpose behind their evening's endeavors and conducted her to chat with the next fashionable lady waiting to have her say.

They caught up with his godmother in the Athelstans' ballroom. Dispatched to fetch refreshments, he left Alicia seated on the chaise beside Lady Amery and shouldered his way into the crowd.

Alicia watched him go, then drew breath and turned to Lady Amery. "I hope you won't think me presumptuous, ma'am, but I need advice, and as the person most nearly concerned is Torrington . . ."

She and Lady Amery were alone on the small chaise; there was no one else close enough to hear—and she might never have another such opportunity to ask the one person in London who held Tony's welfare closest to her heart.

Lady Amery had turned to her; now she smiled radiantly. Reaching for Alicia's hands, she clasped them in hers. "My dear, I'd be delighted to help in any way I can."

Alicia steeled herself to see that sentiment change in the next minutes. Lifting her head, she confessed, "Torrington has asked that I and my household move into his house in Upper Brook Street—his widowed cousin and her daughters will be staying there, too."

Lady Amery's gaze grew distant as she considered, then she refocused on Alicia's face. "*Bon.* Yes, I can see that that would be much more comfortable, especially for him, what with this latest brouhaha." Her eyes twinkled, then, reading Alicia's troubled expression, she grew serious. "But you do not wish this? Would it be difficult to move to Upper Brook Street?"

Alicia stared into her ladyship's transparently sincere eyes. Blinked. "No . . . that is . . ." She dragged in a breath. "I just don't want to do anything to give the gossips food for slander—I don't want inadvertently to do anything to damage his name or his standing."

Lady Amery's concerned expression dissolved into smiles. She patted Alicia's hand. "It is very right that you think of such things—such sentiments do you credit—but I assure you in this case, there is nothing to concern you. The ton understands such matters—*oui, vraiment.*" She nodded encouragingly. "There will be no adverse repercussions to your moving to Upper Brook Street in such circumstances."

The assurance with which she made the statement put the matter beyond argument.

Her expression easing, the weight on her shoulders lightening, Alicia smiled and let herself accept it. Despite her worries, her reservations, everyone—absolutely everyone—insisted Tony's suggestion was not only sound, but an outcome to be desired.

Despite that . . . she said nothing when he returned bearing glasses of champagne. Lady Amery claimed his attention and chatted animatedly about shared acquaintances, to Alicia's relief making no allusion to their discussion or her advice.

Finally, the long evening drew to a close, and they headed home. Geoffrey held to his new habit and accompanied them to their door; Tony, as usual, stayed with them beyond it.

In her bedchamber, they undressed—in silence. She felt herself tensing, waiting for him to ask her again, to press his case . . . instead, he said nothing. She climbed into the big bed; he pinched out the candle, and joined her beneath the covers.

He reached for her, drew her to him, then hesitated. In the dimness, he looked at her face. "You're still considering?"

There was no hint of a frown, of irritation or impatience in his voice; he simply wanted to know.

"Yes." She held his gaze. "But I haven't yet made up my mind."

She felt him sigh, then he tightened his hold on her, lowered his head. "We can discuss it in the morning."

When she awoke the next morning, however, he'd already left her bed. She lay staring at the canopy as minutes, then half an hour ticked by, then she sighed and rose.

Washed, gowned, her hair severely coiled, she headed downstairs.

Pausing in the doorway of the dining parlor, she studied the back of Tony's broad shoulders; she wasn't surprised to find him there, in the chair at the end of the table.

Her brothers saw her and turned; Tony glanced around and rose as she entered. Going past him, she waved him back to his seat, exchanged greetings with her brothers and Adriana—then, to Adriana's amusement, remembered to bid their guest a good morning, too.

He returned it with aplomb, recommending the kedgeree. She poured herself a cup of tea, then rose and crossed to the sideboard. She made her selections, all the while conscious of her brothers' whispers, of the anticipation welling, notch by notch, around the table.

Calmly, she returned to her chair, set down her plate, then sat, thanking Maggs, who held the chair for her.

That done, she picked up her fork—and looked around the table.

At four pairs of expectant eyes. And one black gaze she couldn't read.

She drew in a deep breath, exhaled. "All right. We'll move to Torrington House."

Her brothers cheered; Adriana beamed.

She looked down at her plate, poked at the pile of kedgeree on it. "*But* only when Lord Torrington's cousin is ready to receive us."

The cheering didn't abate, instead it broke up into excited speculation, mixed with whispered plans. She glanced at her brothers, then looked at Tony.

Raised a brow.

Tony knew better than to allow his satisfaction, let alone its depth, to show; looking down the table, holding Alicia's gaze, he inclined his head. "I'll send word when Miranda is recovered from her journey and ready to meet you."

Knowing Miranda, he predicted that would be about ten minutes after she arrived.

SEVENTEEN

AS HE'D PROPHESIED, SO IT PROVED. MIRANDA ARRIVED agog to meet the lady who had finally, as she put it, snared him.

An openhearted lady of considerable charm, her husband's early death had left her sincerely bereft.

"Although I doubt that will last forever." Blond curls framing her heart-shaped face, she looked up at Tony as he stood before the fire in his drawing room. "Meanwhile, I'm on pins, positive pins, waiting to meet this widow of yours. Dare I guess she's ravishingly beautiful?"

Tony fixed her with a not entirely mock-severe glance. "You will behave. Furthermore, you will not regale Alicia with tales of my youth, nor yet of my childhood."

Miranda's grin deepened. "Spoilsport."

He snorted, and turned to the door. The clock on the mantelpiece chimed—twelve *tings*. "I'll go and inform her of your great willingness to make her acquaintance."

At the door, he paused, glanced back. "Just remember—she and I haven't yet formally discussed our marriage." By which he meant she hadn't yet, in so many words, agreed.

Miranda looked both intrigued and delighted. "Don't worry—I won't scuttle your punt."

Feigning disbelief, he left.

* * *

The atmosphere reigning in Waverton Street was as close to pandemonium as anything he'd experienced. He stood in the front hall transfixed by the activity. Crates lay open on the tiles; the green baize door stood propped wide, and a hum of noise pervaded the house. The boys were rushing up and down the stairs, calling to each other, ferrying books and toys, clothes and shoes, stuffing them joyously into the crates before, pausing only to flash him wide grins, racing up the stairs once more.

Through the open dining-room door, he saw Cook and Fitchett carefully wrapping glassware. A sound drew his attention to the gallery; he watched as Maggs, a heavy case on one shoulder, slowly descended the stairs.

"Madhouse, it is." Depositing the case beside two closed crates, Maggs grinned at him. "Almost as bad as one of your mama's journeys."

"Heaven forfend," Tony muttered. "Where's Mrs. Carrington?"

"In her room packing." Maggs stepped aside as the boys came whooping down once more. "Think she's nearly done, but she did say as she'd be out to organize these three devils betimes."

The boys looked up from where they were carefully squeezing slippers and dressing robes in around their toys. They grinned.

Tony fixed them with a direct look. "Do you three devils still need your eldest sister to organize you?"

"'Course not." David shrugged. "But she does anyway."

The other two nodded.

Tony raised his brows. "So if I take her away, you'll be able to manage on your own? My cousin is waiting to meet her, and I thought it might be easier if Alicia came first, on her own."

David and Harry exchanged glances, then nodded encouragingly.

"Good idea," Harry opined. "Then she won't be here to fuss over us."

Matthew looked less certain; Maggs lumbered forward and held out a hand. "Here then, I'll help. We can get you all packed, and meanwhile your sister can go and make Mrs. Althorpe's acquaintance, and make sure she's ready to meet you three, heh?"

Nodding, Matthew took Maggs's hand, but he kept his gaze on Tony's face. "So we'll come to your house later?"

Tony hunkered down, lightly squeezed Matthew's other hand. "I'll send my coach around for you as soon as I get home. It's large enough to take all of you at once, and the luggage can follow. That way, you'll be in Upper Brook Street, in my house, all the sooner."

"Hooray!" David and Harry turned and raced up the stairs. Grinning, reassured, Matthew dashed after them. Maggs brought up the rear.

Tony watched until they disappeared along the corridor, then he went up the stairs and along to Alicia's room.

She was bending over a box at the foot of her bed; straightening with a sigh, she shut the lid.

Smiling, he strolled in. "Finished?"

Alicia looked at him, returned his smile, then glanced distractedly around the room. "Yes—I think that's it for in here."

"Good." Halting before her, he reached for her.

Before she realized what he intended, he'd caught her, bent his head, and was kissing her . . . thoroughly. Her head spun pleasurably . . . then she remembered and struggled.

He ended the kiss; raising his head, he looked down at her. "What?"

She wriggled from his hands, firm about her waist. "The boys!" She peeked around him at the door, but there was no sign of them.

Tony met her warning look with a quizzical one, then he glanced around. "I came to take you to meet Miranda." His gaze returned to her. "She's waiting, so she assured me, on pins."

"Already? Oh." She scanned the room, but she had indeed packed everything. "But the boys aren't yet ready and—"

"The boys assured me they had their packing under control. Maggs has elected to watch over them, and you know Jenkins will as well, and Fitchett and Adriana." He fixed her with a direct look. "So there's no reason you can't come with me now. I'll send my carriage once we reach Upper Brook Street, so they'll all be only an hour or so behind."

She frowned. "But—"

"And don't forget the engagements we have tonight. You'll need to settle in, and then we have a meeting at two o'clock in the library—Jack sent word he's got what we wanted—I'm assuming you still wish to attend?" Innocently, he looked inquiringly at her.

She narrowed her eyes at him. "Of course."

He inclined his head. "And then we've dinner at Lady Martindale's followed by two balls, so we'll be out again within a few hours. I think you should look over the rooms before the others arrive, just in case there's any difficulty, anything you'd like changed."

Lips setting, she looked into his black eyes; she'd seen that expression of immovable purpose before—knew he wouldn't change tack, not easily . . . and perhaps he was right.

She grimaced. "Your cousin—she only has two daughters?"

Tony nodded; taking her elbow, he turned her to the door. "If you're worried she'll have the vapors over the boys' antics, you can rest easy—Miranda was a tomboy to the depths of her soul. We spent much of our childhood together—we were both only children. If anything, she'll be in her element with your brothers—and, incidentally, so will her daughters. If I'm any judge, they'll give your three a run for their money."

That distracted her, enough for him to steer her to the stairs. But—

"I must speak with Fitchett, and Cook, too, before I can leave."

At least she was going down the stairs. He went with her, resigned yet on guard. Stoically, he stuck to her side, determinedly herding her back to the front hall. Finally there, he picked up the pelisse she'd left lying on a chair and helped her into it.

Taking her hand, he drew her out of the front door, pulled it shut, then led her down the steps to where his curricle stood waiting. One of his grooms was holding his matched bays. He helped her in, waited while she'd settled her skirts, then climbed up beside her. Nodding to the groom, he set the horses pacing. Glancing at her, he saw her watching his hands on the reins, watching the horses, still skittish, coquettish.

He realized she was nervous; he kept the horses to a slow trot. "Don't worry—they won't bolt."

She glanced at him. "Oh—I just . . . have rarely had occasion to be behind such beasts. They're very powerful, aren't they?"

"Yes, but I have the reins."

The comment took a moment to sink in, then she relaxed. She looked at him. "You haven't driven me anywhere before."

He shrugged. "There hasn't until now been a need."

But today was different; he wanted her to himself, free of her family. When she first crossed the threshold of his house, he wanted to be with her, just her and him alone, without any distractions. He wanted to have that minute to himself; he refused to waste any time wondering why.

Luckily, she accepted his comment without question;

relaxing a trifle more, she looked around as he took her deeper into the heart of Mayfair.

The moment, when it came, was as simple and as private as he'd wished; only Hungerford was there, holding the door as, his hand at her elbow, Tony guided her into his front hall.

She glanced at Hungerford, nodded, and smiled, then looked up, ahead, and around, and paused, stopped.

Hungerford closed the door, but hung back in the shadows. There was no footman hovering in the hall, no one else to intrude.

Pivoting, she looked around; Tony wondered how she would see it, how she would react to his home.

After a moment, she met his gaze. She sensed his waiting, and smiled. "It's much less intimidating than I'd imagined." Her smile deepened, softened; she glanced around again. "More comfortable. I can see people here—children . . . it's a welcoming house."

Her relief was transparent. It warmed him, eased a small knot of trepidation he hadn't until then acknowledged he carried. Joining her, he took her hand. "This is Hungerford. He's the ultimate authority here."

Hungerford approached and bowed low. "At your service, ma'am. Should you need anything—anything at all—we are at your disposal."

"Thank you."

Hungerford stepped back.

Tony gestured to the drawing-room door. "I'll introduce you to Mrs. Swithins, the housekeeper, later—she can show you the rooms they've prepared. But first, come and meet Miranda."

Buoyed by her impression of the hall, Alicia went forward eagerly. Entering the drawing room, she glanced around—and was again struck by the house's warmth. Without consciously considering it, she'd been expecting a house like him, coolly, austerely elegant, but that wasn't the pervading atmosphere here. The furniture was not new, far from it; every piece looked antique, lovingly polished, the tapestry and brocade upholstery and hangings carrying the rich, jeweled tones of a bygone age.

An age that had valued comfort and convenience as well as luxury, that had expected pleasure and enjoyment to be part of daily life. Hedonistic, but rich, warm, and very much alive.

Like the bright-eyed lady rising from a chair by the hearth. She came forward, smiling widely, hands extended.

"My dear Mrs. Carrington—Alicia—I may call you Alicia, may I not? I'm Miranda, as Tony's doubtless told you. Welcome to Torrington House—may your stay be long and happy."

Miranda's smile was winning; effervescent laughter lurked in her blue eyes. Alicia gave her her hands, smiled back. "Thank you. I hope you won't be too inconvenienced by our descent."

"Oh, *I* certainly won't be, and I doubt anyone could inconvenience Hungerford—he's terrifyingly efficient— all the staff are." Miranda looked at Tony. "You may take yourself off—we want to talk, and we'll do so much more readily without you. I'll take Alicia to meet Mrs. Swithins, so you're relieved on that score, too."

Alicia barely smothered a laugh. She glanced at Tony, saw chagrin briefly flare in his eyes as he sent Miranda a sharp glance, then he turned to her. "I'll send the carriage around for your family."

She smiled. "Thank you."

He hesitated, then, reluctant to the last, nodded and left them.

"Now!" Miranda turned to her, curiosity and delight in her face. "You must tell me all about your family—you have three brothers and a sister, that's all Tony's told me." Waving her to a chair, Miranda resumed her seat.

Alicia sank into the velvet comfort of an armchair, felt a solid sense of safety and security reach for her and wrap her about. Meeting Miranda's expectant gaze, she smiled and assembled her thoughts.

By the time Hungerford brought in the tea tray and she and Miranda had shared a pot, they'd progressed from acquaintances to friends, to newly found bosom-bows. The fictitious nature of her widowhood notwithstanding, they shared many interests—family, country pursuits, household management, and social necessity.

Miranda sent for her daughters; the girls arrived and made their curtsies, then asked polite but curious questions about her brothers. Alicia answered, inwardly heaving a sigh of relief; the girls were well-brought-up, well-bred young ladies, but not in the least sweet, retiring, or weak. They would, indeed, give her brothers pause.

Then it was time to meet Mrs. Swithins and look around the rooms before the others arrived. After performing the introductions, Miranda hung back, letting the housekeeper, a woman of considerable age but imposing presence, softened by a twinkle in her eye, guide Alicia through the house.

"We thought your young brothers would be most comfortable up here, ma'am." Mrs. Swithins led the way into the schoolroom; she waved to rooms opening off the central room. "There's three beds in the long room, and two in the next, so they can sleep together or separate if they wish." She smiled at Alicia. "We weren't sure, so both rooms are prepared."

Alicia frowned. "They're used to being together, but David is twelve."

Mrs. Swithins nodded. "We can leave it to them to decide what's most comfortable."

With a grateful inclination of her head, Alicia allowed

herself to be led on to view the bedrooms for Fitchett and Jenkins.

"So they'll be close enough should the boys have need." With an airy wave, Mrs. Swithins sailed on.

The rooms on the first floor that had been prepared for her and Adriana filled Alicia, not with surprise, for she'd expected something of the sort, but with a sense of having stepped into a fairy tale, or, more specifically, into her own dreams.

Her room lay in the central wing of the mansion, above the long ballroom and overlooking the rear gardens. A wide, spacious chamber, it possessed a sitting area with two chairs before the fireplace, a delicate escritoire against one wall, a bank of large windows with a padded window seat beneath, a gigantic armoire, and a huge four-poster bed hung with pale green silks and covered with an ivory silk coverlet embroidered in green.

"The master mentioned your maid was not with you, so I've assigned Bertha." Mrs. Swithins beckoned to a young girl, who came forward and shyly curtsied. "She knows her way around a lady's wardrobe and is quick with her hands."

Alicia returned Bertha's smile, a trifle shy herself. She'd never had a maid, just Fitchett, not quite the same thing.

"I've hung your gowns in the armoire, ma'am." Bertha's voice was soft, carrying a country burr. Greatly daring, she glanced up and met Alicia's eye. "Absolutely stunning, they be."

"Thank you, Bertha." Alicia hesitated, then added, "I'll need you this evening to help me dress—we've a dinner and two balls to attend."

"Oh?" Miranda pricked up her ears; she came forward to link her arm in Alicia's. "What's this? Tony gadding about in society? Whatever next? You must tell."

Alicia laughed. She thanked Mrs. Swithins, then let Miranda sweep her back downstairs.

The others arrived just in time for luncheon. Emerging from a room Alicia took to be the library, Tony joined the melee in the front hall, then shepherded her family into the dining room, where Miranda waited with her daughters.

Introductions between children could sometimes be awkward; in this case, the arrival of the luncheon dishes cut short any difficult moment. Quickly wriggling onto the chairs to which Tony and Miranda directed them, both her brothers and Miranda's girls were at first on their best behavior, their responses stilted. That lasted only until the platter of sausages was uncovered. Thereafter, needing to ask each other to pass this or that, they quickly lost their shyness in the quest for sustenance.

Margaret and Constance were sturdy young ladies with long blond plaits; both ate heartily, showing no overt sign of consciousness of the boys. That piqued David's and Harry's interest enough for them to extend an invitation to go kite flying in the park.

The girls exchanged looks, then agreed.

When three faces turned up the table to Alicia, and two to Miranda, at the table's other end, the ladies exchanged pleased glances and nodded permission; with just one whoop—from Harry, valiantly smothered—they all pushed back from the table, bobbed curtsies or bowed, then, dismissed with nods, they headed in a bumbling crowd for the door, and Maggs, Jenkins, the park, and the sky.

"Well," Miranda said, turning back from watching them go, "they seem to have fallen on their feet."

Tony shrugged. "Why not?" His gaze went to Alicia, sitting beside him, lingered, then he looked down the table at Adriana, seated beside Miranda. "The others should be arriving any minute." To Miranda, he explained, "We're holding a council of war, so to speak, in the library this afternoon, to discuss the latest developments in our search for A. C."

Miranda's eyes opened wide; she glanced at Alicia. "Is this a private meeting, or can I listen in?"

Tony grimaced. "All in all, it might be as well if you did."

A knock sounded on the front door, and he rose. He didn't trust A. C., not on any level; given Miranda was here with her girls, sharing his roof with Alicia and her family, it was only fair she knew the whole score.

He ushered the three ladies, all determined to attend the gathering, into the front hall as Hungerford opened the door. Members of the Bastion Club streamed in. Tony nodded in greeting; beside him, Miranda murmured, "Well, well—you didn't mention them. And they are?"

The introductions took a few minutes, by which time Tristan and Leonora, Geoffrey, and, most importantly, Jack Hendon and Kit, had arrived. Once everyone was comfortably seated in the library, the large room looked unusually full.

A knock fell on the front door; it opened. A deep voice, not Hungerford's, was heard. An instant later, the library door opened, and Charles walked in. Seeing all eyes on him, he raised his brows. "Am I late?"

Tony waved him to a chair. "I thought you were away."

"No such luck." Charles drew up a chair and sat. "Merely a visit to Surrey with my sisters, sisters-in-law, and dear mama. I got back"—he glanced at the clock— "two hours ago, but matters are so fraught in Bedford Square, I dared not remain. I took refuge at the club, and Gasthorpe told me of the meeting."

His dark gaze, along with a piratical smile, swept the room. "So, what do we have?"

Alicia followed that sweeping glance around the faces, saw in each an impatience, an eagerness, a determination to get on with the business of unmasking A. C. They were quite a crowd, five ladies and eight gentlemen, an intelligent and talented company focused on their common goal.

"So what did you find?" Tony's gaze rested on Jack Hendon.

Jack had settled on a straight-backed chair. "I got the information from Lloyd's, unfortunately not as much as I'd have liked. There's a watchman who goes around every half hour. I could only chance three passes—I had to put out the light every time he came by. Without it, I couldn't see to make copies of the bills of lading." He drew a sheaf of papers from his inside coat pocket. "I got the full details of six ships before I called it a night. However—"

He distributed the papers, handing three to the men on his right, three to his left; the ladies, on the two chaises perpendicular to the hearth, had to contain their curiosity until the men had scanned the pages and passed them their way.

"As you can see," Jack resumed, as the men finished with the papers and looked up, "there's nothing obvious, no particular goods or commodities that were carried on all six ships." He paused, then added. "I'm not sure where that gets us. I was assuming there would be something in common."

The men frowned; they looked at the six sheets, now in the ladies' hands.

"How did you choose which ships to examine?" Christian asked.

"More or less randomly over the years '12 to '15." Jack grimaced. "I thought that would be most useful, but now I wonder whether whatever's the crucial element changes over time. One thing for so many months, another later."

Gervase Tregarth leaned forward, peering at the lists Kit and Alicia had spread on a low table before the chaise. "Is there definitely no item in common?"

Kit, Alicia, and Leonora shook their heads.

One of the men muttered something about the seasons.

Alicia tapped an item on one list. "Three hundred ell of finest muslin. Remember how expensive muslin was?

The price is much better now, but when this was brought in, it would have been worth a small fortune."

"Hmm." Leonora studied the entry. "I never thought of it before—one simply grumbles and pays the price—but it must have been due to the war."

"Supply and demand," Kit said. They were speaking quietly, their lighter voices a counterpoint against the men's rumblings. "Jack says it's the merchants who best supply the demand who get on in business."

"True," Miranda put in, "and during the war, the demand was always there, never satisfied. Anything imported was by definition expensive. Just think how the prices of silks—"

"Let alone tea and coffee." Alicia tapped another entry on one list.

Miranda nodded; so did the others. "All those things became hideously dear. . . ." Her words faded.

Their gazes met. They all exchanged one long wondering glance, then looked at the lists.

"You don't think . . . ?" Adriana leaned nearer.

All five ladies bent over the lists again.

The gentlemen continued to reassess and revisit their reasoning, trying to see a way forward.

Alicia straightened. "That's it." She pointed triumphantly to items listed on each of the six bills of lading. "Tea and coffee!"

"Yes—*of course*!" Kit snatched up one of the lists and checked the entry, then reached for another.

"Ah—I see!" Leonora, face lighting, picked up another list.

Tony, Tristan, and Jack exchanged glances. "What do you see?" Tristan asked.

"The item in common." Alicia picked up another list and pointed to a line. "Tea—one thousands pounds of finest leaves from Assam."

Handing that list to Tony, she picked up another. "On

this one, it's coffee—three hundred pounds of best beans from Colombia."

Kit sat back. "So sometimes it's coffee, and sometimes it's tea—one from the West Indies, the other on ships from the East."

"But they're often both handled by the same merchant," Leonora informed the men as the lists made their way around the circle again. "Not necessarily sold through the same shops, but it's usually the same supplier."

"Which supplier?" Christian asked.

The ladies exchanged glances. "There are many, I imagine," Miranda replied. "It's a profitable area, and fashionable in its way."

"But it's the price that's so important." Alicia looked around the male company. "It's always difficult to get good-quality coffee and tea—there never is enough brought into the country, even now. As Kit said, it's supply and demand, so the price always remains high."

"For good quality," Adriana stressed.

"Indeed." Kit nodded. "And that, perhaps, is where A.C. might have made his money. During the war, certainly over the years '12 to '15, the price of tea and coffee—the better-quality stuff—fluctuated wildly. It was always high, but sometimes it reached astronomical heights."

"Because," Leonora took up the tale, "you men always insist on your coffee at the breakfast table, and we ladies, of course, must have our tea for our tea parties, and the ton wouldn't go around if those things weren't there."

There was an instant's silence as the men all stared at them.

"Are you saying"—Charles leaned forward and fixed them with an intent look—"that during the war, the price of tea and coffee was often driven high—very high—because of sudden shortages?"

All five ladies nodded decisively.

Miranda added, "Only the best-quality merchandise, mind you."

"Indeed. But tea and coffee—the finest quality—appears on each of those lists? One or the other at least?"

Again, the ladies nodded.

"That," Alicia concluded, "seems the only link—the only thing in common, so to speak."

"Held to ransom over our breakfasts." Gervase gathered the lists and shuffled through them. "Doesn't bear thinking of, but it certainly looks—and sounds—right."

Tristan was looking over his shoulder. "Two ships from the West Indies with coffee, the other four, all East Indiamen, carried tea."

"These prices." Jack fixed his wife with a questioning glance. "How much of an increase are we looking at— prices twice as high, three times?"

"For the best coffee?" Kit glanced at Leonora and Alicia. "Anything from ten, to even fifty times the usual price, I would say."

"For tea," Miranda said, "it could easily be from ten to thirty times the price before the war—and even that price was always high."

"How high?" Tristan asked.

The ladies pursed their lips, then tossed around figures that made the men blanch. "Good God!" Charles stopped, calculating. "Why that's . . ."

"One hell of a lot of money!" Jack growled.

"One hell of a lot of profit," Gervase said.

"One very good reason to ensure that the supply failed at critical times." Tony fixed the ladies with an inquisitorial look. "From what you're saying, the person who would stand to gain—"

"Is the merchant who had brought in a cargo of tea and coffee safely just before any shortage occurred."

It was Jack who had spoken. Tony looked at him. "Before?"

Jack nodded. "The warehouses and docks know when a ship and its cargo doesn't arrive, and the merchants mark up the prices of the goods they have in stock accordingly—that I know for fact."

"So . . ." They all sat and thought it over, then Tony called them to order. "Assuming the answer is tea and coffee, how do we go on from here?"

"We first check the waybills of the other ten ships we know were lost courtesy of Ruskin's information." Jack glanced at Tony. "Two of us, now we know what we're looking for, could probably check all the waybills at once."

Tony nodded. "We'll do it tonight."

"Meanwhile," Christian said, "the rest of us can start investigating the merchants who specialize in tea and coffee. The connection to A. C. must be through them." He frowned, then glanced around. "What could the connection between A. C. and a merchant be, given we know, or at least can surmise, that A. C. is one of the ton?"

Charles grimaced. "Can we surmise that, do you think? That he is one of us?"

"I think that's beyond question," Tony answered. "Who else would have known how to manipulate the ton against Alicia? And Dalziel confirmed that the third round of information against her had been laid through the most exclusive gentlemen's clubs. There seems little doubt A. C. is a member not just of the ton, but the haut ton—our circle." A memory floated through his mind; he grimaced. "Indeed, I suspect I've seen him."

"You have?"

"When?"

He briefly explained, describing the man he'd seen through the mists in Park Street all those nights ago.

"Astrakhan—you know, that's not all that common," Jack Warnefleet said. "A point to remember, especially if he didn't know you'd seen him."

"That leaves us still facing the final question," Christian said. "What link could there be between a tea and coffee merchant and a member of the haut ton?"

The room fell silent; only the ticking of the mantelpiece clock could be heard, then Charles looked at Tony. "It couldn't be *that*, could it—the reason behind Ruskin's murder?"

"It's certainly feasible." Tristan leaned back in his chair. "There's many in the ton would move heaven and earth to hide any contact with trade."

"Add to that the illegality involved, let alone its treasonous nature . . ." Gervase glanced around. "That's a powerful motive for removing Ruskin."

"And then going to *any* lengths to cover his tracks." Tony's gaze was fixed on Alicia.

There were slow nods all around. Charles leaned forward, hands clasped. "That's it—we might not yet be able to see the player, but that assuredly is the game. A. C. is directly involved in trade via some tea and coffee merchant."

Suddenly needing to move, Tony rose. Crossing to the fireplace, closer to Alicia, he braced an arm on the mantelpiece and looked around the circle. "Let's recapitulate. A. C. is at the very least a sleeping partner with a merchant who imports the finest tea and coffee. In order to increase profits by driving up prices, he sets out to manipulate the supply of tea and coffee through having ships carrying competitors' supplies taken by the French."

He looked at Jack Hendon. "How did he know which ships to target?"

Jack shrugged. "Easy enough if you're inside the trade. The merchants know each other, and each merchant usually has contracts with only one or at most two shipping lines, and the ships run by each line are listed in a number of registers, none hard to access. It wouldn't have been difficult."

Tony nodded. "So he knows which ships to target to

make his plan work. With the information from Ruskin, he knows when each returning ship will not be under frigate escort, and thus an easy and vulnerable target for a foreign captain."

His voiced hardened. "So A. C. arranges for the target ships to be taken, then sits back in London and counts the inflated return from the cargo he's already landed."

A long silence followed, then Christian straightened. "That's how it worked. We need to identify all possible merchants, then investigate which one had safe cargoes to exploit."

"And from there," Jack Warnefleet murmured, "we dig until we uncover A. C.—there'll be some track leading back to him, one way or another."

The soft menace in his tone was balm to them all.

Christian looked at Tony. "I'll act as coordinator in the search for the merchant, if you like." He glanced at the other members of the club. "We can take that on. I'll let you know the instant we identify the most likely firm."

Tony nodded. "I'll go with Jack tonight and confirm that the link holds good—if there's any ship taken that wasn't carrying tea or coffee, it might give us a link to another aspect of A. C.'s trade interests."

"True." Christian stood. "The more links we can get to A. C.'s trading activities, the easier it'll be to identify him conclusively."

The men rose. The ladies did, too, exchanging plans for meeting that evening at the balls they'd attend.

As the group emerged into the front hall, Charles paused beside Tony, his gaze uncharacteristically bleak. "You know, I might have understood if A. C.'s motive was in some way . . . well, patriotic even if grossly misguided. If he was the sort of traitor who sincerely believed England should lose the war and follow some revolutionary course. But be damned if I can understand how any Englishman could so cold-bloodedly have sent so many English sailors to almost certain death at the hands of the French"—he met Tony's gaze—"all for money."

Tony nodded. "That's one point that sticks in my craw."

Along with the fact A. C. had cast Alicia as his scapegoat.

Expressions grimly determined, they made their farewells and parted, all convinced of one thing. Whoever A. C. was, the man had no soul.

EIGHTEEN

"TAKE CARE!"

In the crush of Lady Carmody's ballroom, Alicia watched Kit lecture her handsome husband, then she turned on Tony, standing beside Alicia.

"And you, too. I suppose I feel responsible after pulling you out of the water all those years ago, but regardless, I would prefer not to have to come to some dockside Watch House and explain to the interested who you both are."

Tony raised his brows. "If we're caught, it'll be your husband's fault—I haven't been retired as long as he."

From the look on Kit's face, she didn't know whether to take umbrage on Jack's behalf or be more worried still. When no eruption ensued, Jack, behind her, glanced around at her face. Sliding his arm around her, he hugged her. "Stop worrying. I'll—we'll—be perfectly safe."

Alicia turned to Tony. She fixed him with her most severe look, the one guaranteed instantly to wring the truth from her brothers. "Is he speaking the truth? *Will* you be all right?"

Tony smiled; lifting her hand, he pressed a warm kiss into her palm. "There's no danger to speak of. Lloyd's is just a coffeehouse—easy pickings."

She wasn't entirely convinced and let it show; his smile deepened.

Glancing around at the jostling throng, at the many

gentlemen moving through its ranks, looking over the available ladies, he murmured, "I'm more concerned about you. Geoffrey will stay close, and Tristan and Leonora will meet you at the Hammonds', then Geoffrey will see you home." He met her gaze. "You face more danger than I." He added, pointedly, "Take care."

It was her turn to smile. "If worse comes to worst, I can always claim Sir Freddie's arm." And perhaps divert him from Adriana's side; the baronet remained assiduously attentive despite Adriana's hints.

Tony grimaced. Jack tapped him on the shoulder; he looked around.

"We'd better go." With a nod, Jack took his leave of her.

Tony's eyes returned to hers, lingered, then he released her hand and turned. With Jack, he moved into the crowd. They were taller than most, yet in seconds, neither Kit nor she could see them.

"Humph!" Kit pulled a face, and linked her arm in Alicia's. "We've been deserted." Surveying Adriana's circle, she set her chin. "This is far too tame—come on." She set off into the crowd, drawing Alicia with her. "Let's find some useful distraction. I don't know about you, but without it, I'll go mad."

Alicia laughed, and let herself be towed into the melée.

Gaining access to the records they sought wasn't quite as easy as Tony had painted it, yet soon enough he and Jack were flicking through files in the offices above the coffee house, searching for, then poring over the bills of lading lodged for the other ten ships Ruskin had identified and which were subsequently taken.

While he worked, Tony's mind revisited their logic, their strategies. "The connection had better not be through Lloyd's itself."

"Unlikely," Jack answered from across the room. "As far as I know, they've never handled tea."

Half an hour later, Tony wondered aloud, "In all of

this"—he waved at the cabinets ringing the room—"do you think there's any chance of identifying ships that docked with cargoes of tea or coffee say in the week before one that was taken?"

Jack looked up, then shook his head. "Needle in a haystack. Virtually every ship that passes through the Port of London will have a waybill in here. That's often hundreds a day. We'd never be able to check enough to identify the ship we want."

He resumed his searching. "Mind you, we *will* be able to confirm the link once we know the merchant and his shipping line."

Tony nodded, and continued flipping through files.

It took them two hours to locate and examine the ten waybills. Then they quietly put the room to rights, eradicating any sign of their visit, and silently retreated from the room and the building.

By the time Tony reached Upper Brook Street, Mayfair was silent, the streets dark with shadows. Miranda, Adriana, and Alicia would have returned home long ago. They should all be asleep in their beds.

Closing the front door, he shot the well-oiled bolts, then crossed the hall. There was no lamp or candle left burning; Hungerford knew him better than that. Quite aside from his excellent night vision, he knew this house like the back of his hand, knew every creak in the stairs, every board that might groan.

At the top of the stairs, he turned away from the gallery leading to the east wing where Miranda, her daughters, and Adriana had their rooms, and headed for the room Alicia had been given, three doors from the master suite. Hand on the doorknob, he paused, struck by a sudden thought.

How had Mrs. Swithins known . . . ?

The answer was obvious. He really was *that* transparent.

Grimacing, he turned the knob.

Alicia was in bed, but not asleep. Cocooned beneath the luxurious embroidered silk coverlet, silk sheets sliding seductively over her skin, she'd been waiting for the past hour, waiting to at least hear Tony's footsteps, passing her door . . . or not, as the case might be.

Unable to sleep, made edgy by her own expectation—that he would come to her, that she wanted him to, even needed him to—an expectation she found somewhat damning—she was after all in his house, an old aristocratic mansion, yet while that fact might inhibit her, she doubted it would influence him—she had forcibly turned her mind to reviewing the day. A long day in which much had happened, and much had changed.

So easily.

That more than anything else, the ease with which the changes had been wrought, the ease with which she'd simply *flowed* into the position he'd created for her, niggled. In some odd way seemed to mock her. Everything had fallen into place so smoothly, she was still struggling to come to grips with the ramifications. As if he'd once more swept her off her feet, and her head had yet to stop whirling.

Not, for her, an uncommon feeling where he was concerned.

It wasn't that she wished things were otherwise; she couldn't convincingly argue against the move, not even to herself. But the uncertainty, the lack of clarity regarding her position here—the lack of sureness made it impossible to feel confident, at ease . . .

She never heard his footsteps; only a faint draft alerted her to the opening door. He was no more than a dark shadow slipping through; she recognized him instantly.

Her eyes had adjusted to the dimness; watching him cross the wide room toward her, she searched his face, all she could see of him, but could detect not even a limp.

Kit's worry had infected her, yet here he was unscathed, moving with his usual fluid grace toward the bed.

He stopped by a chair and sat, reaching down to pull off his boots. She sat up, wriggling in the sheets onto her side; he heard the shushing and glanced across, smiled a touch wearily.

"Did you find the lists? From the other ships?"

He nodded. Setting his boots aside, he stood, stretched. "We found all ten—your theory was right. It's tea and coffee that's the link."

He lowered his arms, weary tension falling from him.

She watched him undress—coat, cravat, waistcoat, and shirt hit the chair. Realizing her mouth was dry, she swallowed, forced her gaze to his face. "So now we have to look for the merchant."

He nodded, looking down, bending down as he stripped off his trousers. "With all of us involved, that won't take long." Straightening, he grimaced. "Maybe a week." He flung the trousers at the chair, then turned to the bed.

Her pulse leapt. "So we're one step away from identifying A. C?"

"One step." Lifting the covers, he slid in beside her. Dropping them, he turned to her. Framed her face with his hands and kissed her.

Deeply, thoroughly, druggingly . . . until she was swept away, her mind whirling on a sensual tide.

Leaving one hand cupping her jaw, with the other Tony reached down and tugged the sheet from between them, then settled his body against hers. Letting the sheets fall, he plundered her soft mouth while with his palm he traced the long, smooth curve from her shoulder, over the supple planes of her back to the swell of her bottom, molding her to him, easing her beneath him, spurred by the realization that her skin was already warm, by the immediate leap of her pulse to the caress, the dewed flush that spread over the silken skin of her bottom, the evidence of her arousal he discovered when he pressed his hand down between them, slid his fingers between her thighs, and found her.

Ready, waiting, urgent for him.

He pressed her back into the bed, parted her thighs with his and filled her, surged slowly into her, taking his time, glorying in the ease with which he could forge in, in the way she tilted her hips and took him deep, to the fluid harmony with which they then moved, sliding into the dance their bodies now knew so well.

A different dance to any he'd enjoyed with any other woman.

Mouths melded, tongues tangling, hot yet languid, their bodies moved, merged, flexed to a rhythm that held a deeper tune, a more powerful cadence.

A heady, dizzying delight, a pleasure that soared higher and reached deeper, that slid past their slick skins, through muscle and bone, past straining sinews and tightening nerves to their cores. To touch, sink into, and hold something there.

Something precious, fragile, yet strong enough to fuse their hearts.

He sensed it before they'd even started to scale the peak. Their bodies held, thrummed with, a driving urgency, yet they had the strength to dally—neither was in any rush, delighting instead in every small touch, each delicate caress.

Slowly, powerfully, he rode her, feeling her body surrender and take him in, feeling the heat of her draw him deeper, tempting him further into her fire. He went, but kept the reins firmly in his hands, as always orchestrating the moment; after all these years, pleasuring women was all but second nature.

Gradually, the tempo built. Beneath him, her body rose, meeting his, matching his, urging him on. Her fingers, on his back, tensed, nails lightly scoring. Without easing the steadily escalating rhythm, he drew back from the kiss, through the dimness studied her face; her eyes were closed, her lips swollen and parted, telltale concentration etched in every line.

He thrust deeper, harder, and she gasped, her body arching greedily under his.

Lifting his shoulders a fraction farther, enough to appreciate the way her body, all sumptuous curves and hot flushed skin, undulated with each thrust, absorbed each forceful penetration as he rode her, filled her, he watched as he pushed her step by slow step closer to sensual fulfillment.

He felt the tension inside her coil, felt her tighten beneath him, her thighs gripping his flanks as release flickered and beckoned. Her ragged breathing filled his ears, a softer sound overlaying his own raspy breaths.

She reached for him, tried to pull him down to her.

Without breaking their rhythm, he shifted his hips, pressing more intimately between hers, then thrust deeper still, harder still.

She gasped, tugged, but the sight of her held him. Eventually lifting his gaze to her face, he saw the glimmer of her eyes beneath her lashes.

Alicia studied his face, licked her lips, felt her world teeter. She was so close to that joyous edge, yet, as always since that first engagement, no matter how desperate the moment, he held to his control, waiting, watching, certain to follow her, yet still . . .

"Come with me." She struggled to find breath enough to add, "Now."

His black eyes, until then hooded, opened wide—enough for her to realize she'd asked something no other ever had.

Her nerves shivered, started to unravel. Dragging in a breath, she lifted a hand to his face, traced his cheek. "*Be* with me. Please."

She wasn't sure how, but she knew what she wanted. Needed.

He knew, too. He gave a shuddering sigh; the tension rippling through him increased, hardening his body as it rode against hers, thrust into hers.

Their gazes remained locked. He shifted his weight, freed a hand, held it open close by her head. "Give me your hand."

She did, shifting her hand from his face, watching as he interdigitated his fingers with hers, then closed them, locking their palms. Then he pressed their linked hands into the pillow.

"Wrap your legs about my waist."

She could barely make out the gravelly command. The silk sheets caressed her skin as she complied, then gasped as he shifted fully over her and drove deep. Her spine bowed, but his weight pinned her, held her down as his hips flexed in a faster, more urgent, more compulsive rhythm.

For an instant, gasping and breathless, she rode it, then she felt his eyes on her face, met his black gaze, once again screened. Felt the flames inside rise, coalesce, fuse to an inferno.

He lowered his head, drove into her harder, faster, more powerfully.

"Now." He breathed the word against her lips, then took them, took her mouth as the conflagration roared— and caught them. Overwhelmed them. Consumed them.

As one. Together, as she'd asked.

Tony felt the reins he'd released whip away, sensed them cinder, all control sundered and gone. For only the second time in his life, he plunged into the heart of that familiar fire *with* a woman, by her side. Her hand was his anchor; he clung to it as her body tightened beneath his, closed powerfully around his, hot, scalding, driving him on, taking him with her into the world beyond the flames, into the pleasure of sexual satiation.

If she wished, so he would; they whirled, joined more intimately than he'd ever been with any other, not just their bodies but their awarenesses fused, experiencing together, simultaneously soaring. Higher, then yet higher.

Until they were both gasping, bodies locked and straining. Until they were there, twined together at the peak.

Until they fell, hearts thundering, senses merged, glory pouring through them. Souls as one.

She was his. Totally, completely, beyond recall.

The words drifted of their own volition across Alicia's brain.

Her body, trapped beneath his, thighs vulnerably wide with him buried so deep inside her, was no longer hers.

Her lips curved in sleepy satisfaction. No matter her thoughts, her will, her determination, logic had no place here. Despite all uncertainty, despite the nebulous unease that even now she could sense, a fog hovering just beyond the bed, even now, despite all, her heart rejoiced.

Lifting the hand he hadn't claimed, she laid it on his hair, then gently stroked. Let her fingers play among the silky strands.

Let her emotions have their way.

Let them well, and fill her mind, fill her throat and her chest, fill her heart, and overflow. Let them slide through her veins and sink into her flesh, a part of her, forever.

He lay heavy upon her; she delighted in his weight. Within her, the warmth of his seed radiated a glow of deep and abiding pleasure. She'd given him all she was; tonight, he'd taken, claimed, but when she'd wanted and needed, he had surrendered and given, too.

No matter what else the days might bring, tonight, he'd been with her.

As totally hers as she'd been his.

The gentle tangling of Alicia's fingers in his hair drew Tony back to earth. To a world that was almost as wonderful as the one they'd visited; her body was a sensual cushion beneath him, her breasts beneath his chest, her hips and thighs cradling his, their bodies still intimately joined.

He was more comfortable than he'd ever thought to be, not just in body but on all other levels. Physically, mentally, emotionally, he was at peace, at home in her arms. Where he was meant to be.

His satisfaction was so profound it was frightening. It lay like a golden sea about him, deep, timeless, ageless, weighing on his limbs, soothing his mind, infinitely precious.

Eyes closed, he savored it, held it, let its waves lap about him—and tried not to think of ever losing it.

Eventually, he felt forced to stir, to draw back from that contented sea. Lifting from Alicia, he ignored her sleepy protest; she seemed as addicted to the moment as he. Settling beside her, he drew her to him, against him, brushing aside her long hair so he could see her face. He looked into her eyes, shadowed pools, mysterious in the night.

Marry me tomorrow.

The words burned his tongue; all the reasons he shouldn't say them—not yet—doused them. Instead, bending his head, he touched his lips to hers, and spoke from his heart.

"Je t'aime." He breathed the words across her lips; closing his eyes, he tasted them. *"Je t'adore."*

He wasn't even conscious of speaking in French; it had always been the language of love to him.

She touched his cheek, returned his kiss, soft, clinging.

Their lips parted; he drew breath, softly asked, "Is everything here as you wish? If there's anything you need—"

She stopped him, laying her fingers across his lips. "There's nothing—everything's perfect." She hesitated, then added, "I like your house."

They were speaking in whispers, as if not to disturb the

blanket of shared pleasure that still surrounded them. It was the deepest part of the night, the small hours of the morning, yet neither was sleepy. Sated, content, they lay in each other's arms, limbs tangled, hands occasionally touching, brushing, stroking.

Time drifted, and with it the tide of their loving. It slowly turned. Returned. Alicia didn't think, but simply flowed with it, knew he did the same.

Effortless. Their communication in that moment needed no words, no careful phrases. It was carried by their hands, their lips, mouths, tongues, every square inch of their bodies.

They moved over and around, worshipping, first one, then the other. Pleasure bloomed, ecstasy blossomed.

He opened her eyes to pleasures she hadn't imagined, sensual delights beyond her ken. In turn, she set aside her inhibitions and let instinct and his guttural murmurs of appreciation guide her.

When at last they joined and again crested the final peak, and found the now-familiar splendor waiting, they were again together, senses open yet wholly merged, deliberately and completely one.

Later, when they lay spent, exhausted, in each other's arms, Alicia heard his words echo in her mind. *I love you. I adore you.*

She wondered if he'd understood her reply.

Tony sank toward sleep, sated to his toes, his mind unfocused. Thoughts drifted, melted into the fogs as they closed in.

He'd told her he loved her, had said the words aloud. He'd surprised himself; he'd always imagined they would be so hard to say.

They'd slipped out, almost without conscious direction, a statement of fact with which he had no argument.

So easy. Now all that remained was to organize their wedding.

They were one step away from identifying A. C. One step away from being free to face their future, to give it their full and undivided attention.

If he had his way—and he was determined he would—the next time they indulged as they just had, they would be in his big bed at Torrington Chase, and Alicia would be his wife.

The following days passed in a frenzy of activity—social commitments on the one hand, covert investigation on the other.

To Alicia's relief, the staff at Torrington House truly were, as Tony had told her, delighted to have three boys rampaging through the house. Once she realized how safe, secure, and cared for the boys now were, with so many benevolently watchful eyes on them, she relaxed her vigilance—one item she didn't need to worry over.

She had plenty of others on her plate.

One was a lovers' spat between Adriana and Geoffrey. It blew over in twenty-four hours, but left Alicia, the recipient of both principals' outpourings, feeling battered. The event precipitated the long-desired meeting between Geoffrey, Adriana, and herself. She and Adriana made their financial situation crystal clear; Geoffrey looked at them as if they were mad, and then asked why they'd thought he would care. Without waiting for an answer, he formally offered for Adriana's hand. Adriana, somewhat stunned by his unwavering singlemindedness, accepted him.

Alicia retired, pleased, relieved, but wrung out. They all agreed that any announcement should wait until Geoffrey had written to his mother in Devon and taken Adriana to meet her. On all other counts, Alicia felt justified in leaving them to plan their own future.

When, later that night, she regaled Tony with a description of the meeting, he laughed, amused. Later still, when she was lying sated and warm in his arms, he murmured, "Did you tell him you weren't a widow?"

"No." He sounded serious; she glanced up. "Should I have?"

He was fiddling with a lock of her hair; he met her gaze, after a moment, replied, "There's no need to tell anyone, not anymore. It doesn't concern anyone but you and me."

She considered, then resettled her cheek on his chest. She listened to his heart beating strongly, steadily, and told herself all was well.

Only it wasn't.

It took her until her fourth day in Torrington House to realize what was wrong, what was increasingly troubling her, converting nebulous unease into a more tangible fear.

In addition to Hungerford's delight at her presence, the open acceptance by the *grandes dames* and hostesses of her sojourn in Upper Brook Street had allayed her concerns on one score. Contrary to her beliefs, it clearly was acceptable for a nobleman's mistress to reside openly under his roof, in certain circumstances. She assumed the ameliorating circumstances included that she was a fashionable widow of whom society approved, that Miranda was present, and that A. C. had attempted to use her as his scapegoat.

Regardless, her initial fears on that point had proved groundless; society took her relocation in its stride. So did everyone else—except her.

Only she was having difficulties, and that in a way she hadn't foreseen. At first, when Miranda had consulted her over this and that, deferring to her suggestions on the menus, the maids, the day-to-day decisions of managing the large household, she'd assumed Miranda was merely trying to ensure she felt at home.

But on the third morning, Miranda threw up her hands. "Oh, stuff and nonsense—this is all so silly. You're hardly an innocent miss with no experience. Here"—she thrust the menus at her—"it's only right and proper *you* should be handling this, and you don't need my help."

With a brilliant smile, Miranda rose, swung her skirts about, and left her to deal with Mrs. Swithins alone. Which, after swallowing her amazement, she did; it was transparent Mrs. Swithins fully expected her to.

From that point, the servants openly deferred to her. From that minute she became, in all reality bar the legal fact, the lady of Torrington House.

Tony's wife.

It was a position she'd never thought to fill; now, she found herself living it. Bad enough. The associated development that transformed the situation into a deeply disturbing, unsettling experience was something she not only hadn't foreseen, but hadn't even dreamed of.

On the fourth morning, the truth hit her like a slap.

Since she'd moved into his house, Tony left her bed only minutes before the maids started their rounds. That morning, she rose from her disarranged couch, only to feel the dragging effects of real tiredness. The first weeks of the Season were packed with entertainments, morning, noon, and night; she, Adriana, and Miranda had attended six events the day before.

When Bertha appeared, she retreated to the bed, and let the little maid tidy away her evening gown. "We've a luncheon at two o'clock—I'll dress for that, but now I'm going to rest. Please tell Mrs. Althorpe and my sister that I'm still sleeping." If they had any sense, they'd be doing the same.

Bertha murmured sympathetically, efficiently tidied, then with a last whispered inquiry if she wished for anything else, which Alicia denied, the maid whisked out.

Left in blissful peace, Alicia snuggled down, closed her eyes. She expected to fall asleep, there was after all no urgent matter awaiting her attention, nothing she need worry about . . .

Her mind emptied, cleared—and the truth was suddenly there, abruptly revealed, rock-solid and absolute. Inescapable and undeniable.

Being the lady of Torrington House was the future her heart truly craved.

The revelation rocked her.

Lying back in the bed, she stared up at the silk canopy and tried to understand. Herself. How, why . . . when had she changed?

The answers trickled into her mind. She hadn't changed, but never before had she allowed herself to think of what she wanted for her own life; she'd spent her life organizing the lives of others, and had deliberately spared no thought for her own. Intentional self-blindness; she knew why she'd done it—it had been easier that way. The wrench of sacrificing dreams . . . one never had to face that deadening choice if one never allowed oneself to dream at all.

Looking back at her younger self, to when she'd made that decision . . . she'd done it to protect her heart against the harsh reality she, even in her relative naïveté, had foreseen. But she was no longer that naive young girl trembling, trepidatious and alone, on the threshold of womanhood, weighed down by responsibilites and cares.

She hadn't changed so much as grown. She was now experienced, assured. Her own actions in formulating and successfully carrying out her plan, and all that had flowed through her association with Tony, had opened her eyes, not just to what might be, but even more powerfully to who she was and what lay within her. Her own strengths, her own will, her abilities.

Beneath all ran a belief, a conviction, in her right to her own life—and a determination, quiet, until now unrecognized and unstated but definitely there, to seize what she wanted.

With the position of Tony's wife hers in all but name . . . the role fitted her like a glove, soothed her by its rightness, fulfilled some deep-seated yearning, an unrealized but essential, fundamental part of her.

That was what she wanted.

Her breath caught; a vise tightened about her heart. Her determination didn't waver.

Yet she was his mistress, not his wife.

He'd said he loved her. Her French was not good—she'd never had time to do more than learn the rudiments; he often murmured phrases during their lovemaking that she couldn't make out, yet she felt confident she hadn't misheard or mistaken those particular words.

She even believed them, or at least believed that he believed them.

What he *meant* by them was another matter.

Marriage had never been part of their arrangement. Just because she now yearned for it, wanted it—and not just because he got along so well with her brothers and had the wherewithal and character to guide and support them precisely as she'd always wished—just because she now realized that marrying him would satisfy every dream she'd never allowed herself to have, she couldn't now turn back the clock.

Couldn't now expect him to think in those terms just because her eyes had been opened. Shouldn't be so naive as to read too much into a simple declaration of love. Pretending to herself would be the ultimate folly, the ultimate way to break her heart.

When Bertha returned at one o'clock, she rose, washed, and dressed. Calmly serene, she went downstairs and threw herself into the social round.

A note arrived from Christian Allardyce just as Tony was about to embark on another round of balls and parties at Alicia's side. Also gathered in his front hall waiting for the coach to be brought around were Adriana, Geoffrey, and Miranda. Lady Castlereagh's was to be their first port of call.

Tony scanned the note. Christian wrote to suggest they should meet at the Bastion Club to review progress. Tony surmised that the others—Christian, Charles, Tristan, Gervase, Jack Warnefleet, and even Jack Hendon—were keen to use the investigation as an excuse to avoid their social obligations.

Even with Alicia's presence as reward, he, too, felt the temptation. For men of their ilk, balls were boring, pointless, and severely drained their never very deep reserves of civility. They'd spent the last decade avoiding fools— why change their ways now?

Noting Alicia, beside him, watching him, he handed her the note. While she read it, he glanced at Geoffrey. If it hadn't been for the little chat they'd had that afternoon, he'd be irritated by Geoffrey's and Adriana's total absorption in the how and where of their nuptials; luckily, Geoffrey had had no argument with his assertion that he and Alicia should marry first, even if by no more than a week.

Given the way Geoffrey was watching over Adriana, as if determined now he'd won her no other would get close, it was clear he, at least, would resist the lure of the investigation.

Tony turned to Alicia as she looked up from the note.

"Are you going?"

He looked into her green eyes, hesitated. "If you would prefer I escort you to the balls tonight, I can put off the meeting until tomorrow."

She looked at him steadily; he couldn't tell what she was thinking. Then she glanced down at the note. "But that would mean actions that could be instigated tomorrow if you met tonight would be delayed, wouldn't it?"

She looked up again. He nodded. Put like that, it was almost incumbent upon him to leave her to Geoffrey's care and devote his attention to unmasking A. C. Still he hesitated, not liking the fact he couldn't follow her thoughts, or see her feelings in her eyes. He usually could. "Are you sure? Geoffrey will stay with you—"

She smiled, confident, and assured. "Yes, of course. Indeed, I'm sure we're starting to be the butt of comments about being forever in each other's pockets." Turning to Miranda, she caught her eye. "Tony's been called away— I'm assuring him we'll be perfectly happy with just Geoffrey as escort."

"Oh, indeed!" Miranda flicked her hand at him. "Go, go!" She grinned, a devilish light in her eye. "I assure you Alicia and I will be *excellently* well entertained."

She meant it in purely teasing vein, yet the barb slipped under Tony's guard and pricked. He glanced at Alicia; turning to him, she gave him her hand.

"I'll bid you a good night, then. I daresay we'll be home long before you get back." She raised her gaze to his face, but not as far as his eyes.

A sudden chill touched him.

Having heard his name and ascertained from Miranda what was going on, Geoffrey turned to him. "Don't worry, I'll bring them all safely back at the end of Lady Selkirk's affair." Meeting Tony's gaze, he quietly added, "Send word tomorrow morning if there's anything I can help with."

Tony nodded. He released Alicia's hand to shake Geoffrey's. When he looked back, he found she'd turned away and was embroiled in a discussion with Adriana.

There seemed no reason to dally. "I'll leave you, then." He made the comment general; with a single nod for everyone, he headed for the door.

What he learned at the club drove all other thoughts temporarily from his mind.

"We've narrowed the field to three possibilities." As he'd suggested, Christian had acted as a central contact, compiling and disseminating information as the others brought it in. They'd all been involved, but in order to keep things moving, they'd simply reported, then got on with the next task, and left Christian to make sense of the whole. This was the first time they'd all gathered since the meeting in Tony's library—the first time they'd heard the results to date.

"Between them, Jack"—Christian nodded at Jack Warnefleet—"and Tristan came up with a list of tea and coffee merchants they've since verified as exhaustive."

"Can one ask how?" Charles asked.

Jack Warnefleet grinned. "Not if you want details. But I'm sure those merchants would be amazed at how much their wives, especially their competitors' wives, know."

"Ah!" Charles turned a limpid glance on Tristan.

Who smiled. "I left that endeavor to Jack. My contribution was verifying the information via the appropriate guilds. By a sleight of argument, I convinced the guild secretaries that I needed to examine their registers for cases of accidental cross-listings, where coffee merchants had been listed as tea merchants, and vice versa."

"Which naturally left you with a list of those who were both. Very nice." Charles looked back up the table.

"The list comprised twenty-three companies," Christian continued. "We eliminated those we know lost cargoes, assuming no merchant is going to send a precious cargo to France just to cover his tracks. That took twelve names out—some of the sixteen ships carried cargoes for the same merchant."

"Poor beggars," Jack Hendon said. "Knowing how close some of them sail to the wind, I'd be surprised if none have gone bankrupt."

"Some have," Gervase answered. "Yet more damage to add to A. C.'s account."

Tony stirred. "So that left us with eleven companies."

Christian nodded. "Courtesy of you all and your chameleon like talents, passing yourselves off as potential coffee-shop proprietors and the like, not to mention your ability to tell barefaced lies, by focusing on who had stock after the last A. C.-induced shortage, we've ended with three names—three merchants. All had stock to sell when the price last soared, and even though that incident was nearly a year ago, we have enough corroboration to conclude that *only* those three had stock to sell at that time."

A general hubbub ensued, centering on whether there was any easy way to narrow the list further.

Tony didn't contribute; reaching out, he took the sheet lying in front of Christian and read the names. "So," his voice fell into the lull as the prospect of a simple next step faded, "A. C. is associated with one of these three."

"Yes, *but*," Christian stressed, "two of the three are not involved. Given what we'll need to do to ferret out a hidden partner, we need to be absolutely certain which of the three it is before we move in."

Tony nodded. "If we get it wrong, we'll alert A. C., and given his record in covering his tracks, all we'll find is another corpse."

Jack Warnefleet sat forward. "So how do we pinpoint the right merchant?"

"The right merchant landed cargoes before each prize was taken." Tony looked across the table at Jack Hendon. "You said once we had a merchant's shipping line, we could verify the safe landing of A. C.'s cargo via the records at Lloyd's. We have three merchants—if we learn which shipping lines they use, could we check all three lines for safe landings in the relevant weeks preceding each prize-taking, and check the cargoes landed?"

Jack held his gaze for a long moment, then asked, "How much time do we have?"

"By my calculation, not a lot. A. C.'s been quiet for nearly a week, but he must know we haven't given up. He'll try something else to deflect the investigation—he won't succeed, but the faster we can conclude it, the better." Tony paused, then added, "Who knows what he might do next?"

It was a point on which he tried not to speculate, yet it

hovered in his mind, a constant threat. To Alicia, to him, to their future.

Jack was thinking, calculating—glancing around the table, he nodded. "Given our number, it's possible. And it might be the best way. The first thing we need to learn is which shipping lines those three companies use, but to do that without alerting the companies, you'll need to ask the shipping lines."

"Can you do that?" Christian asked.

"Not me. As the owner of Hendon Shipping, the instant I start asking questions like that, there'll be hell to pay."

"No matter." Charles shrugged. "You tell us what answers we need, and what questions will best elicit them, and leave it to us."

"Right."

"Easy enough."

The others nodded. It was Tony who asked, "How many shipping lines are there?"

Jack met his gaze. "Seventy-three."

When the others stopped groaning, Jack continued, "I'll put a list together tonight—we can meet here first thing tomorrow. If we push, we should get the information by evening, and then"—he met Tony's gaze again—"we'll first need to get access to the shipping registers and get the ships' names, then we'll revisit Lloyd's. We'll be able to find the answer—which company A.C. is behind—there."

Tony returned Jack's gaze, then nodded. "Let's do it."

NINETEEN

THE NEXT DAY WAS CHAOTIC.

Six members of the Bastion Club attired as no gentleman would normally be met with Jack Hendon in the club's meeting room at eight o'clock. Over breakfast, they divided his list on the basis of the location of the shipping lines' offices, then each took a section and set out. They were masquerading as merchants, all appearing older and a great deal more conservative than they were.

Whoever discovered a link between any of the three merchants and a shipping line would send a messenger back to Jack at the club. They'd decided against calling a halt until all seventy-three shipping lines had been assessed; there was always the possibility that a merchant used more than one, especially if that merchant had something to hide.

Tony had taken a group of fourteen offices congregated around Wapping High Street. Charles, who had drawn the area next to that, shared a hackney down to the docks. They parted, and Tony began his search for a reliable shipping line to bring tea from his uncle's plantations in Ceylon. Once he had a shipping manager keen to secure his fictitious uncle's fictitious cargo, it was easy to ask for references in the form of other tea merchants the line had run cargoes for in the last few years.

By eleven o'clock, he'd visited six offices, and scored

one hit. One line which, so the manager believed, had an exclusive contract with one of their three merchants.

Tony stopped in a tavern to refresh himself with a pint. Sitting at a table by a window, he sipped and looked out. He appeared to be watching the handcarts and drays and the bustling human traffic thronging the street; in reality, he saw none of it, his mind turned inward to more personal vistas.

Things had started to move; the pace always escalated toward the end of a chase. They'd soon have A. C., or at least his name. Dalziel would have his man; Tony would take great delight in delivering him personally.

He needed to keep his eye on the game, yet the very fact it was nearing its apogee had him thinking of what came next. Of Alicia and him, and their future life.

The closer the prospect drew, the more it commanded his attention, the more sensitive to threats to it he became. Last night in the hall, he'd been touched by premonition, by an unfocused, unspecific belief that something was wrong, or at least not right. Something in the way Alicia had reacted had pricked his instincts.

Yet when he'd returned home just after midnight, it was to find the others already back, and Alicia waiting for him in her bed. Explaining that they'd all wished for an early night, she'd encouraged him to tell her all he'd learned; she'd listened, patently interested, to their plans.

Then he'd joined her under the covers and she'd turned to him, welcomed him into her arms, into her body with her usual open and generous ardor. No hesitation, no holding back. No retreat.

When he'd left this morning, she'd still been asleep. He'd brushed a kiss to her lips and left her dreaming.

Perhaps that was all it was—that the social round, now frenetic, combined with the stress of watching over Adriana, was simply wearying her. God knew, it would weary him. When he'd returned to her last night, there'd been no sign of whatever he'd detected earlier, that slight disjunction that had seemed to exist between them.

He spent another five minutes slowly sipping his ale, then downed the rest in two swallows. He had eight more shipping lines to investigate. The sooner they could bring A. C.'s game to a conclusion, the better for them all.

Tony got back to the Bastion Club just after three o'clock. He was one of the last to return; the others were lounging around the table in the meeting room with Jack Hendon waiting impatiently for his report.

"Please say you've found a line working for Martinsons," Jack demanded before Tony could even pull out a chair.

He sat and tossed his list on the table. "Croxtons in Wapping have, so the manager assures me, an exclusive contract."

"Thank God for that." Jack wrote the name down. "I was beginning to think our plan would go awry. We've identified two shipping lines for Drummond, one from the east, one from the west, reasonable in the circumstances, and four—two in each direction—for Ellicot. Croxton runs ships both east and west, so Martinsons can indeed use them exclusively. Now"—he looked down his list—"all we need is for Gervase to confirm none of the three—Martinsons, Ellicot, or Drummond—use any other line."

But when Gervase came striding in fifteen minutes later, it was with different news. "Tatleys and Hencken both carry goods for Ellicot."

They all looked at him; Gervase slowly raised his brows. "What?"

"You're sure?" Jack asked. When Gervase nodded, he opened his eyes wide. "That's six shippers who carry Ellicot's goods, and two of those lines run ships to both the East and West Indies."

Tony caught Jack's eye. "Is it wise to place any great emphasis on that?"

Jack grimaced. "No, but it's tempting. If you wanted to disguise any pattern in shipping around the dates the prizes were taken, then the use of multiple lines and therefore different ships for each safe cargo brought in would totally obscure any link."

"The most likely people to check any connection would be the Admiralty," Gervase said, "yet their records show only the ships and shipping lines. There's no way to detect a link that exists at the level of cargo."

Tony frowned. "Customs and Revenue have records of the cargoes, but even there, the records are sorted by ports, and different lines use different home ports."

"So," Charles said, "this was an extremely well-set-up scheme. It's only because we used Lloyd's that we've been able to put things together."

"Which leads one to conclude," Christian said, "that the scheme's perpetrator knows the administrative ropes well. He knows how the civil services work and which avenues to block."

"We'll still get him." Jack had been reexamining his list. "We have nine shipping lines—more than I'd like, but seven are small. We now need a list of all the vessels each has registered."

"Can we get that before tonight?" Tony asked.

Jack glanced at the clock on the sideboard, then pushed back his chair. "We can but try."

"I'll help." Gervase rose, too. "I know the business well enough to deal with the intricacies of the registers."

"You two concentrate on getting a list of the ships' names," Tony said. "We'll take care of the rest."

Jack and Gervase left, conferring as they went. The others turned to Tony.

"Once we have the list of ships," he said, "we're going to have to search Lloyd's records. We need to identify which merchant consistently brought in a cargo in, say, the week before a prize was taken. Searching in the weeks before three separate incidents should give us one name and one only. If not, we can look at a fourth incident, but chances are three incidents will give us only one merchant who fits our bill."

The others nodded.

"Once we know the particular merchant involved, we should confirm that in each case they did indeed bring in tea or coffee."

"Can we do all that via Lloyd's?" Charles asked.

"Yes. If Jack and Gervase get the ships' names by this evening, I'll revisit Lloyd's tonight."

"I'll come, too" Charles said. "There's this horrendous ball my sisters want to drag me to—I'd much rather hone my filing skills."

"You can count me in," Jack Warnefleet said. "I've never had to track anyone through such a maze before."

They made arrangements to meet later that night.

Only Tristan demurred. "I'll keep a watch on things in the ballrooms. Having had the good sense to get married, I, at least, am safe from the harpies."

Charles grimaced. "Half your luck. I don't know how you managed it so quickly—and now look at Tony. You're both safe. What I want to know is how long *I'm* going to remain dead center in the matchmakers' sights. It's deuced harrowing, I'll have you know."

Both Tony and Tristan made sympathetic noises. The mood of teasing camaraderie disguising their implacable resolve, the meeting broke up and they each headed home.

Tony found Alicia in the garden.

Admitted to the house by Hungerford, he'd slipped upstairs and changed into more normal attire before setting out to search for her.

She was walking alone; Hungerford had told him the

boys were in the park—it was a perfect day for kites. It seemed odd to find Alicia by herself; pensive, head down, deep in thought, she slowly, apparently aimlessly, wandered the lawn.

He watched from the terrace—Torrington House was centuries old, the gardens stretching behind it extensive—then went down the steps and set out to join her. She didn't hear him; not wanting to frighten her by suddenly appearing beside her, he called her name.

Halting, she swung around and smiled. She straightened as he neared. "Did you learn anything?"

He would have taken her in his arms and kissed her, but she held out a hand; the swift glance she cast at the house was a warning.

Reluctantly bowing to her wishes, he took her hand and raised it to his lips. Kissed it, then, noting that her smile had faded, an expression he couldn't read taking its place, he tucked her hand in his arm, anchored it with his. He let a frown show in his eyes. "What's wrong?"

She blinked her eyes wide. "Wrong? Why . . . nothing." She frowned lightly back. "Why did you think there was?"

Because . . .

He felt confused, not a normal feeling, not for him. The expression in her eyes assured him she honestly didn't think anything was wrong, yet . . .

She shook his arm and started to stroll again. "*Did* you learn anything? What has Jack been up to—I met Kit at Lady Hartington's luncheon, and she said he was out, too, looking for A. C.'s connections."

He nodded. "We've all been out for most of the day."

He explained. Alicia listened, put a question here and there, and continued to reiterate to herself: *You are his mistress, his lover, not his wife.*

That, she'd decided, was the only sane way forward, to keep their relationship on a fixed and even keel. If she let herself get seduced—emotionally seduced by her emerging dreams—she'd end hurt beyond measure. She'd accepted the position; if she adhered strictly to that role, she and he could continue as they were. That would have to be enough.

If she was forced to make the choice between being his mistress or not being with him at all, she knew which she'd choose. She never wanted to lose him, to forgo those golden moments when they were so close, when each breath, each thought, each desire was shared. If to hold on to that closeness she had to remain his mistress, so be it. It was, she'd decided, worth the price.

The news he had was exciting; they were clearly closing in on A. C. As they discussed their findings, she was conscious of Tony's gaze on her face, black as ever but not so much intent as keen, sharp. Observant.

Finally, she felt forced to meet his eyes and raise her brows in mute question.

He searched her eyes, then looked forward, steering her along a path leading to a fountain. "Given I need to visit Lloyd's tonight, I won't be able to escort you to whatever entertainments you're scheduled to attend."

She forced herself to smile easily; she patted his arm. "Don't worry—I'm perfectly capable of attending by myself." Even though, in his absence, there was nothing at such events to hold her interest. She didn't even need to watch over Adriana anymore.

She'd learned there were indeed couples, noblemen and their wellborn mistresses, of whose relationship the ton was patently aware, but to which it turned a blind eye. Her and Tony's situation wasn't unusual. However, one relevant and undoubtedly important aspect was that those involved in such accepted affairs never drew attention to their relationship in public.

Such couples did not spend time together in ballrooms or drawing rooms; she should undoubtedly grasp this opportunity to ease their interaction into a more socially acceptable vein.

"You find the balls a bore." She looked ahead at the circular fountain set in the lawn. "There's no reason you need dance attendance on me there. Not anymore."

She glanced at him. There was a frown gathering in his eyes. She needed to discourage him from acting so overtly possessively. She smiled, trying to soften the hint. "And tonight, you need to be elsewhere searching for A. C.—there's no need to feel it's necessary to escort me, or that your absence will bother me—that I'll be in any way discomposed."

Her words were gentle, clear, her expression as always open and honest; Tony heard what she said, but wasn't sure he understood. She was explaining something to him, but what?

His brain couldn't seem to function as incisively as usual. The odd feeling in his chest, a deadening, dulling sensation, didn't help. Halting, he drew in a breath, glanced, unseeing, at the fountain. "If you're sure?"

He looked at her face, into her eyes—and saw something very close to relief in the green.

Her smile was genuine, reassuring. "Yes. I'll be perfectly content."

The assurance he'd asked for, yet not what he'd wanted to hear.

A babel of youthful voices spilled down from the terrace; they both looked and saw the three boys and two girls come tumbling down to the lawns.

Turning, they headed toward the children. As they reached the main lawn, Tony felt Alicia's gaze, glanced down, and met her eyes.

Again, she smiled reassuringly, then patted his arm as she looked ahead. "I'll be here, waiting, when you get home."

He'd accepted the arrangement because he'd had little choice. Yet the suspicion—now hardening to conviction—that something was going awry between them grew, fueled by that part of him that had heard her words as something approaching a dismissal.

A dismissal he'd had neither justification nor opportunity to challenge.

The incident had jolted him in a way he wasn't accustomed to; faced with a raft of unexpected uncertainties, he'd concluded he needed to think before doing anything, before reacting. Yet by one o'clock the next morning, when he silently let himself into his house, his uncertainty had only grown, until he, his usual forceful personality, felt paralyzed.

One thing he'd realized: he didn't have any real idea of what she was thinking, of how she saw their relationship.

He'd told her he loved her; she hadn't reciprocated.

He'd never before said those words to any woman, but in the past he'd been the recipient of such declarations too often for his comfort.

Alicia hadn't said the words. Frowning, he climbed the stairs. Until now, he hadn't thought he needed to hear them; until now, her physical acceptance, all that had passed between them, had been assurrance enough, guarantee enough.

But no more. Now he was uncertain. Of her.

Even though she'd assured him she'd be waiting, he wasn't at all sure what he'd find when he entered her room. But she was indeed there, yet not quite as he'd expected. She wasn't in bed, but standing by the side of the bow window, wrapped in her robe, arms folded beneath her breasts. Shoulder and head resting against the window frame, she looked out on the moonlit gardens.

As usual, she hadn't heard him enter. He made no sound as he closed the door, then stood in the shadows and studied her.

She was deep in thought, her body completely still, her mind elsewhere.

He hesitated, then stepped forward more definitely; she heard him and turned. Through the shadows he saw her gentle smile. She settled back against the window frame. "Did you manage to identify A. C.'s company?"

He halted by the bed. "It's Ellicot."

"The one that used many different shipping lines?"

He nodded; the subject was not the one uppermost in his mind. He eased off his coat. "Tomorrow, we'll start closing in, but we'll need to be careful not to alert A. C. We want him still in England when we learn his name."

He tossed the coat onto a chair, then looked at her. She'd remained at the window, leaning back against the frame, the silk robe draped about her, her arms folded. He sensed she was comfortable, at ease, yet distant.

The bed was behind him; stepping back, he sat on its side. Through the shadows, continued to study her.

He'd manipulated the situation and gained his objective—her, here, under his roof. In his house where he could share her bed easily, where she was protected constantly by his servants. He'd achieved all he'd wanted, all he'd thought they needed, yet . . . something was askew. The situation had developed undercurrents, ones he couldn't read well enough to counter.

She seemed to be drawing back. Not turning away, but sliding from his grasp. Inch by inch, step by tiny step . . .

He needed to hear words, yet he couldn't—didn't know how to—ask for them. Dragging in a short breath, he looked down at his hands, loosely clasped between his thighs. "Perhaps"—keeping his tone ruthlessly even, he looked up—"we should discuss the wedding."

She shook her head—instantly, without the smallest hesitation. "No, not yet. There's no sense making any plans until Geoffrey tells his mother, and they set a date."

He opened his lips to correct her; there was no reason he and she had to wait on Geoffrey and Adriana's arrangements . . .

The realization she'd thought he'd meant Geoffrey and Adriana's wedding, not theirs, burst on him before he uttered a word. It was superseded almost instantly by a blinding insight—the idea of their wedding—that he might be alluding to that—hadn't even occurred to her.

She shifted to stare out of the window once more. "It'll be upon us soon enough, but you needn't worry about the details. I'm sure they'll want to marry in Devon, and that would be wisest . . ." She paused, then softly added, "Considering my deception. A small, private affair would be best . . ."

Alicia let her words trail away. She'd been thinking of the wedding, of Geoffrey and Adriana's growing happiness, and struggling to contain a reaction perilously close to jealousy.

She drew in a slow breath, felt a welling need to rail, not against Geoffrey and Adriana—heaven forbid, she'd worked so hard to bring about her sister's happiness—but against a fate that was so twisted as to make her live through, have to smile through Adriana and Geoffrey's joy while knowing she would never achieve the same. Worse, while knowing she'd willingly and intentionally sacrificed her own chance at such happiness to ensure her sister made the marriage she deserved.

When she'd made the decision to leave behind any thought of marriage and masquerade as a widow, the critical decision from which all else had flowed, she hadn't known what she'd been so ready to turn her back on. Hadn't appreciated her until recently suppressed dreams, hadn't felt their tug.

Now she knew, now she had. Fate was indeed cruel.

Yet among her regrets there was one she didn't have. She didn't regret, couldn't regret, her relationship with Tony. If she couldn't marry him, then she wouldn't marry anyone else, so there was, she'd finally, bitterly, ironically and rather sternly concluded, no point in dwelling on her dreams.

Aside from all else, given his possessiveness, given all she sensed in him, honor notwithstanding, she wasn't at all sure he'd let her go.

Her senses suddenly leapt; she looked up, eyes widening as she found him—as she'd suspected—by her side. Straightening, she faced him.

He met her gaze briefly, searched her face, then his eyes returned to lock on hers. "I'll never let you go."

The words were quiet, steely—infinitely dangerous.

Almost as if he'd been reading her thoughts.

She held his gaze steadily, returned his regard. As always, his black eyes held a measure of heat, yet tonight, she could almost feel the flames. Not simply caressing, languidly artful, but greedily reaching, engulfing, hungry and urgent. Passion fueled them, but tonight there was something else, too, something she couldn't identify— something hotter, more potent, more powerful.

Something that touched her, reached deep, and thrilled her, as nothing had before.

"I know." There was no point in denying the strength of what bound her to him. She held his gaze. "I haven't asked you to."

"Good." The word was guttural in its harshness. His hands closed hard about her waist; she was instantly and shockingly aware of his strength. He pulled her to him, the movement lacking his usual grace. "Don't bother."

That something she couldn't name flared in his eyes.

"You're mine." He bent his head. *"Forever."*

The word was uttered as a vow, with the full force of all he was. Then his lips closed on hers.

He took them, claimed them, then parted them. She offered her mouth, appeasing his demand, ruthless, intent and dominant. His tongue thrust deep, knowing, commanding, then settled to plunder.

Not, as usual, with heated but languid caresses that spun a seductive web, but with unveiled passion, with a driving, ravenous, ruthless desire that stormed her mind and sent her wits careening.

His need hit her, an elemental force that literally shook her to her toes. Before she could react, she felt his hands shift, felt the tug—almost violent—as he jerked the tie of her robe undone. Then his hands, hard and forceful, were at her shoulders, pushing the robe over and down, stripping it away.

He gave her no chance to catch her mental breath. In seconds, the ribbon ties of her chemise were loose, then he pushed the garment down, his hands rough on her skin as he thrust the folds past her hips until they slithered down her legs to the floor.

His hands spread over her naked back and he pulled her fully to him, locked her against him. Angled his head over hers and ravaged her mouth, seizing, taking, ravishing, presaging what was to come.

Hands on his shoulders, fingers sinking into the embroidered silk of his waistcoat, she clung desperately to sanity, held tight as about her the world whirled.

She was naked in his arms, locked against his hard and unquestionably aroused body, her bare skin pressed to his clothes, the steely muscles trapping her screened by fabric. Even in her close-to-witless state, she recognized his clothed state as a deliberate ploy, a sexual taunt expertly aimed. He never cared about his nakedness; him naked she could deal with. Being naked, exposed, disturbed her still, at least beyond the confines of a bed.

He knew it. The way his hands moved over her body, not just possessive but tauntingly so, made that clear. Every touch escalated the tension gripping her, made her even more aware, deepened her feeling of vulnerabilty.

Heightened every sense she possessed until all, every last shred of her awareness, was focused completely on her own body, on what he was doing, on what he made her feel.

His lips held hers trapped as his hard hands moved over her breasts, closing, weighing, kneading, then retreating to play with her tightly budded nipples, causing havoc with nerves already excruciatingly taut. When her breasts were swollen and aching, he moved on, his touch openly hard, demanding, commanding. Not rough, but ruthless, relentless in pushing her on, in demanding and taking from her a surrender beyond all she'd previously given.

She didn't hesitate, didn't draw back. She met his lips, met his ravaging tongue, and let him have his way.

Let him trace her curves as he wished, explore her body as he wanted.

Let him sit on the window seat and lift her over him, let him settle her on her knees straddling his thighs, her own spread wide.

Let him hold her there as he broke from the kiss and trailed hot, burning kisses down her throat. Clinging to his shoulders, she arched her head back, caught her breath as he laved the pulse point at the base of her throat, then moved lower. To the ripe swells of her swollen breasts. To the tight, painful peaks.

He feasted, laving, licking, nibbling, sucking. She slid her fingers into his hair and held tight. Just breathing was a battle, one that only grew worse.

Along with the hot, empty ache deep within her. It welled, swelled, until it seemed to fill her.

Usually, with his hot body pressed to hers, she wasn't so shockingly aware of it. Tonight, held as she was, naked, but with him clothed, her thighs widespread, her body open but unfilled, she felt her own need keenly, clearly, more physically hers, not clouded by his.

Her breasts felt tight, skin hot and burning. He licked one nipple, then rasped it with his tongue; she heard a soft cry, and realized it was hers.

His hands, until then locked about her waist, holding her steady before him, eased; his palms slid down, curved over and around her bottom, then closed, kneading powerfully, evocatively. He continued to tease and taunt her nipples, then releasing her bottom, he ran his cupped hands down the backs of her spread thighs.

Her muscles quivered, then locked; above her knees,

his hands swung around and he pushed both hands, lightly gripping, thumbs cruising the sensitive inner faces, up her thighs.

Slowly. Deliberately.

She stopped breathing when, reaching the tops of her thighs, he paused. Then his hands left her.

She sucked in a breath—lost it when he opened his mouth and drew one tortured nipple deep, and suckled. Her shattered cry echoed through the room.

Then she felt his left hand close about her hip, holding her steady once more. His other hand returned to her mons, with a strong, firm stroke brushed over her curls, then reached beyond.

He opened her, explored her, tracing the entrance to her body while he continued to suckle her breasts, first one, then the other, constantly racking the tension that held her tighter. The emptiness inside her expanded, waiting for him to slake it. Nerves flickering, she waited, breath bated, expecting the slow penetration of his fingers, needing his touch, wanting it.

It didn't come.

She was ready to beg when his hand left her. Desperate, she caught her breath on a sob, felt the fingers wrapped about her hip dig in, anchoring her. Releasing her breast, he lifted his head, found her lips—took them. Ravaged them.

Her world teetered, rocked, then she realized on a rush of quivering relief that his other hand was at his waist, flicking the buttons free. He laid the flap of his trousers open. She immediately went to press closer, to sink down and take him in.

His hands gripped her hips, held her still for an instant, poised as he adjusted himself to her. She felt the broad head of his erection touch her, press fractionally in.

Eyes tight shut, her whole body a mass of urgent, heated need, she tried to gasp through the kiss.

He pulled her down onto him. Impaled her.

Her senses shattered.

He was fully aroused, engorged, more rigid unforgiving iron than velvet.

A low moan escaped her; he lifted her and ruthlessly drew her down again. Further, this time, so she took more of him. He thrust deeper, shifted beneath her, then his hands were at her hips, sculpting her legs, lifting them, rearranging them. As he wished. As he wanted.

He didn't ask, didn't order. He lifted her knees and wound her legs about his waist, leaving her helpless with no purchase to move.

Totally in his control, totally at his mercy.

He showed none; for her part, she asked no quarter.

All she wanted was him deep inside her, and he gave her that, as much as she wished, as much as she wanted.

Arms twined about his neck, she clung as he moved her. He set a steady rhythm, hard and deep, the head of his staff nudging her womb. She felt so full of him, as if he was pressing against her heart—and he only drove deeper, sure and true.

He held her to their kiss, tongues tangling, mouths merged.

Held her on his lap, naked and exposed, more vulnerable in the moonlight than she'd ever been.

More his.

All his.

When he finally released her lips and returned his attentions to her breasts, she let her head fall back, eyes closed.

Tensing as he again teased her nipples until they ached, then suckled anew, hard enough to make her fight to swallow a scream.

The next time, she lost the fight.

He was lifting her, working her on him, around him; simultaneously he was feasting at her breasts. She couldn't take much more stimulation, more of the sensations he was ruthlessly pressing on her, heightened, made infinitely more powerful by their position.

She licked her lips, managed to gasp, "Take me to the bed."

He didn't miss a beat. "No. Here. Like this."

His voice, all she could hear in it, very nearly made her weep.

With joy, with a pleasure that was far beyond the physical.

Need—simple, abiding, far deeper than she'd expected.

Never before had he been like this, never before had he dropped all pretence, every last vestige of sophistication, and allowed her to see so far, so clearly, to see that naked need. To know by her own experience so no lingering doubt could remain what truly drove him.

I love you.

She wanted to say the words. They welled in her chest, pushed up through her throat, but she swallowed them. If she told him that . . .

She had no wits left with which to think; instinct was her only guide. So she left the words unsaid, sobbed instead as her body started to convulse.

And he slowed.

Thrust harder, deeper, but slower.

So she felt every tiny slither as her senses unraveled, felt every last fraction of her helplessness as she climaxed more powerfully than she ever had before.

Tony raised his head and watched her, her ivory limbs silvered by the moonlight as she came apart in his arms. He drank in the sight, one he'd needed, one the prowling beast inside him had simply had to have.

Sunk to the hilt in her body, bathed in its scalding heat, he set his jaw and relentlessly drove her through the longest, most extended climax he'd ever forced on any woman. The soft strangled cries that fell from her lips were balm to his raging soul; the ripples of her release, the contractions that beckoned, her body helplessly gripping and releasing his erection, soothed that most primitive side of him.

It would be an easy matter to finish with her there, but that wasn't what he wanted. Tonight he needed more.

He waited until her muscles relaxed, until she was limp, wholly pliant in his arms. Then he lifted her from him, simultaneously stood, and carried her to the bed. He laid her on the coverlet, then stepped back and stripped off his clothes.

Then he joined her.

Propped beside her, he ran a hand down over her back, over the smooth globes of her bottom. Slowly, surely, he roused her again, then positioned her curled over her knees before him. He entered her slowly, eyes closed, savoring every fraction of an inch as her soft, swollen sheath closed about him.

Then he rode her.

Slowly at first, then without restraint.

Until she was sobbing, hair threshing as she struggled for breath, incoherent in her need, totally wild, completely wanton.

She was usually neither; that last rein of restraint she'd not before released had snapped, broken.

He savored every second of her abandonment, of her complete and absolute surrender, listened to her cries as she fell from the peak—then found his own surrender beckoning.

This time he went willingly. He knew, in some dark corner of his mind, just what he'd been doing. Knew it wouldn't work.

Didn't care.

He'd had to do it—to show her all there was, to tempt that side of her he didn't think she realized she possessed. She was a deeply sensual woman, but exploring her sensuality, opening her eyes to its true nature, had only more clearly demonstrated his own weakness, his own vulnerability.

This was one battlefield on which he was helpless. This was one fight in which there was no enemy.

Only surrender.

On a groan, he did, gave her all he was, all he could ever be.

Spent, he collapsed, then gathered her to him. He'd given her far more than his body. He'd lost his soul. And his heart. And perhaps even more.

TWENTY

HE LEFT ALICIA'S SIDE JUST AFTER DAWN, EARLIER THAN recent habit but after last night, he wanted nothing more than to have done with A. C.

After last night . . . he had even less idea what was wrong between them. Something, yes, but he'd be damned if he had a clue. If he pushed, twelve hours might result in them unmasking A. C., then he would be free to devote himself to the most important endeavor of his life—wooing Alicia, even winning her anew, if that's what was required.

Frowning, he left his apartments. After last night, he could hardly have missed the fact that she was as he'd hoped, openly, generously, totally his. If that was so, then what else was there? From where did their problem, whatever it was, spring?

Confusion reigned. Reaching Alicia's door, he determinedly put it from him, turned the knob, and entered.

She was still asleep. He sat on the bed and looked down at her, then gently shook her shoulder.

"Hmm?" She opened her eyes; he notched up her lack of surprise when she focused on him as a minor victory.

"I'm off to hunt down A. C. We're breakfasting at the club to work out our best approach. We need to learn who owns Ellicot, then proceed from there, but whatever we do—"

"You have to make sure you don't alert A. C." She was

wide-awake now, studying his face, her gaze earnest but watchful.

He hesitated; he wanted to say something about last night, about them, but didn't know what, and couldn't find the words.

"Stay on guard." Squeezing her hand, he rose. "If we stumble and alert him, I'd expect him to run, but . . . he's kept his head until now."

"We'll be careful." She struggled up on her elbows.

"Good." Backing, he raised a hand in farewell. She was naked beneath the covers, now sliding slowly down; he didn't trust himself to kiss her, and stop at just a kiss. Last night had left them both with enough to think about. "I'll be back this evening, if not before."

She nodded. "Take care."

At the door, he glanced back and saw her watching him. He inclined his head, and left.

Closing the door, he turned. David, Harry, and Matthew stood shoulder to shoulder across the corridor staring unblinkingly up at him.

"I was just telling Alicia where I'd be today."

"Oh." David considered his reply to their unspoken question, then nodded and turned to the stairs. "Are you going down to breakfast?"

Harry and Matthew swung around and followed.

Drawing a relieved breath, Tony fell in in their wake. "No—I have to go out straightaway."

Reaching the stairs, David and Harry clattered down.

Matthew stopped and turned to him. "Are you going to marry Alicia?"

Tony looked down into the big eyes fixed innocently on his face. "Yes. Of course."

The other boys had stopped halfway down to listen; now they whooped joyously, and thundered on down.

Matthew simply smiled. "Good." He took Tony's hand and, with simple gravity, accompanied him down the stairs.

* * *

Two hours later, Alicia strolled the lawns in the park, alone but for Maggs, tactfully keeping watch from a distance.

All about her was quiet and serene. It was too early for the fashionable throng; a few latecomers were still exercising their horses on Rotten Row, but most riders had already clattered home while the matrons and their daughters had yet to arrive.

The solitude and fresh air were precisely what she craved.

After the door had closed behind Tony, she'd lain in bed for ten minutes before the insistent refrain playing in her brain had prodded her into action. Ringing for Bertha, she'd washed, dressed, and joined Miranda and Adriana in the breakfast parlor.

Miranda and Adriana had been busy organizing their morning's engagements; she'd excused herself on the grounds of a slight headache and her need for a quiet walk to refresh herself. Accepting her excuse, the other two had left to get ready to visit Lady Carlisle; she'd climbed to the schoolroom and checked on her brothers, then quit the house, Maggs at her heels as per his "master's orders."

She'd accepted his escort with equanimity; she'd grown quite fond of the unprepossessing man. Interpreting his orders to watch over her literally, he'd retreated to stand beneath a large tree, now some distance away, leaving her to her thoughts.

Which were what she'd come to the park to confront.

It—her present tack—wasn't going to work. She'd thought her best way forward was to adhere strictly to her position as Tony's mistress and not wish for more, to rein in her dreams and accept what she'd been given, what he'd freely offered. But that view was fatally flawed—last night had proved it, had illustrated the truth beyond doubt.

The connection between them, so much more, so much stronger than any mere physical link, was not compatible with, would not remain constrained within, the bounds of the relationship of a nobleman and his mistress. Their connection was a vital thing, a living force in and of itself; it was growing, burgeoning, already demanding more.

Last night, she'd nearly told him she loved him, had had to fight to swallow the words. Some night soon she'd lose that fight. One way or another, the truth would out— *in toto*, there was more to it, more depths, more aspects than even that powerful fact.

She might already be carrying his child; it was too early to know, yet the possibility existed. In the beginning, she'd assumed he'd know what to do, would take precautions, yet he hadn't, nor had he expected her to. If she'd been shocked by her wanton behavior last night, her reaction to the idea of bearing Tony's child had only confirmed how little attention she'd paid her to her latent hopes, aspirations, and dreams. Until now.

In her heart, and now very clearly in her mind, she knew what she wanted. The question facing her was how to get it; leaving matters as they were was, she now accepted, no longer an option.

Drawing in a breath, she lifted her head and looked unseeing at some distant trees. She'd taken serious risks to secure Adriana's and her brothers' futures, boldly gambled and won. It was time to act in pursuit of her own future—to realize the dreams she'd never allowed herself to dream but which Tony had brought alive.

She would speak with him. She felt her chin set. Just as soon as A. C. was in custody, she would talk to Tony, explain how she felt about them, about their future. How he would react was the risk, the unknown, yet . . . she had his declaration of love to lean on, and, indeed, more. Their connection itself; through it she sensed how he felt, his need, even if he didn't consciously acknowledge it. In time, he would recognize the truth as she had, and re-assess as she had, and adjust.

Grimacing, she looked down. She would be gambling that their love truly was as she saw it—a huge risk, yet one she felt compelled to take.

The thud of footsteps approaching over the grass reached her. Looking up, she saw a footman in plain black livery striding purposefully her way.

Glancing to the left, she saw Maggs, leaning against the tree trunk, come alert, but as the footman halted and bowed, Maggs relaxed and resumed his unobtrusive watch.

"For you, ma'am."

The footman proffered a note. She took it, opened it, read it, and inwardly cursed. Chickens were coming home to roost thick and fast. Sir Freddie Caudel most formally and politely requested an interview.

She looked across the lawn to the black carriage drawn up on the gravel drive. With a sigh, she tucked the note into her reticule. "Very well."

The footman bowed and escorted her to the carriage. Maggs, closer to the carriage than she, remained where he was, half-obscured by the tree.

Reaching the carriage, the footman opened the door and stood back, clearly expecting her to enter. Puzzled, she looked in, and saw Sir Freddie, dapper and urbanely elegant as usual, sitting inside.

Smiling easily, he half rose and bowed. "My dear, I hope you'll forgive this unusual approach, but for reasons that will become clear as we talk, I wished to speak with you in the strictest privacy. If you will do me the honor of sharing my carriage, I thought we might roll around the Avenue—it's quite peaceful at the moment—and conduct our discussion in relative comfort, out of sight of prying eyes." He smiled, his pale gaze somewhat rueful, gently humorous, and held out his hand. "If you would, my dear?"

Inwardly sighing, she gave him her hand; gathering her skirts, she climbed into the carriage. Sir Freddie released her and she sat opposite him, facing forward. Sir Freddie nodded to his footman. The man shut the door; an instant later, the carriage started slowly rolling.

"Now." Sir Freddie fixed her with a calmly superior smile. "You must let me apologize for this little charade. I'm sure you understand that, given the nature of my interest and thus the reason behind my request for an interview, there would be nothing more unappealing to me than in any way whatever giving the gossipmongers reason to wag their tongues."

Alicia inclined her head; from her experience, now extensive, of Sir Freddie's circumlocutory periods, she knew it was pointless to try to rush him. He would get to his peroration in his own good time. Nevertheless . . . "Now we are here, you perceive me all ears, sir."

"Indeed." Sir Freddie returned her nod. "I should also explain that I did not think it appropriate, in the circumstances, to call at Torrington House." He held up a hand as if to stem a protest she hadn't made. "I'm quite sure I would be treated with all due consideration, indeed graciousness, however, I am aware that Manningham is an old and valued friend of Torrington's." Sir Freddie paused, as if weighing that fact anew. Eventually, he said, "Suffice to say I deemed it impolitic to call on you there."

Again, she inclined her head and wondered how long he would take to come to the point. Given that point—his offer for Adriana's hand—she turned her mind to finding the words with which to refuse him.

Sir Freddie rambled on and on; his voice, polished, light, his accents refined, was easy on the ear. Smoothly, he described his current position, his reasons for looking for a wife, then moved on to Adriana's manifold charms.

The carriage suddenly rocked, the wheel dipping in a pothole; mildly surprised that such a thing existed on the fashionable carriageway, Alicia refocused on Sir Freddie's eloquence, and discovered he was still describing, in phrases both flowery and convoluted, just what it was about her sister that had attracted his notice.

Counseling patience, she folded her hands in her lap, and waited. Her mind slid away . . . she imagined Maggs, under his tree, watching the carriage go around and around the park . . .

Instinct flickered. The carriage blinds had been drawn from the first, she'd assumed to prevent the interested seeing Sir Freddie speaking with her. The carriage rocked again; the blinds swayed—and she caught a glimpse of what lay outside.

It wasn't the park.

She looked at Sir Freddie as the sounds outside registered. They were traveling down some major road, not one lined with trees, not even with shops, but with houses—a road that led not into the city, but out of it.

Her shock, her realization, showed in her face.

Something changed in Sir Freddie's expression, as if a thin, obscuring veil was drawn aside; abruptly she realized that he was watching her closely, a coldly calculating look in his eyes.

He smiled. Before the gesture had been urbanely charming; now it chilled.

"Ah—I did wonder how long it would take." His voice, too, had subtly changed, all pleasantness leaching from it. "However, before you think of making any heroic attempt to escape, I suggest you listen to what I have to say."

His eyes held hers, and they were colder than a snake's. Alicia sat transfixed, her thoughts tumbling, churning. "Escape" implied . . .

"The most important thing you need to bear in mind is that there's another carriage ahead of us on this road. It contains two rather rough men—I wouldn't distinguish them with the title of gentleman—in company with your youngest brother. Matthew, as I'm sure you know, has a habit of slipping outside when he grows bored with his lessons. He did so, with a little encouragement I admit, this morning, just after you'd left the house. He's an enterprising young chap, quite capable of evading all supervision when he chooses." Sir Freddie smiled. "But I'm sure you know that."

Alicia's heart lurched; the blood drained from her face. She did know of Matthew's occasional excursions—just to the area between the house and the street to watch the world rumble by—but since they'd moved to Torrington House, she'd thought they'd stopped. "What do you want with Matthew?"

Sir Freddie's brows rose. "Why nothing, my dear—nothing at all. He's merely a pawn to ensure *you* behave as I wish." His gaze hardened. "If you do as I say, no harm will come to him. Those two men I spoke of have strict orders, ones it's to their advantage to obey. They'll take your brother to a safe place, and wait with him there for word from me. Depending on how matters transpire, I will instruct them either to return him to Upper Brook Street unharmed"—his lips curved lightly, tauntingly, "or to kill him."

He held her gaze. "The instruction I send will depend on you."

Alicia fought to met his gaze levelly, to keep her expression impassive, to keep her fear, her panic, at bay. Icy chills ran up and down her spine. *Matthew* . . . a vise squeezed her heart even as, instinctive and immediate, she searched for the means to free him. Maggs—he would fetch Tony . . . she couldn't work out the how and when, not with Sir Freddie's cold and sharply observant eyes on her.

She licked her lips, forced her lungs to work. "What do you want me to do?" She frowned. "What *is* this all about?" Why kidnap her and Matthew if it was Adriana Sir Freddie wanted?

She allowed her confusion and total incomprehension to show in her face.

Sir Freddie laughed.

The sound chilled her to the marrow.

Then he smiled, and she wanted nothing more than to flee. "This, my dear, is about me covering my tracks, an unfortunate necessity brought on by Ruskin. He couldn't seem to understand that the war was over and the easy pickings with it."

She stared at him. "*You're* A. C?"

"A. C?" Sir Freddie blinked, then his face cleared. "Ah, yes, I'd almost forgotten."

He shifted. With a graceful sweep of his arm, he bowed, the gesture full of his customary elegant charm. Face, lips lightly curved, and manner were all one, but as he straightened, his cold, pale eyes met hers. "Sir Alfred Caudel, my dear, at your service."

Tony returned to Torrington House midmorning. After reviewing their information, the group had agreed that Jack Warnefleet and Christian, neither of whom had been visible thus far in the affair, should visit Ellicot's offices and extract by whatever means they could some idea of who was behind the company.

There was a limit to how unsubtle they could be; there was no guarantee of a quick and favorable outcome. Restless, impatient, sensing matters were nearing a head but with nothing he could reasonably do, Tony had returned home.

He'd only just settled behind his desk when the study door burst open and panic—carried by David, Harry, Matthew, and Jenkins—rushed in.

"*Alicia!*" Matthew shrieked. "You've got to go and save her."

Tony caught him as he charged around the desk and flung himself at him. "Yes, of course," he replied, his gaze locking on the others.

David and Harry had rushed to the desk, gripping the front edge, their expressions as horrified as Matthew's.

Jenkins, close on their heels, was not much better, and out of breath as well.

"My lord," Jenkins puffed, "Maggs sent us to tell you—Mrs. Carrington was inveigled into a carriage which then took off to the west."

Tony swore, started to rise. "Where's Maggs?"

Jenkins struggled for breath. "He's following the carriage. He said he'd send word as he can."

Tony nodded curtly. "Sit down." Lifting Matthew into his arms, he turned his attention to the older boys. "Now, David—tell me what you know, from the beginning."

David dragged in a huge breath, held it for a second, then complied. The story came out in reasonable order: Alicia visiting the schoolroom, mentioning she was going for a walk—Tony had imagined her out with Miranda and Adriana—the boys then prevailing on Jenkins to take their nature lesson in the park; they'd arrived to find Maggs running toward them, swearing and cursing, watching a black carriage that had passed the boys turn out of the park and roll away to the west. Maggs had pounced on them, given them the message, hailed a hackney, and set off after the carriage.

"All right." Tony felt none of their panic; he'd spent the last decade dealing with similarly fraught situations. He welcomed, even relished what he recognized as the call to arms; he couldn't yet see how it related, but he knew a bugle when he heard it. "Did Maggs say who was in the carriage?"

The boys shook their heads. So did Jenkins. "I don't think he saw who it was, my lord."

"It was Sir Freddie someone's carriage." The mumbled words, spoken around a thumb, came from Matthew.

Tony glanced at him, then sat him on the desk so he could see his face. He pulled up his chair and sat, too, so he wasn't towering over the boy. "How do you know that?"

Matthew took his thumb out of his mouth. "Horses.

This time, he had four, but the front two were the ones that always pull his carriage. I know them from when he came to call at the other house."

Tony wondered how much reliance to place on a small boy's observations. He felt a tug on his sleeve and looked into Harry's face.

"Matthew notices things—and he really does know horses."

Tony looked at David, who nodded, then at Jenkins, recovering in a chair. Jenkins nodded, too. "He's very good about details, my lord. Excellent memory."

Tony paused, then swallowed the curse that rose to his lips. Rising, he turned to the bookshelves behind the desk, scanned, then pulled out his copy of *Debrett's*.

A tap fell on the door, then it opened. Geoffrey Manningham strolled in. Across the room, Tony met his gaze.

Instantly, Geoffrey came alert. "What? What's happened?"

"Caudel has kidnapped Alicia." Tony opened the book, swiftly flicking pages. He found the entry for Caudel. He read it, and swore beneath his breath. "Sir *Alfred* Caudel."

He slammed the book shut. "A. C. Currently with the Home Office. From an old if not ancient family, his principal estate is in north Oxfordshire, near Chipping Norton, not far from the tavern where those letters from the French captains were sent."

Geoffrey's mouth had fallen open; he snapped it shut. "*Caudel?* Good God—no wonder he's so desperate to scotch the investigation."

"Indeed, and no wonder he knew so much about the investigation itself." Standing behind the desk, fingers lightly drumming, Tony rapidly assembled a plan, checking and re-checking, mentally listing all the necessary orders. He glanced at the three boys, spared them a reassuring smile. "I'll go after them."

Geoffrey frowned. "You know where they've gone?"

"Maggs has them in his sights—he'll send word as soon as he passes a hostelery." Tony spoke to the boys. "Maggs knows what to do—he won't stop following Alicia. I'll head out as soon as I know which road—Maggs and I have a system we've used before. It'll work, so don't worry that we'll lose the trail." He looked at Geoffrey. "I need you to get word to the others, and then wait here with Adriana, Miranda, and the rest—no need for vapors, I'll bring Alicia back."

Geoffrey nodded. "Right. Who do you want me to get hold of?"

Tony gave him a list. Dalziel first; Tony wrote a short note summarizing the evidence that Sir Freddie was A. C. He handed it to Geoffrey. "Give that to Dalziel—into his hand, don't show it to anyone else. Use my name, that'll get you through his pickets. Then go to Hendon House and tell Jack, then to the club, and tell the majordomo, Gasthorpe. Tell him the others—Deverell's out of town but the other five—all need to know."

While he'd talked, he'd risen and tugged the bellpull. Hungerford appeared; Tony ordered his curricle brought around with the bays put to. Without comment, Hungerford left.

Almost immediately he returned. "A message from Maggs, my lord, brought by an ostler from Hounslow. Maggs says it's the Basingstoke road."

Having assimilated the fact that Sir Freddie was A. C., which he verified beyond doubt by telling her the details of how his scheme had operated, and of how he'd worked since Ruskin's death to turn all blame on her, Alicia still didn't know the answer to her question. She fixed Sir Freddie with a steady gaze. "What do you plan to do now? What do you want me to do?"

"At the moment, nothing." Reaching out, he lifted a window flap, glanced out, then let the flap fall and looked back at her. "We'll be journeying through the night.

When we stop to change horses, you'll remain in the carriage, calm and composed. At no time will you do anything to attract attention. You won't forget that your brother's future lies in your hands, so you will do exactly as I say at all times."

She debated telling him that Tony and his friends knew about Ellicot, but decided to hold her fire, at least until she knew more. "Where are we going?" Through the night suggested deep into the country.

Sir Freddie studied her, then shrugged. "I don't suppose it will hurt to tell you." His tone was cold, unemotional. "Given how forthcoming I've been, I'm sure you've realized by now that this last and, I fancy, winning throw of the dice involves your demise."

She had, but refused to let it panic her. She raised a brow, faintly haughty. "You're going to kill me?"

He smiled his chilling smile. "Most regretfully, I assure you. But before you waste breath trying to tell me such an act won't get me anywhere, let me explain how things will appear once you're no longer about to state your case.

"First, I'm aware of the activities of Torrington and his friends. They really are quite tediously tenacious. Ellicot was an obvious liability—he, naturally, is no longer with us. His family, however, are most likely aware that he had a sleeping partner, so I took care to remove all evidence of my association with him . . . and replaced it with evidence of *your* association with him.

"When Torrington and his friends look, they'll find a circle of evidence that leads them back to you—where their attention should have stayed all along. I'm sure they won't be happy about it, but they won't have any choice in laying the blame at your door. I've become quite adept at bending society and the upper echelons to my bidding; there'll be such irritation that you've escaped, your guilt will be established by default.

"Naturally, you won't be there to answer the charges,

which will only reinforce them. Your disappearance will be seen as an admission of guilt, one your supporters will be at a loss to counter. When your body is eventually found, as I'll ensure it is, everyone will conclude that, weighed down with remorse, with the investigation closing in—something you would know with Torrington as your lover—with social disaster of ever-greater proportions looming over you and your precious family . . . well, you took the only honorable way out for a lady."

She let contempt infuse her voice. "You said you know of Torrington and his friends and how tenacious they are. My death won't convince them—it won't stop their investigation, it'll intensify it." She was perfectly certain of that.

Sir Freddie, however, smiled, coldly condescending. "The key is Torrington, and how he'll react to finding your dead body."

She couldn't stop her lashes from flickering.

Sir Freddie saw; his smile deepened. "He's in love with you, not just a passing fancy, I fear, but well and truly caught. What do you think it will do to him to be the one to discover you dead?"

She refused to react, to give him any indication of what she thought; the arrogant fool had just said the one thing above all others guaranteed to make her fight to the last.

"With you gone and nothing left to save, Torrington will retire to deepest Devon. The others won't be able to sustain the investigation without him." He paused, then added, "And that, my dear, will finally be the end of the story."

She drew breath, but didn't challenge him; there had to be some way to scuttle his plans. She kept her mind focused on that, refusing even to think of defeat. Defeat meant death, and she definitely wasn't ready to die.

Leaning her head against the squabs, she went over his plan. He was right in predicting she would do nothing to put Matthew at risk, but the risk came from Sir Freddie. He'd said his men would hold Matthew *until* they heard from him; if they didn't . . . there'd be time to find them and free Matthew unharmed.

She needed to escape and simultaneously take Sir Freddie captive, ensuring he could send no message. Once they'd turned the tables, Sir Freddie would tell them where Matthew was held . . . she needed Tony for that, but . . .

In her heart, she was sure he'd come for her. Maggs had been watching; he'd probably realized she'd been kidnapped before she had. Maggs would get word to Tony, and Tony would come. However, she couldn't rely on Tony catching up with her before Sir Freddie tried to kill her.

She looked across the carriage. Sir Freddie's eyes were closed, but she didn't think he was asleep. He was some years older than Tony, a few inches shorter, but of heavier build. Indeed, he'd be described as a fine figure of a man, still in his prime; he'd never looked out of place in Adriana's court.

Physically, she couldn't hope to win any tussle, yet if Sir Freddie had any weakness, it was his overweening conceit. He believed he'd get away with everything. If she played to that belief, there might be one moment, almost at the end of the game, when he might be vulnerable. . . .

It would likely be her only chance.

She saw a glint from beneath his lashes; he'd been watching her studying him. "You didn't say where we're going."

He was silent, clearly weighing the risk, then he said, "Exmoor. There's a tiny village I was once stranded in. The evidence will suggest you stopped there, then wandered out onto the moor, threw yourself down a disused mine shaft, and drowned."

Exmoor. Closing her eyes, leaning her head back

again, she focused on that. An isolated moor. They'd have to walk to any mine . . . the coachman would have to stay with the horses . . .

As the day rolled into evening, she behaved precisely as Sir Freddie wished. She considered pretending to fall apart, weeping and despairing, but she wasn't that good an actress, and if Sir Freddie suspected she wasn't resigned to her fate . . . instead, she behaved as she imagined a French duchess would have on her way to the guillotine. Head high, haughtily superior, yet with no hint of any struggle against an overwhelming fate.

He had to believe she'd accepted it, that she'd go haughtily but quietly to her death. Given his background, that was very likely the behavior he'd expect of her, a lady of his class.

The farther they traveled, stopping at inn after inn to change horses, the more evidence she detected of his natural conceit overcoming his caution. He even allowed her to use the convenience at an inn, although she had no chance to speak to anyone, and he remained within sight of the door at all times.

Night fell; four horses pulled the coach steadily on. Closing her eyes, feigning sleep, she felt her nerves tensing and tried to relax. Exmoor, he'd said, and Exeter was still some way ahead; it would be hours yet before she got her chance. Her one chance at the life she now knew beyond doubt she wanted. The life she was prepared to fight for, the life she was determined to have.

Not as Tony's mistress, but as his wife. As his viscountess, the mother of his heir, and other children, too. She had far too much to live for to die.

And she knew he loved her; not only had he said so, but he'd shown her. If she'd had any doubt over what his feelings truly were, the picture Sir Freddie had painted, the question he'd asked: how would Tony react to finding her dead? had blown all such doubts away.

Devastated was too small a word—she knew precisely how he would feel because it was the same way she'd feel in the converse circumstance.

They loved each other, equally completely, equally deeply; she no longer questioned that. Once they were past this, free of Sir Freddie and his deadly scheme, she would speak with Tony. He might not yet see things as she did, but she was perfectly marriageable, after all. He'd established her as his equal in the eyes of the ton; if his mother was anything like Lady Amery and the Duchess of St. Ives, she doubted she'd have any difficulties there.

She wanted to marry him, and if that meant she had to broach the subject herself, then she would. Brazenly. After last night, she could be brazen about anything, at least with him.

The prospect—her future as she would have it with Tony by her side—filled her mind. Joy welled; fear hovered that it would not come to be, but she shunned it, clung to the joy instead.

Held to the vision of a happy future. Let it strengthen her. Her determination to make it happen—that it would be—soared.

Unexpectedly, she slept.

The noisy rattle of the wheels hitting cobblestones jerked Alicia from her doze. It was deepest night, past midnight; she'd heard the sound of a bell tolling twelve as they'd passed through Exeter, now some way behind.

Sir Freddie had fastened back one of the window flaps. Through the window, she glimpsed a hedgerow; beyond it, the ground rose, desolate and empty. The coach slowed, then halted.

"Well, my dear, we're here." Through the gloom, Sir Freddie watched her. Holding to her resolve, she didn't react.

He hesitated, then leaned past her, opened the door,

and climbed down. He turned and gave her his hand; she allowed him to assist her to the cobbles, leaving her cloak on the seat. When the time came to run, she didn't want its folds flapping about her legs. Her skirts would be bad enough.

She'd slipped the cloak off sometime before; Sir Freddie didn't seem to notice—there was no reason he should care. He'd stepped forward to speak to the coachman; she strained her ears and caught the words she'd hoped to hear.

"Wait here until I return."

When she'd first emerged from the coach at an inn, there'd been no footman; she assumed he'd been set down in London. The coachman had avoided her eye; she knew better than to expect help from that quarter. All she needed was for the man to wait until his master returned. If things went her way, his master wouldn't return, not before she did and raised help from the cottages she could see just ahead, lining the road.

Sir Freddie turned to her. Again, he studied her; as she had all along, she met his gaze stonily.

He inclined his head. "Your composure does you credit, my dear. I really do regret putting an end to your life."

She didn't deign to answer. Sir Freddie's lips quirked; with a wave, he indicated a path leading from the narrow road. Within yards of the hedge, the path plunged into a dark wood; beyond, the moors rose, alternately illuminated, then shrouded in gloomy shadow as clouds passed over the moon.

"We have to walk through the wood to reach the moors and the mine."

Sir Freddie reached for her arm, but she forestalled him and turned, and calmly walked to the opening of the path.

* * *

Tony swore; hauling on the reins, he swung the latest pair he'd had harnessed in Exeter onto the road to Hatherleigh.

Why here, for heaven's sake? Was it the isolation?

He'd had hours to consider what Sir Freddie was about while following his path across the country. It had been decades since he'd driven at breakneck speed—he'd been pleased to discover he hadn't forgotten how—but even the exigencies of managing unfamiliar cattle hadn't stopped him from thinking first and foremost of Alicia, of the danger facing her.

Up behind him, Maggs was hanging on grimly, every now and then muttering imprecations under his breath. Tony ignored him. He'd caught up with Maggs at Yeovil; before then, whenever Maggs had stopped to change horses he'd sent a rider wearing a red kerchief back along the road. Tony had stopped each flagged rider, and thus known which road to follow.

As it happened, it was a road he knew well—the same road he'd traveled countless times between Torrington Chase and London. The familiarity had helped; he'd have missed their turning to Hatherleigh if he hadn't known to ask at Okehampton.

Sir Freddie taking Alicia so far from London had been a boon initially, giving him time to catch up. Even though Sir Freddie had been rocketing along, always using four fresh horses, Tony knew he was close on their heels.

While they were traveling, he had no fears for Alicia. Once they stopped . . .

His experience lay in pursuing someone he needed to catch, not save. Every time he thought of Alicia, his heart lurched, his mind stilled, paralyzed; shutting off such thoughts, he concentrated on Sir Freddie instead.

Why this route? Was Sir Freddie intending to drive through to the Bristol Channel and rendezvous with some lugger? Was Alicia a hostage? Or was she intended as the scapegoat Sir Freddie had from the first sought to make her?

That was Tony's blackest fear. The landscape, the desolate sweep of the moors rising up on either side of the road fed it. If Sir Freddie intended to stage Alicia's murder and make it appear a suicide, and thus quash the investigation . . .

Tony set his jaw. Once he got hold of her, he was taking her to Torrington Chase and keeping her there. Forever.

Sending the whip swinging to flick the leader's ear, he drove the horses on.

TWENTY-ONE

ALICIA EMERGED ONTO THE MOOR WITH A SENSE OF RE-
lief; the wood had been dark, the trees very old, the path
uneven and knotted with their roots. Here, at least, she
could breathe—dragging in a breath, she looked up, tracing the path they were following to where it skirted a pile
of rocks and earth, the workings of the disused mine in
which Sir Freddie planned to drown her.

Every nerve taut and alert, she kept walking, head
high, her pace neither too fast nor yet slow enough to
prompt Sir Freddie to hurry her. Scanning the area, she
searched—for a rock, a branch, anything she could use to
overpower him. Closer to the mine would be preferable,
yet the closer they got . . .

She was supremely conscious of him walking steadily
at her heels. He seemed relaxed, just a murderer out to
arrange another death. Quelling a shudder, she looked
again at the mine. The path rose steadily, steeper as it led
up the shoulder of the workings before leveling off as it
skirted the lip of the shaft itself.

The clouds were constantly shifting, drifting; there
was always enough light to see their way, but when the
moon shone clear, details leapt out.

Like the discarded spar she glimpsed, just fleetingly, to
the right of the steepest section of the path.

Her heart leapt; her muscles tensed, ready . . .

Quickly, she thought through what would need to happen. She had to distract Sir Freddie at just the right spot. She'd already decided how, but she needed to set the stage.

Reaching the spot where the steep upward slope commenced, she halted abruptly. Swinging to face Sir Freddie, she found the slope was sufficient for her to meet his gaze levelly. "Do I have your word as a gentleman that my brother won't be harmed? That he'll be released as soon as possible in Upper Brook Street?"

Sir Freddie met her eyes; his lips twisted as, nodding, he looked down. "Of course." After a fractional pause, he added, "You have my word."

She had lived with three males long enough to instantly detect prevarication. Lips thinning, she narrowed her eyes, then tersely asked, "You haven't really got him, have you? There is no second carriage."

She'd wondered, but hadn't dared call his bluff or even question him while trapped in the carriage.

He looked up, raised his brows. Faintly shrugged. "I saw no reason to bother with your brother. I knew the threat alone would be enough to get you to behave."

The relief that surged through her nearly brought her to her knees. The weight on her shoulders evaporated. She was *free*—free to deal with Sir Freddie as she wished, with only her own life at stake. A life she was willing to risk to secure her future—what choice did she have? She fought to keep any hint of her upwelling resolve from her face. She glared at Sir Freddie, then swung on her heel and walked on.

Trusting to his overweening confidence to keep him from wondering at her continued acquiescence for just a few steps more . . .

From behind, she heard a faint chuckle, then his footsteps as he followed. Up ahead to her right lay the wooden spar. Just a *little* farther; she needed the greater steepness, the change in their relative heights . . .

Again she stopped dead, swung to face him.

At the last second let her contempt show. "You *bastard*!"

She slapped him. With the full force of her arm as she delivered the blow, with him lower than she, his face at the right height to take the full brunt of her momentum.

He had no chance to duck; the blow landed perfectly. Her palm stung; he staggered.

She didn't pause but turned and raced, scrambling up the few steps to the spar. She heard him swear foully, heard his boots scrabble on the path. Bending, she locked both hands on the spar, hefted it, and swung around. Driven by resolution laced with very real fear, she put every ounce of strength she possessed behind her swing.

He didn't see it coming.

She wielded the spar like a rounders bat. He was still lower on the path than she; the spar hit him across the side of the head.

The spar cracked, broke, fell from her hands.

He slumped to his knees, groggy, dazed, but not unconscious. He weaved. Desperate, she glanced around.

There were no other spars.

She grabbed up her skirts, stepped around him, and ran. Fled like a fury down the path, leaping down from the workings and streaking across the moor to plunge into the dark wood.

Chest heaving, she forced herself to slow. The roots were treacherous; she couldn't afford to fall. If she could get to the cottages and raise the alarm, she'd be safe. She didn't even have to worry about Matthew anymore.

From behind her came a roar; the thud of heavy footsteps reached her, rapidly gaining.

Fighting down panic, she kept her eyes down, locked on the path, feet dancing over the tree roots—

She ran into a black wall.

She shrieked, then stilled as the familiar scent, the familiar feel of Tony's body against hers, of his arms wrapping about her sank into her senses. She nearly fainted with relief.

He was looking beyond her, over her head. "Where is he?"

His words were a lethal whisper.

"On the path leading up to a disused mine."

He nodded. "I know it. Stay here."

With that he was gone. He moved so swiftly, so silently, surefooted in the darkness, that by the time, dazed, she turned, she'd nearly lost him.

She followed, but carefully, as quiet as he. She'd expected him to wait in the shadows and let Sir Freddie blunder into him as she had, but instead, he paused, waited until Sir Freddie was nearly to the trees, then calmly, determinedly, walked out of the wood.

Sir Freddie saw him. Pure horror crossed his face. He skidded to a halt, turned, and fled.

Back up the path.

Tony was at his heels almost immediately. Following as fast as her skirts would allow, she could see that he could have overhauled Sir Freddie anywhere along the upward slope. Instead, he waited until Sir Freddie gained the level stretch beside the gaping mine shaft before he reached out, spun Sir Freddie around, and plowed his fist into his face.

She heard the sickening thud all the way down the path where she was laboring upward. The first thud was followed by more; she couldn't see either man but felt sure Sir Freddie was on the receiving end. She hoped every blow hurt as badly as they sounded. Gaining the level stretch, she looked, just in time to see Tony slam his fist into Sir Freddie's jaw.

Something cracked. Sir Freddie fell back, onto a pile of rubble. He slumped, winded, but quick as a flash he grabbed a rock and flung it at Tony's head.

She screamed, but Tony hadn't taken his eye from Sir Freddie. He ducked the missile, then, lips curling in a snarl, bent, grabbed Sir Freddie, hauled him to his feet, punched him once in the face, grabbed him again, shook him—and flung him backward into the mine shaft.

There was a huge splash; water sprayed out.

Tony stood where he was, chest heaving until he'd regained his breath, then he stepped forward and looked down just as Alicia joined him.

She cast one brief look at Sir Freddie, spluttering, desperately searching for handholds on the slippery shaft wall, then looked at him. Reached out with both hands and touched him. "Are you all right?"

He looked into her eyes, searched her face—saw she was far more concerned for his well-being than hers—and felt something inside him give. "Yes." He briefly closed his eyes. If she was all right, he was, too.

Opening his eyes, he reached for her, drew her to him. Wrapped her in his arms and gloried in the reality of her warmth against him. Cheek against the silk of her hair, he sent a heartfelt thank-you to fate and the gods, then, easing his hold on her, looked down at Sir Freddie, fighting to hold his head above the dank water. "What do you want to do with him?"

She looked down. Her eyes narrowed. "He told me he'd killed Ellicot, and he was going to kill me. I say we let him drown—poetic justice."

"No!" The protest dissolved into a gurgle as Sir Freddie's terror made his fingers slip. "No," came again as he scrabbled back to the surface. "Torrington," he gasped, "you can't leave me here. What will you tell your masters?"

Tony looked down at him. "That you'd sunk before I reached you?"

Folding her arms, Alicia scowled. "I say we leave him—a hemlocklike taste of his own medicine."

"Hmm." Tony glanced at her. "How about a trial for treason and murder?"

"Trials and executions cost money. Much better just to

leave him to drown. We know he's guilty, and just think—*who* forced him to come here from London? Did *I* make him spin me a tale about kidnapping Matthew?"

Tony stiffened. "He told you that?"

Lips tight, she nodded. "And just think of all the brave sailors he's sent to watery graves! He's a disgusting and debauched worm." She tugged Tony's arm. "Come on— let's go."

She didn't mean it, but she was more than furious with Sir Freddie, and saw no reason not to torture him.

"Wait! Please . . ." Sir Freddie coughed water. "I know someone else."

Tony stilled, then, releasing her, he stepped closer to the edge and crouched down to peer at Sir Freddie. "What did you say?"

"Someone else." Sir Freddie was breathing shallowly; the water in the shaft would be freezing. "Another traitor."

"Who?"

"Get me out of here, and we can talk."

Tony rose; stepping back, he drew Alicia to him, pressed a kiss to her temple, whispered, "Play along." More loudly, he said, "You're right, let's just leave him." His arm around her, he turned them away.

"No!" Spluttering curses floated out of the shaft. "Damm it—I'm not making this up. There *is* someone else."

"Don't listen," Alicia advised. "He's always making things up—just think of his tale about Matthew."

"That was for a reason!"

She glanced over the edge. "And saving your life isn't a reason? Huh!" She stepped back. "Come on, I'm get- ting cold."

They started walking, taking tiny steps so Sir Freddie could hear.

"*Wait*! All right, damm it—it's someone in the Foreign Office. I don't know who—I tried to find out, but he's wilier than I. He's very careful, and he's someone very senior."

Tony sighed; he moved back to crouch at the edge. "Keep talking. I'm listening, but she's not convinced."

In gasps and pants, Sir Freddie talked, answering Tony's questions, revealing how he'd stumbled on the other traitor's trail. Eventually, Tony rose. He nodded at Alicia. "Stand back—I'm going to haul him out."

Tony had to lie full length on the ground to do it, but eventually Sir Freddie lay like a beached whale, shivering, coughing, and convulsing. Neither Alicia nor Tony felt the least bit sympathetic. Yanking Sir Freddie's cravat free, Tony used it to bind his hands before hauling him to his feet and, with a push, starting him back along the path.

Alicia's hand in his, Tony followed his quarry back through the wood and out onto the road. Maggs was waiting beside Sir Freddie's coach.

Alicia looked up at the box. "He had a coachman—he told him to wait."

"Oh, aye. He's waiting right enough, inside the coach." Maggs held out Alicia's cloak and reticule. "Found these when I shoved him in."

"Thank you."

Maggs nodded at Tony. "I was thinking we'd best leave 'em in the cellars at the George. I've had a word to Jim—he's opening up the hatch."

"Excellent idea." Tony prodded Sir Freddie along the road toward the nearby inn. "Bring the coachman."

Maggs had to lug him, for the coachman was unconscious. After a brief discussion with the landlord of the George, they left their prisoners in the cellars under lock and key.

Jim came out and led Sir Freddie's carriage away. Alicia was on the seat of Tony's curricle and he was about to join her when they heard the unmistakable rumble of a carriage heading their way.

Tony exchanged a glance with Maggs, then reached for Alicia. "Just in case, get back down here."

He had her on the ground behind him when the carriage rocked around the corner. The driver saw them and slowed.

"Thank God!" Geoffrey pulled the horses to a halt beside them.

Tony caught the leader's head, quieted the team. "What the devil—?"

In answer the doors of the carriage burst open and Adriana, David, Harry, and Matthew came tumbling out.

They rushed to Alicia, hugged her wildly, a cacophony of questions raining down. They waited for no answers, but danced and jigged, cavorted around Tony, too, but then returned to hug and hang on to their elder sister.

Geoffrey climbed down from the box; he stretched, then came to stand beside Tony. "Don't say I should have stopped them—it was impossible. It's my belief once they take an idea into their heads, Pevenseys are unstoppable." He smiled. "At least Alicia's a Carrington—she's been tamed."

"Hmm," was all Tony said.

Both he and Geoffrey were only children. The performance enacted before them left them both bemused and a trifle envious. They exchanged a glance, for once had no doubt what each other was thinking . . . planning.

"Come on," Tony said. "We'd better get them moving, or we'll be here for the rest of the night."

They rounded up their charges. With joy in their faces, still asking questions, the triumphant Pevenseys eventually climbed back into the carriage. Climbing up to the box, Geoffrey looked at Tony. "The Chase?"

Tony turned from handing Alicia into his curricle. "Where else?" Taking the reins, he climbed up. "It's the only thing Sir Freddie got right."

The comment puzzled Alicia. She waited until they were rolling along, heading farther up the road not back toward town with the heavy carriage rumbling behind. "Where are we going?"

"Home," Tony replied, and whipped up his horses.

She was determined to speak with him, to address the subject of marriage, but no opportunity came her way that night. They traveled for nearly an hour, steadily northward along the country road, then Tony checked the horses and turned in through a pair of tall gateposts with huge wrought-iron gates propped wide.

He'd refused to tell her more about where he was taking her, but she guessed when she saw the house. A large Palladian mansion in pale brown and grey stone with both double-and single-story wings, it sat peacefully in the moonlight, perfectly proportioned, comfortable, and settled within its park.

Tony drew the horses to a halt in the wide gravel forecourt. He leapt down, scanned the house with fond satisfaction, then turned and held out his hand. "Welcome to Torrington Chase."

The next hour went in pleasurable chaos. Servants tumbled from their beds and came rushing, their eagerness a comment on how they viewed their master. Tony flung orders this way and that; in the midst of the flurry, a calm, feminine voice was heard inquiring what her son was up to now.

In the drawing room, Tony exchanged a glance with Geoffrey, then looked at Alicia. Briefly, he lifted her hand to his lips. "Don't panic."

Releasing her, he went out; a moment later, he reappeared with his mother on his arm.

There could never be any doubt of the relationship; the viscountess's dark, dramatic, rather bold beauty was the feminine version of Tony's. Before Alicia could do more than assimilate that, she was enveloped in a warm embrace, then the viscountess—"You will call me Marie, if you please"—was asking questions, meeting the boys, exclaiming over Adriana, all with an understanding that made it clear she was excellently well served by correspondents in London.

Hot milk arrived for the three flagging boys, then they were bundled upstairs to bed. Maggs said he'd stay with them; he lumbered off. The housekeeper—Alicia felt sure the woman must be Mrs. Swithins's sister—came to say that chambers had been prepared for Alicia, Adriana, and Mr. Geoffrey, and that, as usual, the master's apartments lay ready and waiting.

With a recommendation that they all get some sleep, saying she would speak with them all in the morning, the viscountess graciously retired.

Tony asked Mrs. Larkins, the housekeeper, to show Adriana and Geoffrey their rooms. Taking Alicia's hand, he led her up the stairs in their wake, but then turned down another corridor off the main gallery.

He opened a door at the end of the wing and drew her into a large room. It was a private sitting room overlooking the gardens; she got barely a glimpse as he led her through a doorway into a large bedchamber.

She glanced around, taking in the heavy dark blue hangings, the richly carved mahogany furniture, none of it delicate. Her gaze stopped on the huge four-poster bed.

Tony drew her into his arms; she met his gaze. "This is your room."

His eyes held hers for an instant, then he murmured, "I know." He bent his head. "Tonight, very definitely, this is where you belong."

The first brush of his lips, the first touch of his hands as they spread and held her, then moved over her back and pulled her against him, verified the statement, told her how true it was—how very much he needed her.

The raw hunger in his kiss, the undisguised passion, the raging desire that fueled it, spoke eloquently of all he—and she, too—had feared, all they'd known they'd had at risk. Now the threat was behind them, conquered, vanquished, and in the aftermath, in the clear light of their victory, nothing was more apparent than the wonder and rightness of their dreams.

Their strength, their vulnerability—both sprang from the same source. The same overwhelming emotion that laid waste to all barriers and left them burning with one urgent and compulsive need.

Neither questioned it.

They shed clothes in the moonlight, let their inhibitions fall with them to the floor. He lifted her and they came together in a frenzy of need, of lust, of greedy passion, of molten, exultant desire. His need was hers; hers was his. They fed and gave succor, took, yielded, and let the raging tide swell.

Wrapped together, incandescent with glory, they gave themselves up to it, surrendered anew. She gave him all and he returned the pleasure, again and again, over and over until ecstasy built, rose and engulfed them. Caught them, trapped them in its golden fire.

They burned, clung, gasping as they reached the peak and soared, and the flames fell away.

Leaving them somewhere beyond the stars, far beyond the physical world.

Locked together, merged, as one they breathed, and felt, and knew. The moment stretched; full and deep, awareness touched them. Their gazes locked. A moment of heartbreaking stillness held them.

Passion, desire, and love. The smallest word held the greatest power.

This—all of this—was theirs. If they wanted. If they wished.

They both breathed in. The shimmering net released and fell away; the physical world returned and claimed them. With soft murmurs, soothing kisses, and caresses, they sank onto his bed.

Tomorrow, Alicia promised herself as, wrapped in his arms, she drifted into sleep.

* * *

He woke her the next morning, fully dressed, to explain that he'd sent a messenger to London last night, and now had to take Sir Freddie back to the capital.

Watching her as she blinked, valiantly trying to re-assemble her wits, he grimaced. "I'll return as soon as I can. Stay here with the boys. I suspect Geoffrey will want to take Adriana to meet his mother."

He leaned close and kissed her, then rose and strode out.

Alicia stared at the doorway, then heard the door beyond close. *No—wait!* was her instinctive reaction. Instead, she sighed and rolled onto her back.

Foiled again, yet there was no point in ranting. Aside from all else, when she spoke to him of marriage, she wanted Sir Freddie and all his works finished with, no longer in any way hanging over them.

Which left her facing her current situation—in his room, in his bed—and how best to deal with it.

In the end, brazen and resolute, she decided to behave within his house precisely as she meant to go on; she had had enough of deceptions. She rang for water, washed while a round-eyed maid shook and brushed her gown, then, determined to be completely open and honest with Tony's mother, she found her way back to the hall and was deferentially conducted to the breakfast parlor.

There, she found her four siblings in high spirits. Geoffrey rose as she entered; she smiled and waved him back, then bobbed a curtsy to the viscountess, seated at the end of the table.

Marie smiled warmly. "Come and sit here beside me, my dear. We have, I think, much to talk about."

The light in her eyes was delighted, frank, and encouraging; Alicia took her words to heart, piled her plate high at the sideboard, then returned to sit at her side.

She'd barely taken the first bite when Geoffrey asked if

he could take Adriana to visit at his home. "I'd like her to see the house and meet Mama."

The viscountess, busy pouring Alicia a cup of tea, murmured, "Manningham Hall is but two miles away, and Geoffrey's mama, Anne, is waiting to welcome your sister."

Alicia glanced at Adriana, read the eager plea in her eyes. "Yes, of course." With a flicker of her own resolve, she added, "It's only sensible to seize the moment."

Geoffrey and Adriana glowed with happiness; with various assurances, they excused themselves and left.

They passed Maggs in the doorway. He lumbered in, saluting both ladies. "If you're agreeable, ma'am," he addressed Alicia, "I'll be taking these scamps down to the stream. I mentioned it this morning—seems they've been an age without holding a rod, and I'm happy to watch over them."

As Alicia glanced at her brothers, Marie again murmured, "Maggs is entirely trustworthy." She smiled at the large, homely man. "He's been watching over Tony since he was no older than your David."

Alicia regarded her brothers' shining eyes and eager expressions. "If you promise to behave and do exactly as Maggs says . . ." She glanced at Maggs and smiled, too. "You may go."

"H'ray!" Setting down napkins, pushing back their chairs, they rushed to Maggs, pausing only to make their bows to Alicia and the viscountess before happily heading off.

Alicia watched Matthew, his hand in Maggs's, walk confidently out, and felt a rush of emotion. Not just for Matthew, but for the children she would bear; here, like this, with this sort of continuity was how children should be raised.

"Now!' Marie settled back in her chair. At her signal, the young butler departed, leaving them alone. "You can eat, and I will talk, and we will learn all about each other, and you can tell me when your wedding is to be. With his customary flair for avoiding details, Tony hasn't told me."

Lifting her gaze from her plate, Alicia looked into Marie's bright black eyes. "Yes, well . . ." She dragged in a breath; she hadn't expected such a direct approach. "Indeed, that's a subject I wished to discuss with you."

She glanced around, confirming that they were indeed alone. She drew another breath, held it for a moment, then met Marie's gaze. "I'm Tony's mistress, *not* his intended bride."

Marie blinked. A succession of emotions played across her features, then her eyes flared; she pressed her lips tight and reached across to lay her hand on Alicia's arm. "My dear, I greatly fear I must, most contritely, apologize— not for my question, but for my oh-so-tardy son."

Marie shook her head; Alicia realized with some surprise that she was struggling to keep her lips straight. Then Marie met her eyes again. "It seems he hasn't told you either."

Over the next hour, she tried to correct Marie's assumption, but Tony's mother would have none of it.

"No, and no and *non, ma petite.* Believe me, you do not know him as I do. But now you have told me your background, I can well see how you, through his laggardliness, have come to think as you do. You have had no mentor, no guide to rely on—no one to . . . what is the word . . . 'interpret' his behavior for you. Rest assured, he would not have allowed anyone to know of you, much less established you as his consort in the eyes of the ton, or, indeed, brought you here, if he hadn't, from the first, seen you as his bride."

It was increasingly difficult to cling to her argument in the face of Marie's conviction, yet Alicia couldn't— simply could not—believe that all along . . . "From the first?"

"Oui—without doubt." Marie pushed back her chair. "Come—let me show you something, so you will see more clearly."

They left the breakfast parlor; while they walked through the large house, Marie quizzed her on her brothers' education. On the one hand, Alicia's heart soared; this—this house, this sense of family, of immediate and natural care—was the stuff of her dreams. Yet her wits were whirling—she couldn't accept it, couldn't take joy in it, stymied by her uncertainty over Tony's intentions.

Had he always seen her as his wife? Did he *truly* do so now?

Marie led her to a long gallery lined with paintings. "The *famille* Blake. Most we need not consider, but here—here are the ones that might make things clear."

She halted before the last three paintings. The first showed a gentleman in his twenties, dressed in the fashion of a generation before. "Tony's father, the last viscount." The middle picture was of a couple—Marie herself and the previous gentleman, a few years older. "Here is James again, now my husband." She turned to the last painting. "And this is Tony at twenty. Now look, and tell me what you see."

One aspect was obvious. "He looks very much like you."

"Oui—he looks like me. Only his height, his body, did he get from James, and that one does not notice. He looks French, and that is what one sees, but one sees only the surface." Marie caught Alicia's eye. "What a man is, how he behaves—that is not dictated by appearance."

Alicia looked again at the portrait. "You're saying he's more like his father inside?"

"Very much so." Marie linked her arm in hers; turning, they strolled back along the gallery. "In the superficial things, he is clearly French. How he moves, his gestures—he speaks French as well if not better than I. *But* it is always James in the words he speaks, always—without

fail—his Englishness that rules him. So, in deciding the question of did he always mean to marry you or no, the answer is clear."

With a gesture encompassing all the Blakes, Marie said, "You are English yourself. You know of honor. A gentleman's honor—*a true English gentleman's honor*—that is something inviolate. Something one may set one's course by, that one may stake one's life and indeed one's heart on with absolute certainty."

"And that's what rules Tony?"

"That is what is at his core, an inner code that is so much a part of him he does not even stop to think." Marie sighed. "*Ma petite*, you must see that it is not so much a deliberate slight, but an *oversight* that he has not thought to tell you, to ask you to be his bride. To him, his direction is obvious, so, like most men, he expects you to see it as clearly as he."

They'd reached the top of the stairs. Alicia halted. After a moment, she said, "He could have said something—we've been lovers for weeks."

"Oh, he *should* have said something—on that you will get no argument from me." Marie looked at her, frowned. "*Ma petite*, in telling you this, I would not wish you to think that I would counsel you to . . . how do the English say it—let him off easily?"

"Lightly," Alicia absentmindedly returned. She told herself she didn't have a temper, that not being informed she was to marry him—that he intended to marry her, indeed, from the first had so intended—that he'd taken her agreement so completely for granted he hadn't even thought to mention it was neither here nor there . . . she drew a deep breath, felt her jaw firm. "No. I *won't*—"

The boys came clattering into the hall below them. Seeing her and Marie, they came rushing up the stairs; if any shyness toward the viscountess had ever afflicted them, it had already dissipated. A rowdy report of their excellent fishing expedition tumbled from their lips.

Both Alicia and Marie smiled and nodded. Eventually, the boys ran out of exciting news, and paused.

David fixed his bright eyes on Alicia. "When are you and Tony getting married?"

"What he means," Harry put in, jostling his older brother, "is if it's soon, can we stay here?"

Matthew lined up, too. "There's ponies in the stable— Maggs said he'd teach me to ride."

Alicia waited until she was sure she had her voice and expression under control. "How did you know we were going to get married?"

"Tony told us." Harry grinned hugely.

"When?"

"Oh, days ago!" David said. "But can we stay here, please? It's so much fun."

Alicia couldn't think.

Marie stepped in and assured the boys their request would be considered. They grinned, briefly hugged Alicia, then ran off to wash and get ready for lunch.

As their footsteps faded, Marie drew in a long breath. Again, she linked her arm in Alicia's. "*Ma petite*, I think—I really do feel"—she glanced at Alicia—"*not* lightly."

"No." Jaw set, Alicia lifted her head as she and Marie descended the stairs. "And not easily, either."

The coach rocked and swayed. Beyond the flaps, the rain poured down; the wheels splashed through the spreading puddles. Evening had come early over Exmoor, dark clouds roiling up from the Bristol Channel to blanket the moors. Then the clouds had opened.

Alicia felt entirely at one with the weather, but she prayed they wouldn't get bogged. She'd hoped to get a lot farther before halting for the night; now her sights were set on the next town, South Molton, where Maggs had told her they could be sure of a decent inn.

Harry was curled up beside her, asleep with his head in

her lap. He shifted, snuffled, then settled again. Absent-mindedly, she stroked his curls.

Through the unnatural gloom, she looked across the coach at Maggs, burly and bearlike, with Matthew asleep in his arms and David slumped against his side. When he'd heard of her decision to quit Torrington Chase and go home to Little Compton, he'd volunteered to come with her and help with the boys. With no Jenkins or Fitchett, she'd accepted his help gladly.

Once the idea of going home had occurred to her, she'd seized on it and refused to be swayed. Not that Marie had tried; she'd considered, then nodded. "Yes, that will work. He'll have to speak then."

Indeed. Alicia's only question was what he would say, assuming, as both she and Marie had, that Tony would come after her.

Adriana, returning with Geoffrey and an invitation to visit for a few days with Lady Manningham, with whom Adriana had got on well, had been concerned, more about what was going on between Tony and Alicia than anything else. So Adriana was now at Manningham Hall; Marie had smiled and approved the arrangement.

The boys, of course, didn't understand. They'd argued vociferously when she'd informed them they were returning to Little Compton immediately, but Marie had broken in to state, in her most imperious tone, that if they wished to return to the Chase soon, they would go without complaint.

They'd considered Marie, exchanged glances, then consented to accompany Alicia without further grumbling.

Marie had lent her traveling coach and a knowledgeable coachman; she'd also insisted on a groom. "I have no intention of drawing Tony's fire by allowing you to set out insufficiently protected."

So the poor groom, as well as the coachman, was getting drenched up on the box. They would have to stop at South Molton.

She had no idea how long it would be before Tony returned from London. Three days? Four? She hoped to be home in two days.

Head back on the squabs, eyes closed, she tried yet again to calm her chaotic emotions, to bring order to her mind. The greater part was still seething, the rest confused, still innocently querying: he hadn't really intended to marry her, had he? But some part of her knew—he did, he had, from the first. She shouldn't have overlooked how dictatorial he was—how many times had he simply seized her hand and whirled her into a waltz, or into some room? She knew perfectly well how used he was to getting his own way.

In this instance, he still would—she wasn't so far gone in fury she'd deny herself her dreams—but not before, absolutely *not* before he got down on his knees and begged.

Jaw tight, she was imagining the scene when the rhythmic thunder of galloping hooves came out of the night behind them.

The coachman slowed his horses, easing to the side of the road to let the other carriage past. Disturbed by the change in rhythm, the boys stirred, stretched, and opened their eyes.

Listening to the oncoming hooves, Alicia wondered who else was out on such a night, chancing his horses at such a wicked pace.

That pace slowed as the carriage neared, then the sound of hooves lightened further, eventually disappearing beneath the steady drumming of the rain. She strained her ears but heard nothing more.

Then came a shout, indistinguishable from within the coach, but in response the coachman reined his plodding horses to a halt.

The coach rocked on its springs. The boys came alert, eyes wide.

Alicia looked at Maggs. Head on one side, he was listening intently.

No highwayman would use a carriage, surely, and it couldn't be—

The coach door was wrenched open. A tall dark figure was silhouetted in the opening.

Tony glanced once around the coach, then reached in and locked his fingers around Alicia's wrist. "Stay there!"

At his tone, one of rigid authority, the four males jerked upright. He didn't wait to check their expressions, but unceremoniously yanked Alicia—stunned speechless, he noted with uncompromising satisfaction—out of the coach.

He steadied her on her feet, then stalked down the road, towing her behind him. She gasped, but had no option but to go with him.

Courtesy of her totally witless flight, he was already soaked; she was, too, by the time he reached a point out of bellow range of the coach.

Releasing her, he swung around and faced her. He glared at her through the rain. *"What the devil do you think you're doing?"*

The question cracked like a whip. Over the miles, he'd lectured himself not to overreact, to find out why she'd run before reading her the riot act; just the sight of her in a coach leaving him had been enough to lay waste to all such wisdom.

"I'm going home!" Her hair clung to her cheeks, wisps dripping down her neck.

"Your home lies that way!" He jabbed a finger back down the road. "Where I left you—at the Chase."

She drew herself up, folded her arms, tipped up her chin. "I am not continuing as your mistress."

If Alicia had had any doubt that Marie had held to her promise to play the dumb innocent and not explain her complaint, it was put to rest by the expression on Tony's face. Expressions—they flowed in quick succession from totally dumfounded, to incredulous, to believing but unable to follow her reasoning . . . to not liking her reasoning at all . . . then back to absolutely incredulous dumbstruck fury.

"*You*—?" He choked. Black eyes blazing, he jabbed a finger at her. "You are not my bloody mistress!"

She nodded. "Precisely. Which is why I'm going home to Little Compton." Picking up her skirts, she went to swing haughtily about. Her skirts slapped wetly about her legs; catching her arm, he hauled her back to face him.

Held her there. He looked into her face; his, the austere planes wet, his hair plastered to his head, had never looked harsher. "I have no idea what"—he gestured wildly—"*idiot* notion you've taken into your head, but I have never considered you my mistress. I have always— since the first time I saw you—thought of you as my future *wife*!"

"Indeed?" She opened her eyes wide.

"*Yes*, indeed! I've shown you every courtesy, every consideration." He stepped close, actively intimidating; she quelled an instinctive urge to step back. "I've openly protected you, not just through the investigation, not only via your household and mine, but socially, too. As God is my witness I have never treated you other than as my future wife. I've never even *thought* of you as anything else!"

Male aggression radiated from him. Uncowed, she held his black gaze. "That's quite amazing news. A pity you didn't think to inform me earlier—"

"*Of course* I didn't say anything earlier!" The bellow was swallowed by the night. He locked his eyes on hers. "Just refresh my memory," he snarled. "What was the basis of Ruskin's attempt to blackmail you?"

She blinked, recalled, refocused on his face—read the truth blazoned there.

"I didn't want you agreeing to be my wife through any damned sense of gratitude." Tony growled the words; sensing her momentary weakness, he pounced. Lowering his head so they were eye to eye, he pointed a finger at her nose. "I waited—and waited—*forced* myself to wait to ask so you wouldn't feel pressured!"

Panic of a kind he'd never before known clawed at his gut; anger and a largely impotent rage swirled through him; an odd hurt lurked beneath all. He'd thought he'd done the right thing—*all* the right things—yet fate, untrustworthy jade, had still managed to trip him up. Yet the truth was slowly seeping into his brain—he wasn't going to lose her. He just had to find a way through the morass fickle fate had set at his feet.

He scowled at her. "Regardless of what I did or didn't say, or why, what the *devil* did you think the last weeks have been about?" He stepped closer, deliberately crowding her. "What sort of man do you think I am?"

"A nobleman." Alicia refused to budge an inch; elevating her chin, she met him eye to eye. "And men of your class often take mistresses, as all the world knows. Are you going to tell me you've never had one?"

A muscle leapt in his jaw. *"You are not my mistress!"*

The words resonated between them. Slowly, she raised her brows.

He dragged in a breath. Easing back, he released his tight grip on her arm, plowed his hand through his hair, pushing sodden strands from his eyes. "Damn it—the whole bloody ton knows how I see you—*as my wife*!"

"So I've been given to understand. The entire ton, all my acquaintances—even my brothers!—know you intend marrying me. The only person in the entire world who hasn't been informed is *me*!" She narrowed her eyes at him, then more quietly stated, "I haven't even been asked if I'm willing."

Precisely enunciated, the words gave him pause. He

held her gaze for a long moment, then, also more quietly, said, "I told you I loved you." His eyes suddenly widened. "You do understand French?"

"Enough for that, but I didn't catch much else. You speak very rapidly."

"But I said the words, and you understood." His voice gained in strength. "It was *you* who never returned the sentiment."

She lost her temper. "Yes, I *did*! Just not in words." She could feel the heat in her cheeks, refused to let it distract her. "Don't tell me you didn't understand." She gave him a second to do so; when his face only hardened, she jabbed a finger into his chest. "And as for saying the words, *believing* as I did that I was your *mistress*, such a confession would have been entirely unwise."

She realized the implicit admission, sensed by the flare of heat in his gaze that he hadn't missed it.

Lifting her chin, she continued, determined to have all clear between them, "It's all very well to say you love me, but many men doubtless think they love their mistresses, and tell them so—how could I tell what you *meant* by the words?"

For a long moment, he held her gaze, then he gestured, as if brushing the point aside. In the same movement, he reached for her; grasping her elbows, holding her steady, face to face, he locked his eyes with hers. "I need to know—do you love me?"

The question, the look in his eyes, went straight to her heart.

She closed her eyes, then opened them and searched his. The rain was cascading down, the night was wild and black about them, yet he was totally focused on her, as she was on him. She drew breath, shakily said, "In *my* world, love between a man and a woman usually means marriage. In *yours*, that isn't necessarily so. You said one word, but not the other. You knew my background—

knew I wasn't up to snuff. I couldn't tell what you meant, but . . . that didn't make any difference to how I felt about you."

He studied her for a long moment, then released her, stepped close, framed her face with his hands. He looked down into her eyes. *"Je t'aime."* The words resonated with a conviction impossible to doubt. "I love you." He held her gaze. "I want no other woman, not for a day, not for a night—only you. And I want you forever. I want to marry you. I want you in my house, in my bed—you already reside in my heart. You *are* my soul. Please . . ." He paused, still holding her gaze, then more softly continued, "Will you marry me?"

He didn't wait for her answer, but touched his lips to hers. "I never wanted you as my mistress. I only ever wanted you in one role—as my wife."

Another subtle kiss had her closing her eyes, swallowing to get her words out. "Do you think you could see me as the mother of your children?"

He drew back and met her eyes, his expression faintly quizzical. When she said nothing more, he replied, "That's understood."

"Good." She cleared her throat. "In that case . . ."

She paused, holding his black gaze; she still couldn't entirely take it in, that the future of her dreams was here, being offered to her, hers for the taking. He hadn't got down on his knees and begged, yet . . . smiling, she reached up and wrapped her arms about his neck. *"Yes,* I love you, and *yes,* I'll marry you."

"Thank God for that!" He pulled her to him, kissed her thoroughly—let her kiss him back in a wild moment of untrammeled joy with the rain drenching them and the moors a black void about them, then he sighed through the kiss, sank deeper into it, wrapped his arms about her and held her close. Until that moment, she hadn't appreciated just how tense—how keyed up, how uncertain—he'd been.

Through the kiss she sensed their emotions meet, touch, ease—the fraught worry of recent times, the uncertainties, the fears, all faded, submerged beneath a welling tide of unfettered happiness.

When he lifted his head, dragged in a huge breath, and eased his hold on her, all that fraught tension was gone, and he'd reverted to his usual dictatorial self.

"Come." He kissed her hand and turned her back to the coach. His curricle stood across the road, the pair with their heads hanging. "There's a good inn in Chittlehampton, just off the road a little way back. It's closest." Hard hand at her back, urging her along, he glanced at her—met her eyes. "We should get out of these wet clothes before we take a chill."

She seriously doubted, once they got out of their clothes, that they would be in any danger; she could feel the heat in his gaze even through the darkness.

He called orders to the coachman, then opened the coach door and looked in. "We're going back to the Chase."

A chorus of wild cheers and a "Good-oh" from Maggs greeted the pronouncement. She stuck her head past Tony to add, "But we have to stop at an inn for the night. I'm too wet to get back in. I'll follow with Tony."

Her brothers were thrilled, in alt at the prospect of returning to a house she suspected they saw as paradise, and not at all averse to spending the night at an inn along the way.

Tony helped the coachman turn his team, then he drew her protectively back while the coach lurched and started back down the road. In its wake, they walked to his curricle. Closing his hands about her waist, he lifted her to the seat. The rain was easing; she waited until they were rolling along before saying, "About my brothers."

He glanced at her. "What about them? They'll live with us, of course."

She hesitated, then asked, "You're sure?"

"Positive."

She tried to think of what else remained, what else needed to be settled between them . . .

"Good gracious!" She looked at him. "What happened with Sir Freddie?"

Later, kneeling before the fire roaring in the hearth of the best bedchamber of the Sword and Pike in Chittlehampton, one towel wrapped around her while with another she dried her wet hair, she remembered how Tony had laughed.

How delighted he'd been that he—the question of becoming his wife—had exercised her mind to the total exclusion of Sir Freddie.

She had Dalziel to thank for Tony's rapid return. Tony had sent a rider hotfoot to London as soon as they'd reached the Chase the previous night; by return, Dalziel had sent word to bring Sir Freddie to London, but then had changed his mind. He'd met Tony on the road, and taken Sir Freddie into custody; apparently Dalziel wanted to visit Sir Freddie's home in his company.

It seemed clear Dalziel's interest had been sparked by Sir Freddie's claims of another, still unidentified extraitor. For her part, she'd learned enough about extraitors to last her a lifetime.

Yet Tony's reaction out on the road buzzed in her head. Almost as if he hadn't been sure that her connection with him wasn't in some way dependent on the threat of Sir Freddie. That that threat somehow ranked more prominently in her mind than it did.

The latch lifted; Tony entered. He'd taken it upon himself to see her brothers settled; Maggs would sleep in their room, just to make sure.

A smile curved his lips as he paused, studying her, then, smile deepening, he came toward her.

"Stop!" She held up a hand. "You're still dripping. Take off your clothes."

His brows quirked, but he obediently halted. "As you wish."

The purr in his voice was distinctly predatory, the speculation in his eyes equally so. She inwardly grinned, turned back to the fire, and continued to dry her hair.

But the instant he was naked, she rose, crossed the few steps to him. Holding his gaze, with the towel she'd been using on her hair in one hand, with her other hand she whisked the towel she'd wrapped about her free.

One towel in each hand, she started to caress him, to dry him.

She tried to make him keep his hands to himself, but failed. Miserably.

Within minutes, their skins were hotter than the flames, their mouths and hands more greedy. Then she felt his hands close about her waist, his arms tense to lift her. She pulled back from their kiss. "No. On the bed."

She'd never given orders, never taken the lead before, but he acquiesced, releasing her and drawing her to the curtained bed.

He held back the drapes, caught her eye as she climbed through. "How on the bed?"

She smiled, and showed him.

Had him lie flat on his back, and let her straddle him, let her take him in and ride him to oblivion.

She'd taken an hour to ransack his library; as she'd suspected, he had an excellent collection of useful guides. She had every intention of studying them extensively and putting the knowledge to good use.

As she did that night, lavishing pleasure upon him, taking her own from his helpless surrender. Hours later, when the fire had burned low and she lay exhausted, deeply sated in his arms, she murmured, "I love you. Not because you'll protect me and our family, not because you're wealthy, or have a wonderful house. I love you because you're you—because of the man you are."

He was silent for a long moment, then his chest

swelled as he drew breath. "I don't know what love is, only that I feel it. All I know is I love you—and always will."

She lifted her head, found his lips and kissed him, then snuggled down in his arms, where she belonged.

He'd wanted a big wedding. At the Chase, with half the ton and all of the Bastion Club looking on. As he wished, so it was—the only person invited who sent his regrets was Dalziel.

Just over a week later, they all gathered to watch her walk down the aisle of the church in Great Torrington to take her place at Tony's side. Her gown was a confection of ivory silk and pearls that Adriana, her bridesmaid, assisted by Fitchett, Mr. Pennecuik, and numerous others in London, had slaved over to have ready in time. About her throat, three strands of pearls glowed; more pearls circled her wrists and depended from her lobes—a gift from Tony, along with his heart.

As, meeting his black eyes, she placed her hand in his, gave herself into his keeping, she had no doubt which gift was the most precious to her, and in that moment, what was most precious to him.

With him, side by side, she faced the minister, ready and very willing to claim their future.

The ceremony ran smoothly; the wedding breakfast was held on the lawns of the Chase. Everyone from the staff to the Duchess of St. Ives threw themselves into the celebration, resulting in a day filled to overflowing with happiness and simple, unadulterated joy. The boys were in fine fettle; along with Miranda's girls they dodged here and there among the guests, weaving laughter and exuberance through the throng, leaving benevolent smiles in their wake. The horrors of the wars still shadowed many minds; it was at moments like this that the future glowed most brightly.

Late in the afternoon, when the ladies had settled in

chairs on the lawn to chat and take stock, their husbands, released from attendance, gathered under the trees overlooking the lake or wandered down to stroll the shores.

Together with Jack Hendon, who along with Geoffrey had stood as his groomsman, and the other members of the Bastion Club—Christian, Deverell, Tristan, Jack Warnefleet, Gervase, and Charles—Tony retreated to a spot in the pinetum from where they could keep the ladies in view but also talk freely.

The topic that interested them most was Dalziel's absence.

"I've never seen him anywhere in the ton," Christian said. He nodded toward the assembled ladies. "I'm starting to think if he appeared, someone would recognize him."

"What I want to know is how he manages it," Charles said. "He must be in similar straits as we, don't you think?"

"It seems likely," Tristan agreed. "He's definitely 'one of us' in all other respects."

"Speaking of which," Jack Hendon put in, "what happened to Caudel once he was in Dalziel's clutches?"

"Oh, he sang loud and long," Charles replied. "And then sat in his library and put a gun to his head—only way left for a man of his name. Far less messy than a trial and the attendant flap."

"Did he have any immediate family?" Gervase asked.

"Dalziel said a distant cousin will inherit."

Tony looked at Charles. "When did you see him?"

"He called me in." Charles grinned. "Seems this other sod who's been using the war for his own ends has been active for the most part in Cornwall, from Penzance to Plymouth. My neck of the woods. He's in the ministries, most likely the Foreign Office, and he's apparently someone in the higher levels, someone trusted, which is what is most deeply exercising Dalziel. If Caudel was bad, this other has the potential to be even worse."

"Has he been actively spying, or was it something more like Caudel's racket?" Tristan asked.

"Don't know," Charles replied. "That's one of the things I'm supposed to find out. I'm to go in and ask questions, creating the sort of ripples no self-respecting spy wants to know about, and then watch what happens."

Christian grimaced. "A high-risk strategy."

"But oh-so-welcome." Charles glanced at the others, his dark blue eyes alight. "So now I must leave you and be on my way. I'm driving on to Lostwithiel tonight."

He grinned, a touch devilishly. "Courtesy of our erstwhile commander, I have a gold-plated reason to escape London and the ton, and my sisters, sisters-in-law, and dear mama, who are all up for the Season and now fixed in town for the duration. Of course, they expected to spend much of their time organizing me and my future. Instead, I'm on my way home. Alone. There to sit in my library, surrounded by my dogs, put up my feet, and savor a good brandy." He sighed contentedly. "Bliss."

With a rakish smile, he saluted them. "So I must leave you to fight your own battles, gentlemen."

They laughed. Charles turned away.

"Let us know if you need any help," Jack Warnefleet called.

Charles raised a hand. "I will. And if you need to hide, you all know your way to Lostwithiel."

The group under the trees shifted, broke up. Tony, Jack Hendon, and Tristan remained, watching Charles as he glibly made his excuses to Alicia and Tony's mother, then deftly extricated himself from the clutches of the other matrons present.

As Charles headed toward the stables, Tony took note of his jaunty, cocksure stride. He glanced at Jack and Tristan, briefly met their eyes, then all three grinned and looked at their ladies—Alicia, Kit, and Leonora—heads together as they chatted in the sunshine on the lawn.

"I fear," Tony murmured, "that Charles's view of bliss

is severely limited by his restricted experience of the state."

"He doesn't know what he's talking about," Tristan averred.

"True," Jack said.

Tony's grin widened into a smile. "He'll learn."

The three of them stirred and headed out onto the lawn.

STEPHANIE LAURENS's CYNSTER NOVELS
continue in March 2004 with

The Perfect Lover

in paperback from Avon Books

and

The Ideal Bride

in hardcover from William Morrow

Following is an excerpt from The Ideal Bride,
*which tells the tale of Honoria's brother,
Michael Anstruther-Wetherby, and his search
for the wife he so sorely needs.*

Look for the next Bastion Club novel Fall 2004

Eyeworth Manor, Hampshire
Late June, 1825

WIFE, WIFE, WIFE, WIFE.

Michael Anstruther-Wetherby swore beneath his breath. That refrain had plagued him for the last twenty-four hours. When he'd driven away from Amelia Cynster's wedding breakfast, it had run to the rhythm of his curricle's wheels; now it was playing to the steady clop of his bay gelding's hooves.

Lips setting, he wheeled Atlas out of the stableyard, and set out along the drive circling his home.

If he hadn't gone to Cambridgeshire to attend Amelia's wedding, he'd already be one step closer to being an affianced man. But the wedding had been one event he hadn't even thought of missing; aside from the fact his sister Honoria, Duchess of St. Ives, had been the hostess, the wedding had been a family gathering, and he valued family ties.

Rounding the house, a sturdy, three-storied manor house built of grey stone, his gaze went—as it always did when he passed this way—to the monument that stood on the verge halfway between the house and the gates. Set back against the shrubs filling the gaps beneath the tall trees, a contrasting backdrop, the simple stone had stood for fourteen years; it marked the spot where his family—

his parents and younger brother and sister—racing home in a curricle in the teeth of a storm, had been killed by a falling tree. He and Honoria had witnessed the accident from the schoolroom windows.

Perhaps it was simply human nature to value highly something one had lost.

Left shocked and grieving, he and Honoria had still had each other, but with him barely nineteen and she sixteen, they'd had to part. They'd never lost touch—they were, even now, close—but Honoria had since met Devil Cynster; she now had a family of her own.

Slowing Atlas as he approached the stone, Michael was acutely aware he did not. His life was full to bursting, his schedule perennially crammed, yet in moments like this the lack shone clearly, and loneliness jabbed.

He paused, studying the stone, then, jaw setting, faced forward and flicked the reins. Atlas picked up his pace; passing through the gates, Michael held him to a steady canter along the narrow lane.

The nightmarish sound of horses screaming slowly faded.

Today he was determined to take the first step toward establishing a family of his own.

He accepted he had to marry; he'd always assumed he would someday. How else was he to establish the family he craved? Instead, the years had rolled by and he'd become caught up in his career, and through that and his close links with the Cynsters and the haut ton, increasingly cognizant of the breadth of experience the state of marriage encompassed—he'd become less and less inclined to pursue it.

Now, however, his time had come. When Parliament had risen for the summer, he'd been left in no doubt that the Prime Minister expected him to return in autumn with a wife on his arm, thereby enabling his name to be considered in the upcoming cabinet reshuffle. Since April, he'd been actively searching for his ideal bride.

It had been easy to define the qualities he required—passable beauty, loyalty, supportive abilities, such as hostessly talents, and some degree of intelligence lightened with a touch of humor. Finding such a paragon proved another matter, then he'd met Elizabeth Mollison, or rather remet her, for strictly speaking he'd known her all her life. Her father, Geoffrey Mollison, owned nearby Bramshaw House and had been the previous member for the district. Brought low by his wife's unexpected death, Geoffrey had resigned the seat just as Michael had approached the party with his grandfather's and the Cynsters' backing. It had seemed a stroke of fate. Geoffrey had been relieved to hand the reins to someone he knew; even though they were markedly different in character—namely in ambition—he'd found Geoffrey encouraging, always ready to help.

He hoped he'd help now, and support his notion of marrying Elizabeth.

She seemed remarkably close to his ideal. True, she was young—nineteen—but she was also well-bred and unquestionably well-brought-up and, so he judged, quite capable of learning anything she needed to know. Most importantly, however, she had grown up in a political house. Even after her mother had died and her father had retired, Elizabeth had been placed under the wing of her aunt, Augusta, Lady Cunningham, who was married to a senior diplomat.

Even more, her younger aunt, Caroline, had married Camden Sutcliffe, the legendary British ambassador to Portugal. Although Sutcliffe had died two years ago, Elizabeth had also spent time in Lisbon under her aunt Caro's wing.

Elizabeth had lived virtually all her life in political and diplomatic households. He was perfectly certain she'd know how to manage his. And marrying her would strengthen his admittedly already strong position locally;

as by all accounts in future he'd be spending a lot of time on international affairs, a wife who would keep the home fires stoked would be a godsend.

Coldblooded perhaps, yet in his estimation a marriage based on mutual aspirations and affection rather than passion would suit him best.

Despite his close association with the Cynsters, he did not consider himself as one with them when it came to marriage; he was a different sort of man. They were passionate, determined, highhandedly arrogant; he would admit to being determined, he'd long ago learned to disguise his arrogance and he was a politician, ergo not a man given to the wilder passions.

Not a man to allow his heart to rule his head.

A straightforward marriage to a lady close to his ideal—that was what he needed.

The lane wended on, his route to Bramshaw House; a strange impatience rose within him but he held Atlas to his steady pace. Ahead, the trees thinned; beyond, glimpsed through their trunks and the thick undergrowth, he could see the rippling fields lining the Lyndhurst lane.

A feeling of certainty gripped him; it was the right time for him to go forward and marry, to build another family here, the next generation, to put down deeper roots and grow into the next phase of his life.

The lane was a succession of curves, the trees and undergrowth thick enough to screen sounds at any distance; by the time the rattle of the fast approaching carriage, the thud of flying hooves reached him, the carriage was almost upon him.

He only just had time to draw Atlas to the side of the lane before a gig, out of control and careening wildly, exploded around the bend.

It flashed past, heading toward the Manor. Grim-faced, pale as death, a slim woman wrestled with the reins, desperately trying to rein the horse in.

Michael cursed and wheeled Atlas. He was thundering

in the gig's wake before he'd even thought. Then he did, and cursed again. Carriage accidents were his worst nightmare; the threat of witnessing another sank like a spur into his side. He urged Atlas on.

The gig was rocketing, almost flying; the horse would soon tire, but the lane led only to the Manor—and that would be reached too soon.

He'd been born at the Manor, had lived his first nineteen years there; he knew every foot of the lane. Atlas was fresh; he dropped the reins and rode with hands and knees.

They were gaining, but not enough.

Soon the lane would become the drive, which ended with a sharp turn into the forecourt before the Manor steps. The horse would take the curve; the gig wouldn't. It would overturn, the lady would be thrown . . . toward the rocks edging the front beds.

Inwardly cursing, he pushed Atlas on. The big gelding responded, stretching out, legs flashing as they gained inch by inch on the wildly rocking gig. They were almost alongside.

The gates flashed up, then were behind.

No more time.

Gathering himself, Michael sprang from the saddle to the gig. He caught the seat, dragged himself half over it. Lunging across the lady, he grabbed the reins and yanked hard.

The lady screamed.

So did the horse.

Michael hung on, with all his strength hauled back. There was no time—no drive left—to worry about anything but halting the horse.

Hooves skidded; the horse screamed again, swung sideways—and halted. Michael grabbed the brake—too late. Momentum whipped the gig around; pure luck kept it upright.

The lady was flung out onto the grassy verge.

He was thrown after her.

She landed face down; he sprawled half atop her.

For an instant, he couldn't move—couldn't draw breath, couldn't think. Reactions—dozens—poured through him. The slender, fragile body trapped beneath his, delicate yet elementally womanly, sent protectiveness flaring—only to trigger horror and nascent fury over what had so nearly transpired. Over what had been risked.

Then fear welled, black, roiling, irrational and old, deep and dark. It swelled, gripped hard, strangled all else.

Hooves shifted on the gravel—he looked around. The horse, blowing hard, tried to walk, but the gig dragged; the horse stopped. Atlas had halted on the other side of the lawn, and stood watching, ears pricked.

"Ooof!"

Beneath him, the lady struggled. His shoulder lay across her back, his hips anchoring her thighs; she couldn't move until he did. He rolled back, sat up. His gaze fell on the stone monument, two yards away.

The terror of screaming horses filled his mind.

Jaw setting, he drew in a tight breath, and got to his feet. Watched, grim-faced, as the lady pushed back, then swung around to sit.

He reached down, grabbed her hands, and hauled her unceremoniously to her feet. "Of all the stupid, *witless*—" He broke off, fought to shackle his temper, soaring on the wings of that roiling irrational fear. Lost the battle. Hands going to his hips, he glared at its cause. "If you can't handle the reins, you shouldn't be driving." He snapped the words out, didn't care if they cut. "You came within yards of serious injury if not *death!*"

For an instant, he wondered if she was deaf; she gave no indication she'd heard him.

Caroline Sutcliffe dusted her gloved hands, and thanked her stars she'd worn gloves. Ignoring the solid lump of male reverberating with aggravation before her—she had no idea who he was; she hadn't yet seen his face—she shook out her skirts, inwardly grimaced at the grass stains, then straightened the bodice, the sleeves, her gauzy scarf. And finally consented to look up.

And up—he was taller than she'd thought. Wider of shoulder, too . . . the physical shock when he'd landed beside her on the gig's seat, compounded when he'd landed atop her on the grass, flashed back into her mind; she thrust it out again. "Thank you, sir, whoever you are, for your rescue, however ungracious." Her tone would have done a duchess credit—cool, confident, assured and haughty. Precisely the right tone to use on a presumptuous male. "However—"

Her rising gaze reached his face. She blinked. The sun was behind him; she stood in full light, but his face was shadowed.

Raising her hand, she shaded her eyes, and unabashedly peered. At a strong-featured face with a squared jaw and the harsh, angular planes of her own class. A patrician face with a wide brow delimited by straight dark brows over eyes memory painted a soft blue. His hair was thick, dark brown; the silver tracery at his temples only made him more distinguished.

It was a face that held a great deal of character.

It was the face she'd come there to find.

She tilted her head. "Michael? It is Michael Anstruther-Wetherby, isn't it?"

Michael stared—at a heart-shaped face surrounded by a nimbus of fine, sheening brown hair so light it was flyaway, puffed soft as a dandelion crown about her head, at eyes, silver-blue, slightly tip-tilted . . . "Caro?"

She smiled up at him, clearly delighted; for one instant, he—all of him—stilled.

The screaming horses abruptly fell silent.